Modelling Dynamic Systems

PcGive™ 11: Volume II

OxMetrics™

Modelling Dynamic Systems

PcGive™ 11: Volume II

Jurgen A. Doornik
David F. Hendry

Published by Timberlake Consultants Ltd
www.timberlake.co.uk
www.timberlake-consultancy.com
www.oxmetrics.net

British Library Cataloguing-in-Publication Data
A catalogue record of this book is available from the British Library

Library of Congress Cataloguing-in-Publication Data
A catalogue record of this book is available from the Library of Congress
Jurgen A. Doornik and David F. Hendry
p. cm. – (Modelling Dynamic Systems – PcGive 11 Vol II)

ISBN 0-9542603-5-X

Published by
Timberlake Consultants Ltd
Unit B3, Broomsleigh Business Park
London SE26 5BN, UK
http://www.timberlake.co.uk

842 Greenwich Lane,
Union, NJ 07083-7905, U.S.A.
http://www.timberlake-consultancy.com

Contents

Figures

Tables

Preface

Version 11 takes the level of integration of PcGive with OxMetrics (which was called GiveWin previously) one step further: operation is now entirely from OxMetrics. This builds on version 10, which saw the disappearance of the PcFiml name upon the merger with PcGive. Initially, it was necessary to have separate programs for single equation and multiple equation estimation owing to computer hardware restrictions and econometric technology. Over the years these started to disappear and most techniques in PcGive had a multiple-equation equivalent in PcGive. In implementation terms it was increasingly the opposite: a single-equation model is just a multiple-equation model with one equation.

PcGive version 11 for Windows is the latest in a long line of descendants of the original GIVE and FIML programs, and many scholars, researchers and students have contributed to its present form. We are grateful to them all for their help and encouragement.

The release of PcGive Professional version 9 saw a further enhancement of graphical presentations and another shift in approach towards a practical textbook of applied systems modelling (the pre-computer usage of the term 'manual'). With version 10, we substantially rewrote the tutorials, clarifying the role of cointegration analysis in empirical modelling. The documentation comprises very extensive tutorials conducting a complete modelling exercise, teaching econometric modelling conjointly with learning program usage, the econometrics of multiple-equation analysis and a technical summary of the statistical output.

Sections of code in earlier versions were contributed by Neil Ericsson, Adrian Neale, Denis Sargan, Frank Srba and Juri Sylvestrowicz, and their important contributions are gratefully acknowledged. The original mainframe ancestor was written in Fortran, PC versions in a mixture of Fortran, C and Assembler, version 9 was written in C and C++. Version 10 is almost entirely written in Ox, with a few additions in C. Version 10 relies on OxPack for its interface.

A special thanks goes to Gunnar Bårdsen for his detailed checking of early versions of PcFiml 9 as well as the new versions 10 and 11. We also wish to thank Andreas Beyer, Peter Boswijk, Mike Clements, Neil Ericsson, Henrik Hansen, Søren Johansen, Hans-Martin Krolzig, Sophocles Mavroeidis, Grayham Mizon, Bent Nielsen and Marius Ooms, for kindly commenting on various versions of PcFiml and PcGive. We wish to thank Maureen Baker and Nuffield College for their support.

The documentation for GIVE has evolved dramatically over the years. We are indebted to Mary Morgan and Frank Srba for their help in preparing the first (mainframe) version of a manual. Our thanks also to Manuel Arellano, Giorgio Bodo, Peter Boswijk, Julia Campos, Mike Clements, Neil Ericsson, Carlo Favero, Chris Gilbert, Henrik Hansen, Søren Johansen, Marius Ooms, Adrian Neale, Ed Nelson, Bent Nielsen, Robert Parks, Jean-François Richard, Timo Teräsvirta and Giovanni Urga for their many helpful comments on the documentation.

MikTex, in combination with dvips and Scientific Word eased the development of the documentation in LaTeX. The editing was almost entirely undertaken using OxEdit, which allowed flexible incorporation of PcFiml output and LaTeX compilation, and HyperSnap-DX which enabled the screen captures (with bmp2eps for conversion to PostScript).

Over the years, many users and generations of students have written with helpful suggestions for improving and extending the software, and while this version will undoubtedly not yet satisfy all of their wishes, we remain grateful for their comments and hope that they will continue to write with good ideas and *report any bugs*!

DFH owes a considerable debt to Evelyn and Vivien during the time he has spent on this project: their support and encouragement were essential, even though they could benefit but indirectly from the end product. In a similar fashion, JAD is delighted to thank Kate for her support and encouragement. We hope the benefits derived by others compensate.

We wish you enjoyable and productive use of

PcGive for Windows

Part I

Prologue

Chapter 1

Introduction to Volume II

1.1 The PcGive system

PcGive is an interactive menu-driven program for econometric modelling. Version 11 for Windows, to which this documentation refers, runs on Intel-compatible machines operating under Windows XP/2000. PcGive originated from the AUTOREG Library (see Hendry and Srba, 1980, Hendry, 1986, 1993, Doornik and Hendry, 1992, and Doornik and Hendry, 1994), and is part of the OxMetrics family.

The econometric techniques of the PcGive system can be divided by the type of data to which they are (usually) applied. The documentation is comprised of three volumes, and the overview below gives in parenthesis whether the method is described in Volume I, II or III. Volume IV refers to the PcNaive book.

- **Models for cross-section data**
  - Cross-section Regression (I)
- **Models for discrete data**
  - Binary Discrete Choice (III): Logit and Probit
  - Multinomial Discrete Choice (III): Multinomial Logit
  - Count data (III): Poisson and Negative Binomial
- **Models for financial data**
  - GARCH Models (III): GARCH in mean, GARCH with Student-t, EGARCH, Estimation with Nelson&Cao restrictions
- **Models for panel data**
  - Static Panel Methods (III): within groups, between groups
  - Dynamic Panel Methods (III): Arellano-Bond GMM estimators
- **Models for time-series data**
  - Single-equation Dynamic Modelling (I)
  - Multiple-equation Dynamic Modelling (II): VAR and cointegration, simultaneous equations analysis

  - ARFIMA Models (III): exact maximum likelihood, modified-profile likelihood or non-linear least squares
  - Seasonal adjustment using X12Arima (III): regARIMA modelling, Automatic model selection, Census X-11 seasonal adjustment.

- **Monte Carlo**
  - AR(1) Experiment using PcNaive (IV)
  - Static Experiment using PcNaive (IV)
  - Advanced Experiment using PcNaive & Ox Professional (IV)
- **Other models**
  - Nonlinear Modelling (I)
  - Descriptive Statistics (I)

The current book, **Volume II**, describes **multiple-equation dynamic modelling**. This part of PcGive used to be called **PcFiml**. Starting from version 10, PcFiml has been merged into the main PcGive program.

PcGive uses OxMetrics for data input and graphical and text output. OxMetrics is described in a separate book (Doornik and Hendry, 2006). Even though PcGive is largely written in Ox (Doornik, 2006), it does not require Ox to function.

1.2 Multiple-equation dynamic modelling

The multiple-equation component of PcGive is designed for modelling multivariate time-series data when the precise formulation of the economic system under analysis is not known *a priori*. The current version is for systems that are linear in variables, which could comprise jointly determined, weakly or strongly exogenous, predetermined and lagged endogenous variables. A wide range of system and model estimation methods is available; stochastic and identity equations are handled. Particular features of the program are its ease of use, familiar interface, flexible data handling, structured approach, extensive set of preprogrammed diagnostic tests, its focus on recursive methods, and its powerful graphics. An extensive batch language is also supported.

The main design concepts underlying this part of PcGive centre on the need to avoid information overload when modelling a system of dynamic equations (as the number of parameters can become very large), to remain easy and enjoyable to use, to offer the frontier techniques, and to implement a coherent modelling strategy. Specifically, it seeks to achieve all of these objectives simultaneously. The size of system that can be analyzed pushes the limits of PCs capacities, data availability, econometric technique and comprehension of dynamic models. The documentation is especially extensive to fully explain the econometric methods, the modelling approach and the techniques used, as well as bridge the vast gap between the theory and practice in this area by a detailed description of a modelling exercise in operation. Like the companion volume on single-equation modelling (see Volume I: Hendry and Doornik, 2006), this book transcends the old ideas of 'textbooks' and 'computer manuals' by linking the learning of econometric methods and concepts to the outcomes achieved when they are applied by the user at the computer. Because the program is so easy to learn and use, the main focus is on its econometrics and application to data analysis. Detailed tutorials in Chapters 3–8 teach econometric modelling of dynamic systems for possibly non-stationary data by walking the user through the program in organized steps. This is supported by clear explanations of the associated econometric methods in Chapters 9–14. The material spans the level from introductory to frontier research, with an emphatic orientation to practical modelling. The exact definitions of all statistics calculated are described in Chapter 15. The appendices in Chapters A1–A2 are for reference to details about the batch language, and data sets. The context-sensitive help system supports this approach by offering help on both the program and the econometrics at every stage.

This chapter describes the special features of multiple-equation modelling in PcGive, discusses how to use the documentation, provides background information on data storage, interactive operation, help, results storage and filenames, sketches the basics of how to use the program and describes its graphics capabilities, illustrated throughout later chapters.

1.3 The special features

Many of the special features of PcGive are listed in Volume I. Here we concentrate on the special features which are available for multiple-equation modelling:

(1) *Ease of use*

(2) *Advanced graphics*

(3) *Flexible data handling in OxMetrics*

(4) *Efficient modelling*

- The underlying **Ox algorithms** are **fast, efficient, accurate** and carefully **tested**; all **data are stored in double precision**.

- This part of PcGive is specially designed for **modelling multivariate time-series** data, and analyzes dynamic responses and long-run relations with ease; it is simple to change sample, or forecast, periods or estimation methods: models are retained for further analysis, and general-to-specific sequential simplifications are monitored for reduction tests.

- The **structured modelling approach** is fully discussed in this book, and guides the ordering of menus and dialogs, but application of the program is completely at the user's control.

- A **vast range of estimators** is supported, including multivariate least squares, system cointegration techniques, and most simultaneous equations estimators (centered around FIML), providing automatic handling of identities and checking of identification, and allowing non-linear cross-equation constraints; powerful numerical optimization algorithms are embedded in the program with easy user control, and most methods can be calculated recursively over the available sample.

- PcGive offers **powerful preprogrammed testing facilities** for a wide range of specification hypotheses, including tests for dynamic specification, lag length, cointegration, tests on cointegration vectors and parsimonious encompassing; Wald tests of linear and non-linear restrictions are easily conducted.

- **System and model revision is straightforward** since PcGive remembers as much as possible of the previous specification for the next formulation.

- A **batch language** allows storage for automatic estimation and evaluation of models, and can be used to prepare a PcGive session for teaching.

(5) *Powerful evaluation*

- **System and simultaneous-equations mis-specification tests are automatically provided**, including vector residual autocorrelation, vector heteroscedasticity, system functional form mis-specification, and vector normality.

- **Individual equation diagnostic information** is also provided including ARCH and (e.g.) plots of correlograms and residual density functions.

- The **recursive estimators provide easy graphing** of residuals with their confidence intervals, log-likelihoods, and parameter-constancy statistics (scaled by selected nominal significance levels); these are calculated for systems, cointegration analyses and models – see recursive FIML in action.

- All estimators provide **graphs** of fitted/actual values, residuals, and **forecasts** with error bars or bands for 1-step (against outcomes in that case), h-step and dynamic forecasts; perturbation and impulse response analyses are also supported.

(6) *Extensive batch language*

- **PcGive formulates the batch commands** needed to rerun a system and model as an interactive session proceeds – all you have to do is save the file if desired.

- The **batch language** supports commands for data loading; transformation; system formulation, estimation and testing; cointegration analyses and tests; model formulation, estimation and testing; imposing restrictions. All these can be stored as simple batch commands, to be extended, revised and/or edited with ease. Batch files can be run in whole or in part from within an interactive session.

(7) *Well-presented output*

- **Graphs can be saved** in several file formats for later recall and further editing, or printing and importing into many popular word processors, as well as directly by 'cut and paste'.
- **Results window** information can be saved as a text document for input to most word processors, or directly input by 'copy and paste'.

We now consider some of these special features in greater detail.

Efficient modelling sequence

- Modelling dynamic econometric systems involves creating and naming lags, controlling sample periods, assigning the appropriate status to variables (endogenous, non-modelled etc.), so such operations are either automatic or very easy. The basic operator is a lag polynomial matrix. Long-run system solutions, cointegration tests, the significance of blocks of lagged variables, the choice between deterministic or stochastic dynamics, and roots of long-run and lag-polynomial matrices are all calculated. When the recommended general-to-specific approach is adopted, the sequence of reductions is monitored for both systems and models, and reduction F-tests and system information criteria are reported.
- This **extensive book** seeks to bridge the gap between econometric theory and empirical modelling: the tutorials in Part II walk the user through every step from inputting data to the final selected econometric model of the vector of variables under analysis. The econometrics chapters in Part III explain all the necessary econometrics for system modelling and evaluation with reference to the program, offering detailed explanations of all the estimators and tests. The statistical output chapter carefully defines all the estimators and tests.
- The **ordering of the menus and dialogs** is determined by the underlying theory: first establish a data-coherent, constant-parameter dynamic system; then investigate cointegration, and reduce the system to a stationary, near orthogonal and simplified representation; next develop a model to characterize that system in a parsimonious and interpretable form; and finally check for parsimonious encompassing of the system: see Hendry, Neale and Srba (1988), Hendry and Mizon (1993) and Hendry (1993, 1995) for further details. Nevertheless, the application and sequence of the program's facilities remain completely under the user's control.
- The estimators supported are based on the estimator generating equation approach in Hendry (1976), and include handling of identities and automatic checking of identification. Estimation methods include Multivariate Ordinary (OLS)

and Recursive Least Squares (RLS); Johansen's reduced-rank cointegration analysis for systems with both its recursive and constrained implementations; Single-equation OLS (for large systems and small samples, denoted 1SLS), Two-Stage Least Squares (2SLS), Three-Stage Least Squares (3SLS), Limited-Information Instrumental Variables (LIVE), Full-Information Instrumental Variables (FIVE), Limited-Information Maximum Likelihood (LIML), Full-Information Maximum Likelihood (FIML), Recursive FIML (RFIML), and constrained FIML (CFIML: with possibly non-linear cross-equation constraints for models; also available recursively, and denoted RCFIML). Systems and models are easily revised, transformed and simplified since as much as possible of a previous specification is retained. Up to 100 models are remembered for easy recall and progress evaluation.

- Powerful testing facilities for a wide range of specification hypotheses of interest to econometricians and economists undertaking substantive empirical research are preprogrammed for automatic calculation. Available tests include dynamic specification, lag length, cointegration rank, hypothesis tests on cointegration vectors and/or adjustment coefficients, and tests of reduction or parsimonious encompassing. Wald tests of (non-)linear restrictions are easily conducted using the constraints editor and such constraints can be imposed for estimation by cutting and pasting, then using CFIML.

Powerful evaluation

- Much of the output is provided in **graphical form** which is why it is an interactive (rather than a batch) program. The option to see multiple graphs allows for efficient processing of large amounts of information. Blocks of graphs for up to 36 equations can be viewed simultaneously, incorporating descriptive results (fitted and actual values, scaled residuals etc.), recursive statistics, cointegration output (time series of cointegration vectors, or recursive eigenvalues), single-equation diagnostic test information, cross-equation relationships (such as residual cross-plots), single-parameter likelihood grids, and a wide range of forecasts.

- **Evaluation tests** can be either automatically calculated, calculated in a block as a summary test option, or implemented singly or in sets merely by selecting the relevant dialog option. A comprehensive and powerful range of mis-specification tests is offered in order to sustain the methodological recommendations about model evaluation. System and simultaneous-equations models mis-specification tests include vector residual autocorrelation, vector heteroscedasticity, system functional form mis-specification and vector normality (the test proposed in Doornik and Hansen, 1994). Individual-equation diagnostic information is also provided, including scalar versions of all the above tests as well as ARCH, and (for example) plots of correlograms and residual density functions. When the system is in fact a single equation, multivariate tests have been designed to deliver the same answer with the same degrees of freedom as the single equation tests.

- Much of the power of PcGive resides in its extensive use of **recursive estimators** for systems, cointegration analyses and models. The output can be voluminous (1-step residuals and their standard errors, constancy tests etc. at every sample size for every equation), but recursive statistics can be graphed for easy presentation and appraisal (up to 36 graphs simultaneously). The size of systems is really only restricted by the available memory and length of data samples. **Recursive cointegration** analysis and **recursive FIML** are surprisingly easy and amazingly fast – given the enormous numbers of calculations involved.
- All estimators provide time-series graphs of residuals, fitted and actual values and their cross-plots. 1-step forecasts and outcomes with 95% confidence intervals shown by error bars or bands can be graphed, as can dynamic simulation (within sample), dynamic forecasts (*ex ante*) or even h-step ahead forecasts for any choice of h – all with approximate 95% confidence bars. Forecasts can be conducted under alternative scenarios.

Considerable experience has demonstrated the practicality and value of using PcGive live in classroom teaching as a complementary adjunct to theoretical derivations. On the research side, the incisive recursive estimators and the wide range of preprogrammed tests make PcGive the most powerful interactive econometric modelling program available. Part II records its application to a practical econometric modelling problem. These roles are enhanced by the flexible and informative graphics options provided.

1.4 Documentation conventions

The convention for instructions that you should type is that they are shown in `Typewriter` font. Capitals and lower case are only distinguished as the names of variables in the program and the mathematical formulae you type. Once OxMetrics has started, then from the keyboard, the `Alt` key accesses line menus (at the top of the screen); from a mouse, click on the item to be selected using the left button. Common commands have a shortcut on the toolbar, the purpose of which can be ascertained by placing the mouse on the relevant icon. Icons that can currently operate are highlighted. Commands on menus, toolbar buttons, and dialog items (buttons, checkboxes etc.) are shown in Sans Serif font: click on highlighted options to implement.

Equations are numbered as (chapter.number); for example, (8.1) refers to equation 8.1, which is the first equation in Chapter 8. References to sections have the form

§chapter.section, for example, §8.1 is Section 8.1 in Chapter 8. Tables and Figures are shown as Figure chapter.number; for example, Figure 5.2 for the second Figure in Chapter 5. Multiple graphs are numbered from left to right and top to bottom, so (b) is the top-right graph of four, and (c) the bottom left.

1.5 Using Volume II

Volume II comes in five main parts: Part I comprises this introductory chapter, and instructions on starting the program. Part II has five extensive tutorials on dynamic system modelling; these emphasize the modelling aspects yet explain program usage en route. Part III has six chapters discussing the econometrics of PcGive from system formulation to dynamic forecasting. Part IV offers a detailed description of the statistical and econometric output. Finally, Part V contains appendices. The documentation ends with references, and author and subject indices. As discussed above, the aim is to provide a practical textbook of systems modelling, linking the econometrics of PcGive to empirical practice through tutorials which implement an applied modelling exercise. In more detail:

(1) A separate book explains and documents the companion program **OxMetrics** which records the output and provides the data loading and graphing facilities.

(2) Volume I provides tutorials for single-equation modelling, and contains an accompanying econometrics text book.

(3) The **Prologue** introduces the main features provided for multiple-equation modelling, sketches how to use the program and illustrates some of its output.

(4) The **Tutorials** in Chapters 3 to 8 are specifically designed for joint learning of the econometric analyses and use of the program. They describe system formulation, estimation and evaluation; cointegration procedures; reduction of the system to a stationary representation; econometric modelling of that system; and advanced features. By implementing a complete empirical research exercise, they allow rapid mastery of PcGive while acquiring an understanding of how the econometric theory operates in practice.

(5) The **Econometric Overview** in Chapter 9 reviews the various econometric procedures for multiple-equation modelling.

(6) The **Econometric Theory** in Chapters 10 to 13 explain in technical detail the econometrics of multiple-equation modelling.

(7) Chapters 14 and 15 concern numerical optimization and the detailed description of the statistical output. Chapter 15 is to some extent self-contained, as it briefly repeats the basic notation employed in Chapters 10 to 13.

(8) The **Appendices** in Chapters A1 to A2 document the remaining functions. Chapter A1 documents the various languages (such as Algebra and Batch) used in PcGive. Most information about menus, dialogs etc., is available in the on-line help. These chapters should be needed for reference only, but it may be helpful to read them once.

The appropriate sequence is first to follow the instructions in the **installation procedure** to install PcGive Professional on your system. Next, read the remainder of this introduction, then follow the step-by-step guidance given in the **tutorials** in Volume I and II to become familiar with the operation of PcGive. The **appendices** should be needed for reference only, but it may be helpful to read them once, especially A1. The technical description of the econometrics procedures is provided in Part III.

To use the documentation, either check the index for the subject, topic, menu, or dialog that seems relevant, or look up the part relevant to your current activity (for example, econometrics, tutorials or manuals) in the **Contents**, and scan for the most likely keyword. The references point to relevant publications that analyze the methodology and methods embodied in PcGive.

1.6 Citation

To facilitate replication and validation of empirical findings, PcGive should be cited in all reports and publications involving its application. The appropriate form is to cite PcGive in the list of references.

1.7 World Wide Web

Consult `www.oxmetrics.com` or `www.pcgive.com` pointers to additional information relevant to the current and future versions of PcGive. Upgrades are made available for downloading if required, and a demonstration version is also made available.

1.8 Some data sets

The data used in Hendry (1995) is provided in the files `UKM1.in7/UKM1.bn7`. The DHSY data (see Davidson, Hendry, Srba and Yeo, 1978) is supplied in the files `DHSY.in7/DHSY.bn7`. An algebra file, `DHSY.alg`, contains code to create variables used in the paper. A batch file, `DHSY.fl`, loads the data, executes algebra code, and estimates the two final equations reported in the paper.

For the data sets used in Hendry and Morgan (1995), consult:
`www.nuff.ox.ac.uk/users/hendry`.

Part II

Tutorials on Multiple-Equation Modelling

Chapter 2

Tutorial Data

2.1 Introduction

The operation of multiple-equation modelling is similar to single-equation modelling, and both share the OxMetrics edit window for results and its graphics. We assume that users have previously followed the tutorials in Volume I. For detailed instructions on how to load and transform data using the calculator or algebra, and create sophisticated graphs, consult the OxMetrics book. If at any time you get stuck, press `F1` for context-sensitive help. Or access the Help menu to find out about specific topics (including relevant econometric information).

2.2 The tutorial data set

Most of the tutorial chapters use the data set `MulTut1.in7/MulTut1.bn7`. The data set comprises four stochastic variables, denoted *Ya*, *Yb*, *Yc* and *Yd*; a *Constant*, *Seasonal* and *Trend* are automatically created by PcGive when required. The data are computer-generated, to mimic a realization of a quarterly vector stochastic process representable by a (log)linear dynamic system. The tutorials will analyze and model these four variables over their sample period of 200 observations, 1951 (1) to 2000 (4). We retain the data points 2000(1)–2004(4) for multi-step forecasting exercises (but, because we have simulated data, we already now the future outcomes). The series are a replication from the DGP used in Doornik, Hendry and Nielsen (1998), and the modelling tutorials in this book closely follow the steps taken in that article. If you wish to use real data instead, you could follow the tutorials alonng with the UKM1 data set, comparing the results to those reported in Doornik, Hendry and Nielsen (1998).

To start, load the data set in **OxMetrics**, and graph the four variables as in Figure 2.1. We assume the first three series are in logarithms. In terms of units, the first could be the log of the real money stock, and the second the log of real GNP. The third could be the growth rate of prices (i.e. inflation), and the final series an interest rate measure. There appears to a break in the trend growth of *Yb*, *Yc* and *Yd* in the 1970's. Such behaviour is compatible with the series being integrated (possibly of order 1, denoted

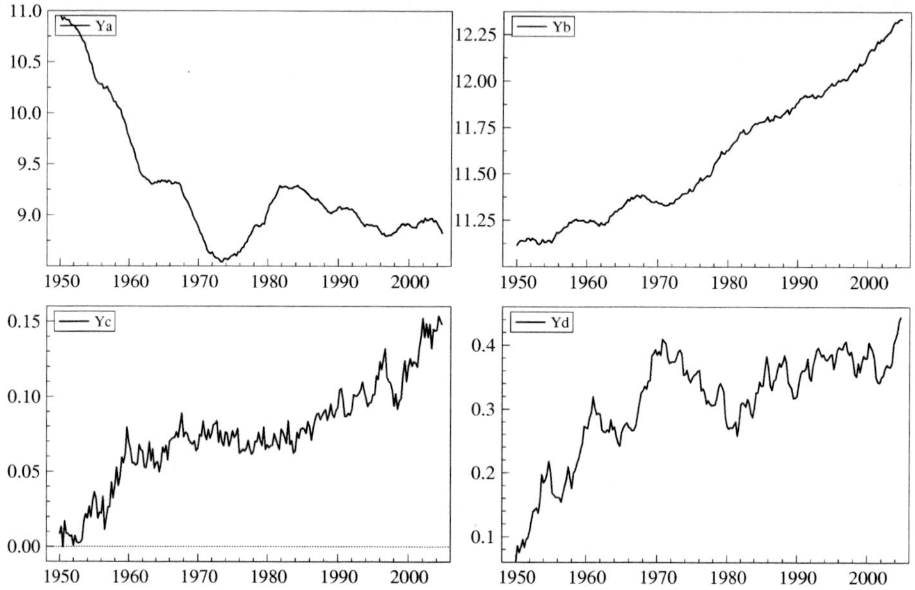

Figure 2.1 Time-series of the four variables.

by I(1)), but does not preclude other explanations (for example, stationary around a deterministic – but perhaps split – trend). However, there is no obvious seasonality in the data.

Next, we will plot the data both over time and against each other, in pairs (*Ya*,*Yb*) and (*Yc*,*Yd*). The outcome is shown in Figure 2.2 (again perhaps subject to minor differences: we have matched the time series of *Ya* and *Yb* for both scale and range, did the same for *Yc*, *Yd*, and added a regression line).

Clearly, the two sets are highly correlated within pairs, but behave differently between. Further, (*Yc*,*Yd*) seem to have moved closely together at the start of the sample, but diverged in the 1970's and again at the end of the sample.

Now, create first differences of all variables in the data set, either using the OxMetrics Calculator or Algebra: *DYa*, *DYb*, *DYc*, and *DYd*. Repeat Figure 2.2, but now for the differenced series. This leads to Figure 2.3. The differences do not seem to be integrated, although (*DYa*,*DYb*) show noticeable serial and cross correlation. Since the differences are autocorrelated, a lag length of 2 is the minimum needed to characterize the outcomes.

This completes the exploratory graphical analysis of the tutorial data set. In the next chapter we commence econometric modelling of the dynamic system.

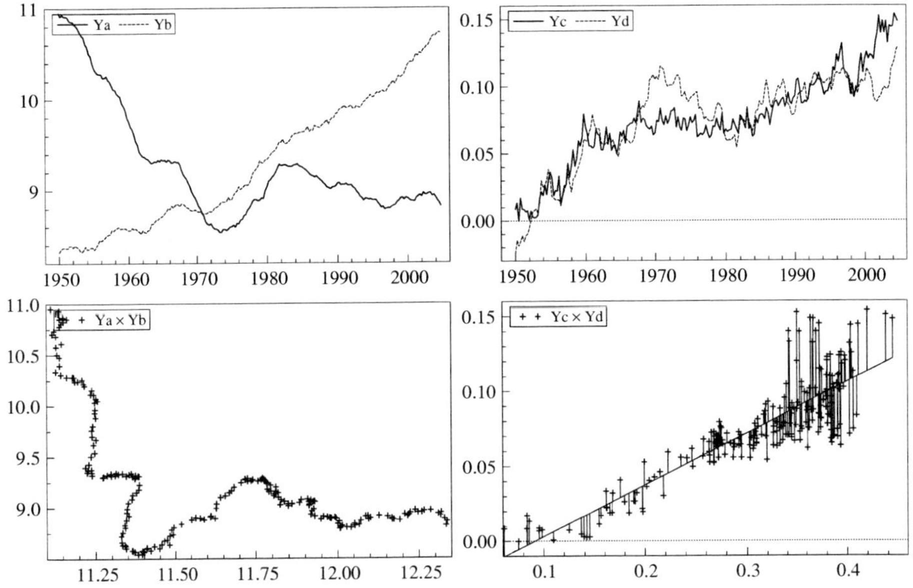

Figure 2.2 Time series and scatter plots for pairs of variables.

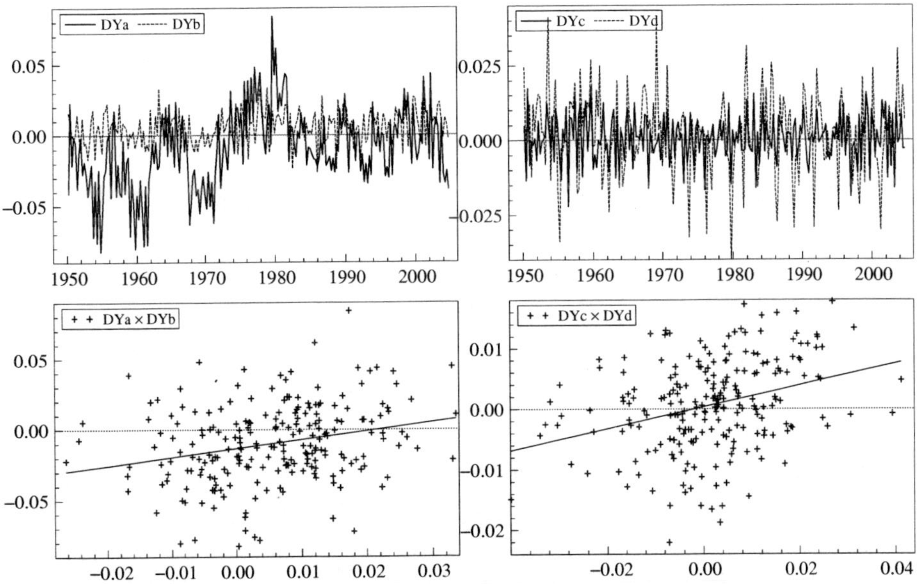

Figure 2.3 Time series and scatter plots for pairs of differences.

Chapter 3

Tutorial on Unrestricted System Estimation and Evaluation

3.1 Introduction to dynamic systems

The modelling process in PcGive starts by focusing on the *system*, often called the *unrestricted reduced form* (URF), which can be written as (using simple dynamics):

$$\mathbf{y}_t = \boldsymbol{\pi}_1 \mathbf{y}_{t-1} + \boldsymbol{\Phi}\mathbf{q}_t + \boldsymbol{\Gamma}_1 \mathbf{z}_t + \mathbf{v}_t, \mathbf{v}_t \sim \mathsf{IN}_n\left[\mathbf{0}, \boldsymbol{\Omega}\right], \tag{3.1}$$

where $\mathbf{y}_t, \mathbf{z}_t$ are respectively $n \times 1$ and $q \times 1$ vectors of observations at time t, for $t = 1, \ldots, T$, on the endogenous variables $\mathbf{y}$ and non-modelled variables $\mathbf{z}$; $\mathbf{q}_t$ holds the deterministic variables such as the *Constant* and *Trend*. $\mathsf{IN}_n[\mathbf{0}, \boldsymbol{\Omega}]$ denotes an n-dimensional independent, normal density with mean zero and covariance matrix $\boldsymbol{\Omega}$ (symmetric, positive definite). In (3.1), the parameters $(\boldsymbol{\pi}_1, \boldsymbol{\Phi}, \boldsymbol{\Gamma}_1, \boldsymbol{\Omega})$ are assumed to be constant and variation free, with sufficient observations to sustain estimation and inference.

Modelling in this tutorial starts with a *closed* linear dynamic system, using two lags:

$$\mathbf{y}_t = \boldsymbol{\pi}_1 \mathbf{y}_{t-1} + \boldsymbol{\pi}_2 \mathbf{y}_{t-2} + \boldsymbol{\Phi}\mathbf{q}_t + \mathbf{v}_t, \mathbf{v}_t \sim \mathsf{IN}_n\left[\mathbf{0}, \boldsymbol{\Omega}\right], \tag{3.2}$$

which is called a *vector autoregression* (VAR) when all $\mathbf{y}$ variables have the same lag length. An example of a two-equation VAR(2) is:

$$\begin{array}{rcl} Ya_t & = & \delta_0 + \delta_1 Ya_{t-1} + \delta_2 Ya_{t-2} + \delta_3 Yb_{t-1} + \delta_4 Yb_{t-2} + v_{1t}, \\ Yb_t & = & \delta_5 + \delta_6 Ya_{t-1} + \delta_7 Ya_{t-2} + \delta_8 Yb_{t-1} + \delta_9 Yb_{t-2} + v_{2t}. \end{array} \tag{3.3}$$

A more compact way of writing the system (3.1) is:

$$\mathbf{y}_t = \boldsymbol{\Pi}_u \mathbf{w}_t + \mathbf{v}_t, \tag{3.4}$$

where $\mathbf{w}$ contains $\mathbf{z}$, lags of $\mathbf{z}$, lags of $\mathbf{y}$ and the deterministic variables $\mathbf{q}$.

An in-depth discussion of the econometric analysis of a dynamic system is given in Chapter 11.

3.2 Formulating a system

Load the MulTut1 tutorial data set in OxMetrics. If you haven't done so, start the Model process in OxMetrics, and select Multiple Equation Dynamic Modelling using PcGive on the Model dialog:

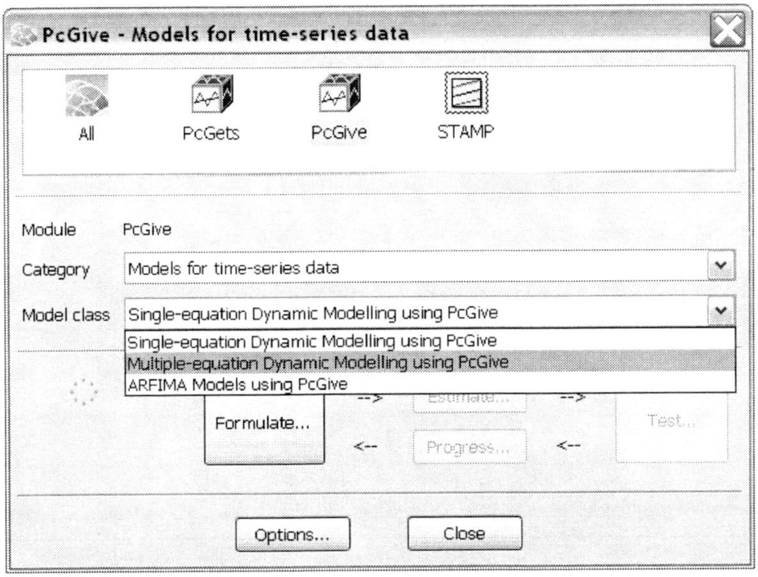

Click on Formulate to go directly to the Data selection dialog. The key information required by PcGive in order to formulate the system comprises:

- the menu of endogenous (Y) variables (here *Ya* to *Yd*);
- their lag lengths (here 3; a common length is needed for cointegration analysis);
- the choice of deterministic variables (e.g., Constant and Trend);
- and their status (unrestricted, which is relevant for cointegration analysis);
- any additional unmodelled (Z) variables (none here).
- Later, estimation choices will need to specify the sample period and the method of estimation. The next three dialogs elicit this information in a direct way.

First set the lag length to three (in the bottom right corner). Mark *Ya*, *Yb*, *Yc*, *Yd* in the list of database variables (remember, you can select multiple variables with the keyboard using the Shift key, or with the mouse by using Shift+click orCtrl+click), press the Add button. Repeat for the *Trend* in the list of special variables. Current-dated variables are automatically denoted as Y (endogenous) unless they are selected from the list of special variables; a *Constant* is automatically added (but can be deleted if so required). The special variables are *Constant*, *Trend*, *Seasonal*, and *CSeasonal*; The constant and seasonals are by default classified as U(nrestricted). The next two sections discuss these issues. Check that the status of *Trend* is indeed *not* marked as

U(nrestricted) (so it can be restricted in a later tutorial to enter the long run only, precluding a quadratic trend in the levels if some of the variables are found to have unit roots). The following capture shows the dialog just before pressing OK:

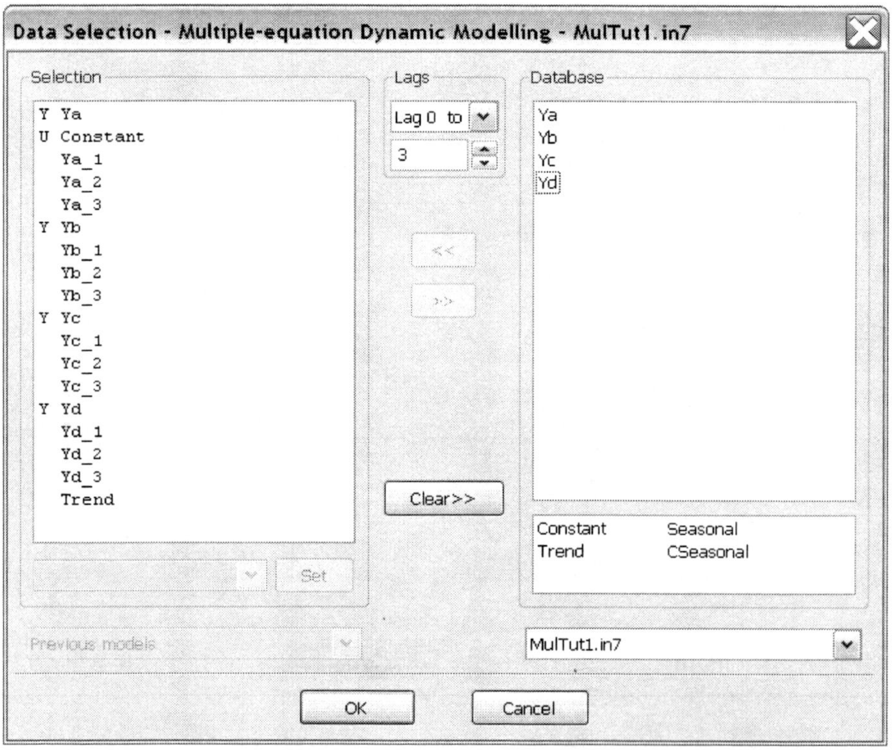

Other mouse-based operations are: double clicking on a variable in the database or a special variable will add that variable to the model specification; double clicking on a model variable will remove it, while right-clicking can be used to change the status.

3.3 Unrestricted variables

Variables can be classified as *unrestricted*. Such variables will be partialled out, prior to FIML estimation, and their coefficients will be reconstructed afterwards. Suppose, for example, that the constant in the above example is set to unrestricted. Then *Ya*, *Ya*_1, *Yb*_1, *Ya*_2, *Yb*_2 and *Yc* are regressed on the constant; in subsequent estimation, PcGive will use the residuals from these regressions and omit the constant (the coefficients $\delta_1 \ldots \delta_5$ and $\delta_7 \ldots \delta_{11}$ in (3.3) are unaffected).

Although unrestricted variables do not affect the basic estimation, there are some important differences in subsequent output:

(1) Following estimation: the R^2 measures and corresponding F-test are relative to the unrestricted variables.
(2) In cointegration analysis: unrestricted variables are partialled out together with the short-run dynamics, whereas restricted variables (other than lags of the endogenous variables) are restricted to lie in the cointegrating space.
(3) In recursive FIML and CFIML estimation: the coefficients of unrestricted variables are fixed at the full sample values.
(4) In FIML estimation: again, the result does not depend on the fact whether a variable is unrestricted or not, but estimation of the smaller model could improve convergence properties of the non-linear estimation process.
(5) In heteroscedasticity tests: squares and cross-products of unrestricted variables are not included in the tests.

3.4 Special variables

The list of special variables contains the deterministic variables which are frequently used in a model. For annual data, these are the *Constant* and the *Trend*. The constant always has the value 1. The trend is 1 for the first database observation, 2 for the second, and so forth.

For non-annual data, PcGive automatically creates a seasonal. The Seasonal is non-centered, whereas CSeasonal is centered (mean 0). Seasonal will always be 1 in quarter 1, independent of the first observation in the sample. When adding the seasonal to a model which already has a constant term, PcGive will add Seasonal, Seasonal_1 and Seasonal_2. That corresponds to Q1, Q2 and Q3. When there is no constant, Seasonal_3 is also added. An example for quarterly data is:

	Trend	Seasonal	CSeasonal	Seasonal_1	Seasonal_2	Seasonal_3
1980 (1)	1	1	0.75	0	0	0
1980 (2)	2	0	−0.25	1	0	0
1980 (3)	3	0	−0.25	0	1	0
1980 (4)	4	0	−0.25	0	0	1
1981 (1)	5	1	0.75	0	0	0
1981 (2)	6	0	−0.25	1	0	0
1981 (3)	7	0	−0.25	0	1	0
1981 (4)	8	0	−0.25	0	0	1

3.5 Estimating an unrestricted system

After pressing the OK button to accept the system as formulated, PcGive brings up the Model Settings dialog:

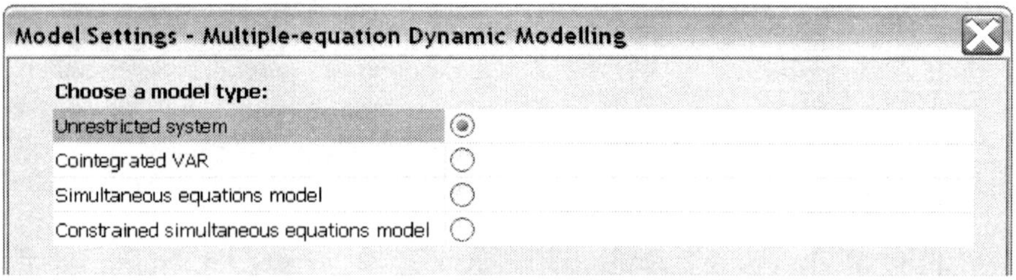

Select Unrestricted system, and press OK to move to the Estimate Model dialog:

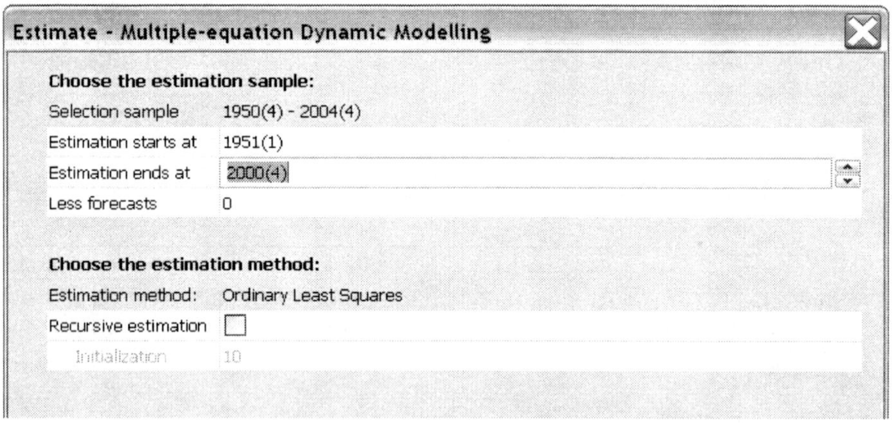

Check that the estimation sample is set to 1951(1)–2000(4) (200 observations), to ensure a common sample for all that follows. Ordinary Least Squares (OLS) should be highlighted: click on OK to produce the estimation output.

Even in such a small system as the present one, a fair volume of output appears: yet we have in fact set the Options dialog to produce minimum output, and adding tests, forecasts etc., will magnify the output considerably. Recursive estimation will produce a potentially enormous output. If there are n endogenous variables with m lags, and q non-modelled variables with r lags, then each equation has $k = nm + (r+1)q$ regressors. With T observations and $M-1$ retained for initialization, there will be $nk(T-M+1)$ coefficients, standard errors etc. plus $\frac{1}{2}n(n+1)(T-M+1)$ error variances. Here, that would produce about 10 000 basic numbers to handle – hardly 'data reduction', and hardly comprehensible if presented as pure numerical information. This problem of InfoGlut is tackled in PcGive by using graphical presentations as far as possible to guide modelling. We will draw on and report here only those items of most relevance as they are required. Thus, we now consider a few of the summary statistics.

First, the goodness of fit is best measured by the standard deviations of the residuals, as these are either in the same units as the associated dependent variables, or for log models, are a proportion. Moreover, they are invariant under linear transforms of the variables in each equation. They are presented with each equation as σ and collected at the end of the equation output. Here we have marked the diagonal for readability:

```
correlation of URF residuals (standard deviations on diagonal)
                 Ya            Yb            Yc            Yd
Ya         0.016680 <   -0.013268      -0.54810      -0.56481
Yb        -0.013268    0.0098245 <     -0.13913      0.037555
Yc         -0.54810     -0.13913     0.0068800 <     0.41436
Yd         -0.56481     0.037555       0.41436     0.012924 <
```

Consequently, the residual standard deviations are about 1.7%, 1.0%, 0.7% and 1.3% respectively. Assuming that three lags were sufficient to produce white noise errors on the system (an issue considered shortly), then these provide the baseline innovation standard errors.

Next, the correlations between the residuals are shown in the off-diagonal elements. There is one large positive correlation between *Yc* and *Yd* and two large negative correlations between *Ya* and *Yc*, and *Ya* and *Yd* respectively. Such features invite modelling. Finally, the correlations between fitted values and outcomes in each equation are:

```
correlation between actual and fitted
             Ya            Yb            Yc            Yd
        0.99963       0.99954       0.97104       0.98702
```

The squares of these correlations are the nearest equivalent to R^2 in a multivariate context, and as least-squares on each equation is valid here, their squares do coincide with the conventional coefficient of multiple correlation squared R^2. The correlation of actual and fitted remains useful when a model is developed, but no unique R^2 measure is calculable. The extremely high values reflect the non-stationarity apparent in the data and do not by themselves ensure a sensible model.

3.6 Graphic analysis and multivariate testing

Rather than peruse the detailed output of coefficients, standard errors and so on to try and interpret the system, we will now view the graphical output. Click on the Model/Test menu in OxMetrics and select the Graphic Analysis item, as shown on the next page. Mark the first three options, namely Actual and fitted, Cross plot of actual and fitted, and Residuals (scaled).

Press OK on the graphics dialog. With four endogenous variables, there will be 12 graphs. The graphs will appear all at once in OxMetrics as shown in Figure 3.1. (When graphs get small, the legends are automatically removed; double click on a graph and use the legends dialog page to reinstate the legends if desired.)

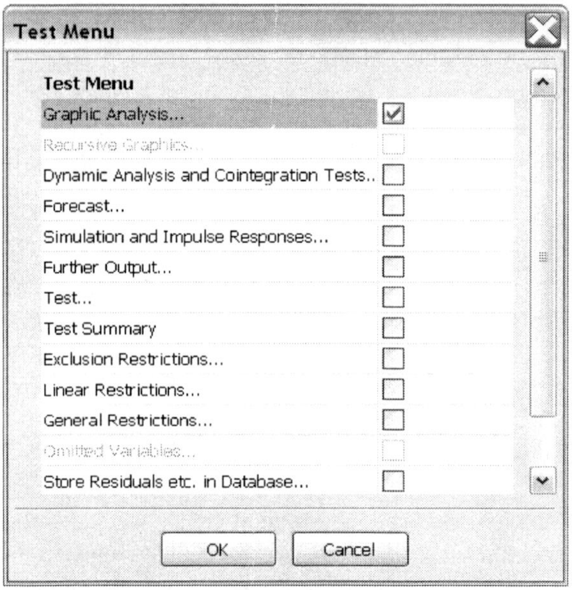

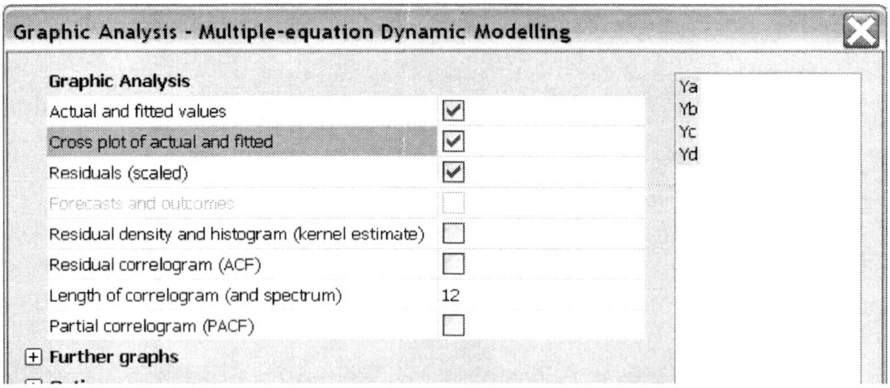

The obvious features of the graphs in Figure 3.1 are the very close fits (owing to the integrated and non-stationary nature of the variables and, as before, should not be taken as evidence for the goodness of the system representation); the close tracking of the apparent changes in trend (again, a *post-hoc* feature which least-squares essentially ensures will occur irrespective of the correctness of the model); and the relatively random (white noise) appearance of the residuals in the final column. Further, the residuals seem to be relatively homoscedastic with few outliers visible, the main exception being the *Ya* residuals, where a large outlier appears in 1979(4).

We can investigate some of these aspects further by returning to the Graphic analysis, but now selecting only Residual density and histogram and Residual correlogram (ACF); remember to deselect actual and fitted and residuals. The resulting 8 graphs are shown Figure 3.2.

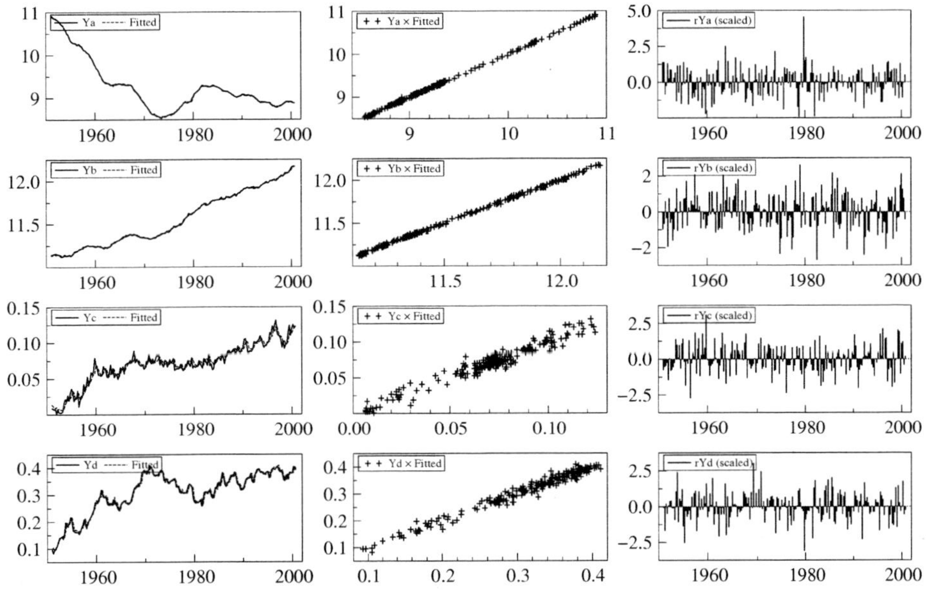

Figure 3.1 Actual and fitted values, their cross plots, and scaled residuals.

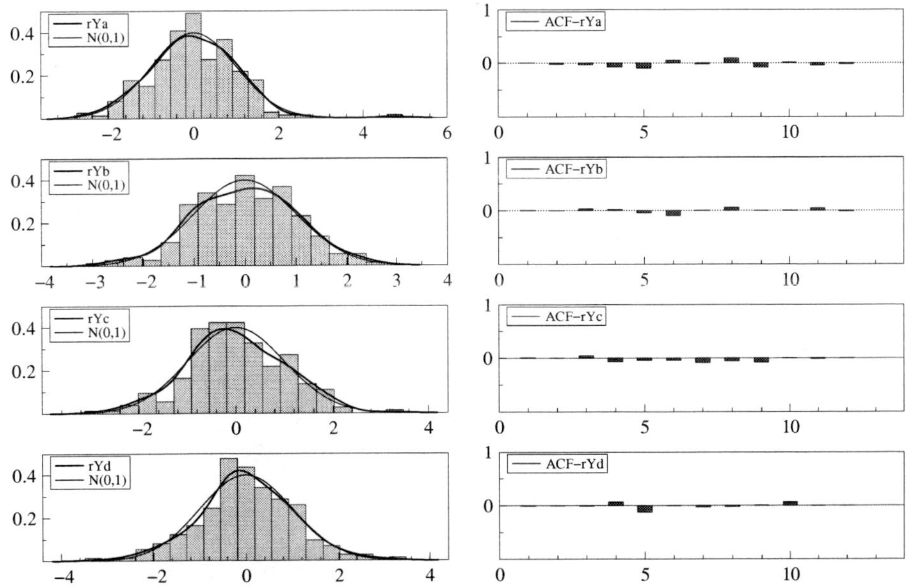

Figure 3.2 Residual correlograms, densities and histograms.

The white-noise nature of the residuals is loosely confirmed by the absence of any residual serial correlations in the correlograms, and normality seems a fair approximation to the distributional shape. The *Ya* residuals appear normal except for the one outlier which can be seen on the right. Note that the non-parametrically estimated densities are plotted beside the N[0, 1] for comparison.

These are single equation diagnostics, and appropriate system mis-specification tests must be conducted for data congruency before proceeding.

Select the Test menu, choose Test, then mark the first four entries, and select the Vector tests radio button:

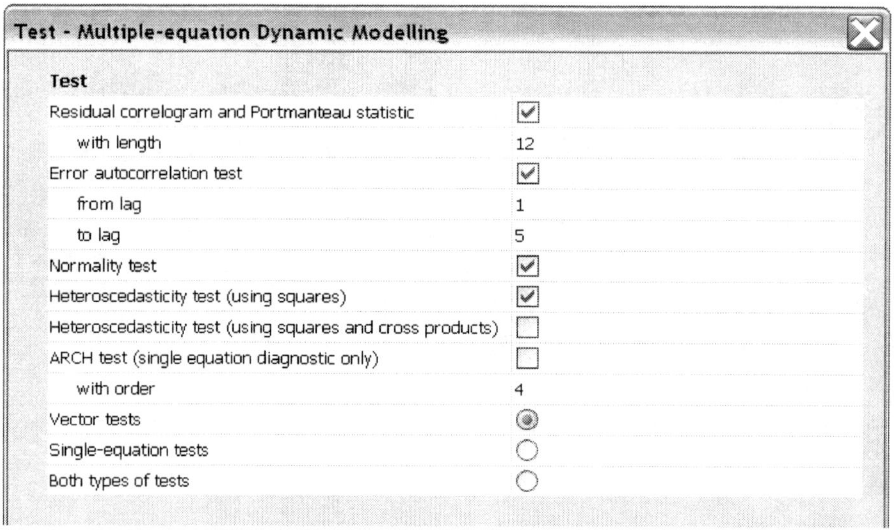

to obtain (after a suitable computational delay for the calculation of these more demanding statistics):

```
Vector Portmanteau statistic for 12 lags and 200 observations: 148.518

Testing for Vector error autocorrelation from lags 1 to 5
 Chi^2(80)=   76.899 [0.5775]   and F-form F(80,645)=  0.87519 [0.7695]

Vector Normality test for Residuals
Skewness
      0.29071     -0.056267     -0.075580      0.064325
Excess kurtosis
       3.9478        2.9789        3.0413        3.1549
Skewness (transformed)
       1.7050      -0.33584      -0.45085       0.38385
Excess kurtosis (transformed)
       2.3507       0.30030       0.47290       0.82882
Vector Normality test:   Chi^2(8) =   9.8973 [0.2723]

Testing for Vector heteroscedasticity using squares
 Chi^2(260)=  253.49 [0.6021]  and F-form F(260,1430)= 0.88188 [0.8992]
```

If you run the single-equation tests, you'll see that the only rejection is normality for the *Ya* equation. In practical situations, one may consider adding an unrestricted dummy for that particular observation. However, because the system version of the test is insignificant, we treat the system as data congruent for the time being. The degrees of freedom of these tests tend to be very large, so considerable mis-specification could be hidden within an insignificant test, but without some notion as to its form, little more can be done. Should many individual tests be conducted, it is important to control the overall size of the procedure. However, we have also ignored the integrated (I(1)) nature of the data in setting implicit critical values: since these should usually be larger, and no hypothesis as yet suggests rejection, no practical problems result. Wooldridge (1999) shows that the diagnostic tests remain valid.

3.7 System reduction

We now return to the system specification-test information, and consider the F-tests for the various variables in the system, which were printed as part of the initial regression output. The tests for the overall significance in the system of each regressor in turn (that is, its contribution to all four equations taken together) are:

```
F-tests on retained regressors, F(4,183) =
        Ya_1         16.5680 [0.000]**         Ya_2          3.57113 [0.008]**
        Ya_3         1.50794 [0.202]           Yb_1          27.4530 [0.000]**
        Yb_2        0.781160 [0.539]           Yb_3         0.399901 [0.809]
        Yc_1         14.3843 [0.000]**         Yc_2          2.08716 [0.084]
        Yc_3        0.819438 [0.514]           Yd_1          52.3821 [0.000]**
        Yd_2         3.40769 [0.010]*          Yd_3         0.493406 [0.741]
       Trend         7.15357 [0.000]**    Constant U         8.00744 [0.000]**
```

Seven system regressors are significant at the 1% level, and a further two at (nearly) the 5% level, with the *Trend* highly significant. Conversely, all third lags and *Yb_2* have high probability values (that is, are not at all significant) and seem redundant. Care is needed when eliminating variables that are highly intercorrelated (for example, *Yd_2* and *Yd_3*), and since a common lag length is needed for the cointegration analysis, we first investigate deleting all lags at length 3, since none is very significant. Thus, select Model, Formulate, and mark *Ya_3*, *Yb_3*, *Yc_3* and *Yd_3*, and then Delete. Accept the reduced system, *keeping the estimation sample period unchanged*, estimate and the output appears. Again the details are reported at the end of this chapter, and here we note the same summary statistics as before:

```
correlation of URF residuals (standard deviations on diagonal)
                  Ya           Yb           Yc           Yd
Ya          0.016541    -0.018395     -0.54692     -0.56326
Yb         -0.018395    0.0098044     -0.12842     0.049441
Yc          -0.54692     -0.12842    0.0068527      0.42397
Yd          -0.56326     0.049441      0.42397     0.013009
```

```
correlation between actual and fitted
            Ya            Yb            Yc            Yd
       0.99963       0.99953       0.97065       0.98657
```

The residual standard deviations are essentially unaltered, confirming the unimportance for fit of the eliminated variables.

Next select Model, Progress to check the statistical relevance of the deletions. The Progress dialog is:

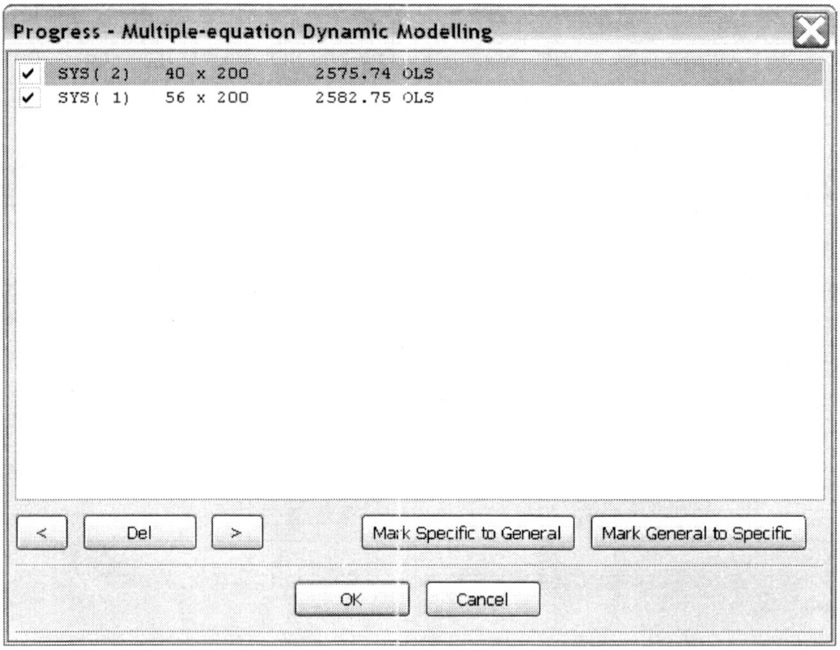

Accept to see the output:

```
Progress to date
Model          T     p        log-likelihood          SC         HQ        AIC
SYS( 1)      200    56  OLS        2582.7528     -24.344    -24.894    -25.268
SYS( 2)      200    40  OLS        2575.7408     -24.698<   -25.090<   -25.357<

Tests of model reduction
SYS( 1) --> SYS( 2): F(16,559)=  0.81220 [0.6723]
```

The reduction by 16 parameters for eliminating lag length 3 is acceptable on the overall F-test, and reduces the 'costs' as measured by the model-selection criteria which seek to balance fit with degrees of freedom.

The summary F-statistics suggest that some lag-2 variables matter greatly, and the *Trend* remains borderline significant using conventional significance levels, so we retain it until after the more appropriate cointegration analysis in the next tutorial.

```
F-tests on retained regressors, F(4,187) =
          Ya_1       20.0751 [0.000]**          Ya_2         6.28850 [0.000]**
          Yb_1       28.1894 [0.000]**          Yb_2         1.19728 [0.313]
          Yc_1       16.5842 [0.000]**          Yc_2         3.19859 [0.014]*
          Yd_1       54.9586 [0.000]**          Yd_2         2.71702 [0.031]*
         Trend       7.93233 [0.000]**     Constant U        9.03718 [0.000]**
```

3.8 Dynamic analysis

As a prelude to cointegration analysis, we consider several features of the dynamics of the system. Chapter 11 explains the mathematics. Select Test/Dynamic Analysis, and mark Static-long run solution and Plot roots of companion matrix.

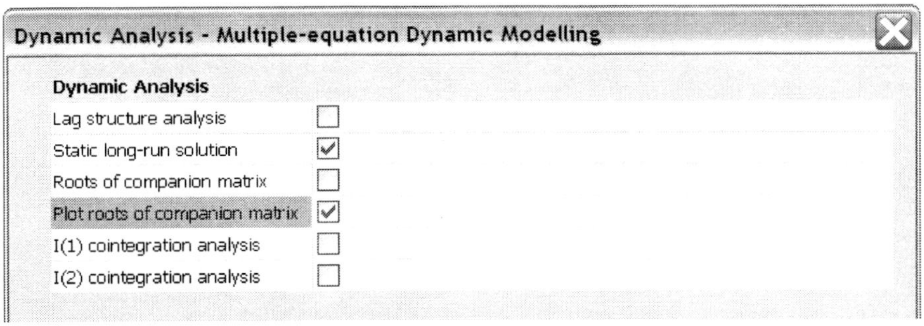

which will produce extensive output as follows:

```
Long-run matrix Pi(1)-I = Po
                 Ya            Yb            Yc            Yd
Ya         -0.10542      0.034061      -0.56666      -0.81271
Yb        0.0087339      -0.20631       0.38600      -0.24463
Yc       -0.0060918      0.061448      -0.23078      0.044220
Yd        0.0073431     -0.038269       0.24051     -0.067974

Long-run covariance
                 Ya            Yb            Yc            Yd
Ya           7.1894       0.85063      -0.16998      -0.74057
Yb          0.85063       0.11627     -0.015486     -0.090387
Yc         -0.16998     -0.015486     0.0055835      0.016610
Yd         -0.74057     -0.090387      0.016610      0.077003

Static long run
              Trend      Constant
Ya       -0.0014309        8.5200
Yb        0.0061396        10.872
Yc       0.00039009      0.063465
Yd       0.00066191       0.31232

Standard errors of static long run
              Trend      Constant
Ya        0.0045475        1.0699
```

```
Yb        0.00057830      0.13606
Yc        0.00012673     0.029817
Yd        0.00047063      0.11073

Mean-lag matrix sum pi_i:
                  Ya            Yb            Yc            Yd
Ya            1.2617      -0.17395      -0.30937      -0.91999
Yb          0.010025       0.85410       0.49334      -0.28166
Yc         -0.036173       0.11715       0.91991      0.073673
Yd         -0.075414     -0.017779       0.21902       0.76213

Eigenvalues of long-run matrix:
       real        imag     modulus
    -0.4345      0.0000      0.4345
   -0.05790    -0.04791     0.07516
   -0.05790     0.04791     0.07516
   -0.06014      0.0000     0.06014

I(2) matrix Gamma:
                  Ya            Yb            Yc            Yd
Ya            1.3671      -0.20802       0.25729      -0.10727
Yb         0.0012916        1.0604       0.10734     -0.037031
Yc         -0.030082      0.055705        1.1507      0.029453
Yd         -0.082757      0.020490     -0.021496       0.83011
```

From the eigenvalues of $\widehat{\mathbf{P}}_0 = \widehat{\pi}(1) - \mathbf{I}_n = \widehat{\pi}_1 + \widehat{\pi}_2 - \mathbf{I}_n$, the rank of the long-run matrix seems to be less than 4 (there are three small eigenvalues), consistent with the apparent non-stationarity of the data. However, the rank is also greater than zero, suggesting some long-run relations, or cointegration, between the variables. Figure 3.3 shows that the companion matrix has no roots outside the unit circle, which might signal an explosive system, nor more roots close to unity than the dimension of the long-run matrix, consistent with the system being I(1), rather than I(2). Nevertheless, the three eigenvalues greater than 0.9 suggest at most 2 long-run relations: any more would cast doubt on our tentative classification. The non-stationarity is reflected in the huge values on the diagonal of the long-run covariance matrix, and the poorly determined static long run. However, the long-run trend is nearly significant for *Ya*, supporting retaining it as a system regressor.

3.9 Recursive estimation

The next main feature to be described concerns graphical examination of parameter constancy using recursive methods. Select Model, Estimate, and tick the box for Recursive estimation (we used 36 observations to initialize here). The output in the results window will be identical to OLS, but selecting Test reveals that Recursive Graphics is now a feasible selection. Choose it to bring up the Recursive Graphics dialog (also available by clicking on the 'Chow-test' icon – the red graph with the straight line):

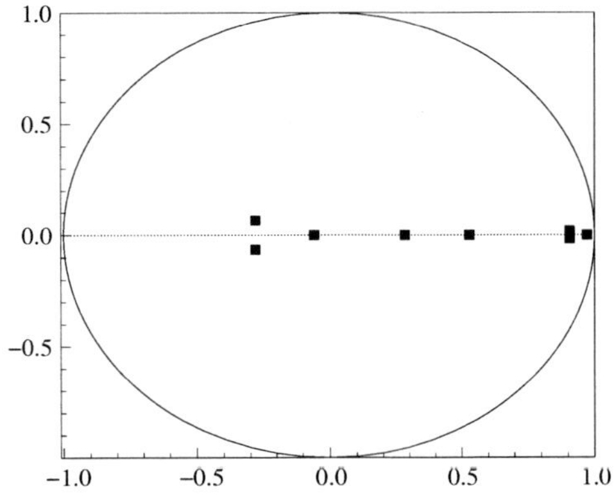

Figure 3.3 Roots of companion matrix.

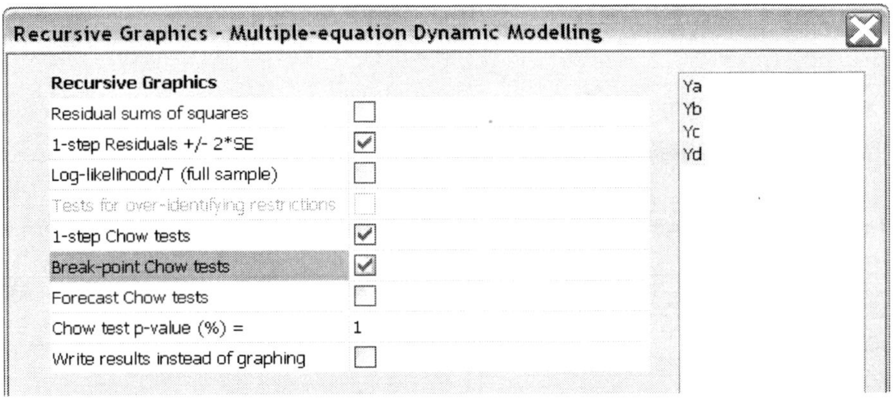

Mark 1-step residuals, 1-step Chow tests, and break-point Chow tests; keep the significance level at 1% given that there are close to 200 statistics per equation. There will be 14 graphs: 1-step residuals, 1-step and $N\downarrow$ (or break-point) Chows for each of the four equations, plus 1-step and $N\downarrow$ Chows for the system as a whole (called 'Chow' in the Figure). The output looks like Figure 3.4. The vast majority of the 1-step residuals lie within their anticipated 95% confidence intervals (that is, $0 \pm 2\widetilde{\sigma}_t$). About 1% of the 1-step tests should be significant etc. Overall, constancy is not rejected, so the system with two lags seems acceptable on the analysis thus far.

The next stage is to consider the integration and cointegration properties of the system, which is the subject of the second tutorial. Prior to that, we look at batch files, and note the use of PcGive for forecasting — although in econometric terms, that would be best undertaken after the system has been reduced to I(0).

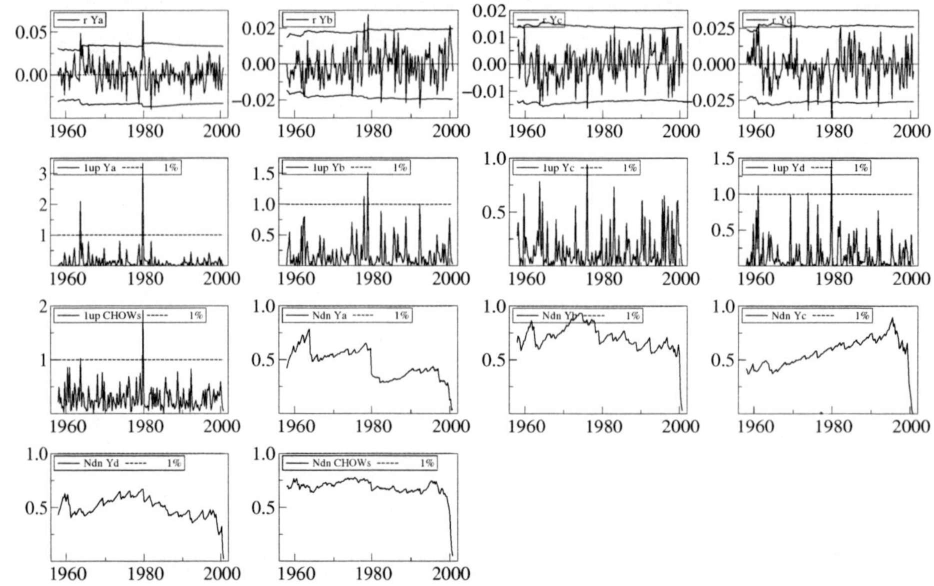

Figure 3.4 Recursive estimation statistics.

3.10 Batch editor

While we have been formulating our system, PcGive has been quietly recording the resulting instructions, and these can be viewed in the batch editor. Activate the Batch Editor in OxMetrics (its icon is the OxMetrics picture with a red arrow) to see the system record in batch code:

```
module("PcGive");
package("PcGive", "Multiple-equation");
usedata("MulTut1.in7");
system
{
    Y = Ya, Yb, Yc, Yd;
    Z = Ya_1, Ya_2, Yb_1, Yb_2, Yc_1, Yc_2, Yd_1, Yd_2, Trend;
    U = Constant;
}
estimate("OLS", 1951, 1, 2000, 4, 0, 28);
```

This batch file can be saved before exiting the batch editor, so that it can be rerun on restarting to resume the analysis wherever it was terminated.

As can be seen, the information in the batch file relates to the specification of the system (which variables are involved, their classification into endogenous, non-modelled and unrestricted variables, and the method of estimation with its associated sample period and recursive initialization). To run a batch file, click on OK in the OxMetrics Batch editor. A full overview of the relevant batch commands is given in

Appendix A1.

Click on Load History in the Batch Editor to see the code for theentire modelling history. Here we make a few changes. We keep the recursive estimation (to remove it, change the number 28 in `estimate` to 0), but add in some batch code to create first differences, which we will use later. The final code is:

```
module("PcGive");
package("PcGive", "Multiple-equation");
usedata("MulTut1.in7");
algebra
{
  DYa = diff(Ya, 1);
  DYb = diff(Yb, 1);
  DYc = diff(Yc, 1);
  DYd = diff(Yd, 1);
}
system
{
  Y = Ya, Yb, Yc, Yd;
  Z = Ya_1, Ya_2, Yb_1, Yb_2, Yc_1, Yc_2, Yd_1, Yd_2, Trend;
  U = Constant;
}
estimate("OLS", 1951, 1, 2000, 4, 0, 28);
```

There is no need to save this file, as it is supplied with PcGive as `MulTut1.fl` in the batch folder.

3.11 Forecasting

PcGive supports three distinct types of forecast analysis. First, within the available data sample, sequences of 1-step-ahead out-of-estimation-sample forecasts can be generated. Select Model, Estimate, deselect recursive estimation and set the number of forecasts to 20, then accept. The following summary statistics are reported (Test/Further Output can be used to print more extensive output):

```
1-step (ex post) forecast analysis 1996 (1) to 2000 (4)
Parameter constancy forecast tests:
using Omega  Chi^2(80)=   94.199 [0.1326]   F(80,170)=    1.1775 [0.1891]
using  V[e]  Chi^2(80)=   86.798 [0.2826]   F(80,170)=    1.0850 [0.3265]
using  V[E]  Chi^2(80)=   87.503 [0.2650]   F(80,170)=    1.0938 [0.3113]
```

Again, graphics provide a convenient medium, so select Test, Graphic Analysis, and mark Forecasts and outcomes, as well as Forecast Chow tests (the latter is under the Further graphs section), creating five graphs. The output is in Figure 3.5. The forecasts lie within their 95% confidence intervals (shown by the vertical error bars of ±2SE, based on the 1-step ahead forecast error variances; the factor two can be changed when the graph is displayed in OxMetrics using the Line Attributes graph edit page). The system constancy test is not significant at the 5% level at any horizon (this is an unscaled χ^2 test, with the 5% significance line as shown).

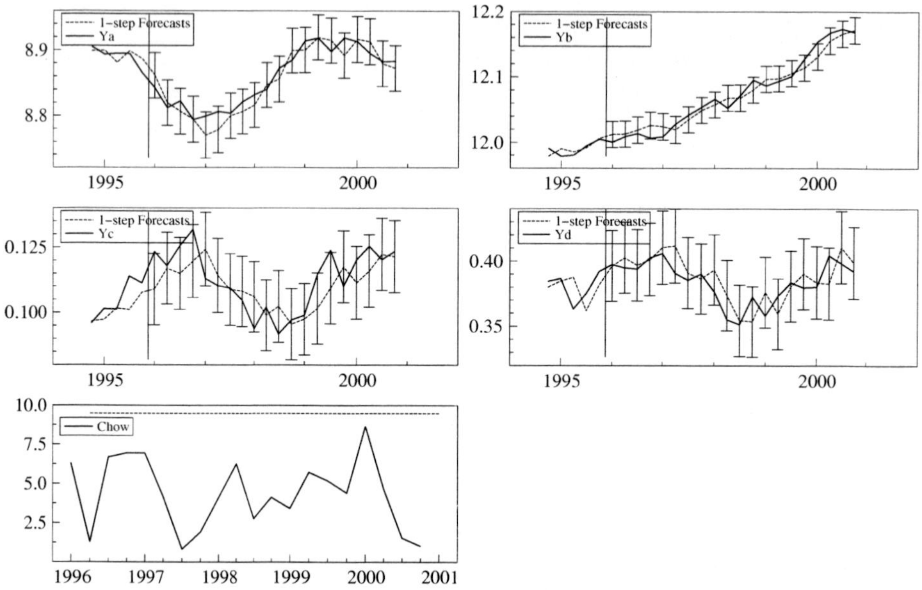

Figure 3.5 1-step forecast statistics.

For purely *ex ante* dynamic forecasts, select Forecast from the Test menu. The two types of forecasts available here are:

(1) Dynamic forecasts
(2) h-step forecasts
Up to h forecasts, the graphs will be identical to the dynamic forecasts. Thereafter, h-step forecasts will be graphed: at $T+h$ the dynamic forecast for $T+h$ starting from T, at $T+h+1$ the dynamic forecast for that period starting at $T+1$, at $T+h+2$ the dynamic forecast starting at $T+2$, etc.

Forecasts are drawn with or without 95% error bars or bands, but by default only the innovation uncertainty (error variance) is allowed for in the computed forecast error variances. Optionally, parameter uncertainty can be taken into account when computing the forecast error variances.

In the dialog, set 44 periods, and mark the error variance option, choose error fans (showing darker colours as the probability rises):[1]

[1]The Bank of England popularized this form of forecast error reporting: see e.g., Britton, Fisher and Whitley (1998). Because they used red for errors around inflation forecasts, and green for GNP forecasts, these charts became known as 'rivers of blood and bile': see Coyle (2001) for an amusing discussion.

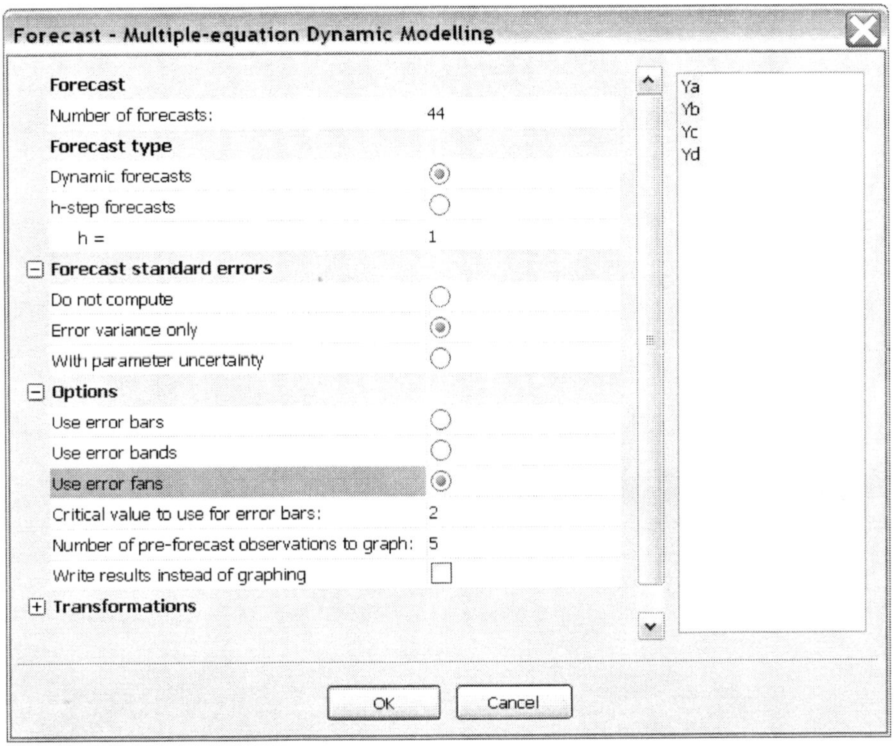

and accept to produce Figure 3.6. Note that you can switch between showing error bars, fans and bands in the Options section of the Forecast dialog. Once a graph is on screen, you can also switch between error fans, bands and bars as follows: double click on the graph, select the appropriate area and vector (Forecasts x (time) here), and make a choice under Error bars.

We have highlighted the *ex ante* period. The uncertainty about the future increases rapidly, and little confidence can be held in the end-of-sample predictions. This is a natural consequence of the implicit unit roots in the system, and matches the large increases seen above between the conditional 1-step residual variances and the long-run variances. The data were actually available for the first 36 'out of sample' values, and as shown in Figure 3.6, reveal the large potential departures between multi-step forecasts and outcomes that are compatible with a considerable degree of forecast uncertainty.

The final forecast mode shown in Figure 3.7 is a sequence of h-step-ahead out-of-estimation-sample forecasts for any choice of h. Select Test, Forecast. The selection now follows the same path as the previous choice except that h-step must be marked in the Forecast dialog, and the desired value of h entered (set $h = 12$ here, given that the frequency is monthly). Thus, keep 44 periods, mark the error bars and 1-step, but set the number of steps to 12. The output will coincide with that from dynamic forecasts for the first 12 steps, then continue at 12 steps for the remainder up to 12 periods beyond. In

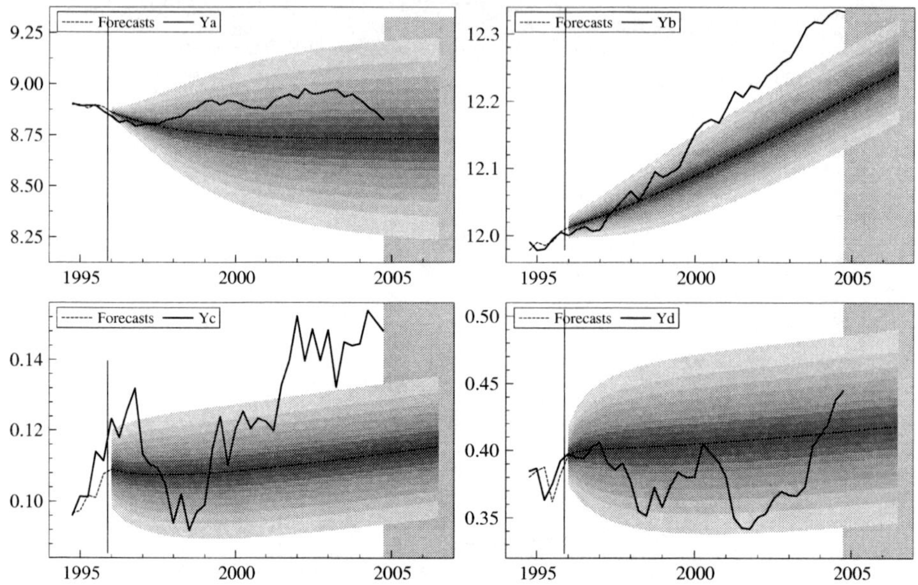

Figure 3.6 Dynamic forecasts.

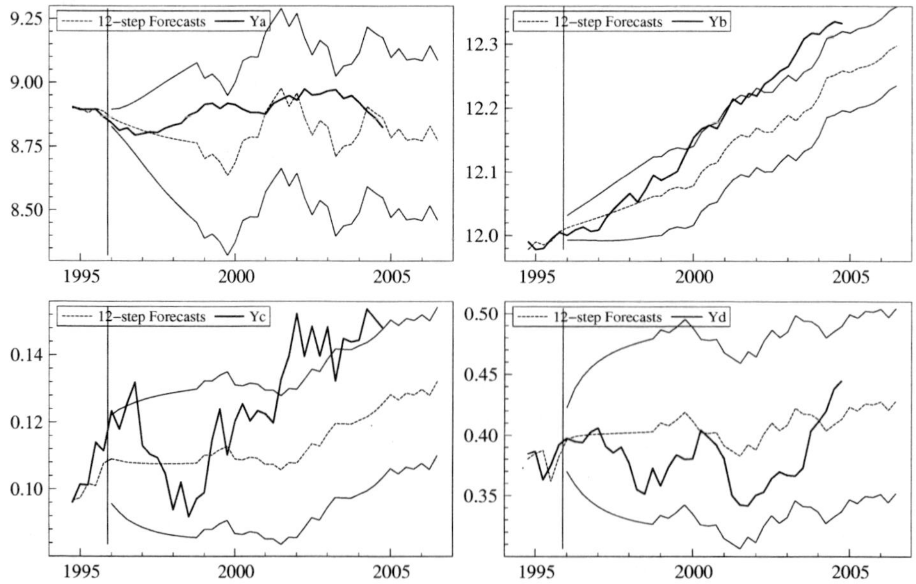

Figure 3.7 12-step forecasts.

effect, therefore, dynamic forecasts correspond to setting h equal to the forecast period. The uncertainty remains constant from 12 steps onwards in Fig. 3.7, and the forecasts start to behave more like the actual data. This happens because the 13th forecast is actually the 12-step forecast starting at $T+2$, etc.

The outcomes are rather poor, even though the system in fact coincides with the reduced form of the data generation process (whose form is a secret we shall not reveal at this stage). The error bands are based on an asymptotic approximation which neglects parameter uncertainty, and this could underestimate forecast error variances in small samples. One potential advantage of a more restricted model of the system is that parameter variability may be considerably reduced.

3.12 Equilibrium-correction representation

This is a simple yet useful transform of a dynamic system which can facilitate the interpretation of systems by mapping from $\mathbf{y}_t, \mathbf{y}_{t-1}, \mathbf{y}_{t-2}$ to $\Delta\mathbf{y}_t$, $\Delta\mathbf{y}_{t-1}$, and $\mathbf{y}_{t-1}$ where only the first lag remains in levels. Linear systems are invariant under linear transforms in that the likelihood is unaltered, and if $\widehat{\mathbf{\Pi}}$ is the original estimate of a coefficient matrix $\mathbf{\Pi}$, and we map to $\mathbf{A\Pi}$, then the estimate of the transformed matrix $\widehat{\mathbf{A\Pi}}$ is equal to $\mathbf{A}\widehat{\mathbf{\Pi}}$. Unit roots are still estimated if any are present, but graphs and many specification test statistics are easier to interpret. Since the residuals are unaltered, diagnostic tests are not changed, nor are such calculations as dynamic analysis (provided the link between Δy_t and y_t is taken into account), dynamic forecasting and dynamic simulation. However, graphical analysis (such as actual and fitted, static forecasts etc.) will change to match the use of a dependent variable in differences. Note that this transformation was called error-correction form in the previous edition of this book.

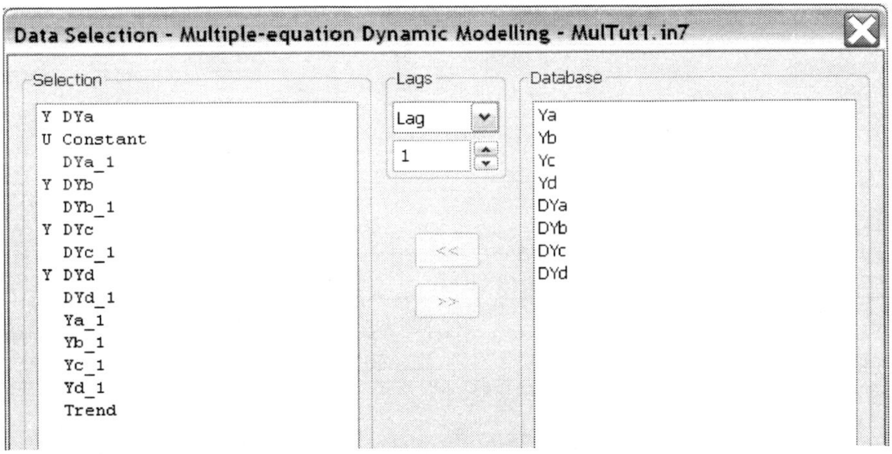

If you have not yet created the differences of *Ya*, *Yb*, *Yc*, and *Yd*, do this now using the default names *DYa*, *DYb*, *DYc*, *DYd*. Then formulate the previous model in differences: for each variable, enter the differences as endogenous variables, using one lagged difference, as well as the one-period lagged levels. Don't forget to add the *Trend*, as shown above.

It is important to bear in mind that *PcGive will not recognize the relation between the lagged level and the differenced level* in the differenced system. As a consequence some results will not match between the two representations. In particular, the dynamic analysis will be different. All misspecification tests will be identical, with the exception of the heteroscedasticity tests, which uses the squared endogenous variables as regressors.

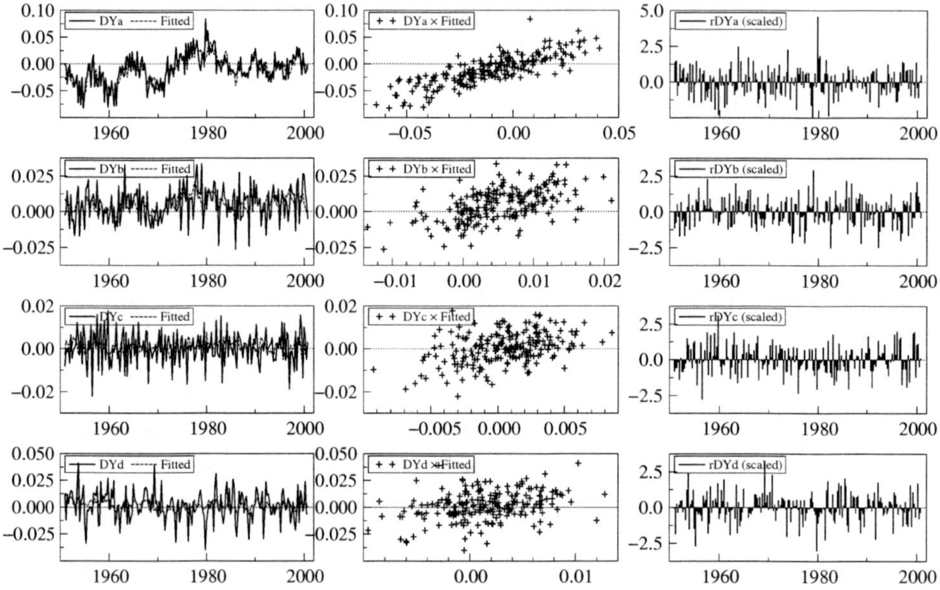

Figure 3.8 Fitted and actual values for differences.

Choose OLS with 0 forecasts, still starting in 1951 (1), then accept. We only note the summary information on F-tests and the correlation between actual and fitted as most other statistics are unaltered.

```
F-tests on retained regressors, F(4,187) =
        DYa_1        6.28850 [0.000]**        DYb_1          1.19728 [0.313]
        DYc_1        3.19859 [0.014]*         DYd_1          2.71702 [0.031]*
         Ya_1        34.6163 [0.000]**         Yb_1          7.76914 [0.000]**
         Yc_1        13.8266 [0.000]**         Yd_1          54.1003 [0.000]**
        Trend        7.93233 [0.000]**   Constant U          9.03718 [0.000]**
correlation between actual and fitted
           DYa            DYb            DYc            DYd
       0.81175        0.52949        0.40986        0.30598
```

The actual and fitted graphs are perhaps the most changed as Figure 3.8 shows. The less than spectacular fits are clear, especially the much lower correlations implicit in the cross plots, even though the scaled residuals graphs are identical to those shown above.

There are many aspects that can now be explored without further guidance from us: try the test summary for additional single-equation diagnostics; try forecasting without error confidence intervals shown, noting how misleading such results are, and compare them with the output from dynamic simulation.

This concludes the first tutorial on formulating, estimating, testing, and analyzing a dynamic system. If you wish, you can save the Results window, but there is no need to save the database: remember that we only changed it by creating differences; we shall recreate these in Chapter 6. The batch file is already provided, but otherwise it is easy to save the algebra file, or better still, add the required algebra commands to the start of a batch file.

Chapter 4

Tutorial on Cointegration Analysis

4.1 Introduction to cointegration analysis

As discussed in §3.12, the system (3.2) can be written in equilibrium-correction form as:

$$\Delta \mathbf{y}_t = (\boldsymbol{\pi}_1 + \boldsymbol{\pi}_2 - \mathbf{I}_n)\,\mathbf{y}_{t-1} - \boldsymbol{\pi}_2 \Delta \mathbf{y}_{t-1} + \boldsymbol{\Phi}\mathbf{q}_t + \mathbf{v}_t,$$

or, writing $\mathbf{P}_0 = \boldsymbol{\pi}_1 + \boldsymbol{\pi}_2 - \mathbf{I}$, and $\boldsymbol{\delta}_1 = -\boldsymbol{\pi}$:

$$\Delta \mathbf{y}_t = \mathbf{P}_0 \mathbf{y}_{t-1} + \boldsymbol{\delta}_1 \Delta \mathbf{y}_{t-1} + \boldsymbol{\Phi}\mathbf{q}_t + \mathbf{v}_t. \tag{4.1}$$

Equation (4.1) shows that the matrix $\mathbf{P}_0$ determines how the level of the process $\mathbf{y}$ enters the system: for example, when $\mathbf{P}_0 = \mathbf{0}$, the dynamic evolution does not depend on the levels of any of the variables. This indicates the importance of the rank of $\mathbf{P}_0$ in the analysis. $\mathbf{P}_0 = \sum \boldsymbol{\pi}_i - \mathbf{I}_n$ is the matrix of long-run responses. The statistical hypothesis of cointegration is:

$$\mathsf{H}(p)\text{:}\;\; \text{rank}\;(\mathbf{P}_0) \leq p.$$

Under this hypothesis, $\mathbf{P}_0$ can be written as the product of two matrices:

$$\mathbf{P}_0 = \boldsymbol{\alpha}\boldsymbol{\beta}',$$

where $\boldsymbol{\alpha}$ and $\boldsymbol{\beta}$ have dimension $n \times p$, and vary freely. As suggested by Johansen (1988, 1995b), such a restriction can be analyzed by maximum likelihood methods.

So, although $\mathbf{v}_t \sim \mathsf{IN}_n[\mathbf{0}, \boldsymbol{\Omega}]$, and hence is stationary, the n variables in $\mathbf{y}_t$ need not all be stationary. The rank p of $\mathbf{P}_0$ determines how many linear combinations of variables are I(0). If $p = n$, all variables in $\mathbf{y}_t$ are I(0), whereas $p = 0$ implies that $\Delta\mathbf{y}_t$ is I(0). For $0 < p < n$ there are p cointegrating relations $\boldsymbol{\beta}'\mathbf{y}_t$ which are I(0). At this stage, we are not discussing I(2)-ness, other than assuming it is not present.

The approach in PcGive to determining cointegration rank, and the associated cointegrating vectors, is based on Johansen (1988), extended for various tests as described below. Chapter 12 explains the mathematics and statistics. Other useful references

```
 H0:rank<=  Trace test  pvalue
     0          239.27 [0.000] **
     1          57.058 [0.001] **
     2          13.667 [0.688]
     3          4.3804 [0.689]

Asymptotic p-values based on: Restricted trend, unrestricted constant
Unrestricted variables:
[0] = Constant
Restricted variables:
[0] = Trend
Number of lags used in the analysis: 2

beta (scaled on diagonal; cointegrating vectors in columns))
Ya             1.0000      -0.12022      -0.59067        1.1218
Yb          -0.034236        1.0000        4.7611       -7.1907
Yc             5.2236       -2.8748        1.0000       -11.471
Yd             8.4541       0.64638       -3.4438        1.0000
Trend    -0.0059925    -0.0056181     -0.028187      0.049566

alpha
Ya           -0.10068      0.030138    -0.0068447    -0.0045982
Yb          -0.016845      -0.17602    -0.0026109     0.0025638
Yc         0.00057796      0.070334     0.0026466     0.0029856
Yd          0.0025727     -0.081061      0.011275     0.0015021

long-run matrix, rank 4
                   Ya            Yb            Yc            Yd         Trend
Ya           -0.10542      0.034061      -0.56666      -0.81271    0.00039902
Yb          0.0087339      -0.20631       0.38600      -0.24463     0.0012905
Yc         -0.0060918      0.061448      -0.23078      0.044220   -0.00032523
Yd          0.0073431     -0.038269       0.24051     -0.067974    0.00019663
```

The output consists of the cointegrating vectors $\widehat{\boldsymbol{\beta}}$, the feedback coefficients (also called loading matrix) $\widehat{\boldsymbol{\alpha}}$, the long-run matrix $\widehat{\mathbf{P}}_0 = \widehat{\boldsymbol{\alpha}}\widehat{\boldsymbol{\beta}}'$, and eigenvalues and test statistics.

There are two very small eigenvalues and two judged significant at the 1% level on the p-values (see Doornik, 1998 for the distribution approximations). This outcome determines the rank of $\widehat{\mathbf{P}}_0$ as 2 (that is, we reject H_0: $p = 0$ and H_0: $p \leq 1$).

The columns of $\widehat{\boldsymbol{\beta}}$ are the cointegrating vectors. Note that for any non-singular matrix $\mathbf{Q}$:

$$\widehat{\boldsymbol{\alpha}}\mathbf{Q}\mathbf{Q}^{-1}\widehat{\boldsymbol{\beta}}' = \widehat{\boldsymbol{\alpha}}\widehat{\boldsymbol{\beta}}', \tag{4.2}$$

so the long-run matrix is unaffected by a rotation of the cointegrating space. The output therefore (arbitrarily) standardizes the output so that $\widehat{\boldsymbol{\beta}}$ has ones on the diagonal.

At this stage the long-run matrix is still the same as that obtained from dynamic analysis in the previous chapter.

4.6 Intercepts and linear deterministic trends II

Two additional models arise when we consider the additional options for entering the *Constant* and *Trend*:

Hypothesis	y	β'y	trend	constant
$\mathsf{H}_{ql}(p)$	quadratic	linear	unrestricted	unrestricted
$\mathsf{H}_{l}(p)$	linear	linear	restricted	unrestricted
$\mathsf{H}_{l}(p)$	linear	constant	not present	unrestricted
$\mathsf{H}_{c}(p)$	constant	constant	not present	restricted
$\mathsf{H}_{z}(p)$	zero	zero	not present	not present

As discussed in Doornik, Hendry and Nielsen (1998), likelihood-ratio test statistics for the two additional models have also been derived by Johansen (1995b). The asymptotic distribution under $\mathsf{H}_{ql}(p)$ depends on nuisance parameters, and this complicates the rank determination considerably (*op. cit.,* Theorem 6.2). To develop a consistent test procedure, the idea is to only test $\mathsf{H}_{ql}(p)$ if $\mathsf{H}_{l}(p)$ has been rejected (*op. cit.,* Ch. 12). The relevant hypotheses are nested as:

$$\begin{array}{ccccccccc} \mathsf{H}_{ql}(0) & \subset & \cdots & \subset & \mathsf{H}_{ql}(p) & \subset & \cdots & \subset & \mathsf{H}_{ql}(n) \\ \cup & & & & \cup & & & & \parallel \\ \mathsf{H}_{l}(0) & \subset & \cdots & \subset & \mathsf{H}_{l}(p) & \subset & \cdots & \subset & \mathsf{H}_{l}(n). \end{array} \tag{4.3}$$

By testing the hypotheses

$$\mathsf{H}_{l}(0), \mathsf{H}_{ql}(0), \mathsf{H}_{l}(1), \mathsf{H}_{ql}(1), \ldots, \mathsf{H}_{l}(n-1), \mathsf{H}_{ql}(n-1),$$

sequentially against the unrestricted alternative and stopping whenever the hypothesis is accepted, a consistent procedure is obtained.

A corresponding complication arises with $\mathsf{H}_{lc}(r)$. The test procedure is then based on:

$$\begin{array}{ccccccccc} \mathsf{H}_{lc}(0) & \subset & \cdots & \subset & \mathsf{H}_{lc}(p) & \subset & \cdots & \subset & \mathsf{H}_{lc}(n) \\ \cup & & & & \cup & & & & \parallel \\ \mathsf{H}_{c}(0) & \subset & \cdots & \subset & \mathsf{H}_{c}(r) & \subset & \cdots & \subset & \mathsf{H}_{c}(n). \end{array} \tag{4.4}$$

When we allow for a quadratic trend in the current model we find for the trace test:

$$\left[\begin{array}{ccccc} & p=0 & p\leq 1 & p\leq 2 & p\leq 3 \\ \mathsf{H}_{ql}(p) & 229^{**} & 53.9^{**} & 10.8 & 4.1^{*} \\ \mathsf{H}_{l}(p) & 239^{**} & 57.1^{**} & 13.7 & 4.4 \end{array}\right].$$

We encounter 239^{**}, 229^{**}, 57.1^{**}, 53.9^{**}, 13.7, so that the first hypothesis to be accepted is $\mathsf{H}_{l}(2)$. Therefore the quadratic trend is rejected, and the conclusion is as before. We ignore the final test statistic for $\mathsf{H}_{ql}(p)$, which is just significant at the 5% level.

4.7 Recursive eigenvalues

Recursive estimation can also be a valuable tool in assessing constancy in cointegrated models. To activate recursive cointegrating, we need to move from the unrestricted reduced form to the cointegrated VAR, so at the Model Settings stage select the latter:

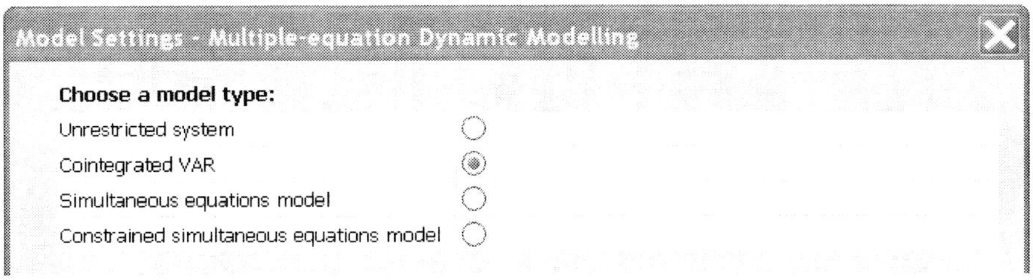

The next dialog asks for the cointegrated VAR settings. Set the rank to four, and keep No additional restrictions:

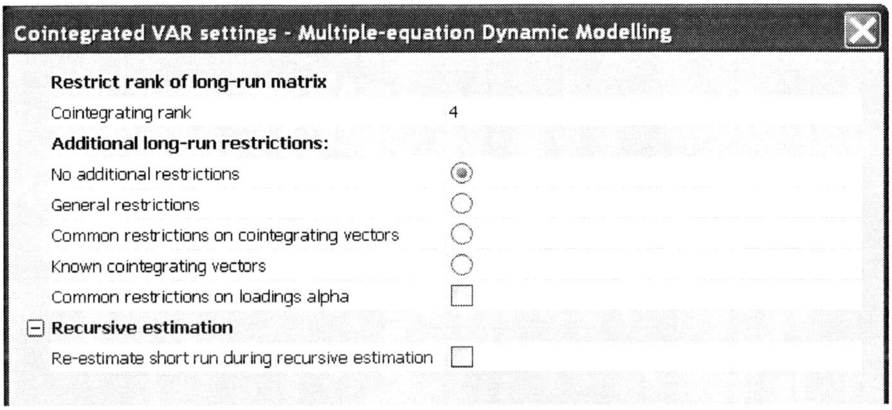

This results in exactly the same model as before, because no rank restrictions have been imposed yet. In the next dialog, start estimation at 1951(1) as before, and select recursive estimation with 28 observations to initialize. The output omits the test statistics for the rank: it is assumed that the rank of the cointegration space is fixed.

Test/Recursive Graphics shows the recursive eigenvalue – Figure 4.1a has them all in one graph. The eigenvalues are relatively constant, the first two at non-zero values, the third much smaller but visibly above zero, and the last at close to zero throughout. However, these are conditional on having partialled out the full-sample dynamics and unrestricted variables, so are more 'constant' than would have been found at the time on a smaller sample.

To obtain eigenvalues for each sample size with re-estimation of the full analysis, tick the option under recursive estimation in the cointegrated VAR settings.

Estimation now takes somewhat longer: for each $t = M, \dots, T$ the complete analysis is redone. The results in Fig. 4.1b show larger changes, equivalent to what an investigator at the time would have found.

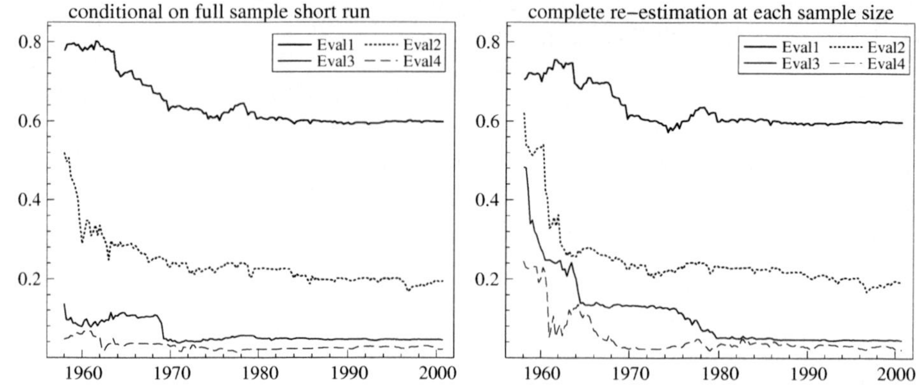

Figure 4.1 Recursive eigenvalues.

4.8 Cointegration graphics

Select Test and Graphic Analysis, which has an additional section for cointegration graphics.

Mark the first two entries for Cointegration relations and Actual and fitted. Then click OK to see Figure 4.2.

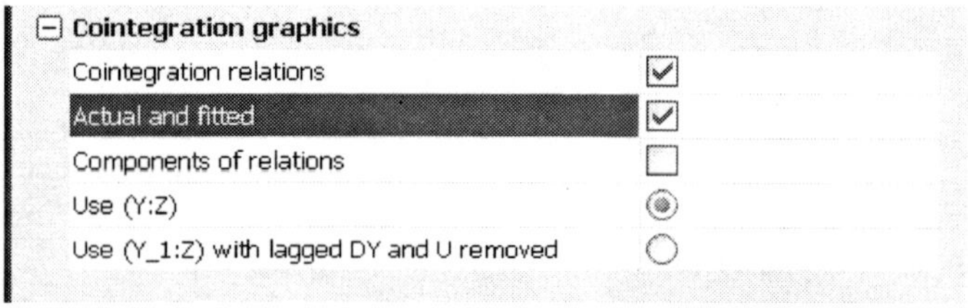

The first four graphs of Figure 4.2 show the linear combinations $\widehat{\boldsymbol{\beta}}'\mathbf{y}_t$, the next four plot the sum of the non-normalized coefficients (with the opposite sign as in regression, namely $-\sum_{j\neq i}\widehat{\beta}_j y_{jt}$) against the normalized variable (that is, long-run fitted and actual). The first two cointegration vectors look fairly stationary, with fitted and actual tracking each other reasonably closely. The last two look less non-stationary, with not much relation between fitted and actuals.

The $\widehat{\boldsymbol{\beta}}'\mathbf{x}_t$ do not correct for short-run dynamics, so would look more stationary still if the Use (Y_1:Z) with lagged DY and U removed option was marked in the dialog, see Figure 4.3.

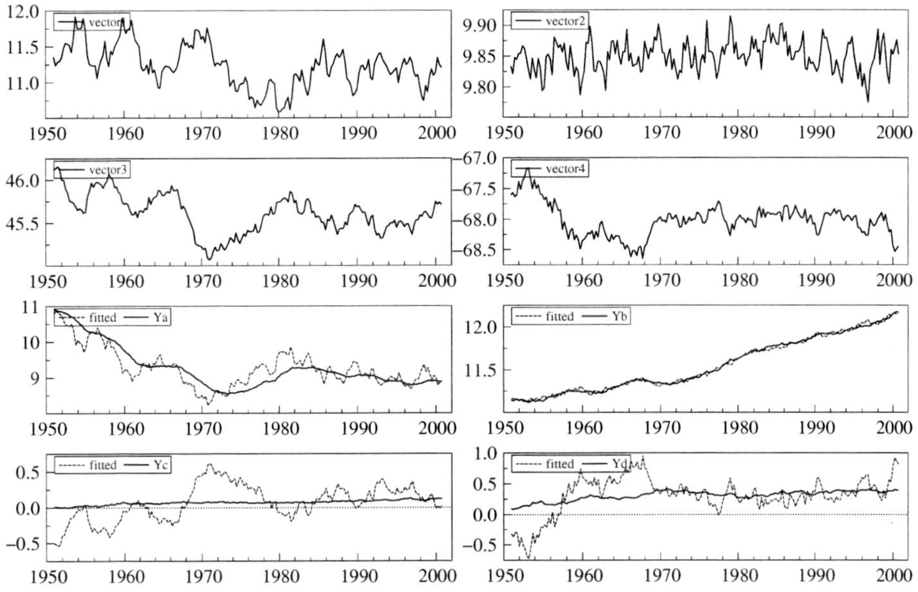

Figure 4.2 Time series of cointegration vectors.

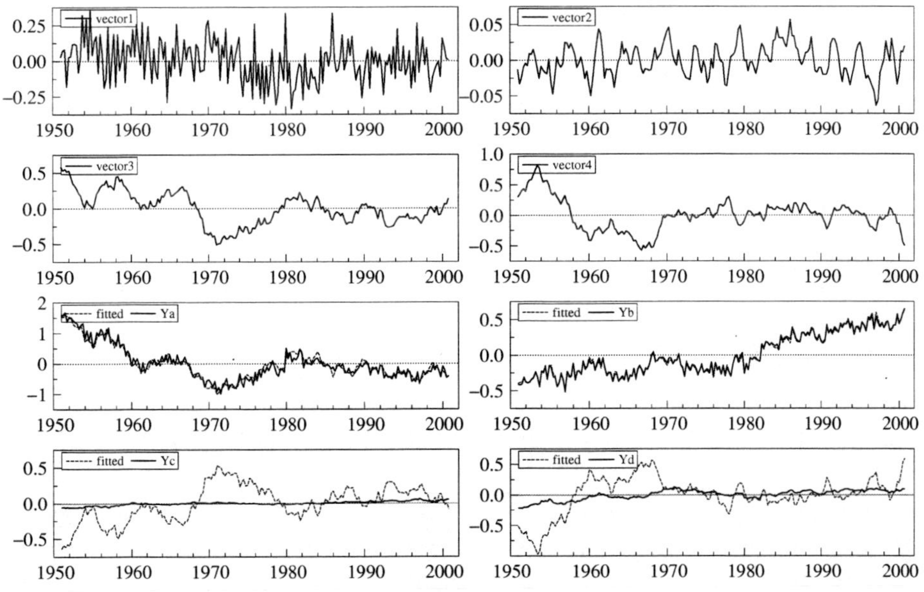

Figure 4.3 Time series of cointegration vectors, corrected for short-run dynamics.

Chapter 5

Tutorial on Cointegrated VARs

5.1 Introduction

The results from the previous chapter suggested a cointegration space with rank 2. One possibility is just to accept this with the corresponding cointegrating vectors, but these are unlikely to coincide with the structural relations. Another, which we follow, is to uniquely determine the cointegration vectors based on economic theory, but supported by statistical testing. This requires knowledge about the economic analysis being undertaken, which is difficult to accomplish for artificial data.

Doornik, Hendry and Nielsen (1998) designed the DGP from which the data are a replication to mimic their final model for UK money demand. Accordingly, *Ya* corresponds to the logarithm of real money demand ($m-p$), *Yb* equals the logs of total final expenditure (i), *Yc* is inflation (Δp), and *Yd* measures the opportunity costs of holding money (R_n).

5.2 Imposing the rank of the cointegration space

The first step is to compute $\widehat{\mathbf{P}}_0$ when only a rank restriction is imposed: here we wish to set $p = 2$. If you start afresh, formulate the model as a VAR(2) in the four *Ya*,...,*Yd* variables, with unrestricted *Constant* and restricted *Trend* (i.e., the *Trend* is not unrestricted, which is the default). Follow §4.7 by selecting Cointegrated VAR at the Model Settings stage, then setting the rank to 2, but imposing no further restrictions:

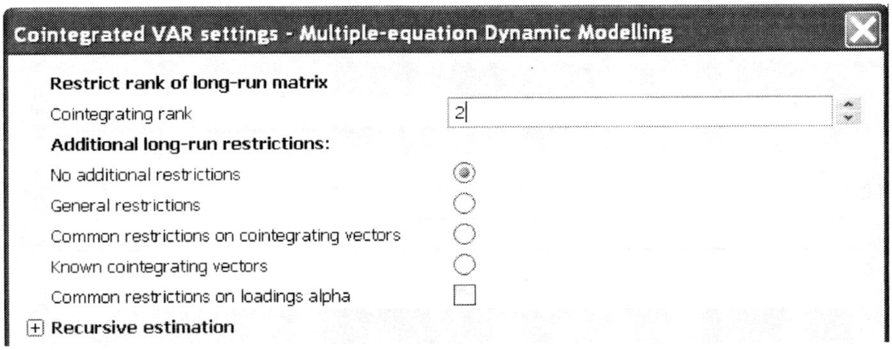

Estimate over the same 200 observations (1951-1 to 2000-4), without recursive estimation. The output does not report the coefficients of the short-run dynamics (Δy_{t-1} here), nor the coefficients of the unrestricted variables (the *Constant* in this model).

```
SYS( 1) Cointegrated VAR (using MulTut1.in7)
        The estimation sample is: 1951(1) - 2000(4)

Cointegrated VAR(2) in:
[0] = Ya
[1] = Yb
[2] = Yc
[3] = Yd

Unrestricted variables:
[0] = Constant
Restricted variables:
[0] = Trend

Number of lags used in the analysis: 2

beta
Ya            1.0000     -0.12022
Yb         -0.034236       1.0000
Yc            5.2236      -2.8748
Yd            8.4541      0.64638
Trend     -0.0059925   -0.0056181

alpha
Ya          -0.10068     0.030138
Yb         -0.016845     -0.17602
Yc        0.00057796     0.070334
Yd         0.0025727    -0.081061

Standard errors of alpha
Ya         0.0081392     0.054271
Yb         0.0048097     0.032070
Yc         0.0033833     0.022559
Yd         0.0064879     0.043260
```

```
Restricted long-run matrix, rank 2
                   Ya            Yb            Yc            Yd         Trend
Ya           -0.10430      0.033585      -0.61256      -0.83169    0.00043401
Yb          0.0043157      -0.17544       0.41802      -0.25619     0.0010898
Yc         -0.0078776      0.070315      -0.19918      0.050349   -0.00039861
Yd           0.012318     -0.081149       0.24647     -0.030647    0.00043999

Standard errors of long-run matrix
Ya           0.010431      0.054272       0.16171      0.077236    0.00030878
Yb          0.0061642      0.032071      0.095556      0.045641    0.00018246
Yc          0.0043361      0.022560      0.067218      0.032105    0.00012835
Yd          0.0083151      0.043261       0.12890      0.061566    0.00024613

Reduced form beta
Ya            -1.0000       0.00000
Yb            0.00000       -1.0000
Yc            -5.1464        2.2561
Yd            -8.5113       -1.6696
Trend       0.0062104     0.0063647
Standard errors of reduced form beta
Ya            0.00000       0.00000
Yb            0.00000       0.00000
Yc            0.99592       0.38888
Yd            0.25410      0.099219
Trend      0.00037897    0.00014798

Moving average impact matrix
     -0.33216       0.85487       -4.9634       -6.2864
     -0.14183       0.64169      0.089129       -1.3688
    -0.023478       0.14515       0.32544     -0.041532
     0.053222      -0.18820       0.38637       0.76370

log-likelihood       2568.90703  -T/2log|Omega|      3704.05786
no. of observations         200  no. of parameters           34
rank of long-run matrix       2  no. long-run restrictions    0
beta is not identified
No restrictions imposed
```

When $p = 2$ is imposed, $\widehat{\mathbf{P}}_0$ is different from its counterpart calculated without any rank restrictions which was reported in §4.5. The difference appears to be small, consistent with the insignificance of the test for the rank restriction (remember that this test did not have a simple χ^2 distribution). Note that the estimated $\widehat{\boldsymbol{\alpha}}$ and $\widehat{\boldsymbol{\beta}}$ are simply the first two columns from the matrices in §4.5, with the long-run matrix computed as:

$$\begin{pmatrix} \widehat{\boldsymbol{\alpha}}_1 & \widehat{\boldsymbol{\alpha}}_2 \end{pmatrix} \begin{pmatrix} \widehat{\boldsymbol{\beta}}_1' \\ \widehat{\boldsymbol{\beta}}_2' \end{pmatrix}.$$

Some care is required when interpreting the standard errors of $\widehat{\boldsymbol{\alpha}}$ at this stage: the calculations essentially assume that the cointegrating vectors (the $\widehat{\boldsymbol{\beta}}$) are known, so that all uncertainty is attributed to the loadings. No such problem exists with the standard errors of the long-run matrix.

The reduced-form cointegration vectors correspond to the triangular representation (see Phillips, 1991). We will discuss the moving-average impact matrix in §5.6 below.

The summary table at the bottom of the output contains the log-likelihood, which matches the value for $p = 2$ found at the testing stage. The number of parameters is computed as follows:

short-run coefficients, Δy_{t-1}	4×4	=	16
unrestricted *Constant*	1×4	=	4
feed-back coefficients, $\widehat{\alpha}$	4×2	=	8
coefficients in cointegrating vectors, $\widehat{\beta}$	5×2	=	10
adjustment for double counting	2×2	=	-4
total			**34**

The adjustment is based on (4.2): in this case, we can insert an arbitrary 2×2 matrix $\mathbf{Q}$, and we must subtract the number of elements in $\mathbf{Q}$ to avoid double counting. The reported standard errors use the residual variance matrix $\widehat{\boldsymbol{\Omega}}^{-1}$ which is based on the residual sum of squares matrix:

$$\widehat{\boldsymbol{\Omega}} = \frac{\widehat{\mathbf{V}}'\widehat{\mathbf{V}}}{T-c}.$$

As elsewhere in PcGive, T is the sample size (200 here), and c is the adjustment for degrees of freedom: the number of estimated parameters per equation, rounded down to the nearest integer. In the current model $c = \lceil 34/4 \rceil = 8$.

5.3 Intercepts and linear deterministic trends III

We argued in §4.2 that a *Trend* should be entered restrictedly if there is any evidence of trending behaviour. The corresponding cointegration hypothesis is $\mathsf{H}_l(p)$ which has the desirable property of (asymptotic) similarity, so the critical values of tests do not depend on the deterministic effects. It was shown in §4.6 how to handle the not-so-well-behaved tests. Now that we have fixed the rank of the cointegration space, we can test if the *Trend* is significant. Therefore re-estimate the cointegrated VAR without the `Trend` and rank two. Use Progress to test the restriction:

```
Progress to date
Model        T     p          log-likelihood         SC         HQ        AIC
SYS( 1)    200    34   COINT      2568.9070   -24.788<   -25.122<   -25.349<
SYS( 2)    200    32   COINT      2556.2587   -24.715    -25.029    -25.243

Tests of model reduction
SYS( 1) --> SYS( 2): Chi^2(2) =    25.297 [0.0000]**
```

The likelihood-ratio test has a standard $\chi^2(2)$ distribution (we are keeping the rank of the long-run matrix fixed). So dropping the *Trend* is strongly rejected.

5.4 Cointegration restrictions

PcGive offers a uniform approach to testing all forms of restrictions on both cointegration vectors and feedback coefficients. It is based on the transparency of explicitly setting the restrictions to be imposed on elements of $\boldsymbol{\alpha}$ and $\boldsymbol{\beta}$. A restrictions editor is provided, which shows the numbering of all the elements, and within which restrictions are defined by statements of the form &4=0 to set the element corresponding to parameter 5 to zero (numbering commences with &0). Several examples will now be provided, and related to alternative approaches (such as Johansen and Juselius, 1990, and Johansen, 1991, discussed in the addendum to this chapter).

Coefficient restrictions can have three effects:

(1) **rotate** the cointegrating space;
(2) contribute to **identification** of the cointegrating space;
(3) **restrict** the cointegrating space without contributing to identification.

As an illustration, consider a cointegrated VAR with $n = 3$, $p = 1$ and a restricted *Trend*:

$$\mathbf{P}_0 = \begin{pmatrix} \alpha_1 \\ \alpha_2 \\ \alpha_3 \end{pmatrix} \begin{pmatrix} \beta_1 & \beta_2 & \beta_3 & \beta_4 \end{pmatrix}.$$

First consider imposing $\beta_1 = 1$:

(1) $\beta_1 = 1$ is a rotation of the cointegrating space, leaving $\mathbf{P}_0$ unchanged:

$$\mathbf{P}_0 = \begin{pmatrix} \alpha_1\beta_1 \\ \alpha_2\beta_1 \\ \alpha_3\beta_1 \end{pmatrix} \begin{pmatrix} 1 & \beta_2/\beta_1 & \beta_3/\beta_1 & \beta_4/\beta_1 \end{pmatrix}.$$

(2) $\beta_1 = 1$ also makes the cointegrating space identified: the only feasible $\mathbf{QQ}^{-1}$ we can insert between $\boldsymbol{\alpha\beta}'$ is $Q = 1$.
(3) $\beta_1 = 1$ does not impose any restrictions on the cointegrating space so the likelihood of the model is unchanged.

Next, consider imposing $\beta_1 = 0$:

(1) $\beta_1 = 0$ is a restriction of the cointegrating space, changing $\mathbf{P}_0$, and therefore the likelihood. So we can test if it is a valid restriction.
(2) $\beta_1 = 0$ cannot be achieved by a rotation, but itself is unaffected by any rotation. As a consequence, rotation is still allowed, and the cointegration space is not identified.

When $p > 1$ the counting involved to decide the effect of coefficient 'restrictions' is very difficult. For example, before PcGive could do this, our manual efforts were regularly wrong. Fortunately, PcGive implements the algorithm of Doornik (1995b), and we can let the computer do the hard work.

To illustrate how the general approach in PcGive operates, we consider the normalization of the cointegrating vector on the diagonal. Keep the VAR formulation with the restricted *Trend*, select Model/Model settings, Cointegrated VAR, and then on the Cointegrated VAR settings, set the General restrictions radio button:

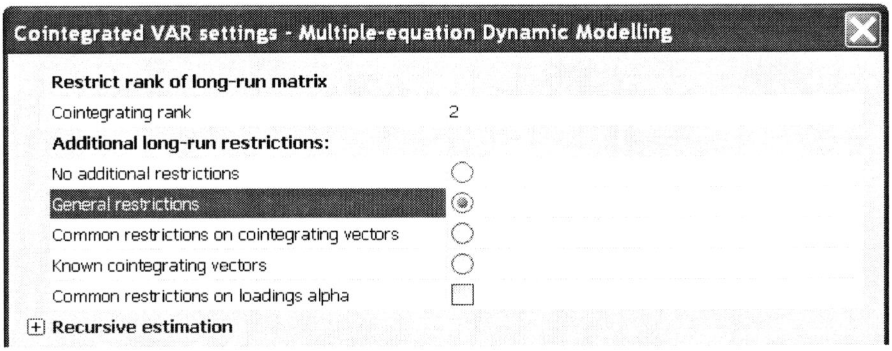

Pressing OK in produces the General Restrictions Editor:

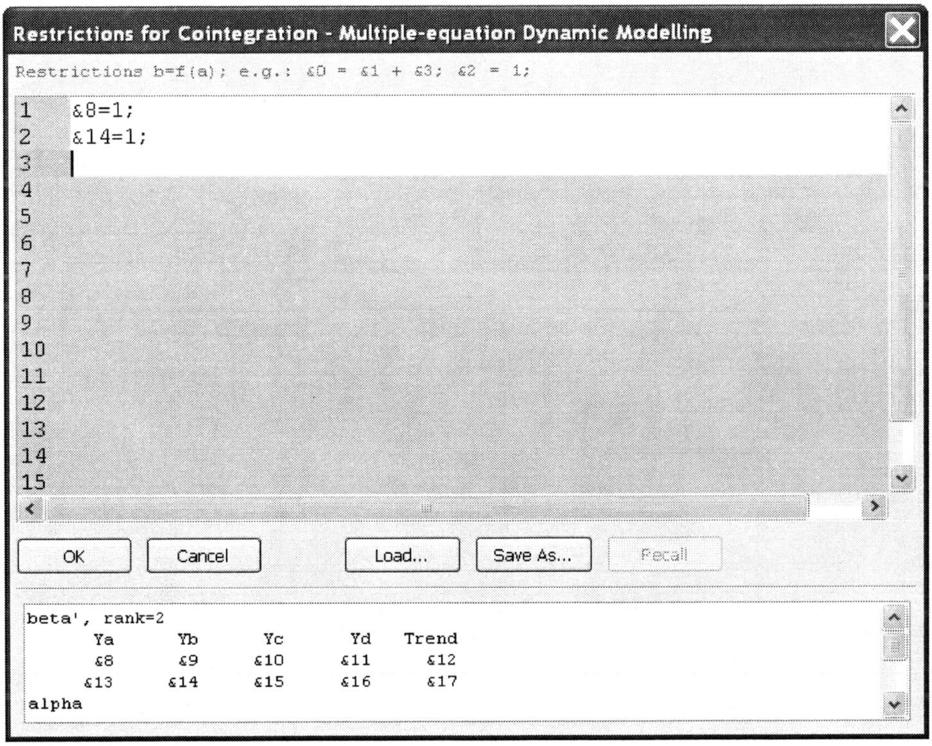

To normalize $\widehat{\beta}$ on the diagonal enter the restrictions as shown above. The output confirms that this rotation has no effect on the log-likelihood:

```
log-likelihood      2568.90703  -T/2log|Omega|      3704.05786
no. of observations        200  no. of parameters           34
rank of long-run matrix      2  no. long-run restrictions    0
beta is not identified
No restrictions imposed

General cointegration restrictions:
&8 = 1;
&14= 1;
```

When the cointegration rank is p, the elements of α are notionally numbered from 0 to $np-1$ in the form (for $n=4, p=2$):

```
&0  &1
&2  &3
&4  &5
&6  &7
```

The elements of β are then numbered in rows from np to $np+p(n+q_r)-1$ for q_r non-modelled variables in the cointegration vector. For $n=4, p=2$ and $q_r=1$:

```
&8   &9   &10  &11  &12
&13  &14  ...
```

Note that the numbering of the elements alters as the rank of $\mathbf{P}_0$ changes.

5.5 Determining unique cointegration relations

To uniquely determine the two cointegration vectors, given their possible interpretations as excess demands for money and goods respectively, we remove the *Trend* from the first, and *Ya* (interpreted as $m-p$) from the second:

```
&8 = 1; &12 = 0;
&13= 0; &14 = 1;
```

This can be achieved through a rotation of the space, and no restrictions have been imposed. However, the cointegrating space is now just identified, and any further parameter restriction can be tested.

Restrict the income (i, corresponding to *Yb*) coefficient to -1 in the first vector (converting it to an inverse-velocity relation):

```
&8 = 1; &9 = -1; &12 = 0;
&13= 0; &14 = 1;

log-likelihood      2568.83873  -T/2log|Omega|      3703.98956
no. of observations        200  no. of parameters           33
rank of long-run matrix      2  no. long-run restrictions    1
beta is identified

LR test of restrictions: Chi^2(1) =   0.13660 [0.7117]
```

Now suppose that in the first vector inflation and the interest rate have the same coefficient:

```
&8 = 1; &9 = -1; &10 = &11; &12 = 0;
&13= 0; &14 = 1;
```

This is again not rejected:

```
log-likelihood         2568.4813   -T/2log|Omega|        3703.63212
no. of observations          200   no. of parameters             32
rank of long-run matrix        2   no. long-run restrictions      2
beta is identified

LR test of restrictions: Chi^2(2) =   0.85147 [0.6533]
```

Finally, we set the feedbacks to zero for the second vector on the first equation, and the first on the last three equations (related to long-run weak exogeneity):

```
&8 = 1; &9 =-1; &10 = &11; &12 = 0;
&13= 0; &14= 1;
&1 = 0;
&2 = 0; &4 = 0; &6 = 0;
```

With the test of the restrictions being $\chi^2(6) = 11.638$ [p $= 0.07$] this is only just accepted. The final results are:

$$\begin{bmatrix} \widehat{\alpha} & 1 & 2 \\ m-p & \underset{(0.007)}{-0.109} & \underset{(-)}{0} \\ i & \underset{(-)}{0} & \underset{(0.024)}{-0.156} \\ \Delta p & \underset{(-)}{0} & \underset{(0.015)}{0.034} \\ R_n & \underset{(-)}{0} & \underset{(0.028)}{-0.068} \end{bmatrix},$$

$$\begin{bmatrix} \widehat{\beta}' & m-p & i & \Delta p & R_n & t \\ 1 & \underset{(-)}{1} & \underset{(-)}{-1} & \underset{(-)}{7.06} & \underset{(0.08)}{7.06} & \underset{(-)}{0} \\ 2 & \underset{(-)}{0} & \underset{(-)}{1} & \underset{(0.47)}{-2.49} & \underset{(0.12)}{1.70} & \underset{(0.00018)}{-0.0063} \end{bmatrix}. \quad (5.1)$$

5.6 Moving-average impact matrix

The moving-average impact matrix shows the alternative representation of a cointegrated process. Consider the VAR representation of an I(1) process $\mathbf{y}_t$:

$$\mathbf{y}_t = \boldsymbol{\mu} + \sum_{i=1}^{m} \boldsymbol{\pi}_i \mathbf{y}_{t-i} + \boldsymbol{\epsilon}_t.$$

Since the process is I(1), the lag polynomial contains a unit root, which can be extracted to leave a lag polynomial with all its eigenvalues inside the unit circle. Consequently, the remainder lag polynomial matrix can be inverted, and the differenced process can be expressed in a moving-average form as:

$$\Delta \mathbf{y}_t = \mathbf{C}(L)(\boldsymbol{\mu} + \boldsymbol{\epsilon}_t).$$

and solving for levels:

$$\mathbf{y}_t = \mathbf{y}_0 + \mathbf{C}(1)\boldsymbol{\mu}t + \mathbf{C}(1)\sum_{i=1}^{t}\boldsymbol{\epsilon}_i + \mathbf{C}^*(L)\boldsymbol{\epsilon}_t.$$

Then $\mathbf{C}(1)$ is the moving-average impact matrix. It is computed in PcGive from:

$$\mathbf{C}(1) = \boldsymbol{\beta}_\perp \left(\boldsymbol{\alpha}'_\perp \boldsymbol{\Upsilon} \boldsymbol{\beta}_\perp\right)^{-1} \boldsymbol{\alpha}'_\perp$$

where

$$\mathrm{r}\left(\boldsymbol{\alpha}'_\perp \boldsymbol{\Upsilon} \boldsymbol{\beta}_\perp\right) = n - p \qquad (5.2)$$

(see Chapter 12, Banerjee, Dolado, Galbraith and Hendry, 1993, and Johansen, 1995b).

For the current specification we find:

```
Moving-average impact matrix
       0.00000         1.2934        -4.7669        -5.3435
       0.00000        0.61466        0.58769        -1.1190
       0.00000        0.10757        0.44859      -0.023701
       0.00000       -0.20370        0.30985        0.62207
```

Although it cannot be seen immediately, the MA representation $\widehat{\mathbf{C}}(1)$ has rank 2 as required.

5.7 Cointegration graphics

If one is willing to wait a short time, then the recursive restricted cointegration coefficients can be graphed. The options also allow a transform of the likelihood, and the test of the overidentifying restrictions to be graphed. In this case we keep the short-run fixed (remember: this is set in the Cointegrated VAR Settings dialog).

Figure 5.1 shows the graphs of the three remaining unrestricted $\widehat{\beta}_{i,j,t}$, using 60 initial values (otherwise, the variation at the start swamps that later), together with the sequence of χ^2 tests of the overidentifying cointegration restrictions; their 5% critical values are shown (alternative p-values can be set).

It is important to note that the graph labelled 'loglik/T' does not depict the likelihood as it would be found at the time. Instead it excludes the likelihood constant and shows

$$\hat{l}_t/T = -\tfrac{1}{2}\log\left|\tfrac{1}{T}\sum_{i=1}^{t}\widehat{\mathbf{V}}'_i\widehat{\mathbf{V}}_i\right|,$$

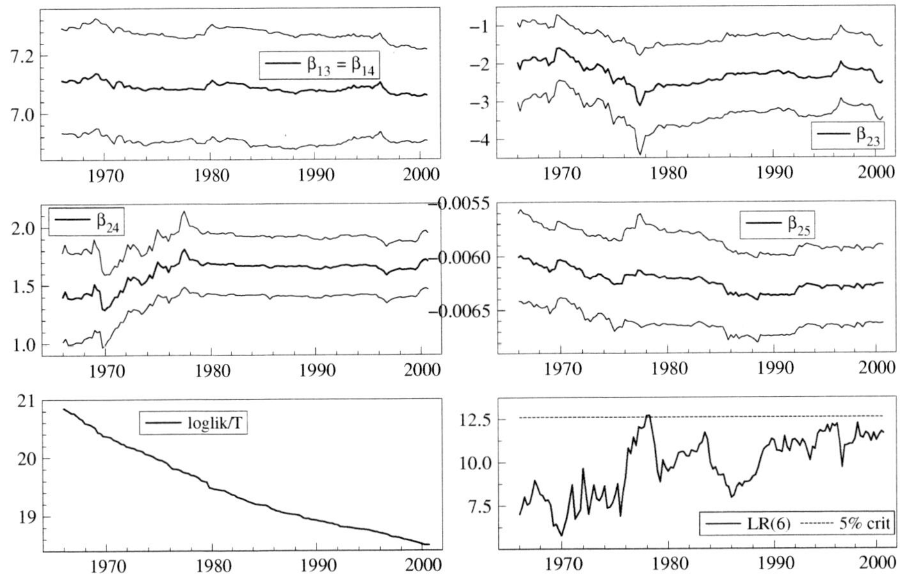

Figure 5.1 Time series of restricted cointegration coefficients.

which corresponds to a full-sample log-likelihood if $\widehat{\mathbf{V}}_i$ is zero for $i = t+1, \ldots, T$. The actual likelihood up to t is proportional to:

$$\hat{\ell}_t/t = -\tfrac{1}{2}\log\left|\tfrac{1}{t}\sum_{i=1}^{t}\widehat{\mathbf{V}}_i'\widehat{\mathbf{V}}_i\right| = -\tfrac{1}{2}\log\left|\widehat{\mathbf{\Omega}}_i\right|.$$

This concludes the tutorial on cointegration. The next stage is to map the data in the system to I(0), and that is the topic of Chapter 6.

A batch file corresponding to this chapter is provided in a file called MulTut2.fl. There are various ways to create such a file, for example by activating the batch editor in OxMetrics, and saving the specification:

```
// Batch code for the final specification of Tutorial on Cointegration:
module("PcGive");
package("PcGive", "Multiple-equation");
loaddata("MulTut1.in7");
system
{
    Y = Ya, Yb, Yc, Yd;
    Z = Ya_1, Ya_2, Yb_1, Yb_2, Yc_1, Yc_2, Yd_1, Yd_2, Trend;
    U = Constant;
}
rank(2);
option("shortrun", 0);
constraints
{
```

```
    &8=1;  &9=-1; &10=&11; &12=0;
    &13=0; &14=1;
    &1=0;  &2=0;  &4=0;
    &6=0;
}
//estimate("COINT", 1951, 1, 2000, 4, 0, 28);// for recursive estimation
estimate("COINT", 1951, 1, 2000, 4);
```

The original batch code implements recursive restricted cointegration analysis, removed here, by setting the '28' in `estimate` to 0. Finally, in MulTut2.fl we changed the `usedata` command (which just selects an already loaded database) to `loaddata` (which will attempt to load the database into OxMetrics).

5.8 Addendum: A and H matrices

Up to this point, we have completely ignored the other two choices for restricted cointegration analysis. This section turns to the final two methods, which will not involve iterative estimation.

The only linear restriction we consider is whether the cointegration vector $(0, 1, -1, 0, 0)$ lies in the cointegration space. The $\mathbf{H}$ matrix discussed in Chapter 12 then has the form $(0, 1, -1, 0, 0)'$ and is set as follows. Select Model, Formulate, Model Settings, and at Cointegrated VAR settings choose Known cointegrated vectors. Input a rank of 2, and press OK. In the subsequent matrix editor alter the dimensions of $\mathbf{H}$ to $5{\times}1$, typing in the elements of $\mathbf{H}$ as $(0, 1, -1, 0, 0)'$ in the first column:

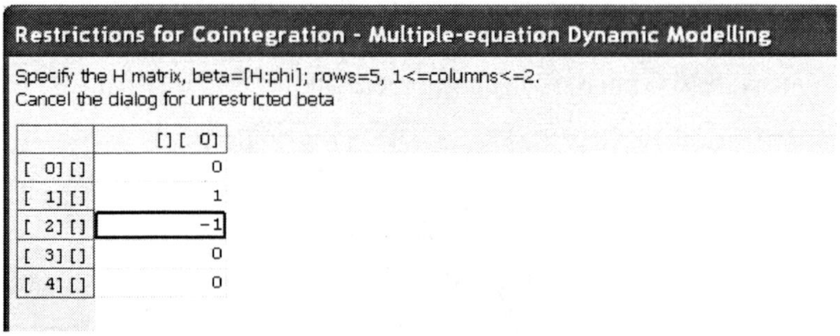

The output is similar to the unrestricted analysis, except for the standard errors of the coefficients. In this case the hypothesis is decisively rejected. Since $p = 2$ is preserved, these tests have conventional asymptotic χ^2-distributions.

Note that the β eigenvectors are not normalized here, but as the second is not unique, any linear combination is acceptable.

Chapter 6

Tutorial on Reduction to I(0)

6.1 Introduction

The next important step in model construction is to map the data to I(0) series, by differencing and cointegrating combinations. We have determined two unique cointegrating vectors in Chapter 4 and can construct the data analogues either by the algebra, or the calculator. We choose the former.

If you start afresh, load the tutorial data set `MulTut1.in7`.

First, we use the algebra editor to create the cointegrating vectors corresponding to (5.1). In OxMetrics, type `Alt+a` and enter the algebra code as follows (or save typing and load the algebra file called MulTut3.alg)

```
CIa = Ya - Yb + 7.1 * Yc + 7.1 * Yd;
CIb = Yb - 2.5 * Yc + 1.7 * Yd - 0.0063 * trend();

DYa = diff(Ya, 1);
DYb = diff(Yb, 1);
DYc = diff(Yc, 1);
DYd = diff(Yd, 1);
```

We shall also need the differences of all the Y variables in this chapter. We created them using the calculator as explained in §2.2, but they are included in the Algebra code for convenience.

We can now formulate an I(0) system that excludes all I(1) variables, and effectuate the reduction equivalent to the rank 2 restriction on $\mathbf{P}_0$. The time-series graphs of the restricted cointegrating vectors are shown in Figure 6.1.

Now select Model, Multiple Equation Dynamic Modelling, Formulate. Press the Clear button to clear the existing system, if any. Select one lag, mark *DYa*, *DYb*, *DYc*, *DYd*, *CIa*, *CIb*, press <<. Note that one lag of a difference includes the second lag of the level, matching the reduction to 2 lags obtained in Chapter 3. In this chapter we keep the *Constant* as unrestricted. Next, mark *CIa*, *CIb* and delete them. The final result should look like:

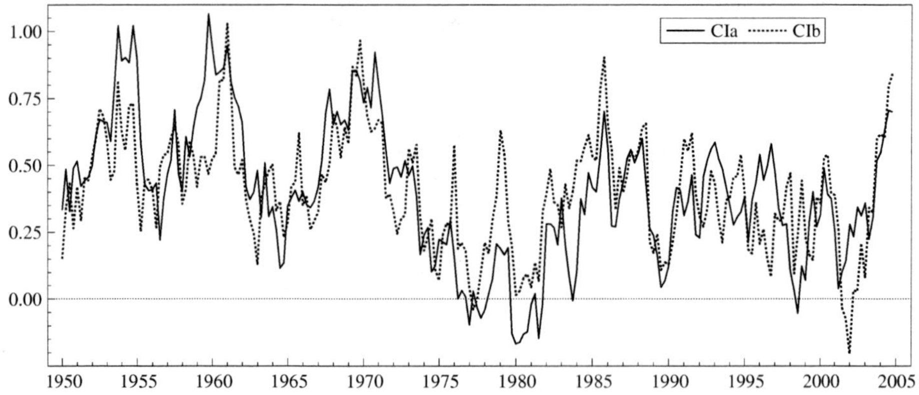

Figure 6.1 Restricted cointegrating relations.

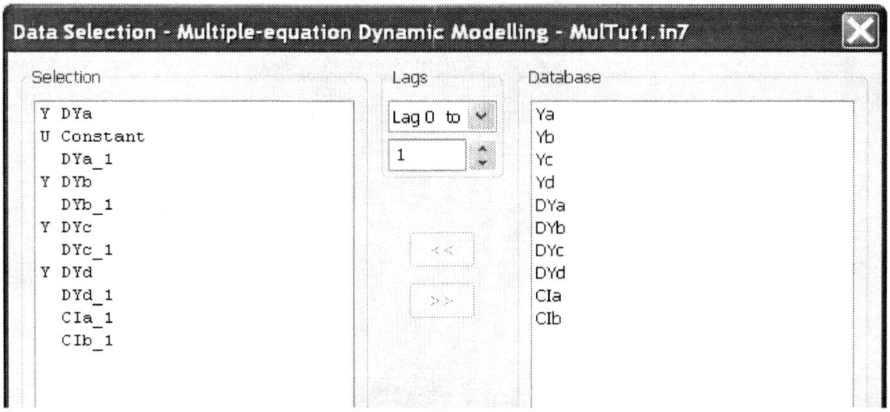

Accept, select the Unrestricted system model type, and estimate by ordinary least squares using recursive estimation (), since henceforth all tests are in I(0) form, and so have conventional critical values. To exactly match our output, check that the first data point in the estimation sample is 1951(1), ending at 2000(4). The impact of the two reductions (shorter lag and cointegration) has been to diminish the total number of parameters from 66 ($4 \times 14 + 10$) to 38 ($4 \times 7 + 10$). It is incorrect to conduct a direct likelihood-ratio test against the initial system, since that would be a mixture of I(1) distributions (corresponding to estimated unit roots) and conventional (deleting the second-lag differences). However, the equation standard errors are in fact very close to those obtained in Chapter 3, consistent with the validity of the rank restriction.

```
SYS( 1) Estimating the system by OLS (using MulTut1.in7)
        The estimation sample is: 1951(1) - 2000(4)

URF equation for: DYa
                  Coefficient  Std.Error  t-value  t-prob
DYa_1               -0.361724    0.08172    -4.43   0.000
DYb_1                0.207510     0.1184     1.75   0.081
DYc_1               -0.266326     0.1993    -1.34   0.183
DYd_1               0.0970494     0.1080    0.898   0.370
CIa_1               -0.102817    0.01030    -9.98   0.000
CIb_1              -0.0635232    0.04687    -1.36   0.177
Constant        U    0.741448     0.5250     1.41   0.159

sigma = 0.0166518    RSS = 0.05351523076

URF equation for: DYb
                  Coefficient  Std.Error  t-value  t-prob
DYa_1             0.000845350    0.04808   0.0176   0.986
DYb_1              -0.0837649    0.06963    -1.20   0.230
DYc_1               -0.121905     0.1172    -1.04   0.300
DYd_1               0.0289575    0.06356    0.456   0.649
CIa_1              0.00305339   0.006059    0.504   0.615
CIb_1               -0.161631    0.02757    -5.86   0.000
Constant        U     1.82190     0.3088     5.90   0.000

sigma = 0.00979602    RSS = 0.01852067807

URF equation for: DYc
                  Coefficient  Std.Error  t-value  t-prob
DYa_1               0.0290789    0.03363    0.865   0.388
DYb_1              -0.0621194    0.04871    -1.28   0.204
DYc_1               -0.153002    0.08202    -1.87   0.064
DYd_1              -0.0301411    0.04446   -0.678   0.499
CIa_1             -0.00811361   0.004239    -1.91   0.057
CIb_1               0.0635006    0.01929     3.29   0.001
Constant        U   -0.709454     0.2160    -3.28   0.001

sigma = 0.00685321    RSS = 0.009064543557

URF equation for: DYd
                  Coefficient  Std.Error  t-value  t-prob
DYa_1               0.0760642    0.06480     1.17   0.242
DYb_1             -0.00410509    0.09385  -0.0437   0.965
DYc_1               0.0368430     0.1580    0.233   0.816
DYd_1                0.179957    0.08567     2.10   0.037
CIa_1              0.00996420   0.008167     1.22   0.224
CIb_1              -0.0616365    0.03716    -1.66   0.099
Constant        U    0.691057     0.4163     1.66   0.098

sigma = 0.0132038    RSS = 0.03364745099

log-likelihood      2568.14654  -T/2log|Omega|      3703.29737
|Omega|        8.25626995e-017  log|Y'Y/T|         -35.0006237
```

```
R^2(LR)                  0.868973  R^2(LM)                  0.298236
no. of observations           200  no. of parameters              28

F-test on regressors except unrestricted: F(24,664) = 21.8757 [0.0000] **
F-tests on retained regressors, F(4,190) =
        DYa_1        6.21141 [0.000]**       DYb_1        1.61535 [0.172]
        DYc_1        3.46363 [0.009]**       DYd_1        2.87861 [0.024]*
        CIa_1        48.5812 [0.000]**       CIb_1        12.6274 [0.000]**
     Constant U      12.7712 [0.000]**

correlation of URF residuals (standard deviations on diagonal)
                   DYa          DYb           DYc           DYd
DYa           0.016652    -0.017332      -0.55424      -0.57625
DYb          -0.017332    0.0097960      -0.12154      0.039991
DYc           -0.55424     -0.12154     0.0068532       0.43181
DYd           -0.57625     0.039991       0.43181      0.013204
correlation between actual and fitted
             DYa          DYb           DYc           DYd
         0.80554      0.51986       0.39334       0.22703
```

The coefficients are now becoming interpretable in part. Consider each equation in turn:

(1) *DYa*: *DYb_1*, *DYc_1* and *DYd_1* seem irrelevant as does *CIb_1*, matching the earlier cointegration tests on $\boldsymbol{\alpha}$.
(2) *DYb*: all stochastic variables seem irrelevant, except for the cointegrating vector *CIb_1*, consistent with our previous findings about $\boldsymbol{\alpha}$.
(3) *DYc*: the only significant stochastic variables is *CIb_1*, with *CIa_1* and *DYc_1* on the borderline of significance.
(4) *DYd*: except for the autoregressive coefficient, apparently nothing is significant!

The F-tests confirm that *DYb_1* is not significant in the system as a whole. The correlations of actual and fitted are much lower in I(0) space.

Select Test, Graphic analysis, and mark the first three entries in the Graphic analysis dialog, and click OK. Figure 6.2 shows the resulting time series of fitted and actual values, their cross plots, and the scaled residuals for the four endogenous variables. The different goodness of fit of the four equations time-series is not apparent, since fine detail cannot be discerned (it is clearer on a colour screen), but the cross-plots show the markedly different correlation scatters. There is no evidence that the outcomes are markedly affected by any influential observations, nor do the residuals manifest outliers or obvious patterns.

It is sensible to diagnostically test our reduced system, so we briefly reconsider constancy and data congruence. Select Test, Graphic analysis, and mark Residual density and histogram and Residual correlogram in the Graphic analysis dialog, leading to Figure 6.3. There is no evidence of within-equation residual serial correlation, and the densities and distributions are close to normality except for the single large outliers found earlier.

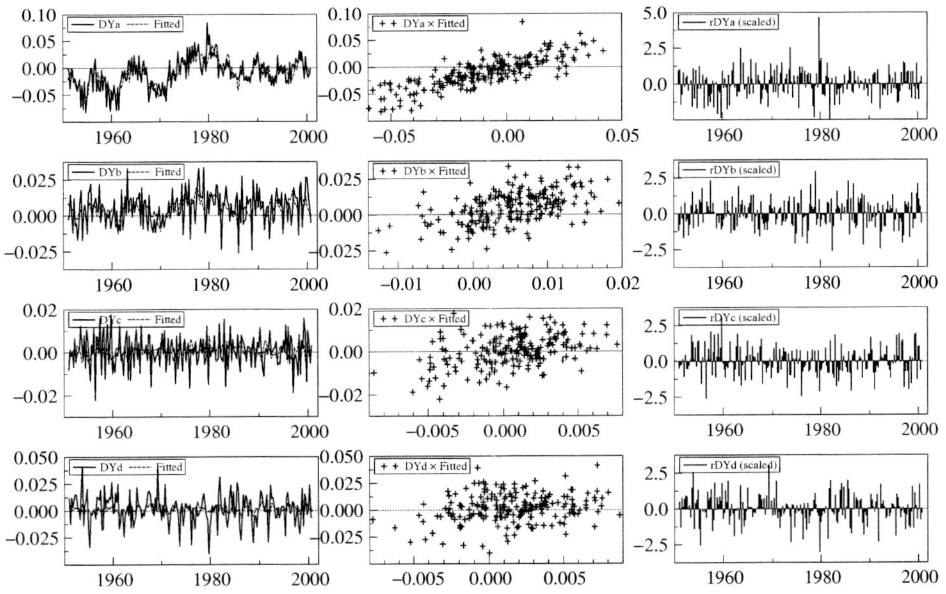

Figure 6.2 Fitted and actual values and scaled residuals.

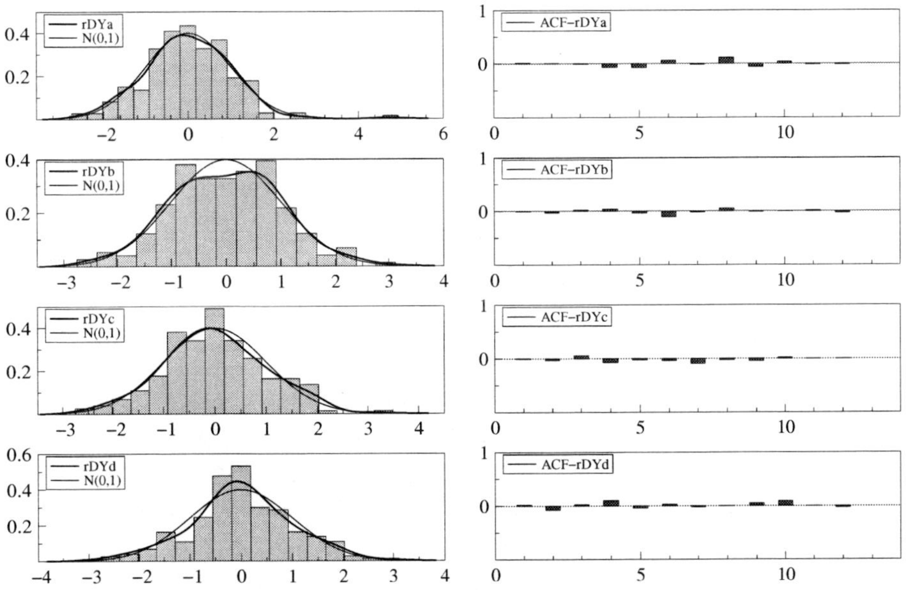

Figure 6.3 Individual-equation graphical diagnostics.

A more powerful diagnostic is given by selecting Test, Test summary which yields:

```
DYa        : Portmanteau(12):  6.83059
DYb        : Portmanteau(12):  4.1626
DYc        : Portmanteau(12):  4.77481
DYd        : Portmanteau(12):  6.4972
DYa        : AR 1-5 test:       F(5,188)  =  0.53076  [0.7528]
DYb        : AR 1-5 test:       F(5,188)  =  0.30714  [0.9082]
DYc        : AR 1-5 test:       F(5,188)  =  0.45314  [0.8107]
DYd        : AR 1-5 test:       F(5,188)  =  0.90527  [0.4788]
DYa        : Normality test:    Chi^2(2)  =   19.994  [0.0000]**
DYb        : Normality test:    Chi^2(2)  = 0.043564  [0.9785]
DYc        : Normality test:    Chi^2(2)  =  0.35152  [0.8388]
DYd        : Normality test:    Chi^2(2)  =   3.3216  [0.1900]
DYa        : ARCH 1-4 test:     F(4,185)  =  0.51936  [0.7216]
DYb        : ARCH 1-4 test:     F(4,185)  =   1.9359  [0.1063]
DYc        : ARCH 1-4 test:     F(4,185)  =  0.70485  [0.5896]
DYd        : ARCH 1-4 test:     F(4,185)  =   1.2644  [0.2856]
DYa        : hetero test:       F(12,180)=    1.0655  [0.3918]
DYb        : hetero test:       F(12,180)=   0.45196  [0.9396]
DYc        : hetero test:       F(12,180)=    1.3620  [0.1879]
DYd        : hetero test:       F(12,180)=    1.2770  [0.2355]
DYa        : hetero-X test:     F(27,165)=   0.86482  [0.6605]
DYb        : hetero-X test:     F(27,165)=   0.72513  [0.8361]
DYc        : hetero-X test:     F(27,165)=   0.91901  [0.5844]
DYd        : hetero-X test:     F(27,165)=    1.1900  [0.2504]

Vector Portmanteau(12):  166.497
Vector AR 1-5 test:       F(80,673)=  0.67164 [0.9865]
Vector Normality test:    Chi^2(8) =   10.483 [0.2328]
Vector hetero test:       F(120,1341)=  0.99611 [0.4965]
Vector hetero-X test:     F(270,1493)=  0.97300 [0.6064]
```

The first block shows single equation statistics, and the second the system tests. None of the tests is significant at the 1% level, except the normality statistic for *DYa*, which may need reconsideration when a model of the system has been constructed and evaluated.

Finally, select Test, Recursive graphics (or click on its icon). Mark the entries in the dialog for 1-step residuals and break-point Chow tests with a 1% significance level, and accept to see Figure 6.4. The 1-step errors lie within their approximate 95% confidence bands with constant standard errors (the first four plots), and no break-point Chow test is anywhere significant (the 1% line is the top of each of the last five boxes). The last plot is the overall system constancy test. Thus, constancy cannot be rejected, suggesting that the system is in fact managing to 'explain' the changes of growth as an endogenous feature.

6.2 A parsimonious VAR

The only major remaining reduction to a parsimonious VAR that can be implemented at the level of the system is to eliminate *DYb_1*. This is because variables must be dropped

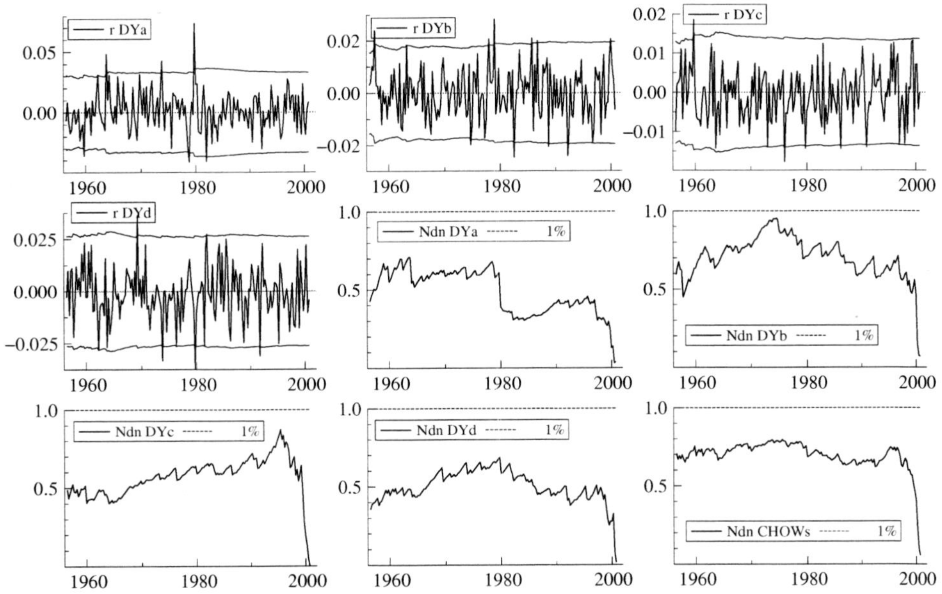

Figure 6.4 Recursive constancy statistics.

from the system altogether since all equations have the same formulation by construction; later, when we construct a model of the system, the equations can differ in their specifications. Nevertheless, the resulting system provides a stiff competitor for any model thereof, since there are no redundant variables to camouflage poor restrictions in other directions.

Select Model, Formulate System, mark *DYb_1* and delete it, then re-estimate by OLS (deselecting recursive estimation).

```
SYS( 2) Estimating the system by OLS (using MulTut1.in7)
        The estimation sample is: 1951 (1) to 2000 (4)

URF equation for: DYa
                    Coefficient  Std.Error  t-value  t-prob
DYa_1                 -0.377648    0.08165    -4.63   0.000
DYc_1                 -0.318658     0.1981    -1.61   0.109
DYd_1                  0.147751     0.1046     1.41   0.160
CIa_1                 -0.108686   0.009792    -11.1   0.000
CIb_1                -0.0572335    0.04698    -1.22   0.225
Constant      U        0.673981     0.5263     1.28   0.202

sigma = 0.0167405   RSS = 0.05436753506

URF equation for: DYb
                    Coefficient  Std.Error  t-value  t-prob
DYa_1                0.00727345    0.04783    0.152   0.879
DYc_1                 -0.100781     0.1161   -0.868   0.386
```

```
DYd_1                  0.00849077      0.06131      0.138    0.890
CIa_1                  0.00542276     0.005737      0.945    0.346
CIb_1                   -0.164170      0.02752      -5.96    0.000
Constant         U        1.84913       0.3083       6.00    0.000

sigma = 0.00980731    RSS = 0.01865955855

URF equation for: DYc
                      Coefficient  Std.Error  t-value  t-prob
DYa_1                   0.0338460    0.03348     1.01   0.313
DYc_1                   -0.137336    0.08123    -1.69   0.092
DYd_1                  -0.0453191    0.04291    -1.06   0.292
CIa_1                 -0.00635650   0.004015    -1.58   0.115
CIb_1                   0.0616178    0.01926     3.20   0.002
Constant         U      -0.689257     0.2158    -3.19   0.002

sigma = 0.00686427    RSS = 0.009140922104

URF equation for: DYd
                      Coefficient  Std.Error  t-value  t-prob
DYa_1                   0.0763792    0.06423     1.19   0.236
DYc_1                   0.0378782     0.1558    0.243   0.808
DYd_1                    0.178954    0.08233     2.17   0.031
CIa_1                   0.0100803   0.007703     1.31   0.192
CIb_1                  -0.0617609    0.03696    -1.67   0.096
Constant         U       0.692392     0.4141     1.67   0.096

sigma = 0.0131697   RSS = 0.03364778454

log-likelihood      2564.80235  -T/2log|Omega|      3699.95317
|Omega|         8.53704438e-017  log|Y'Y/T|        -35.0006237
R^2(LR)               0.864517  R^2(LM)               0.291746
no. of observations        200  no. of parameters           24

F-test on regressors except unrestricted: F(20,634) = 26.2345 [0.0000] **
F-tests on retained regressors, F(4,191) =
      DYa_1          6.70718 [0.000]**         DYc_1          3.54518 [0.008]**
      DYd_1          3.95504 [0.004]**         CIa_1          57.5154 [0.000]**
      CIb_1          12.7415 [0.000]**     Constant U         12.8788 [0.000]**

correlation of URF residuals (standard deviations on diagonal)
                 DYa          DYb          DYc          DYd
DYa         0.016741    -0.027933     -0.55902     -0.57210
DYb        -0.027933    0.0098073     -0.11269     0.040113
DYc         -0.55902     -0.11269    0.0068643      0.43029
DYd         -0.57210     0.040113      0.43029     0.013170
correlation between actual and fitted
         DYa          DYb          DYc          DYd
     0.80207      0.51457      0.38418      0.22701
```

Every variable now matters to the system, if not to every equation in it, but the fit has changed little.

6.3 A restricted system

It is possible to remain in the context of VAR modelling, yet impose specific restrictions on each equation. To do so, however, requires formulating a model of the system, and initially PcGive takes that model to be the system itself (augmented with any necessary identities, as discussed in the next chapter).

The total number of variables involved in a system must be less than the estimation sample size, but otherwise the size of the system is only limited by available memory.

Now, select Model, Formulate, accept and in the Model Settings select Simultaneous equations model:

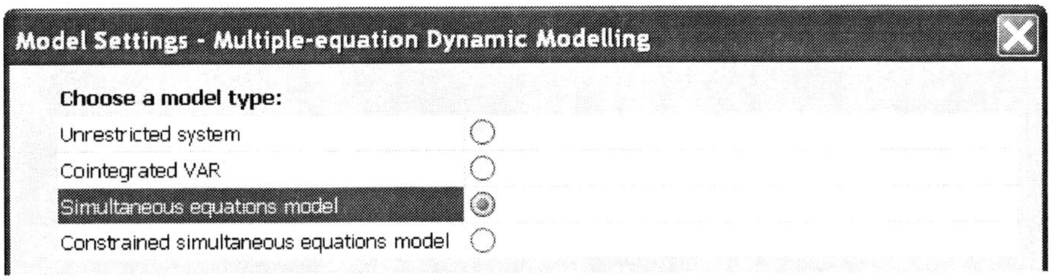

The next stage brings up the Model Formulation dialog for simultaneous equations:

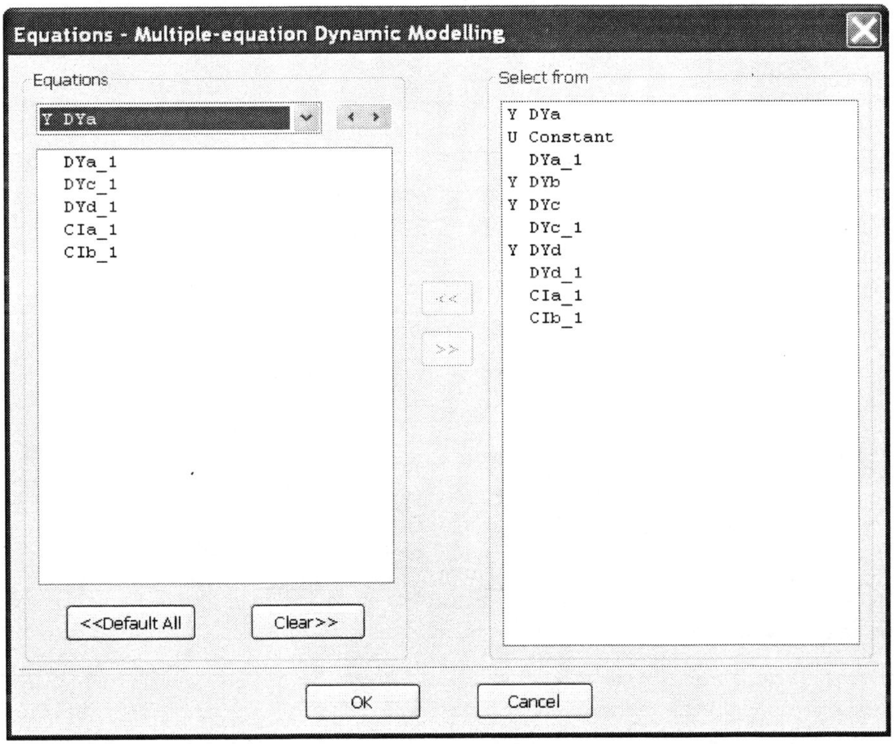

NOTE: If no model existed before, the default specification is the system, with any identities still unspecified. Otherwise PcGive will try to reuse the previous model specification, even if it belonged to another system (this might lead to the default displaying an unidentified model: only variables that are in the system can appear in the model).

The leftmost column starts with a choice of equation: which endogenous variable is under analysis; below that is the current model of that endogenous variable; and the next right column shows the system currently under analysis. We start by deleting all lagged endogenous variables with a t-value less than one: from the *DYb* equation remove *DYa*_1, *DYc*_1, *DYd*_1, and from *DYd* equation remove *DYc*_1. Now accept (click OK), and the model estimation dialog appears.

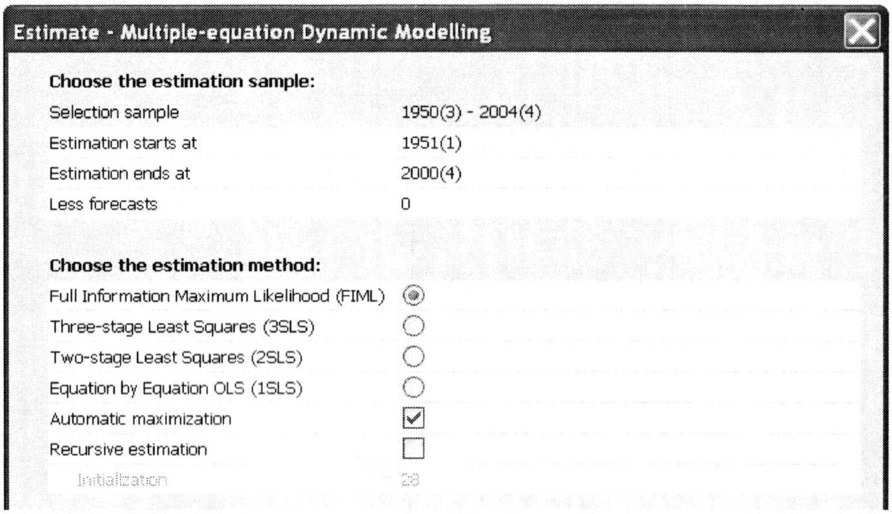

If necessary, mark Full Information Maximum Likelihood (FIML), clear the recursive estimation box, and accept.

```
MOD( 3) Estimating the model by FIML (using MulTut1.in7)
        The estimation sample is: 1951(1) - 2000(4)

Equation for: DYa
                     Coefficient  Std.Error  t-value  t-prob
DYa_1                  -0.375080    0.08102    -4.63   0.000
DYc_1                  -0.292092     0.1621    -1.80   0.073
DYd_1                   0.141835     0.1018     1.39   0.165
CIa_1                  -0.108811   0.009730    -11.2   0.000
CIb_1                 -0.0540969    0.04493    -1.20   0.230
Constant        U       0.638781     0.5033     1.27   0.206

sigma = 0.0166983
```

```
Equation for: DYb
                    Coefficient  Std.Error  t-value  t-prob
CIa_1                0.00320873   0.003715    0.864   0.389
CIb_1                 -0.152488    0.02378    -6.41   0.000
Constant         U      1.71856     0.2663     6.45   0.000

sigma = 0.00980469

Equation for: DYc
                    Coefficient  Std.Error  t-value  t-prob
DYa_1                 0.0337335    0.03309     1.02   0.309
DYc_1                 -0.155048    0.07237    -2.14   0.033
DYd_1                -0.0426863    0.04193    -1.02   0.310
CIa_1               -0.00610962   0.003982    -1.53   0.127
CIb_1                 0.0595486    0.01873     3.18   0.002
Constant         U    -0.666086     0.2098    -3.17   0.002

sigma = 0.00684751

Equation for: DYd
                    Coefficient  Std.Error  t-value  t-prob
DYa_1                 0.0729349    0.06307     1.16   0.249
DYd_1                  0.187209    0.07585     2.47   0.014
CIa_1                 0.0102815   0.007596     1.35   0.177
CIb_1                -0.0662305    0.03200    -2.07   0.040
Constant         U     0.742545     0.3584     2.07   0.040

sigma = 0.0131379

log-likelihood       2564.30187  -T/2log|Omega|        3699.4527
no. of observations         200  no. of parameters            20

LR test of over-identifying restrictions: Chi^2(4) =   1.0009 [0.9097]
BFGS using analytical derivatives (eps1=0.0001; eps2=0.005):
Strong convergence

correlation of structural residuals (standard deviations on diagonal)
                 DYa          DYb          DYc          DYd
DYa         0.016698    -0.027289     -0.55907     -0.57216
DYb        -0.027289    0.0098047     -0.11348     0.038958
DYc         -0.55907     -0.11348    0.0068475      0.43044
DYd         -0.57216     0.038958      0.43044     0.013138
```

A full description of FIML output is also reserved for the next chapter: here we merely note that the test for over-identifying restrictions, corresponding to the deletion of the four variables, is insignificant.

As a next step, delete the cointegrating vectors to impose the long-run weak exogeneity found in the previous chapter: delete *CIa_1* from all equations except the first, and delete *CIb_1* from the first equation.

```
MOD( 4) Estimating the model by FIML (using MulTut1.in7)
        The estimation sample is: 1951 (1) to 2000 (4)

Equation for: DYa
                  Coefficient  Std.Error  t-value  t-prob
DYa_1               -0.358078    0.06932    -5.17   0.000
DYc_1               -0.183105     0.1462    -1.25   0.212
DYd_1                0.107668    0.09863     1.09   0.276
CIa_1               -0.112656   0.006656    -16.9   0.000
Constant       U    0.0321975   0.002508     12.8   0.000

sigma = 0.0167206

Equation for: DYb
                  Coefficient  Std.Error  t-value  t-prob
CIb_1               -0.138162    0.01667    -8.29   0.000
Constant       U      1.55878     0.1875     8.31   0.000

sigma = 0.00979834

Equation for: DYc
                  Coefficient  Std.Error  t-value  t-prob
DYa_1               0.0584115    0.02254     2.59   0.010
DYc_1               -0.194370    0.07131    -2.73   0.007
DYd_1              -0.0379947    0.04163   -0.913   0.363
CIb_1               0.0343037    0.01430     2.40   0.017
Constant       U    -0.384436     0.1607    -2.39   0.018

sigma = 0.00688309

Equation for: DYd
                  Coefficient  Std.Error  t-value  t-prob
DYa_1             -0.00202958    0.04112  -0.0494   0.961
DYd_1                0.207178    0.07522     2.75   0.006
CIb_1              -0.0608980    0.02480    -2.46   0.015
Constant       U     0.685985     0.2787     2.46   0.015

sigma = 0.0131769

log-likelihood       2559.69288  -T/2log|Omega|      3694.84371
no. of observations         200  no. of parameters           16

LR test of over-identifying restrictions: Chi^2(8) =   10.219 [0.2500]
BFGS using analytical derivatives (eps1=0.0001; eps2=0.005):
Strong convergence

correlation of structural residuals (standard deviations on diagonal)
                DYa          DYb          DYc          DYd
DYa        0.016721    -0.022263     -0.56019     -0.56813
DYb       -0.022263    0.0097983     -0.12150     0.043773
DYc        -0.56019     -0.12150    0.0068831      0.41668
DYd        -0.56813     0.043773      0.41668     0.013177
```

For dynamic forecasting, select Test, Forecast and set 16 periods (two years), marking all four variables (we are using error bars, a choice made under Options), to see Figure 6.5.

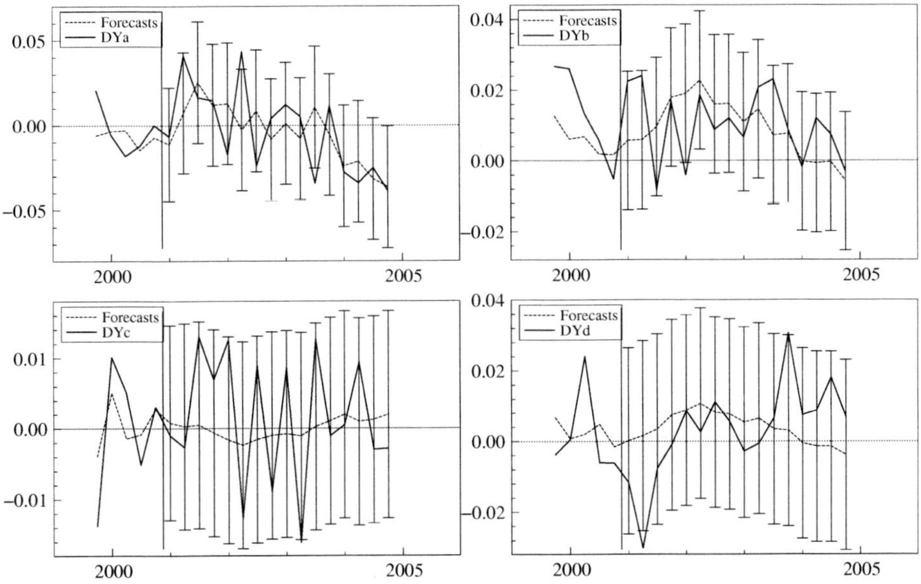

Figure 6.5 Dynamic forecasts in I(0) space.

This reveals the shortcomings of the current approach:

(1) The forecasts look more like 1-step forecasts because the cointegrating vectors are fixed at their actual values, instead of being forecasted themselves.
(2) We can only make 16 forecasts, because the cointegrating vectors are not known beyond that.
(3) We can only forecast differences, while we may be interested in forecasting the levels of the variables.

The first two are manifestations of the same issue: if we can tell PcGive how the cointegrating vectors are constructed, then we can create proper dynamic forecasts, with error bands that reflect the uncertainty more appropriately. This can be achieved using identities, which we introduce in the next chapter.

It is possible to redo this estimation recursively (this executes remarkably quickly), which gives further useful information in the recursive graphics. Then select Test/recursive Graphics:

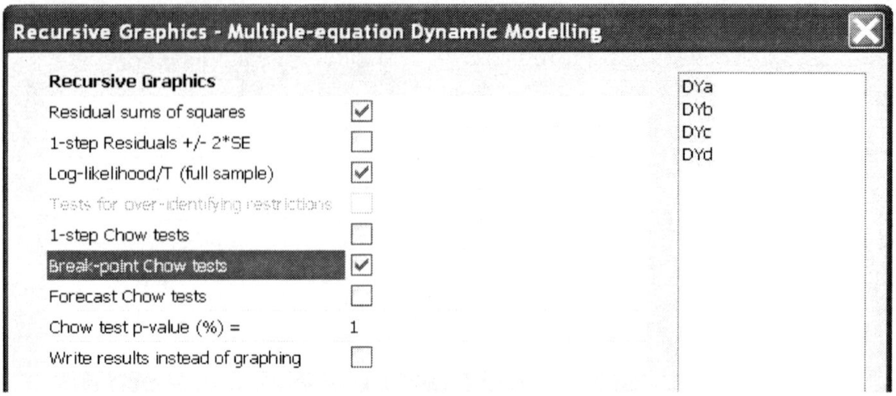

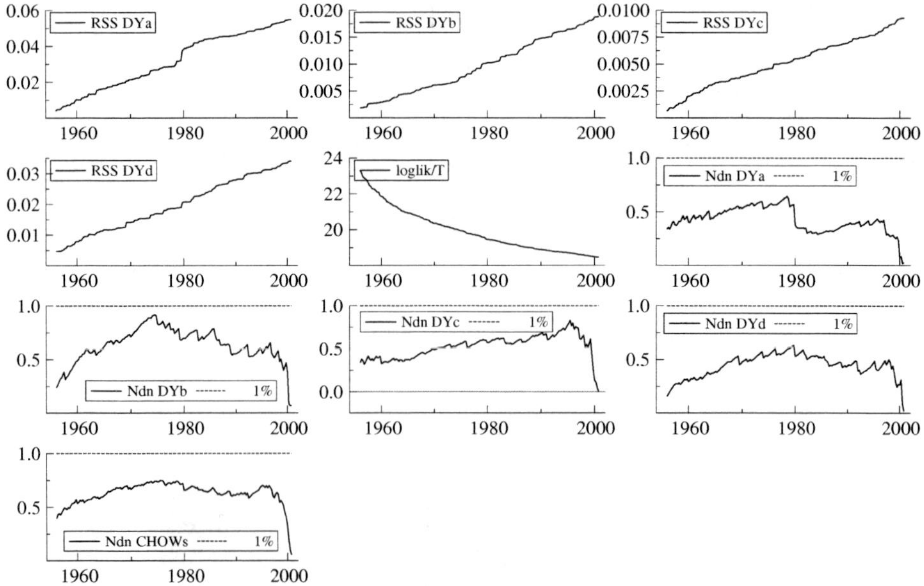

Figure 6.6 Recursive model statistics.

Select the settings shown, to produce Figure 6.6. The first row shows the now familiar recursive residuals with $\pm 2\widehat{\sigma}_t$; the second shows the scaled log-likelihood function as T increases (as for recursive cointegrated VARs, see §5.7), the sequence of scaled tests of the hypothesis that the model parsimoniously encompasses the system (i.e., the recursively-computed likelihood-ratio test of the overidentifying restrictions), and the sequence of break-point Chow tests scaled by their 1% significance (one-off) level. There is no evidence against the specification at this stage (check that the test summary remains acceptable). Note that, the unrestricted constant is partialled out from the full sample before computation of the recursive estimation.

6.4 Progress

Select Progress from the Model menu (`Alt+m,p`) to conduct a formal test of the last two reductions of both the system and its model. The screen capture below assumes that you started PcGive afresh in this chapter. If not, your progress dialog will also list previous models: in that case just select the most recent four matching the capture. (An alternative approach would be to write the batch code of these models using the Progress dialog and then rerun that).

Eligible I(0) systems are marked; the nested cases, where variables have been deleted is represented by the model thereof, on which the individual-equation restrictions have been imposed.

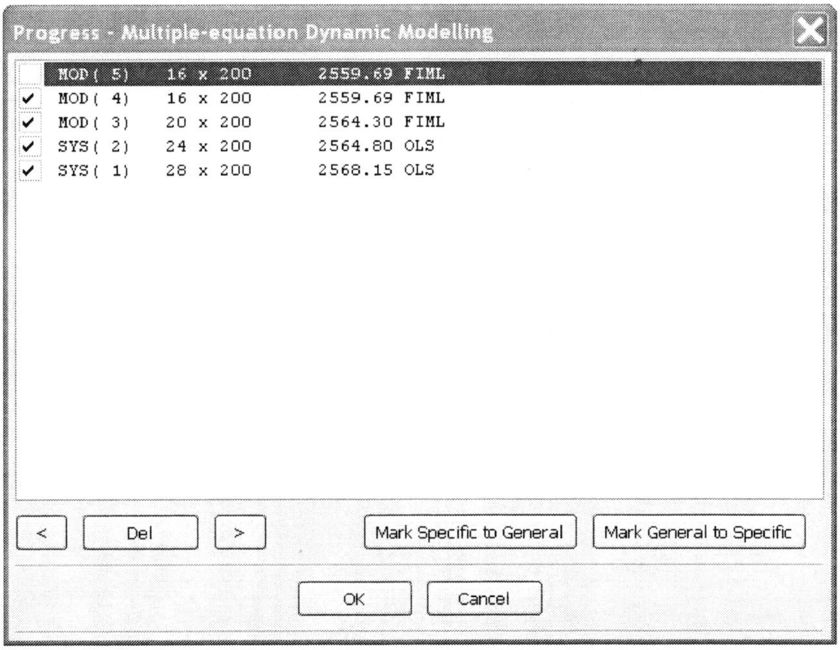

In our case, MOD(5) is a recursive re-estimation of MOD(4), so we unselected it. Then accept to obtain:

```
Progress to date
Model        T    p        log-likelihood        SC        HQ       AIC
SYS( 1)    200   28  OLS        2568.1465   -24.940   -25.215   -25.401
SYS( 2)    200   24  OLS        2564.8023   -25.012   -25.248   -25.408
MOD( 3)    200   20  FIML       2564.3019   -25.113   -25.310   -25.443<
MOD( 4)    200   16  FIML       2559.6929   -25.173<  -25.330<  -25.437

Tests of model reduction
SYS( 1) --> SYS( 2): F(4,190) =    1.6154 [0.1720]
SYS( 1) --> MOD( 3): Chi^2(8) =    7.6893 [0.4644]
SYS( 1) --> MOD( 4): Chi^2(12)=    16.907 [0.1531]
```

```
SYS( 2) --> MOD( 3): Chi^2(4) =    1.0009 [0.9097]
SYS( 2) --> MOD( 4): Chi^2(8) =    10.219 [0.2500]

MOD( 3) --> MOD( 4): Chi^2(4) =    9.2180 [0.0559]
```

Thus, both reductions are accepted, so the individual insignificance of the F-tests on *DYa_1* and *DYd_1* did not camouflage their joint significance as revealed by the last statistic.

Finally, we create a batch file corresponding to this chapter. The Load history button in Batch editor can be used to write the Batch code for all previously estimated models. Here we have added the Algebra code, and removed the redundant repetition of the system for the models. The final result is in MulTut3.fl:

```
module("PcGive");
package("PcGive");
loaddata("MulTut1.in7");
algebra
{
    CIa = Ya - Yb + 7.1 * Yc + 7.1 * Yd;
    CIb = Yb - 2.5 * Yc + 1.7 * Yd - 0.0063 * trend();

    DYa = diff(Ya, 1);
    DYb = diff(Yb, 1);
    DYc = diff(Yc, 1);
    DYd = diff(Yd, 1);
}
system
{
    Y = DYa, DYb, DYc, DYd;
    Z = DYa_1, DYb_1, DYc_1, DYd_1, CIa_1, CIb_1;
    U = Constant;
}
estimate("OLS", 1951, 1, 2000, 4);
system
{
    Y = DYa, DYb, DYc, DYd;
    Z = DYa_1, DYc_1, DYd_1, CIa_1, CIb_1;
    U = Constant;
}
estimate("OLS", 1951, 1, 2000, 4);
model
{
    DYa = DYa_1, DYc_1, DYd_1, CIa_1, CIb_1;
    DYb = CIa_1, CIb_1;
    DYc = DYa_1, DYc_1, DYd_1, CIa_1, CIb_1;
    DYd = DYa_1, DYd_1, CIa_1, CIb_1;
}
estimate("FIML", 1951, 1, 2000, 4);
model
{
    DYa = DYa_1, DYc_1, DYd_1, CIa_1;
```

```
    DYb = CIb_1;
    DYc = DYa_1, DYc_1, DYd_1, CIb_1;
    DYd = DYa_1, DYd_1, CIb_1;
}
estimate("FIML", 1951, 1, 2000, 4);
progress;
```

Before exiting, try deleting every regressor from *DYd* to see the identification failure; that course is not viable here because PcGive requires at least one regressor in each equation. The next chapter will consider conditioning to produce an open system, and a simultaneous equations model thereof. This concludes the tutorial on mapping to I(0).

Chapter 7

Tutorial on Simultaneous Equations Models

7.1 Introduction to dynamic models

Dynamic model formulation specifies a model of the system in terms of structural equations. If you select Simultaneous equations model (SEM) at the model settings, a dialog will be offered in which you can formulate the individual equations in the Model Formulation dialog box. When you press OK, you will be taken automatically to the Estimate Model dialog, see §6.3. We now briefly describe the econometrics of these stages.

To obtain a *simultaneous dynamic model*, premultiply the system (3.4) given in §3.1 by a non-singular, non-diagonal matrix $\mathbf{B}$, which yields:

$$\mathbf{B}\mathbf{y}_t = \mathbf{B}\mathbf{\Pi}_u\mathbf{w}_t + \mathbf{B}\mathbf{v}_{u,t}.$$

We shall write this formulation as:

$$\mathbf{B}\mathbf{y}_t + \mathbf{C}\mathbf{w}_t = \mathbf{u}_t, \ \mathbf{u}_t \sim \mathsf{IN}_n\left[\mathbf{0}, \mathbf{\Sigma}\right]$$

with $t = 1, \ldots, T$; or using $\mathbf{A} = (\mathbf{B} : \mathbf{C})$ in which $\mathbf{B}$ is $(n \times n)$ and $\mathbf{C}$ is $(n \times k)$:

$$\mathbf{A}\mathbf{x}_t = \mathbf{u}_t.$$

The *restricted reduced form* (RRF) corresponding to this model is obtained as the solution:

$$\mathbf{y}_t = \mathbf{\Pi}_r\mathbf{w}_t + \mathbf{v}_{r,t}, \text{ with } \mathbf{\Pi}_r = -\mathbf{B}^{-1}\mathbf{C}.$$

The estimated variance of $\mathbf{u}_t$ is:

$$\widetilde{\mathbf{\Sigma}} = \frac{\widehat{\mathbf{A}}\mathbf{X}'\mathbf{X}\widehat{\mathbf{A}}'}{T-c}.$$

There is a degrees-of-freedom correction c, which equals the average number of parameters per equation (rounded towards 0); this would be k for the system (also see §5.2).

Identification of the model, achieved through imposing within-equation restrictions on $\mathbf{A}$, is required for estimation. The *order condition* for identification is only a necessary condition imposed on each equation. PcGive checks this as each equation is formulated. The *rank condition* is necessary and sufficient, and is checked prior to model estimation by setting each non-zero coefficient to unity plus a uniform random number.

Some equations of the model could be *identities*, which are exact linear combinations of variables equal to zero. Identities in PcGive are created by marking identity endogenous variables as such during system formulation. These are ignored during system estimation and analysis. Identities come in at the model formulation level, where the identity is specified just like other equations. However, there is no need to specify the coefficients of the identity equation, as PcGive automatically derives these by estimating the equation.

An example of a model with (3.3) as the unrestricted reduced form is:

$$\begin{aligned} Ya_t &= \beta_0 + \beta_1 Ya_{t-1} + \beta_2 Yb_t \\ Yb_t &= \beta_3 + \beta_4 Yb_{t-1}. \end{aligned}$$

In terms of (3.3), the lag two coefficients (δ_2, δ_4, δ_7, δ_9) are all restricted to zero, as is δ_6, and $\delta_3 = \beta_2 \times \beta_4$.

A model in PcGive is formulated by:

(1) which *variables* enter every equation, including identities;
(2) coefficients of identity equations need not be specified, as PcGive automatically derives these by estimating the equation (provided $\mathsf{R}^2 \geq .99$);
(3) *constraints*, if the model is to be estimated by constrained FIML (CFIML).

7.2 The cointegrated VAR in I(0) space

Although we assume you have read both Chapters 5 and 6, we will pick up our thread from the end of Chapter 5. The reason for this is that we can ask PcGive to formulate the initial mapping from a cointegrated VAR to a parsimonious VAR (PVAR) in I(0) space. This simplifies the work which was undertaken in Chapter 6.

If you've just started modelling using OxMetrics, make sure the model category is set to Models for time-series data and the category to Multiple-equation dynamic modelling. Also make sure the `MulTut1.in7` data file is loaded into OxMetrics, and then run the batch file from Chapter 5, which is called `MulTut2.fl`. This batch file reruns the final cointegrated VAR from that chapter. Referring back, we imposed rank two on the long-run matrix, with six additional restrictions:

```
beta
Ya            1.0000       0.00000
Yb           -1.0000        1.0000
Yc            7.0601       -2.4871
Yd            7.0601        1.7041
Trend        0.00000    -0.0062609

alpha
Ya          -0.10851       0.00000
Yb           0.00000      -0.15559
Yc           0.00000      0.033729
Yd           0.00000     -0.067749

log-likelihood      2563.08826  -T/2log|Omega|      3698.23909
no. of observations        200  no. of parameters           28
rank of long-run matrix      2  no. long-run restrictions    6
beta is identified

LR test of restrictions: Chi^2(6) =    11.638 [0.0706]
```

Following successful estimation of the CVAR, go to Test/Further Output and select Batch code to map CVAR to I(0) model. This prints:

```
// Batch code to map CVAR to model with identities in I(0) space
algebra
{
    DYa = diff(Ya, 1);
    DYb = diff(Yb, 1);
    DYc = diff(Yc, 1);
    DYd = diff(Yd, 1);
    CIa = Ya -Yb +7.06007 * Yc +7.06007 * Yd;
    CIb = Yb -2.48711 * Yc +1.70407 * Yd -0.00626095 * trend();
}
system
{
    Y = DYa, DYb, DYc, DYd;
    I = CIa, CIb;
    Z = DYa_1, DYb_1, DYc_1, DYd_1,
        CIa_1, CIb_1, Constant;
    U = ;
}
model
{
    DYa = DYa_1, DYb_1, DYc_1, DYd_1, CIa_1, CIb_1, Constant;
    DYb = DYa_1, DYb_1, DYc_1, DYd_1, CIa_1, CIb_1, Constant;
    DYc = DYa_1, DYb_1, DYc_1, DYd_1, CIa_1, CIb_1, Constant;
    DYd = DYa_1, DYb_1, DYc_1, DYd_1, CIa_1, CIb_1, Constant;
    CIa = DYa, DYb, DYc, DYd, CIa_1;
    CIb = DYb, DYc, DYd, Constant, CIb_1;
}
estimate("FIML", 1951, 1, 2000, 4, 0, 0);
```

The identities correspond to the cointegrating relations:

$$\begin{aligned} CIa_t &= Ya_t - Yb_t + \beta_{13} Yc_t + \beta_{13} Yd_t, \\ CIb_t &= Yb_t + \beta_{23} Yc_t + \beta_{24} Yd_t + \beta_{25} t. \end{aligned}$$

However, because the stochastic equations are formulated in terms of the first differences, we must do the same with the cointegrating vectors. Pre-multiplying by the first-difference operator Δ gives:

$$\begin{aligned} CIa_t &= CIa_{t-1} + \Delta Ya_t - \Delta Yb_t + \Delta\beta_{13} Yc_t + \Delta\beta_{13} Yd_t, \\ CIb_t &= CIb_{t-1} + \Delta Yb_t + \Delta\beta_{23} Yc_t + \Delta\beta_{24} Yd_t + \beta_{25}, \end{aligned}$$

which is the form used in the batch code above. The differenced trend is a constant, which is why we do not include the *Constant* unrestrictedly in the model. The inclusion of identities is a convenient way to approach modelling with cointegrated variables since it avoids having to eliminate two of the differences in terms of levels and differences of cointegrating vectors. Then, for example, dynamic analysis or dynamic forecasts can be conducted.

Modify the batch code in the OxMetrics results window to reflect the simplification steps of Chapter 6:

(1) delete *DYb_1* from all equations;
(2) delete *CIb_1* from the *DYa* equation and *CIa_1* from the others;
(3) delete all regressors except *CIb_1* and the constant from the *DYb* equation;
(4) delete *DYc_1* from the *DYd* equation.

The model section of the code should look like this:

```
model
{
    DYa = DYa_1, DYc_1, DYd_1, CIa_1, Constant;
    DYb = CIb_1, Constant;
    DYc = DYa_1, DYc_1, DYd_1, CIb_1, Constant;
    DYd = DYa_1, DYd_1, CIb_1, Constant;
    CIa = DYa, DYb, DYc, DYd, CIa_1;
    CIb = DYb, DYc, DYd, Constant, CIb_1;
}
```

To get identical results as before, we need to set exactly the same coefficients in the cointegrating vectors as before:

```
    CIa = Ya -Yb +7.1 * Yc +7.1 * Yd;
    CIb = Yb -2.5 * Yc +1.7 * Yd -0.0063 * trend();
```

After making these changes, you can select the whole section of batch code, from the `algebra` statement to `estimate`, and run it by pressing `Ctrl+B`. Alternatively, you can run the supplied batch file `MulTut3id.fl`. This estimates the final model of Chapter 6, with the addition of the two identities for which the specification is listed just before the model output:

```
Identity for CIa
DYa          1.0000
DYb         -1.0000
DYc          7.1000
DYd          7.1000
CIa_1        1.0000
R^2 = 1 over 1951 (1) to 2000 (4)

Identity for CIb
DYb             1.0000
DYc            -2.5000
DYd             1.7000
CIb_1           1.0000
Constant   -0.0063000
R^2 = 1 over 1951 (1) to 2000 (4)
```

Provided you adjusted the coefficients in the cointegrating vectors, the log-likelihood is identical to that in §6.3:

```
log-likelihood        2559.69289  -T/2log|Omega|       3694.84371
no. of observations          200  no. of parameters            16
LR test of over-identifying restrictions: Chi^2(12)=   16.907 [0.1531]

correlation of structural residuals (standard deviations on diagonal)
                DYa           DYb           DYc           DYd
DYa        0.016721     -0.022260      -0.56019      -0.56813
DYb       -0.022260     0.0097983      -0.12150      0.043771
DYc        -0.56019      -0.12150     0.0068831       0.41668
DYd        -0.56813      0.043771       0.41668      0.013177
```

Note that the test for over-identifying restrictions has changed because we have a slightly different URF. If you wish, you can estimate this URF and use Progress to calculate the statistic in a different way (to do this you will need to estimate the URF, then move it below the model in Progress, and double click on the URF to select it for the progress report).

Further simplification leads us to delete both *DYc_1* and *DYd_1* from *DYa*, then *DYd_1* from *DYc*, and finally *DYa_1* from the *DYd* equation. The final parsimonious VAR is:

```
MOD( 4) Estimating the model by FIML (using MulTut1.in7)
        The estimation sample is: 1951 (1) to 2000 (4)

Equation for: DYa
                      Coefficient  Std.Error  t-value  t-prob
DYa_1                   -0.349132    0.06260    -5.58   0.000
CIa_1                   -0.111349   0.006508    -17.1   0.000
Constant                0.0318185   0.002485     12.8   0.000

sigma = 0.0167625

Equation for: DYb
                      Coefficient  Std.Error  t-value  t-prob
CIb_1                   -0.137948    0.01663    -8.29   0.000
```

```
Constant                  1.55636      0.1870      8.32    0.000

sigma = 0.00977343

Equation for: DYc
                      Coefficient  Std.Error  t-value  t-prob
DYa_1                   0.0583258    0.02097     2.78   0.006
DYc_1                   -0.242065    0.05997    -4.04   0.000
CIb_1                   0.0321119    0.01349     2.38   0.018
Constant                -0.359823     0.1516    -2.37   0.019

sigma = 0.00688795

Equation for: DYd
                      Coefficient  Std.Error  t-value  t-prob
DYd_1                    0.238268    0.06052     3.94   0.000
CIb_1                  -0.0564784    0.02083    -2.71   0.007
Constant                 0.636257     0.2342     2.72   0.007

sigma = 0.0131465

log-likelihood      2558.45031  -T/2log|Omega|      3693.60114
no. of observations        200  no. of parameters           12

LR test of over-identifying restrictions: Chi^2(16)=   19.392 [0.2488]
BFGS using analytical derivatives (eps1=0.0001; eps2=0.005):
Strong convergence

correlation of structural residuals (standard deviations on diagonal)
                 DYa          DYb          DYc          DYd
DYa         0.016762    -0.020084     -0.56272     -0.56841
DYb        -0.020084    0.0097734     -0.12272     0.043877
DYc         -0.56272     -0.12272    0.0068880      0.41753
DYd         -0.56841     0.043877      0.41753     0.013147
```

Model evaluation is as before. The vector tests from the test summary report no problems:

```
Vector Portmanteau(12):  183.513
Vector EGE-AR 1-5 test:   F(80,688)=   0.77569 [0.9229]
Vector Normality test:    Chi^2(8) =    5.2487 [0.7307]
Vector hetero test:       F(120,1372)=    1.0233 [0.4172]
Vector hetero-X test:     F(270,1530)=    1.0415 [0.3230]
```

whereas there is still significant non-normality owing to the outlier in the *DYa* equation.

7.3 Dynamic analysis and dynamic forecasting

Since the complete structure of the system is now known, aspects such as dynamic analysis and dynamic forecasts can be implemented. Select Test, Dynamic Analysis then Static long-run solution and Roots of companion matrix to produce (we replaced the numbers smaller than 10^{-17} by zeros):

Long-run matrix Pi(1)-I = Po

	DYa	DYb	DYc	DYd	CIa
DYa	-1.3491	0.00000	0.00000	0.00000	-0.11135
DYb	0.00000	-1.0000	0.00000	0.00000	0.00000
DYc	0.058332	0.00000	-1.2421	0.00000	0.00000
DYd	0.00000	0.00000	0.00000	-0.76171	0.00000
CIa	0.065018	0.00000	-1.7186	1.6919	-0.11135
CIb	-0.14583	0.00000	0.60513	0.40509	0.00000

	CIb
DYa	0.00000
DYb	-0.13794
DYc	0.032113
DYd	-0.056499
CIa	-0.035198
CIb	-0.31428

Long-run covariance

	DYa	DYb	DYc	DYd	CIa
DYa	0.0089164	0.0012038	-0.00015306	-0.00093322	-0.098836
DYb	0.0012038	0.00024059	2.3704e-006	-0.00013804	-0.013589
DYc	-0.00015306	2.3704e-006	9.4255e-006	1.2467e-005	0.0016244
DYd	-0.00093322	-0.00013804	1.2467e-005	9.9531e-005	0.010382
CIa	-0.098836	-0.013589	0.0016244	0.010382	1.1088
CIb	-0.0078608	-0.0013885	3.8397e-005	0.00087321	0.087804

	CIb
DYa	-0.0078608
DYb	-0.0013885
DYc	3.8397e-005
DYd	0.00087321
CIa	0.087804
CIb	0.012507

Static long run

	Constant
DYa	-0.0097057
DYb	0.0051424
DYc	0.00057086
DYd	0.0015204
CIa	0.40335
CIb	11.245

Standard errors of static long run

	Constant
DYa	0.0066773
DYb	0.0010968
DYc	0.00021715
DYd	0.00070547
CIa	0.074460
CIb	0.0079082

Mean-lag matrix sum pi_i:

	DYa	DYb	DYc	DYd	CIa
DYa	-0.34914	0.00000	0.00000	0.00000	-0.11135

DYb	0.00000	0.00000	0.00000	0.00000	0.00000
DYc	0.058332	0.00000	-0.24205	0.00000	0.00000
DYd	0.00000	0.00000	0.00000	0.23829	0.00000
CIa	0.065018	0.00000	-1.7186	1.6919	0.88865
CIb	-0.14583	0.00000	0.60513	0.40509	0.00000

	CIb
DYa	0.00000
DYb	-0.13794
DYc	0.032113
DYd	-0.056499
CIa	-0.035198
CIb	0.68572

Eigenvalues of long-run matrix:

real	imag	modulus
-1.307	0.09377	1.310
-1.307	-0.09377	1.310
-1.000	0.0000	1.000
-0.7145	0.0000	0.7145
-0.3293	0.0000	0.3293
-0.1205	0.0000	0.1205

Eigenvalues of companion matrix:

real	imag	modulus
0.8795	0.0000	0.8795
0.6707	0.0000	0.6707
-0.3071	-0.09377	0.3211
-0.3071	0.09377	0.3211
0.2855	0.0000	0.2855
0.0000	0.0000	0.0000

Since the system is stationary, the long-run outcomes are interpretable (some are redundant given the simplicity of the dynamics in this system). Note that the roots of $\widehat{\pi}(1) - \mathbf{I}_n$ are one minus the roots of the companion matrix, and that the long-run *Constant* is highly significant in every equation except *DYa*. The *Constant* coefficients for the differenced variables are, of course, their long-run trends, and when multiplied by 400, deliver the annual growth rates as a percentage.

The long-run covariances are not easy to interpret when the identities are retained, since the 6×6 matrix only has rank 4. Here, the 'non-singular' long-run system is given by, for example, *DYa*, *DYb*, *CIa*, *CIb*, which is a valid (full rank) representation.

For dynamic forecasting, select Test, Forecast, Dynamic forecasts and set 16 periods (two years), marking all six variables, to see Figure 7.1.

This greatly improves on Figure 6.5, because the cointegrating vectors are now endogenous to the simultaneous equations model. The error bars for *DYc* and *DYd* reach their unconditional values almost at once whereas those for *DYa* and *DYb* continue to increase for about eight periods, as do the error bars for the cointegrating vectors. The variables therefore rapidly converge to their unconditional means and variances, where the former are non-zero except for *DYc* and *DYd*, and have 'realistic' values.

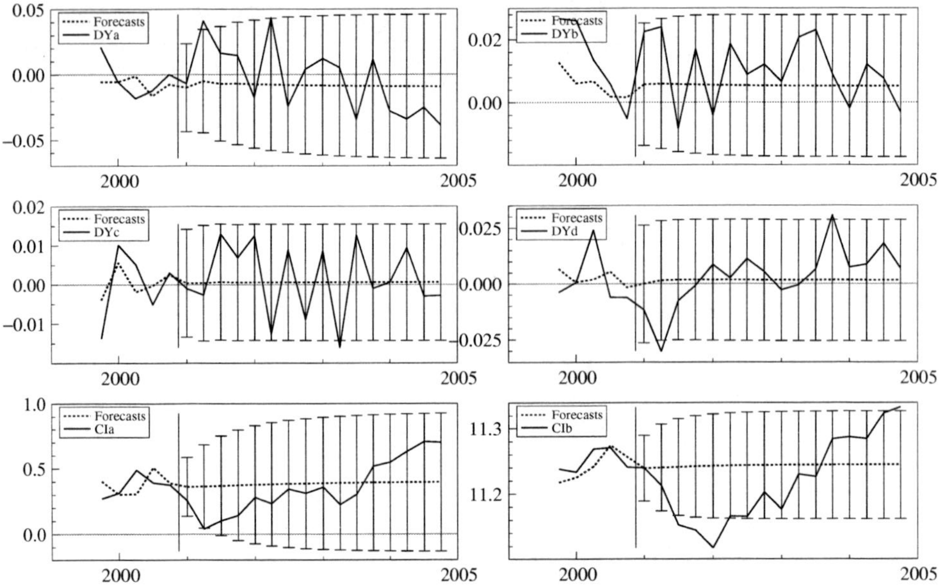

Figure 7.1 Dynamic forecasts in I(0) space.

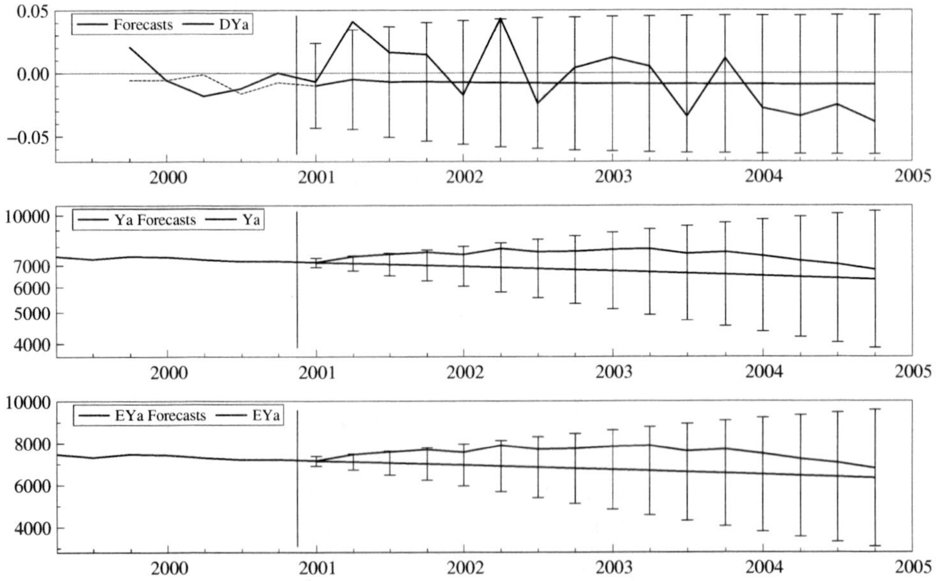

Figure 7.2 Dynamic forecasts in I(0) and I(1) space.

The contrast with the dynamic forecast graphs of Figure 3.5 is marked, and the current model is a much better representation of the information content of the system.

Note that the error bars will not converge to zero even when there are columns of zeros in the long-run covariance matrix. The reason is that the error bars are based (as $h \rightarrow \infty$) on the unconditional error covariance matrix (of the form $\sum_i \mathbf{A}^i \boldsymbol{\Omega} \mathbf{A}^{i\prime}$) whereas the long-run covariance is $(\mathbf{I}_n - \mathbf{A})^{-1} \boldsymbol{\Omega} (\mathbf{I}_n - \mathbf{A}')^{-1}$. See Chapter 11 for a more precise description.

Dynamic forecasting also allows forecasting derived functions of the original variables, by specifying Algebra code. For example, we can forecast the levels of `Ya` by integrating the difference (as an alternative to creating an identity for `Ya`):

```
Ya = cum(DYa) + 8.88265;
```

where we integrate from the actual level at 2000(4). Actually, since `Ya` is in logs, we can also undo the logarithm:

```
Ya = cum(DYa) + 8.88265;   EYa = exp(Ya);
```

so enter the code in the dialog as follows:

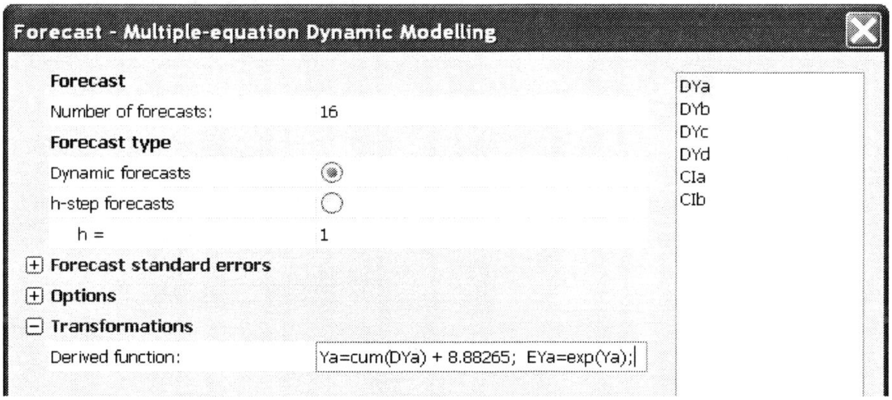

Also mark only the *DYa* equation to create just three graphs.

The result is in Figure 7.2, which involved some manipulation: we added the actual values to the bottom two graphs. This required changing the default areas to get visually meaningful graphs. In the middle graph, we also changed the style of the Y axis to `logs (data is in logs)`. Consequently the bottom two graphs are essentially the same, although the standard errors will differ in general.[1]

[1] The middle graph uses a 'naive' transformation of the error bands: if $\hat{y}_t, t = T+1, \ldots, T+H$ denotes the forecasts, and $f^{-1}(\cdot)$ the reverse data transformation, then the graph shows $f^{-1}(\hat{y}_t)$ with bands at $f^{-1}(\hat{y}_t - 2\hat{e}_t)$ and $f^{-1}(\hat{y}_t + 2\hat{e}_t)$. This, however, does not take into account the covariance which may be induced by the (reverse) transformation. When the reverse transformation is explicitly specified in the `Derived function` box, the standard errors of the forecast error are computing numerically, which takes the Jacobian of the transformation into account.

7.4 Modelling the parsimonious VAR

Why model a PVAR? Hendry and Doornik (1994) argue that the main reason is to simultaneously reduce the sample dependence of the estimated system and increase its invariance to change. The former arises because of the high dimensionality of a VAR, so that combinations of lagged variables accidentally coincide with data 'blips', inducing dependence on transient empirical phenomena: later re-estimation over a longer sample period should reveal this difficulty by driving the extended estimates towards insignificance despite more information. The second factor requires parameterizing in terms of the autonomous relations and eliminating the accidental features.

As before, when we identified the cointegration space, we needed to know about the economic content of the subject matter. Remember that *Ya*, *Yb*, *Yc*, *Yd* correspond respectively to the logarithms of real money $(m - p)$ and total final expenditure (i), inflation (Δp), and an interest rate differential which measures the opportunity costs of holding money (R_n). In §5.5, we already examined the long-run weak exogeneity of $(y_t, \Delta p_t, R_{n,t})$ for the parameters of the first cointegrating relation (under the assertion that this is the correct order of hypothesis testing). This supports the interpretation of the first equation as a contingent model of money demand, in which agents decide their money holdings once current inflation, income and opportunity costs are known, although Δp_t and $R_{n,t}$ could represent 'random walk' predictors of next period's values. Then the remaining three equations model those variables, consistent with narrow money not greatly influencing their behaviour. The second cointegration vector represents the excess demand for goods and services on this interpretation, which is one factor affecting inflation and output growth, and possibly interest-rate setting behaviour by the central bank (for a more extensive analysis, see Hendry, 2001).

To interpret the model more usefully, we first reparametrize the cointegration vectors to have zero means, so the intercepts that remain become growth rates. Here the sample means of *CIa* and *CIb* are 0.4 and 11.25 respectively, so subtract these:

```
CIam = CIa - 0.4; CIbm = CIb - 11.25;
```

and reformulate the system in terms of these zero-mean cointegration vectors. The only *change* in the estimates should be in the intercept values. Because there should be no 'autonomous' growth in either inflation or interest rates, their constants should be set to zero; whereas the intercepts in the first two equations should deliver the same long-run growth (since we have imposed a unit elasticity of real money with respect to real expenditure via the first cointegration relation). Implementing the first two delivers a test of over-identifying restrictions of $\chi^2(18) = 26.3$ [p $=$ 0.09]. The estimates now are (easily obtained in LaTeX form by using Test, Further Output, Write model results):

$$\mathit{DYa} = -\underset{(0.0618)}{0.326}\,\mathit{DYa}_{t-1} - \underset{(0.00647)}{0.11}\,\mathit{CIam}_{t-1} - \underset{(0.00105)}{0.011}$$

$$\mathit{DYb} = -\underset{(0.0166)}{0.137}\,\mathit{CIbm}_{t-1} + \underset{(0.000687)}{0.00466}$$

$$DYc = \underset{(0.0187)}{0.0337}\ DYa_{t-1} - \underset{(0.0599)}{0.266}\ DYc_{t-1} + \underset{(0.0128)}{0.0202}\ CIbm_{t-1}$$

$$DYd = \underset{(0.0598)}{0.24}\ DYd_{t-1} - \underset{(0.0205)}{0.0558}\ CIbm_{t-1}$$

The remaining restriction requires CFIML, but is clearly invalid, since the first intercept is negative, but real expenditure has grown, at about 2.2% p.a. (400×0.0055). This is due to an 'unlucky draw of the data', since the restriction is in fact true in the DGP (see §7.6).

The final features of the data that merit modelling are the large negative residual correlations between money with the inflation and interest-rate equations, consistent with the contingent model of money demand noted above. OLS estimation of such a specification yields:

$$\begin{aligned} DYa = &- \underset{(0.0616)}{0.28}\ DYa_{t-1} - \underset{(0.133)}{0.891}\ DYc_t - \underset{(0.072)}{0.518}\ DYd_t \\ &- \underset{(0.00109)}{0.0108} - \underset{(0.00637)}{0.108}\ CIam_{t-1} \end{aligned}$$

Both contemporaneous variables are highly significant. However, when the corresponding equation is estimated with DYc_t and DYd_t endogenized, we obtain:

$$\begin{aligned} DYa = &- \underset{(0.0746)}{0.363}\ DYa_{t-1} - \underset{(0.00677)}{0.11}\ CIam_{t-1} - \underset{(0.00106)}{0.0112} \\ &+ \underset{(0.658)}{0.73}\ DYc_t + \underset{(0.428)}{0.391}\ DYd_t \end{aligned}$$

Neither variable is significant, and their signs are uninterpretable, confirming that data variation can be important. Indeed, a glance back at Figure 3.1 reveals the problem: real money holdings fell in the sample analyzed, whereas real expenditure rose, and indeed both inflation and interest rates had quite strong chance trends.

We complete this set of tutorials with a look at maximization control, and a comparison of our modelled equations with the actual DGP. The final tutorial in Chapter 8 looks at some advanced features. If you wish, you could leave that for later reading — we trust you now have sufficient experience to start modelling with actual data.

7.5 Maximization control

When deselect Automatic maximization in the Estimation dialog, you are presented with the Optimization Control dialog (for the model prior to formulating the mean-zero cointegration vectors, i.e. the model of `MulTut4.fl`):

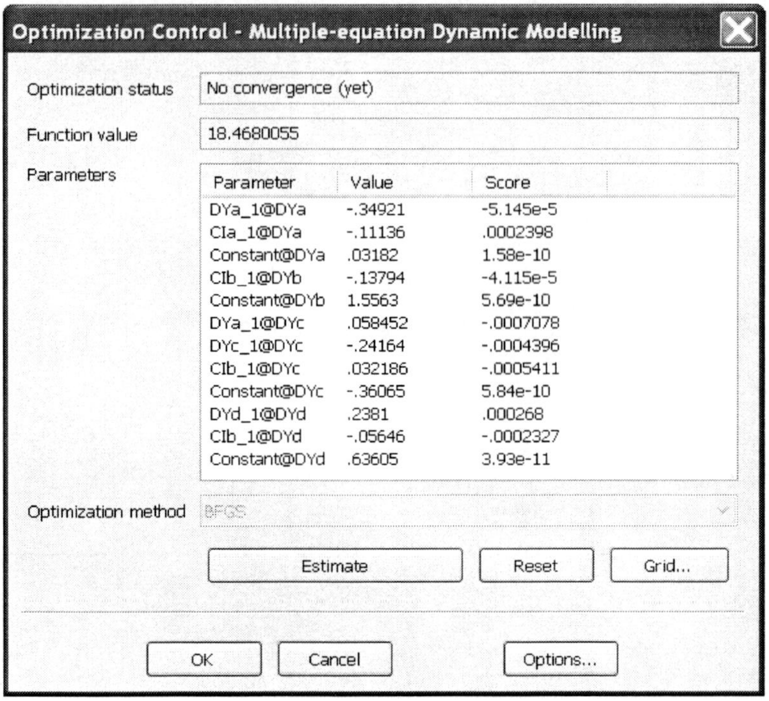

Note that we resized the dialog somewhat to display all free parameters. The available options are:

(1) Coefficient values can be set to any particular desired value by double clicking on the coefficient in the list box.
(2) Reset the initial values to those at dialog entry.
(3) Estimate, to optimize the objective function starting from the listed coefficient values.
(4) Press Options to control the maximization process:
    - Change the maximum number of iterations (that is, steps in which the function value reduces); if this number is reached, the optimization process will abort, despite not yet finding the minimum.
    - Specify how often (if at all) iteration output is printed; and
    - Set the convergence criterion.
(5) Conduct a Grid search over the model parameters.

The starting values for FIML are provided by 3SLS estimation, which usually is a good initial point. To continue, press the Estimate button to maximize the log-likelihood, which happens nearly instantaneously. Next, we will draw some parameter grids.

There are two methods available to generate a parameter grid:

(1) Maximize over remaining parameters.
This involves a complete log-likelihood maximization over the other parameters. For example, in a two parameter case, where the grid is over α:

$$\widehat{\ell}(\alpha_i, \widehat{\beta})/T = \max_{\beta} \ell(\alpha_i, \beta)/T, \quad \alpha_i = \alpha_1, \ldots, \alpha_n,$$

where α_i are the selected grid points.

(2) Keep all remaining parameters fixed.
The fixed grid only involves likelihood evaluations, keeping the second parameter fixed at its current value, while computing the first over the grid coordinates:

$$\ell(\alpha_i, \beta \mid \beta = \beta^*)/T, \quad \alpha_i = \alpha_1, \ldots, \alpha_n,$$

Therefore, the former method can be much slower, especially for a 3D (bivariate) grid. For example, a 20 by 20 grid would require 400 likelihood maximizations (i.e., 400 FIML estimates).

For an illustrative graph, we first compute a one-dimensional fixed grid of all parameters. To start, press Estimate to maximize, then press the Grid button:

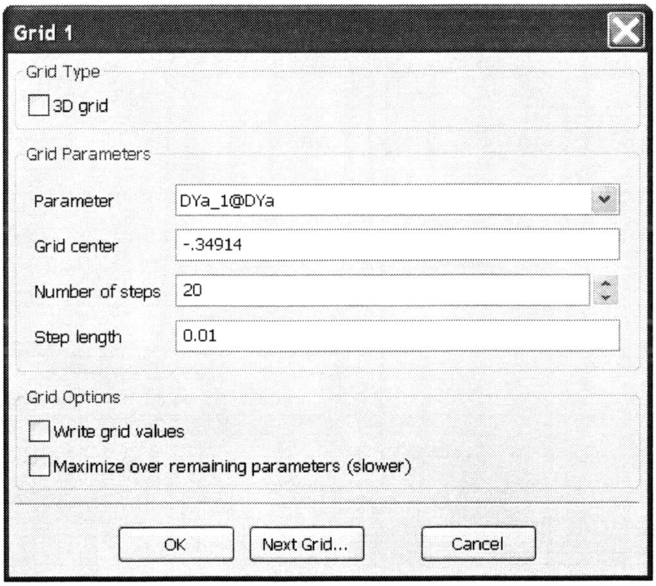

and then press Next Grid eleven times, until the title says ‘Grid 12’, for which the listed parameter is the Constant. Then press OK (don’t press Cancel if you go too far: that will abort the whole procedure, not creating any graphs). The result should look like Figure 7.3

For some examples of two-dimensional grids it is useful to move somewhat away from the maximum: double click on the first parameter, and change its value to -0.5.

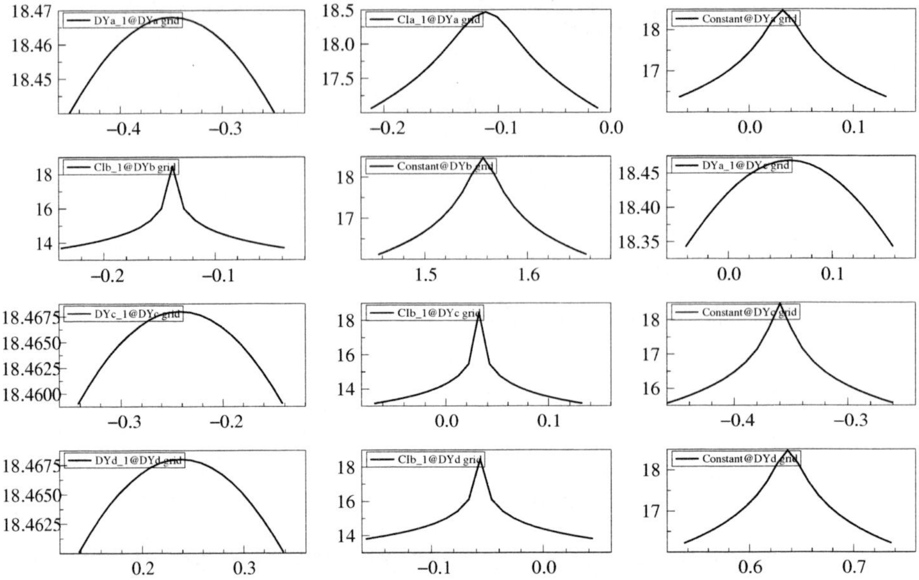

Figure 7.3 Likelihood function projections for one parameter.

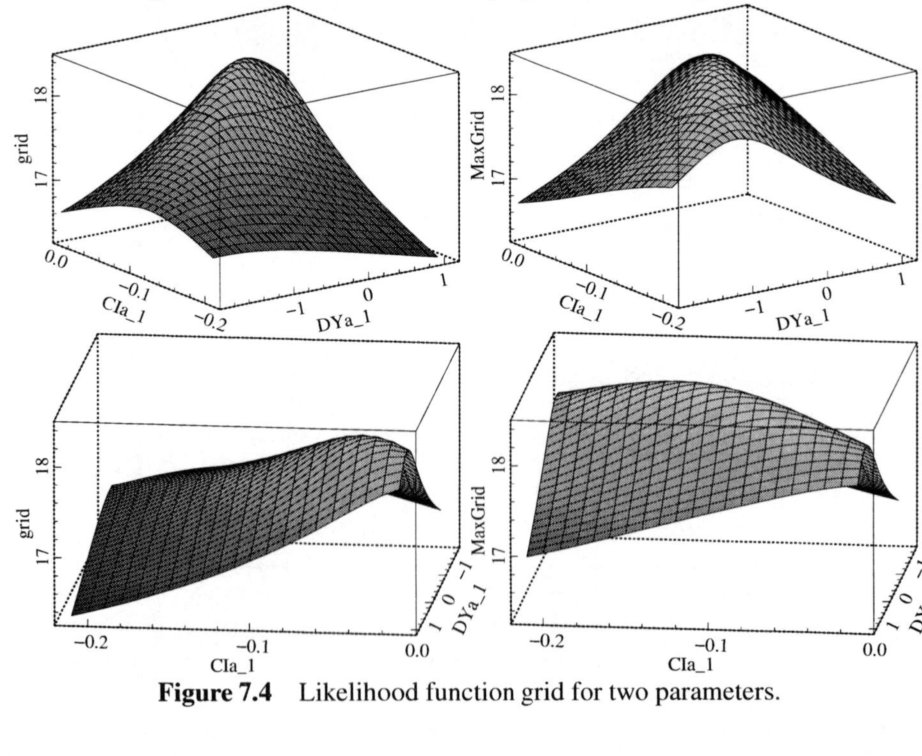

Figure 7.4 Likelihood function grid for two parameters.

All the gradients will change as a consequence — it is clear that this is not the maximum. Also set the third parameter (the first *Constant*) to zero.

For the three-dimensional grid plots, which are a function of two parameters, we look at the first two coefficients. Activate the grid, and click on 3D grid. For the first parameter, that of *DYa*_1, set the number of steps to 30, and the step size to 0.1. Select *CIa*_1 for the second parameter, setting the number of steps for to 20 with step size 0.01:

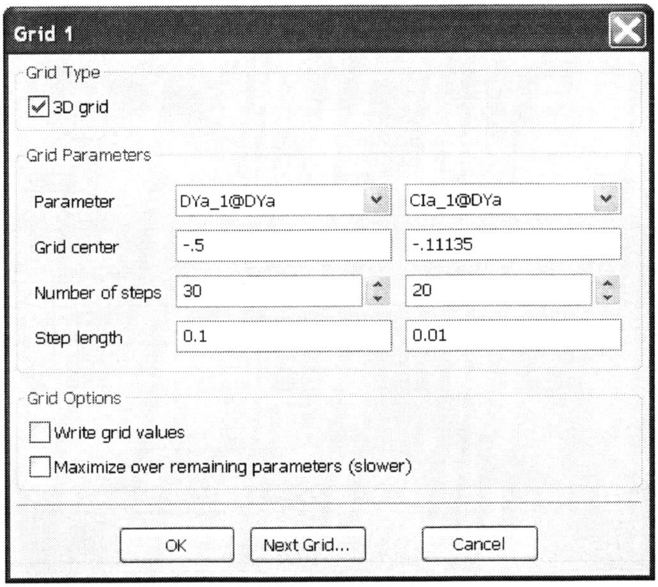

Click on Next Grid, and reset to the same grid as before, but now select Maximize over remaining parameters. The first grid is in Figure 7.4a, with the second, using full re-estimation for every grid point, in Figure 7.4b.

Figure 7.4c and d correspond to 7.4a and b respectively, but they are both rotated in the same way to expose the curvature along *CIa* more clearly. This illustrates the difference between the two grids: in the max grid case, we can read the actual likelihood maximum of the graph (roughly at -0.1 for the *CIa*_1 coefficient). This cannot be done for fixed grid graph: there the maximum appears to be at a value near -0.02, with a clearly lower log-likelihood value: at the fixed graph, the coefficient of the *Constant* is kept at zero, while the max graph re-estimates it every time.

7.6 How well did we do?

The tutorial data are generated artificially, from the data generation process (DGP) in Doornik, Hendry and Nielsen (1998), so we can check on the closeness of the selected model to the DGP.

In fact the system was:

$$\Delta \mathbf{x}_t = \begin{pmatrix} -0.102 & 0 \\ 0 & -0.149 \\ 0 & 0.036 \\ 0 & -0.04 \end{pmatrix} \begin{pmatrix} 1 & -1 & 6.41 & 7.16 & 0 & -0.209 \\ 0 & 1 & -2.13 & 1.48 & -0.0063 & -11.186 \end{pmatrix}$$

$$\times \begin{pmatrix} \mathbf{x}_{t-1} \\ t \\ 1 \end{pmatrix} + \begin{pmatrix} 0.0063 \\ 0.0063 \\ 0 \\ 0 \end{pmatrix} + \begin{pmatrix} -0.3 & 0 & 0 & -0.06 \\ 0 & 0 & 0 & 0 \\ 0.068 & 0 & -0.26 & 0 \\ 0 & 0 & 0 & 0.17 \end{pmatrix} \Delta \mathbf{x}_{t-1} + \boldsymbol{\nu}_t,$$

when:

$$\boldsymbol{\nu}_t \sim \mathsf{IN}_4 \left[\mathbf{0}, \boldsymbol{\Sigma} \right], \text{ where } \boldsymbol{\Sigma}^* = \begin{pmatrix} 1.6\% & & & \\ -0.08 & 1\% & & \\ -0.51 & 0.03 & 0.69\% & \\ -0.49 & 0.09 & 0.31 & 1.3\% \end{pmatrix},$$

using the lower triangle of $\boldsymbol{\Sigma}^*$ to show the cross correlations of the errors, and:

$$\begin{pmatrix} \mathbf{x}'_{-1} \\ \mathbf{x}'_0 \end{pmatrix} = \begin{pmatrix} 10.9445 & 11.1169 & 0.000779 & 0.048967 \\ 10.9369 & 11.1306 & 0.013567 & 0.050 \end{pmatrix}.$$

Note that, despite the way the DGP is written, the constant is actually not restricted to the cointegration space, thus satisfying $\mathsf{H}_l(2)$.

So we actually did very well, coming close to recovering the actual DGP! The only restriction we imposed which was not in the DGP is $\beta_{13} = \beta_{23}$ in the cointegrating vector. Another problem was caused by the negative growth rate of real money in this draw, as discussed in §7.4. Of course, we were fortunate that our initial general model had the DGP nested within it — in practice, one cannot expect to be so lucky.

Chapter 8

Tutorial on Advanced VAR Modelling

8.1 Introduction

In Chapter 3 we formulated and estimated a system which was a vector autoregression. The modelling sequence progressed as:

VAR in I(1) space
↓
Cointegrated VAR in I(1) space
↓
Cointegrated VAR in I(0) space
↓
Parsimonious CVAR
↓
Structural model

This chapter discusses some of the features of PcGive that were not addressed in the previous tutorials. It is assumed that you have some familiarity with the material in the preceding tutorials: required mouse actions or keystrokes are often not given here.

The basis for this chapter is Lütkepohl (1991) (in the remainder referred to as Lütkepohl). Using a data set listed there, we shall replicate many of the calculations and graphs. The purpose is to discuss remaining features of PcGive, show its flexibility, and explain any differences in results. The emphasis will be on technique, rather than interpretation.

8.2 Loading the Lütkepohl data

The data are listed in Table E.1 of Appendix E in Lütkepohl, and are provided with PcGive in the file `MulTutVAR.in7`. Start OxMetrics and load this file (if the default installation was used, the file will be in `\Program files\OxMetrics4\data`).

The data are quarterly, and have sample period 1960(1)–1979(4) (with one year used for forecasting):

I investment,
Y income,
C consumption.

These are seasonally adjusted data for West Germany, the units are billions of DM. The levels are graphed in Figure 8.1.

The calculator was used to create logarithms of the variables: $i = \log(I)$, $y = \log(Y)$, $c = \log(C)$, as well as first differences: $Di = \Delta i$, $Dy = \Delta y$, $Dc = \Delta c$:

```
i = log(I);
y = log(Y);
c = log(C);
Di = diff(i, 1);
Dy = diff(y, 1);
Dc = diff(c, 1);
```

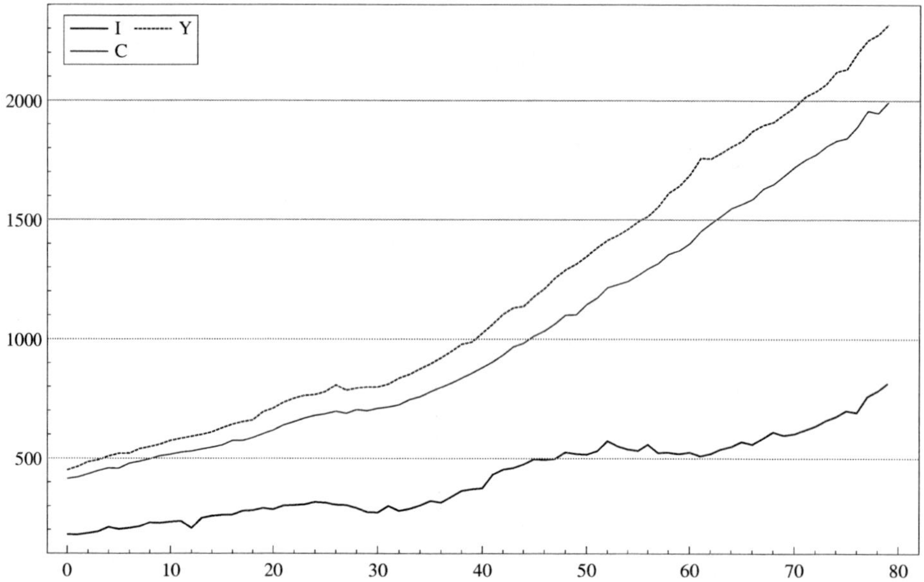

Figure 8.1 Levels of investment, income and consumption.

8.3 Estimating a VAR

Activate Model, Formulate System and set up a two-lag VAR with unrestricted constant. Reduce the estimation sample by one year (that is, estimate up to 1978 (4); estimation yields:

```
SYS( 1) Estimating the system by OLS (using MulTutVAR.in7)
        The estimation sample is: 1960(4) - 1978(4)
```

```
URF equation for: Di
                 Coefficient   Std.Error  t-value  t-prob
Di_1               -0.319631      0.1255    -2.55   0.013
Di_2               -0.160551      0.1249    -1.29   0.203
Dy_1                0.145989      0.5457    0.268   0.790
Dy_2                0.114605      0.5346    0.214   0.831
Dc_1                0.961219      0.6643     1.45   0.153
Dc_2                0.934394      0.6651     1.40   0.165
Constant      U   -0.0167220     0.01723   -0.971   0.335

sigma = 0.0461479   RSS = 0.1405555086

URF equation for: Dy
                 Coefficient   Std.Error  t-value  t-prob
Di_1               0.0439311     0.03186     1.38   0.173
Di_2               0.0500308     0.03172     1.58   0.120
Dy_1               -0.152732      0.1386    -1.10   0.274
Dy_2               0.0191658      0.1358    0.141   0.888
Dc_1                0.288502      0.1687     1.71   0.092
Dc_2              -0.0102049      0.1689  -0.0604   0.952
Constant      U    0.0157672    0.004375     3.60   0.001

sigma = 0.0117191   RSS = 0.009064290022

URF equation for: Dc
                 Coefficient   Std.Error  t-value  t-prob
Di_1             -0.00242267     0.02568  -0.0944   0.925
Di_2               0.0338804     0.02556     1.33   0.190
Dy_1                0.224813      0.1117     2.01   0.048
Dy_2                0.354912      0.1094     3.24   0.002
Dc_1               -0.263968      0.1360    -1.94   0.056
Dc_2              -0.0222301      0.1361   -0.163   0.871
Constant      U    0.0129259    0.003526     3.67   0.000

sigma = 0.00944476   RSS = 0.00588743192

log-likelihood        606.306968  -T/2log|Omega|       917.054506
|Omega|          1.22587519e-011  log|Y'Y/T|          -24.4249756
R^2(LR)                 0.503318  R^2(LM)                0.198829
no. of observations           73  no. of parameters            21

F-test on regressors except unrestricted: F(18,181) = 2.83062 [0.0002] **
F-tests on retained regressors, F(3,64) =
        Di_1        3.10599 [0.033]*       Di_2        1.83313 [0.150]
        Dy_1        3.66382 [0.017]*       Dy_2        4.89344 [0.004]**
        Dc_1        6.39472 [0.001]**      Dc_2       0.750599 [0.526]
    Constant U      6.83391 [0.000]**

correlation of URF residuals (standard deviations on diagonal)
                  Di             Dy            Dc
Di          0.046148        0.13242       0.28275
Dy           0.13242       0.011719       0.55526
```

```
Dc              0.28275         0.55526      0.0094448
correlation between actual and fitted
              Di               Dy               Dc
       0.35855          0.33793          0.50128
```

Here we have $T = 73$, $k = 7$, so that the t-probabilities come from a Student-t distribution with 66 degrees of freedom. Most statistics (such as the standard errors, standard deviations of URF residuals and correlation of URF residuals) are based on $\widetilde{\Omega}$. To compute σ without degrees-of-freedom correction for the first equation, for example:

$$\widehat{\sigma} = \sqrt{\frac{T-k}{T}}\widetilde{\sigma} = 0.9508 * 0.04615 = 0.0439.$$

8.4 Dynamic analysis

Select Test, Dynamic analysis, select static long-run solution and roots of companion matrix. The output includes:

```
Long-run matrix Pi(1)-I = Po
                    Di              Dy              Dc
Di             -1.4802         0.26059          1.8956
Dy            0.093962         -1.1336         0.27830
Dc            0.031458         0.57973         -1.2862

Long-run covariance
                    Di              Dy              Dc
Di           0.0019289      0.00049528      0.00047269
Dy          0.00049528      0.00024515      0.00020511
Dc          0.00047269      0.00020511      0.00020007

Mean-lag matrix sum pi_i:
                    Di              Dy              Dc
Di            -0.64073         0.37520          2.8300
Dy             0.14399        -0.11440         0.26809
Dc            0.065338         0.93464        -0.30843

Eigenvalues of long-run matrix:
         real        imag     modulus
       -1.639      0.2614       1.659
       -1.639     -0.2614       1.659
      -0.6228      0.0000      0.6228

Eigenvalues of companion matrix
lambda_i real      imag    modulus        z_i real        imag     modulus
      0.5705     0.0000     0.5705  |         1.75        0.00        1.75
     -0.3906     0.3891     0.5513  |        -1.29       -1.28        1.81
     -0.3906    -0.3891     0.5513  |        -1.29        1.28        1.81
    -0.07725     0.4856     0.4917  |       -0.320       -2.01        2.03
    -0.07725    -0.4856     0.4917  |       -0.320        2.01        2.03
     -0.3712     0.0000     0.3712  |        -2.69        0.00        2.69
```

The companion matrix for the VAR(2) model $\mathbf{y}_t = \boldsymbol{\pi}_1 \mathbf{y}_{t-1} + \boldsymbol{\pi}_2 \mathbf{y}_{t-2} + \mathbf{v}_t$ is:

$$\begin{pmatrix} \widehat{\pi}_1 & \widehat{\pi}_2 \\ \mathbf{I}_3 & \mathbf{0} \end{pmatrix} = \begin{pmatrix} -0.320 & 0.044 & -0.0024 & -0.161 & 0.0500 & 0.034 \\ 0.146 & -0.153 & 0.225 & 0.115 & 0.0192 & 0.355 \\ 0.961 & 0.289 & -0.264 & 0.934 & -0.0102 & -0.022 \\ 1 & 0 & 0 & 0 & 0 & 0 \\ 0 & 1 & 0 & 0 & 0 & 0 \\ 0 & 0 & 1 & 0 & 0 & 0 \end{pmatrix}$$

All the roots, λ_i, of the companion matrix are inside the unit circle (modulus[1] is less than 1). Or in terms of $z_i = 1/\lambda_i$, all roots are outside the unit circle. The numbers for z_i have been added to the output.

8.5 Forecasting

Static forecasting is possible only if we retain observations for that purpose, so is not feasible given our present selection (if you selected the data sample as described above). However, it is easy to re-estimate the system reserving some observations for static forecasting. Dynamic forecasting requires data over the forecast period on any non-modelled, stochastic variables. When the system is closed, it is feasible computationally to dynamically forecast well beyond the available data period, but the practical value of such an exercise is doubtful for long horizons.

Re-estimate the VAR on the sample to 1979(4), withholding the four new observations for forecasting, by requiring 4 forecasts. Then use Test/Further Output/Static (1-step) forecasts to print the full output. The extra information in the results window is:

```
1-step (ex post) forecast analysis 1979(1) - 1979(4)
Parameter constancy forecast tests:
using Omega  Chi^2(12)=    16.366 [0.1750]    F(12,66) =    1.3638 [0.2059]
using  V[e]  Chi^2(12)=    15.113 [0.2353]    F(12,66) =    1.2594 [0.2638]
using  V[E]  Chi^2(12)=    15.155 [0.2331]    F(12,66) =    1.2629 [0.2616]

1-step forecasts for Di (SE with parameter uncertainty)
   Horizon        Forecast          SE         Actual         Error   t-value
    1979-2     -0.0108109     0.04805     -0.0114944  -0.000683436    -0.014
    1979-3      0.0165471     0.04779      0.0924158     0.0758687     1.587
    1979-4      0.0206854     0.04783      0.0298530    0.00916755     0.192
    1980-1    -0.00873230     0.04957      0.0425596     0.0512919     1.035
   mean(Error) =      0.033911    RMSE =      0.046020
   SD(Error)   =      0.031111    MAPE =        298.00
```

[1]Modulus is defined as: $|a+ib| = \sqrt{(a^2+b^2)}$. If $x.z = (a+ib)(c+id) = 1$ then $c = a/|x|^2$ and $d = -b/|x|^2$.

```
1-step forecasts for Dy (SE with parameter uncertainty)
  Horizon       Forecast          SE        Actual          Error   t-value
   1979-2     0.0199108     0.01220    0.0309422      0.0110314     0.904
   1979-3     0.0198156     0.01214    0.0242599     0.00444439     0.366
   1979-4     0.0260749     0.01215    0.0101569     -0.0159180    -1.311
   1980-1     0.0187781     0.01259    0.0182852   -0.000492824    -0.039
  mean(Error) =  -0.00023377    RMSE =   0.0099382
  SD(Error)   =    0.0099354    MAPE =      25.763

1-step forecasts for Dc (SE with parameter uncertainty)
  Horizon       Forecast          SE        Actual          Error   t-value
   1979-2     0.0216287    0.009835    0.0257249     0.00409616     0.416
   1979-3     0.0160543    0.009781    0.0353467      0.0192924     1.972
   1979-4     0.0188460    0.009789  -0.00512034     -0.0239663    -2.448
   1980-1     0.0274440     0.01014    0.0233395    -0.00410454    -0.405
  mean(Error) =   -0.0011706    RMSE =    0.015654
  SD(Error)   =     0.015610    MAPE =      50.009

Forecast tests using V[e]:
1979-1         Chi^2(3) =  0.84043 [0.8398]
1979-2         Chi^2(3) =   5.7548 [0.1242]
1979-3         Chi^2(3) =   6.8511 [0.0768]
1979-4         Chi^2(3) =   1.6668 [0.6443]
```

The Graphic analysis dialog can be used to plot the outcomes: mark Forecasts and outcomes as well as Forecast chow tests. Figure 8.2 shows the graph.

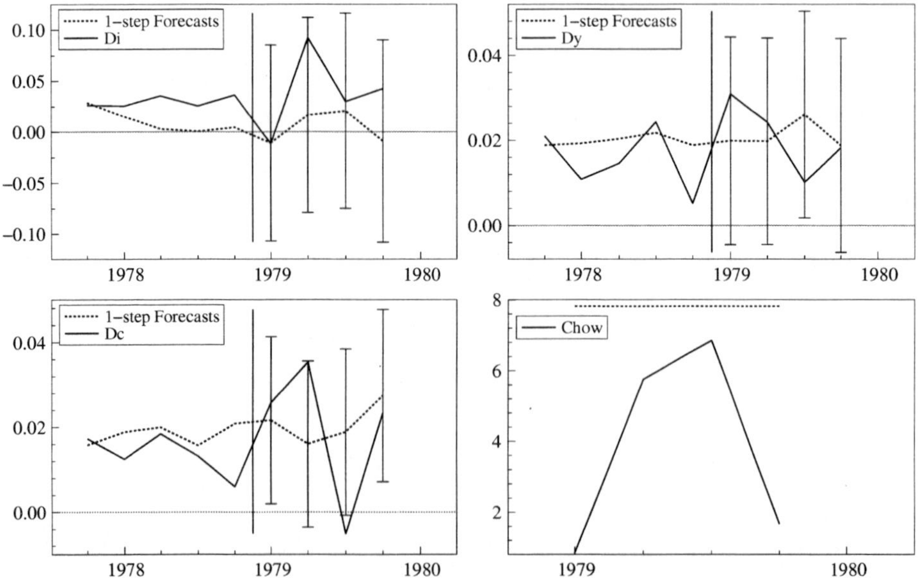

Figure 8.2 1-step forecasts with error and parameter-variance based error bars.

We can compare these results to the output from dynamic forecasting. Access its dialog, select four 1-step forecasts, and Write results instead of graphing in the Options section to obtain the second set of 1-step forecast standard errors. Next, select four dynamic forecasts in the Forecast dialog and Write:

```
1-step forecasts for Di (SE based on error variance only)
   Horizon       Forecast          SE        Actual          Error    t-value
    1979-1     -0.0108109     0.04615    -0.0114944   -0.000683436     -0.015
    1979-2      0.0165471     0.04615     0.0924158      0.0758687      1.644
    1979-3      0.0206854     0.04615     0.0298530     0.00916755      0.199
    1979-4    -0.00873230     0.04615     0.0425596      0.0512919      1.111

1-step forecasts for Dy (SE based on error variance only)
   Horizon       Forecast          SE        Actual          Error    t-value
    1979-1      0.0199108     0.01172     0.0309422      0.0110314      0.941
    1979-2      0.0198156     0.01172     0.0242599     0.00444439      0.379
    1979-3      0.0260749     0.01172     0.0101569     -0.0159180     -1.358
    1979-4      0.0187781     0.01172     0.0182852   -0.000492824     -0.042

1-step forecasts for Dc (SE based on error variance only)
   Horizon       Forecast          SE        Actual          Error    t-value
    1979-1      0.0216287    0.009445     0.0257249     0.00409616      0.434
    1979-2      0.0160543    0.009445     0.0353467      0.0192924      2.043
    1979-3      0.0188460    0.009445   -0.00512034     -0.0239663     -2.538
    1979-4      0.0274440    0.009445     0.0233395    -0.00410454     -0.435

Dynamic (ex ante) forecasts for Di (SE based on error variance only)
   Horizon       Forecast          SE        Actual          Error    t-value
    1979-1     -0.0108109     0.04615    -0.0114944   -0.000683436     -0.015
    1979-2      0.0107809     0.04866     0.0924158      0.0816349      1.678
    1979-3      0.0211157     0.04903     0.0298530     0.00873726      0.178
    1979-4      0.0123583     0.04942     0.0425596      0.0302013      0.611

Dynamic (ex ante) forecasts for Dy (SE based on error variance only)
   Horizon       Forecast          SE        Actual          Error    t-value
    1979-1      0.0199108     0.01172     0.0309422      0.0110314      0.941
    1979-2      0.0203487     0.01220     0.0242599     0.00391127      0.321
    1979-3      0.0169806     0.01231     0.0101569    -0.00682373     -0.554
    1979-4      0.0206009     0.01243     0.0182852    -0.00231571     -0.186

Dynamic (ex ante) forecasts for Dc (SE based on error variance only)
   Horizon       Forecast          SE        Actual          Error    t-value
    1979-1      0.0216287    0.009445     0.0257249     0.00409616      0.434
    1979-2      0.0146539    0.009755     0.0353467      0.0206928      2.121
    1979-3      0.0198257     0.01079   -0.00512034     -0.0249461     -2.313
    1979-4      0.0187203     0.01083     0.0233395     0.00461917      0.426
```

The first set of 1-step forecast standard errors (labelled 'SE with parameter uncertainty') takes parameter uncertainty into account, the second set (created with the Forecast dialog) does not. Hence in the latter, the standard errors remain constant (at $\widetilde{\sigma}$), and are smaller than the full forecast standard errors. Figure 8.3 gives four dynamic forecasts with these constant error bars, together with some pre-forecast data. Compared to Figure 8.2, the bars are noticeably smaller only for *Dc*.

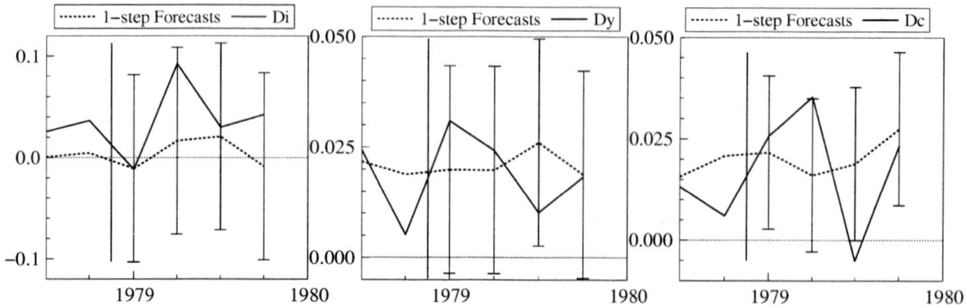

Figure 8.3 1-step forecasts with error-variance based bars.

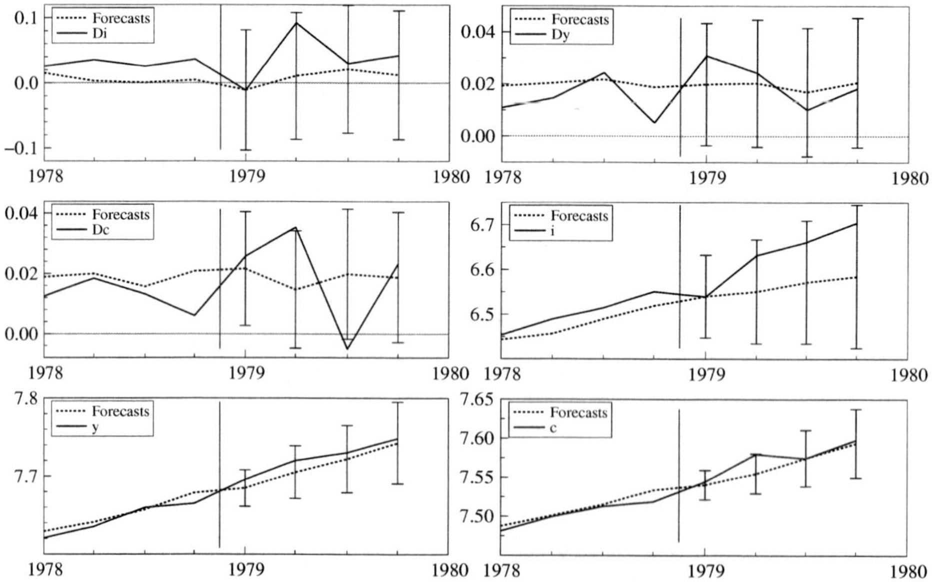

Figure 8.4 Dynamic forecasts of levels and differences.

It is often interesting to have forecasts of both the levels and the differences. This can be achieved using identities. Add *i, y, c* with one lag to the system, and mark the current-dated levels as I(dentities). Activate Simultaneous equations model in the, Model Settings, and define the three identities as:

$$i = i\_1, Di,$$
$$y = y\_1, Dy,$$
$$c = c\_1, Dc.$$

Also delete any lagged levels from the stochastic equations, so these remain in differences. Re-estimate by FIML keeping four forecasts. The results should be as before. Figure 8.4 shows four dynamic forecasts, with error bars, both for the differences and the levels (the identities have to be marked in the dialog). Note the rapid increase in the height of the error bars for the levels.

This approach can be compared to that underlying Figure 7.2, where Algebra code was used to obtain levels forecasts. The advantage of the current approach is that forecast standard errors can be computed analytically, rather than numerically. Here we could add code to undo the logarithms: `I=exp(i); Y=exp(y); C=exp(c);`.

8.6 Dynamic simulation and impulse response analysis

Dynamic simulation in PcGive is similar to dynamic forecasting, but starting at a point inside the estimation sample. Select Simulation and Impulses:

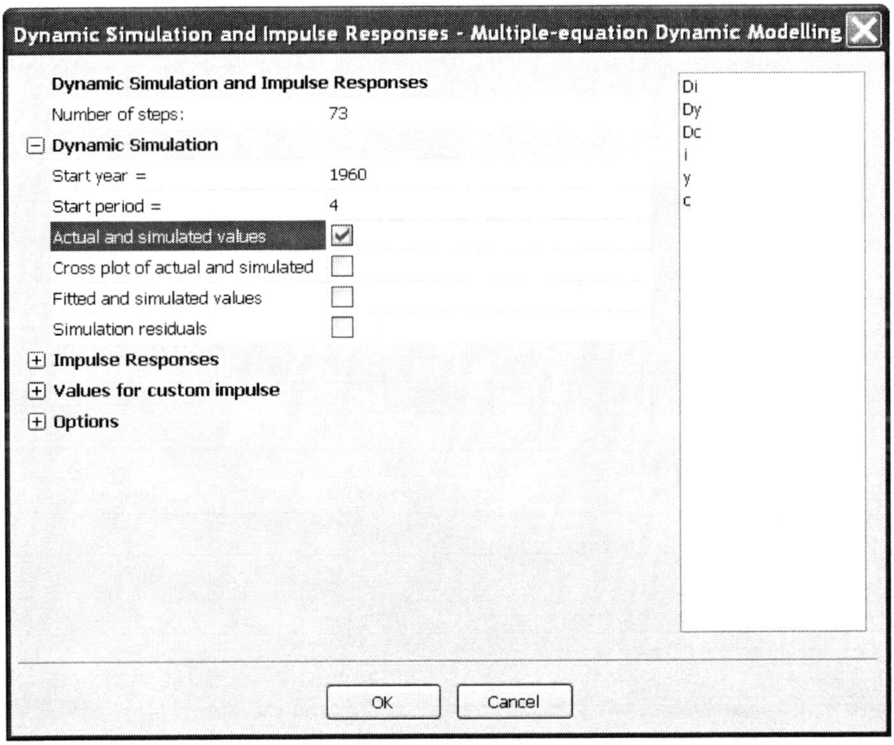

Marking Actual and simulated values and all equations gives Figure 8.5.
Notice the complete lack of explanatory power for simulated differences after the first couple of data points, apart from the mean. That the levels appear to track well is therefore essentially an artefact due to the residuals summing to zero (see Pagan, 1989).

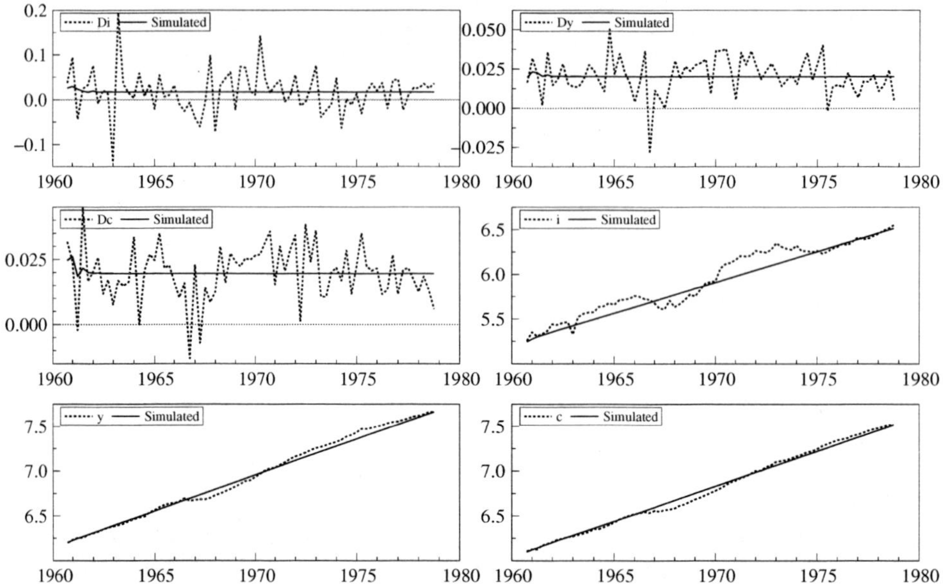

Figure 8.5 Dynamic simulation for levels and differences.

8.6.1 Impulse response analysis

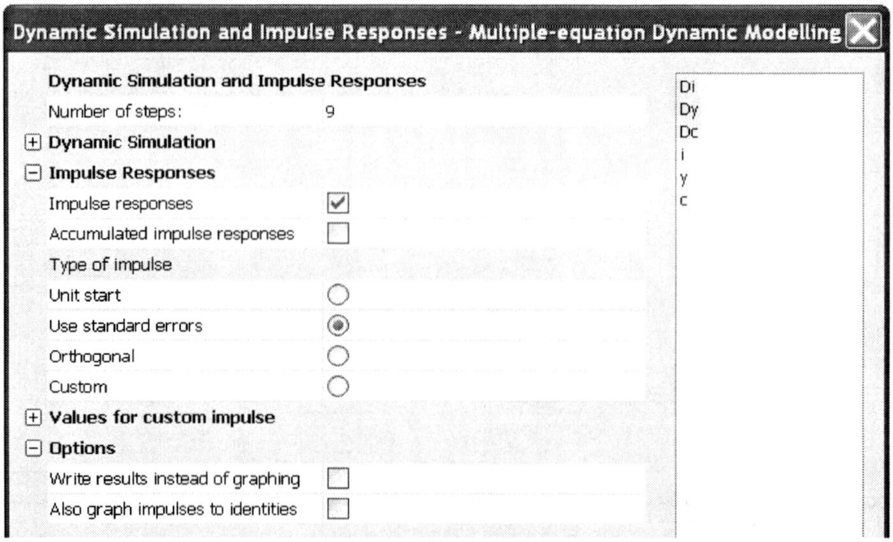

Impulse response analysis amounts to dynamic simulation from an initial value of zero, where a shock at $t = 1$ in a variable is traced through. This amounts to graphing powers of the companion matrix. As with dynamic simulation, for linear systems, most information is given in the dynamic analysis, but graphs might be easier to interpret than numbers.

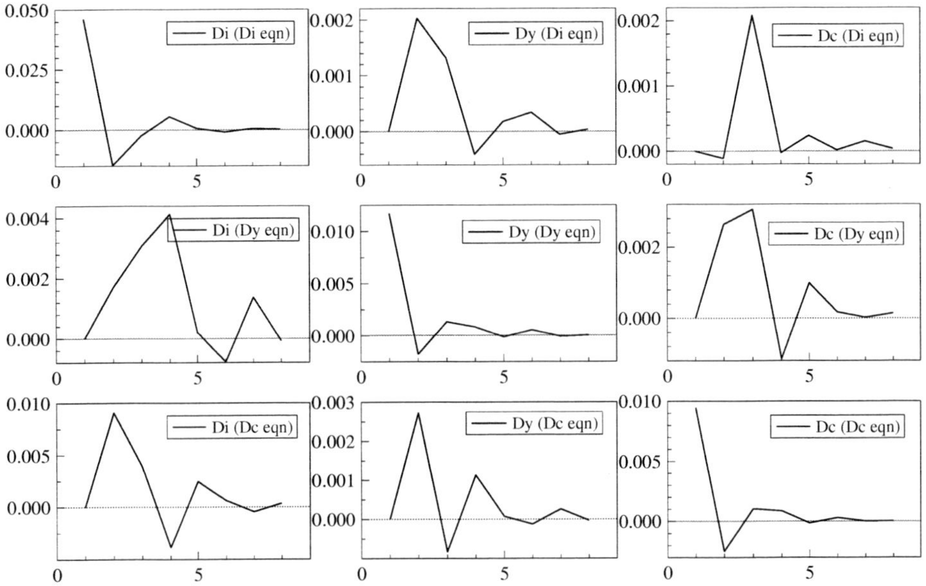

Figure 8.6 Impulse responses.

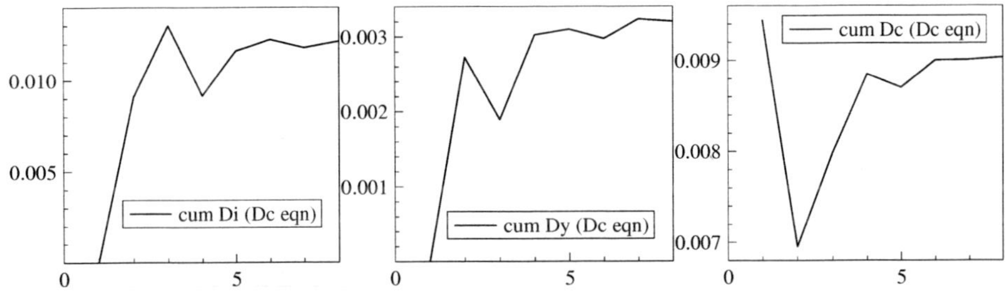

Figure 8.7 Accumulated responses to an impulse in *Dc*.

Select Test/Simulation and Impulse Responses, set the number of steps to eight collapse the Dynamic Simulation group, expand Impulse Responses, and mark Impulse Responses and Use standard errors. Finally, deselect Also graph impulses to identities as shown above. The result is Figure 8.6. Selecting unit initial values only affects the scaling of the graphs. Accumulated responses are also available. Mark Accumulated responses and unmark *Di* and *Dy* in the list box. The resulting Figure 8.7 gives the accumulated responses to a standard error impulse in *Dc*. Orthogonalized responses are available, but these alter the conditioning assumptions, and care is required to avoid violating weak exogeneity conditions (see e.g., Ericsson, Hendry and Mizon, 1996).

8.7 Sequential reduction and information criteria

Re-estimate the initial VAR in differences with four lags and U(nrestricted) *Constant* and without identities, with sample 1961(2) – 1978(4) for estimation. Select Lag structure analysis from Test/Dynamic analysis to see:

```
Tests on the significance of each variable
Variable      F-test          Value [  Prob]
Di            F(12,148)=    1.7075 [0.0704]
Dy            F(12,148)=    1.4961 [0.1315]
Dc            F(12,148)=    1.4616 [0.1449]
Constant      F(3,56)   =   2.5526 [0.0646]


Tests on the significance of each lag
Lag 4         F(9,136) =    1.3212 [0.2314]
Lag 3         F(9,136) =   0.55863 [0.8288]
Lag 2         F(9,136) =    2.0976 [0.0337]*
Lag 1         F(9,136) =    2.7265 [0.0059]**

Tests on the significance of all lags up to 4
Variable      F-test          Value [  Prob]              AIC           SC
Full model                                           -15.7593     -14.5165
Lag 4 - 4     F(9,136) =    1.3212 [0.2314]          -15.8095     -14.8534
Lag 3 - 4     F(18,158)=   0.88530 [0.5970]          -15.9960     -15.3268
Lag 2 - 4     F(27,164)=    1.4410 [0.0863]          -15.8988     -15.5164
Lag 1 - 4     F(36,166)=    1.7475 [0.0101]*         -15.8249     -15.7293
```

The middle block of F-tests considers each lag on its own. The last block considers models with decreasing lag length. The line labelled full model gives the information criteria with all lags in the model. The next line drops lag 4, the next drops lags 3 and 4, etc. In each case, the F-test is the test on the significance of those lags. So lags 3–4 are neither jointly nor individually significant. The second lag is significant, but only marginally when tested together with lags three and four.

Similar results can be obtained by omitting one lag at a time, and then re-estimating, while keeping the sample unchanged. From the output for each VAR we find ($T = 71$ in each case):

lags	log-likelihood	$-T/2 \log \lvert\text{Omega}\rvert$	$\log \lvert\text{Omega}\rvert$	$\lvert\text{Omega}\rvert$
4	598.45649	900.690396	−25.3715604	9.57792214^{-12}
3	591.23731	893.471222	−25.1682034	1.17378385^{-11}
2	588.85911	891.093022	−25.1012119	1.25511114^{-11}
1	576.40866	878.642571	−24.7504949	1.78236489^{-11}
0	564.78424	867.018150	−24.4230465	2.47289502^{-11}

Remember that these are based on $\widehat{\mathbf{\Omega}} = \frac{1}{T}\widehat{\mathbf{V}}'\widehat{\mathbf{V}}$, whereas most other statistics use $\widetilde{\mathbf{\Omega}} = \frac{1}{T-k}\widehat{\mathbf{V}}'\widehat{\mathbf{V}}$ ($\widetilde{\Sigma}_u$ in Lütkepohl). Conversion for an n-dimensional VAR is:

$$\log\left|\widetilde{\mathbf{\Omega}}\right| = \log\left|\widehat{\mathbf{\Omega}}\right| + n\log\left(\frac{T}{T-k}\right).$$

Model/Progress lists the log-likelihoods, Schwarz, Hannan–Quinn and Akaike information criteria, and F-tests for the model reduction.

```
Progress to date
Model          T    p       log-likelihood          SC        HQ       AIC
SYS( 1)       71   39  OLS       598.45649     -14.516   -15.265   -15.759
SYS( 2)       71   30  OLS       591.23731     -14.853   -15.429   -15.810
SYS( 3)       71   21  OLS       588.85911     -15.327   -15.730   -15.996<
SYS( 4)       71   12  OLS       576.40866     -15.516   -15.747   -15.899
SYS( 5)       71    3  OLS       564.78424     -15.729<  -15.787<  -15.825

Tests of model reduction (please ensure models are nested for test validity)
SYS( 1) --> SYS( 2): F(9,136) =   1.3212 [0.2314]
SYS( 1) --> SYS( 3): F(18,158)=  0.88530 [0.5970]
SYS( 1) --> SYS( 4): F(27,164)=   1.4410 [0.0863]
SYS( 1) --> SYS( 5): F(36,166)=   1.7475 [0.0101]*

SYS( 2) --> SYS( 3): F(9,143) =  0.44573 [0.9079]
SYS( 2) --> SYS( 4): F(18,167)=   1.4797 [0.1028]
SYS( 2) --> SYS( 5): F(27,172)=   1.8618 [0.0094]**

SYS( 3) --> SYS( 4): F(9,151) =   2.6014 [0.0081]**
SYS( 3) --> SYS( 5): F(18,175)=   2.6470 [0.0006]**

SYS( 4) --> SYS( 5): F(9,158) =   2.5338 [0.0097]**
```

The F-form of the likelihood ratio test (see §11.8) is expected to have better small-sample behaviour than the uncorrected χ^2 form (these can be easily computed by hand, then use OxMetrics's Data, Tail probability to check significance). Sequential reduction based on the F-tests would accept system $1 \to 2 \to 3$, but reject further reduction to system 4. A direct reduction from system $1 \to 4$ only has a p-value of 8.6%; the large number of restrictions somewhat hides the significance of the second lags. Thus, we began with an appropriate reduction when using 2 lags.

PcGive includes all parameters (including coefficient of the constant) in the computation of the information criteria. The outcomes are easily verified, using the equations in (15.19) and the T and k as listed. Here both SC and HQ have a minimum for system 5, which only has a constant term: that seems an excessive simplification, and would certainly fail on diagnostic testing (try and see: Vector AR 1-2 $\mathsf{F}(18, 175) = 2.4318[0.0016]^{**}$ for example).

8.8 Diagnostic checking

Re-estimate the VAR using two lags (use Recall to find it on the System formulation), and the estimation sample 1960(4)–1978(4).

Residual correlograms, see Figure 8.8, are obtained through the graphic analysis, here shown up to lag 12 (residual-based vector tests featured in the tutorial sections 3.2 and 6.1). Activate Test, Test, and mark Residual correlogram and portmanteau statistic selecting 12 lags, and Normality test, and select Vector tests only.

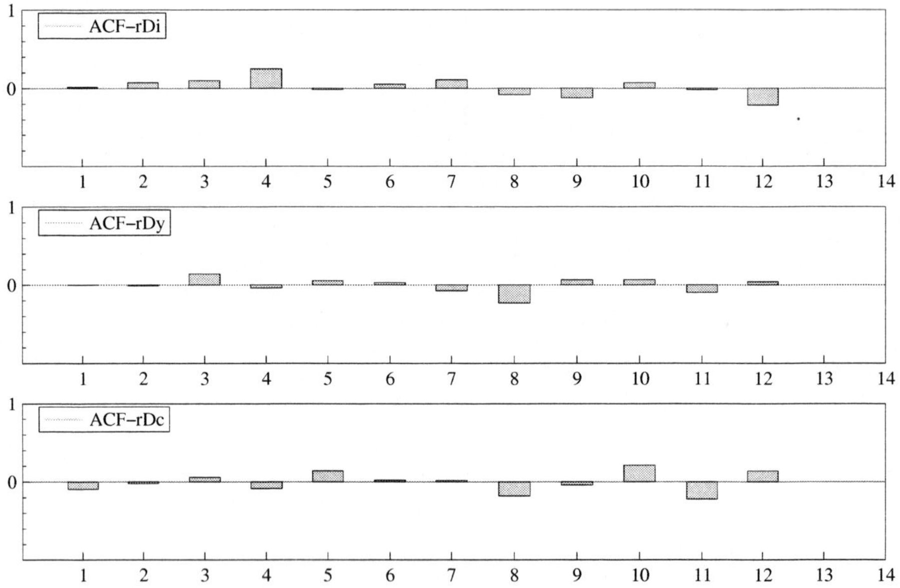

Figure 8.8 Residual correlograms.

```
Vector Portmanteau statistic for 12 lags and 73 observations: 81.9337

Vector Normality test for Residuals
Skewness
      0.28111     -0.25831      -0.79946
Excess kurtosis
       4.8159       3.3070        4.2370
Skewness (transformed)
       1.0479     -0.96504       -2.7431
Excess kurtosis (transformed)
       3.3502      0.93428       0.18474
Vector Normality test:   Chi^2(6) =    21.685 [0.0014]**
```

These tests are discussed in §11.9.2.1 and §11.9.2.3 respectively. The reported skewness and excess kurtosis are both for the individual residuals, and the transformed residuals. The latter are approximately standard normally distributed; here one of each is significant. Overall, normality is clearly rejected. More detail on the vector normality test is provided in Doornik and Hansen (1994). It is preferred to the test in Lütkepohl for two reasons. First, the test reported by PcGive employs a small-sample correction. Second, Lütkepohl's test uses Choleski decomposition, resulting in a test which is not invariant to reordering the dependent variables, for example:

$$\begin{aligned} Di, Dy, Dc &: \chi^2(6) = 7.84 \ [0.2501] \\ Dc, Dy, Di &: \chi^2(6) = 25.6 \ [0.0003] ** \end{aligned}$$

The reported portmanteau statistic is already corrected for degrees of freedom. A more appropriate test for vector error autocorrelation is the LM test offered through the Test dialog. Select three lags:

```
Testing for Vector error autocorrelation from lags 1 to 3
 Chi^2(27)=   32.807 [0.2035]   and F-form F(27,161)=    1.1448 [0.2962]
```

We shall try to replicate this manually. First save the residuals of the VAR: Test, Store in database. Select Residuals and accept the default names *VDi, VDy, VDc* (remember to return to OxMetrics to accept names). Access the database and replace the initial three missing values of these residuals by 0. We wish to label the lagged dependent variables as unrestricted. However, PcGive does not allow this. To bypass this restriction, create lags in the Calculator, removing the underscore from the name (the code is in `MulTutVAR.alg`):

```
Di1 = lag(Di, 1);
Di2 = lag(Di, 2);
Dy1 = lag(Dy, 1);
Dy2 = lag(Dy, 2);
Dc1 = lag(Dc, 1);
Dc2 = lag(Dc, 2);
```

Access Formulate, remove the lagged dependent variables and add the newly created variables. Change the classification from endogenous to unrestricted. Also classify the *Constant* as unrestricted. Add three lags of the residuals, removing the current variables. Estimate this system, again over 1960 (4) to 1978 (4):

```
log-likelihood        624.998959  -T/2log|Omega|       935.746498
|Omega|           7.34581503e-012  log|Y'Y/T|          -25.124781
R^2(LR)                  0.40077  R^2(LM)                0.149802
no. of observations           73  no. of parameters            48

F-test on regressors except unrestricted: F(27,161) = 1.14479 [0.2962]
F-tests on retained regressors, F(3,55) =
      VDi_1       0.119026 [0.949]         VDi_2         3.20095 [0.030]*
      VDi_3        1.72735 [0.172]         VDy_1         3.04572 [0.036]*
      VDy_2        1.32545 [0.275]         VDy_3         4.54787 [0.006]**
      VDc_1        3.17154 [0.031]*        VDc_2        0.131043 [0.941]
      VDc_3        2.03838 [0.119]      Constant U       2.22153 [0.096]
        Di1 U     0.146988 [0.931]           Dy1 U       5.03299 [0.004]**
        Dc1 U      5.26900 [0.003]**         Di2 U       3.27341 [0.028]*
        Dy2 U      3.36121 [0.025]*          Dc2 U       4.25374 [0.009]**
```

Now remove the lagged residuals, re-estimate, and ask for a progress, keeping only the two most recent systems marked:

```
Progress to date
Model        T    p      log-likelihood          SC        HQ       AIC
SYS(11)     73   48  OLS      624.99896     -14.302   -15.208   -15.808
SYS(12)     73   21  OLS      606.30697     -15.377   -15.773   -16.036

Tests of model reduction
SYS(11) --> SYS(12): F(27,161)=    1.1448 [0.2962]
```

The original F-form has been replicated twice, and is computed as in (11.111)–(11.113), here:

$$\frac{1-(1-\mathsf{R}^2(\mathtt{LR}))^{1/2.92}}{\mathsf{R}^2(\mathtt{LR})^{1/2.92}} * \frac{59.5*2.92-12.5}{3*9}.$$

The LM test follows from (11.132):

$$73*3*\mathsf{R}^2(\mathtt{LM}).$$

8.9 Parameter constancy

Chow tests for constancy are readily computed and graphed following recursive estimation. For a system, both single equation and system tests are computed, whereas for a model only the system tests are available. Estimate the original VAR(2) over 1960(4)–1978(4) by RLS using 40 observations for initialization. Don't use any unrestricted variables (which would have their coefficients fixed at the full sample values). Then estimate the same system by recursive OLS. In Recursive graphics, deselect all variables (click on one, and then Ctrl+click on the same). The system Chow tests and log-likelihood/T (see §5.7) are graphed in Figure 8.9.

The values in these graphs can be written to the results editor. To make the amount of data more manageable, estimate up to 1974(2) with 51 observations for initialization. This gives four recursive estimates. Again: make sure that there are no unrestricted variables. Activate the Recursive graphics dialog, mark log-likehood/T and the three Chow tests (again deselecting all variables) and select the Write results instead of graphing button:

```
             -- residuals t+1,..,T are zero --
                loglik/T     (t)          loglik     actual loglik
1973-3           12.5913 (  52)          692.523           650.374
1973-4           12.5720 (  53)          691.462           663.373
1974-1           12.5676 (  54)          691.218           677.164
1974-2           12.5359 (  55)          689.474           689.474

System: 1-step Chow tests
1973-3        F(  3, 42) =        0.83707  [0.4812]
1973-4        F(  3, 43) =        0.56380  [0.6418]
```

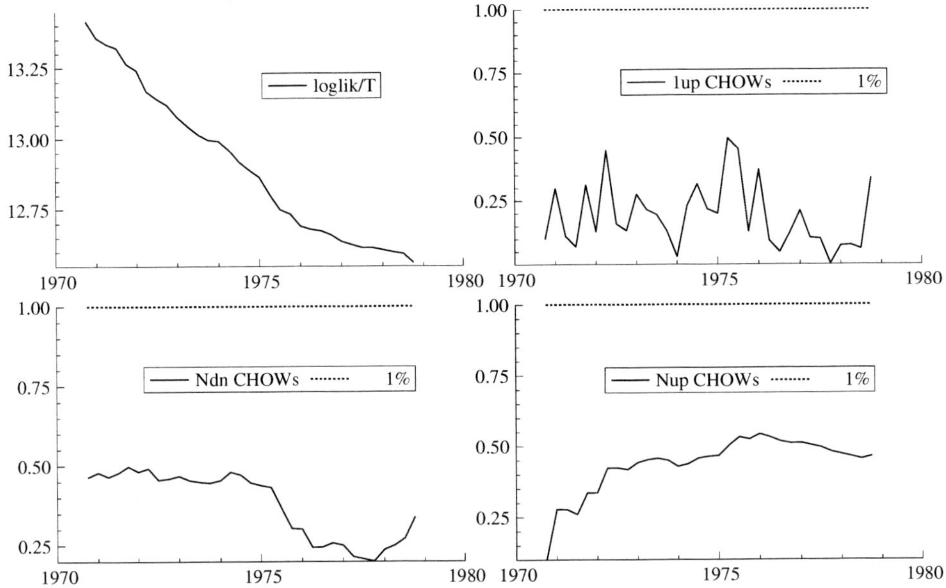

Figure 8.9 Log-likelihood/T and system Chow tests.

```
1974-1      F(  3, 44) =       0.13087  [0.9412]
1974-2      F(  3, 45) =       0.98173  [0.4098]

System: Breakpoint (N-down) Chow tests
1973-3      F( 12,111) =       0.61214  [0.8281]
1973-4      F(  9,104) =       0.54269  [0.8402]
1974-1      F(  6, 88) =       0.53974  [0.7766]
1974-2      F(  3, 45) =       0.98173  [0.4098]

System: Forecast (N-up) Chow tests
1973-3      F(  3, 42) =       0.83707  [0.4812]
1973-4      F(  6, 84) =       0.69318  [0.6557]
1974-1      F(  9,102) =       0.50407  [0.8686]
1974-2      F( 12,111) =       0.61214  [0.8281]
```

These results can be replicated using dummy variables. Use the calculator to create four impulse dummy variables (in the calculator, click the Dummy button, then enter period of the impulse, accept and name as shown below, copied from our results file, and usable in the algebra, or use `MulTutVARdum.alg`):

```
i1973p3 = dummy(1973,3, 1973,3);
i1973p4 = dummy(1973,4, 1973,4);
i1974p1 = dummy(1974,1, 1974,1);
i1974p2 = dummy(1974,2, 1974,2);
```

Add the four dummies to the VAR, no lags, and clear their status. Estimate by OLS up to 1974(2). This effectively removes the last four observations. The 1-step Chow test amounts to adding one observation at a time, and testing its significance.

Towards the end of the output, you will see for the i1973p3 dummy:

```
F-tests on retained regressors, F(3,42) =
     i1973p3       0.837065 [0.481]
```

Deleting that dummy, re-estimating gives the same result in the progress:

```
SYS( 4) --> SYS( 5): F(3,42)  =  0.83707 [0.4812]
```

Next delete the remaining dummies one dummy at a time, starting with *i1973p4*:

system

8	:	constant;				
7	:	constant,				i1974p2;
6	:	constant,			i1974p1,	i1974p2;
5	:	constant,		i1973p4	, i1974p1,	i1974p2;
4	:	constant,	i1973p3,	i1973p4	, i1974p1,	i1974p2.

The progress report, after some reordering of the F-tests is:

```
Progress to date
Model      T    p       log-likelihood         SC        HQ       AIC
SYS( 4)   55   33  OLS      459.99499     -14.323   -15.061   -15.527
SYS( 5)   55   30  OLS      458.39804     -14.483   -15.155   -15.578
SYS( 6)   55   27  OLS      457.33706     -14.663   -15.268   -15.649
SYS( 7)   55   24  OLS      457.09277     -14.873   -15.410   -15.749
SYS( 8)   55   21  OLS      455.34939     -15.028   -15.498   -15.795

Tests of model reduction
SYS( 4) --> SYS( 8): F(12,111)=  0.61214 [0.8281]
SYS( 5) --> SYS( 8): F(9,104) =  0.54269 [0.8402]
SYS( 6) --> SYS( 8): F(6,88)  =  0.53974 [0.7766]
SYS( 7) --> SYS( 8): F(3,45)  =  0.98173 [0.4098]
```

The forecast Chow tests correspond to testing the significance of *i1973p3* in the system with all the dummies, then of both *i1973p3* and *i1973p4*, then of the first three dummies etc. In other words, the first statistic tests stability for one period, the next for two periods, then for three periods, etc. (the forecast horizon increases). The break-point Chow tests have a shrinking forecast horizon: four from 1973(2), three from 1973(3), etc.

Estimation up to 1973(2) is equivalent to estimation up to 1974(2) with four dummies. However, we cannot do a likelihood ratio test for constancy by comparing reported log-likelihood values for the different periods, as these are based on different Ts. For example (note that $\widehat{\ell}$ excludes the likelihood constant K_c):

$$1960(4) - 1973(2): \ \widehat{\ell}_1 = 637.86208 \ T_1 = 51,$$
$$1960(4) - 1973(3): \ \widehat{\ell}_1 = 650.37394 \ T_1 = 52,$$

would give a negative likelihood-ratio test. To 'rebase' $\widehat{\ell}_1$ to T_2, compute:

$$\left(\frac{-2}{T_1}\widehat{\ell}_1 + n\log\left(\frac{T_1}{T_2}\right)\right)\frac{T_2}{-2}.$$

Using $T_2 = 55$ and yields the loglik values as given in the penultimate column oof the recursive output. To match the log-likelihood from progress still requires taking account of the likelihood constant $K_c = -Tn/2(1 + \log 2\pi)$.

The parameter constancy tests that are reported when observations are withheld for forecasting test the same hypothesis as the forecast system Chow test, but are based on the Wald principle. Estimation with 1973(3) and 1973(3)–1973(4) as forecasts respectively yields:

```
1-step (ex post) forecast analysis 1973(3) - 1973(3)
Parameter constancy forecast tests:
using Omega  Chi^2(3) =    2.9742 [0.3956]    F(3,44)   =    0.9914 [0.4057]
using  V[e]  Chi^2(3) =    2.6308 [0.4521]    F(3,44)   =   0.87693 [0.4603]
using  V[E]  Chi^2(3) =    2.6308 [0.4521]    F(3,44)   =   0.87693 [0.4603]

1-step (ex post) forecast analysis 1973(3) - 1973(4)
Parameter constancy forecast tests:
using Omega  Chi^2(6) =    4.8958 [0.5573]    F(6,44)   =   0.81596 [0.5634]
using  V[e]  Chi^2(6) =    4.3874 [0.6244]    F(6,44)   =   0.73123 [0.6270]
using  V[E]  Chi^2(6) =    4.3903 [0.6240]    F(6,44)   =   0.73172 [0.6266]
```

Estimation with *i1973p3* up to 1973(3), and both *i1973p3* and *i1973p4* estimated up to 1973(4), allows us to test the significance of the dummies through the general restrictions test option:

```
Test for excluding:
[0]  = i1973p3@Di
[1]  = i1973p3@Dy
[2]  = i1973p3@Dc
Subset Chi^2(3) = 2.63078 [0.4521]

Test for excluding:
[0]  = i1973p3@Di
[1]  = i1973p4@Di
[2]  = i1973p3@Dy
[3]  = i1973p4@Dy
[4]  = i1973p3@Dc
[5]  = i1973p4@Dc
Subset Chi^2(6) = 4.39033 [0.6240]
```

Finally, note that the small sample correction to obtain the F-test in PcGive is different from that in Lütkepohl. The test statistic ξ_1 of (11.46) is identical to $\widehat{\lambda}_h$ of equation (4.6.13) in Lütkepohl. PcGive computes (ξ_1 already has a degrees of freedom correction)

$$\eta_1 = \frac{\xi_1}{nH}$$

in contrast to

$$\bar{\lambda}_h = \widehat{\lambda}_h \frac{T}{nH\,(T+k)}.$$

The F-tests from recursive estimation and progress use Rao's approximation, see (11.111)–(11.113).

8.10 Non-linear parameter constraints

Reduced-rank VAR models can be estimated through CFIML, which is FIML with non-linear parameter constraints. Consider the two-lag VAR $\mathbf{y}_t = \boldsymbol{\pi}_1\mathbf{y}_{t-1} + \boldsymbol{\pi}_2\mathbf{y}_{t-2} + \mathbf{v}_t$ imposing rank-one restrictions on $\boldsymbol{\pi}_1$ and $\boldsymbol{\pi}_2$:

$$\boldsymbol{\pi}_1 = \mathbf{bc}' = \begin{pmatrix} b_1c_1 & b_1c_2 & b_1c_3 \\ b_2c_1 & b_2c_2 & b_2c_3 \\ b_3c_1 & b_3c_2 & b_3c_3 \end{pmatrix}, \quad \boldsymbol{\pi}_2 = \mathbf{bd}' = \begin{pmatrix} b_1d_1 & b_1d_2 & b_1d_3 \\ b_2d_1 & b_2d_2 & b_2d_3 \\ b_3d_1 & b_3d_2 & b_3d_3 \end{pmatrix}.$$

Note that this is different from the cointegration analysis, which is reduced rank estimation of the long-run matrix (Chapter 4). Numbering the coefficients as

$$(\boldsymbol{\pi}_1\ \boldsymbol{\pi}_2) = \begin{pmatrix} \&0 & \&1 & \&2 & \&3 & \&4 & \&5 \\ \&6 & \&7 & \&8 & \&9 & \&10 & \&11 \\ \&12 & \&13 & \&14 & \&15 & \&16 & \&17 \end{pmatrix}$$

this corresponds to the following restrictions (in MulTutVAR.res):

```
&0=&6*&1/&7;  &2=&8*&1/&7;   &12=&6*&13/&7;  &14=&8*&13/&7;
&3=&9*&1/&7;  &5=&11*&1/&7;  &15=&9*&13/&7;  &17=&11*&13/&7;
&4=&10*&1/&7; &16=&10*&13/&7;
```

For the computations we follow Lütkepohl, and first remove the means from the variables (the complete code can also be found in `MulTutVAR.fl`). Setup a system which regresses *Di, Dy, Dc* on a *Constant* (clear status) over 1960(2)–1978(4):

```
SYS(13) Estimating the system by OLS (using MulTutVAR.in7)
        The estimation sample is: 1960(2) - 1978(4)

URF equation for: Di
                  Coefficient  Std.Error  t-value  t-prob
Constant            0.0181083   0.005404     3.35   0.001

URF equation for: Dy
                  Coefficient  Std.Error  t-value  t-prob
Constant            0.0207113   0.001395     14.8   0.000

URF equation for: Dc
                  Coefficient  Std.Error  t-value  t-prob
Constant            0.0198710   0.001201     16.5   0.000
```

Then save the residuals as *VDi, VDy, VDc* – you may choose overwrite if these already exist in the database. Setup the two-lag VAR in *VDi* etc., but without a constant. First add up to lag 1, and then add the second lag. This way, when it comes to the model, the first lags will appear before the second lags in each equation. This is required for the restrictions code below. When estimating as a simultaneous equations model over 1960(4)–1978(4), the model will have log-likelihood 606.219308.

Next, enter Constrained simultaneous equation model in the Model Settings. Check that the regressors are ordered as *VDi_1*, *VDy_1*, *VDc_1*, *VDi_2*, *VDy_2*, *VDc_2*. The next stage leads to the General restrictions editor: enter the above restrictions (or load them from the file MulTutVAR.res, supplied with PcGive). Estimate the model (strong convergence is quickly reached).

The restrictions involve division by &7, and a grid reveals the singularity when parameter 3 (&7) is zero, see Figure 8.10. The grid computations could fail if the third parameter gets too close to zero. Starting from version 9, PcGive uses analytical differentiation throughout, and the maximization procedure works better: the area of numerical singularity around &7 has been reduced considerably. To experiment, you could try setting &7 to a small negative or positive number and see what happens. When too close to zero, the algorithm results in very large parameters, with failure to improve in the line search.

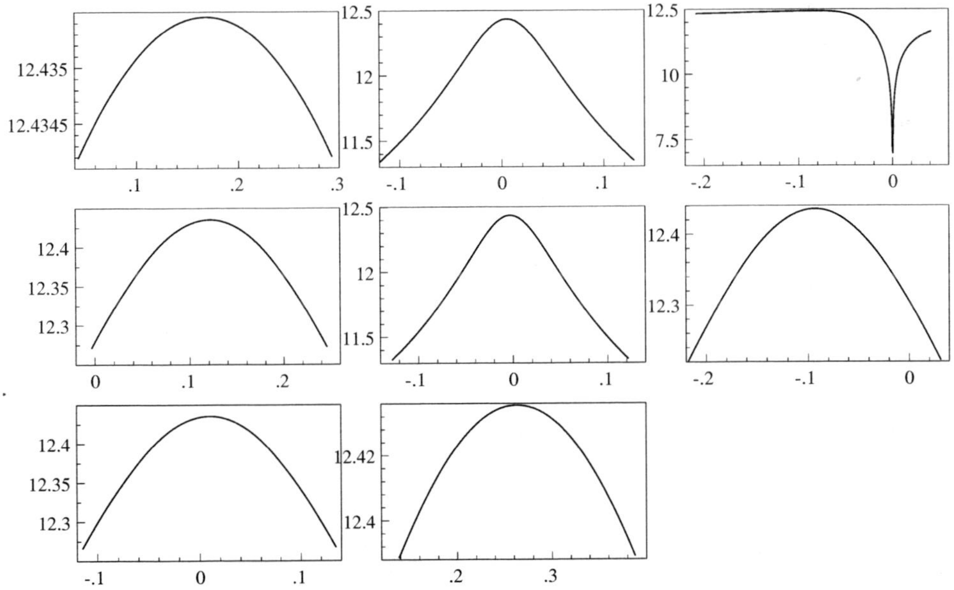

Figure 8.10 Grid of reduced rank VAR.

The output is:

```
MOD( 2) Estimating the model by CFIML (using MulTutVAR.in7)
        The estimation sample is: 1960(4) - 1978(4)

Equation for: VDi
                    Coefficient  Std.Error  t-value  t-prob
VDi_1                -0.0106552        ---
VDy_1                  0.168361     0.3089    0.545   0.588
VDc_1                 -0.245365        ---
VDi_2                0.00541090        ---
VDy_2                  0.187979        ---
VDc_2                -0.0206638        ---

sigma = 0.0475615

Equation for: VDy
                    Coefficient  Std.Error  t-value  t-prob
VDi_1                0.00527015   0.007330    0.719   0.475
VDy_1                -0.0832730    0.07933    -1.05   0.298
VDc_1                  0.121360     0.1140     1.06   0.291
VDi_2               -0.00267628   0.006041   -0.443   0.659
VDy_2                -0.0929759    0.08763    -1.06   0.292
VDc_2                 0.0102205    0.03086    0.331   0.742

sigma = 0.0119145

Equation for: VDc
                    Coefficient  Std.Error  t-value  t-prob
VDi_1                -0.0166783        ---
VDy_1                  0.263532    0.08790     3.00   0.004
VDc_1                 -0.384065        ---
VDi_2                0.00846958        ---
VDy_2                  0.294239        ---
VDc_2                -0.0323446        ---

sigma = 0.00933562

log-likelihood      597.040617  -T/2log|Omega|      907.788156
no. of observations         73  no. of parameters            8

LR test of over-identifying restrictions: Chi^2(10)=   18.357 [0.0492]*
BFGS using analytical derivatives (eps1=0.0001; eps2=0.005):
Strong convergence

Constraints:
&0=&6*&1/&7;&2=&8*&1/&7;
&12=&6*&13/&7;&14=&8*&13/&7;
&3=&9*&1/&7;&5=&11*&1/&7;
&15=&9*&13/&7;&17=&11*&13/&7;
&4=&10*&1/&7;&16=&10*&13/&7;

correlation of structural residuals (standard deviations on diagonal)
```

```
                VDi            VDy           VDc
VDi        0.047561        0.10106       0.26111
VDy         0.10106       0.011915       0.58193
VDc         0.26111        0.58193     0.0093356
```

This model can be further explored. For example, eigenvalues of the companion matrix reveal that it is rank 2:

```
Eigenvalues of companion matrix:
        real          imag     modulus
     -0.2390       -0.2506      0.3463
     -0.2390        0.2506      0.3463
-8.521e-017-3.402e-009 3.402e-009
-8.521e-017 3.402e-009 3.402e-009
-4.896e-018        0.0000 4.896e-018
-2.557e-018        0.0000 2.557e-018
```

Another option is recursive estimation. Many possibilities remain, but we leave you now to explore on your own.

Part III

The Econometrics of Multiple Equation Modelling

Chapter 9

An Introduction to the Dynamic Econometric Systems

9.1 Summary of Part III

Linear system modelling is structured from the general to the specific. The general model is a dynamic statistical system. This is the maintained model, defined by the variables of interest, their distributions, whether they are modelled or non-modelled, and their lag polynomials. Thus, for example, four variables may be modelled as linearly dependent on another two, intercept and linear deterministic trend, with a maximum of three lags. System formulation, the status of the variables therein, dynamic specification, estimation, and evaluation are all discussed. Because of their central role, integration and cointegration are analyzed in a separate chapter. Once a congruent system is available, a postulated econometric model can be evaluated against it, or a model of the system developed.

An econometric model is usually a simultaneous equations structure, which is treated as a model of the system. It is intended to isolate autonomous, parsimonious relationships based on economic theory. The system must adequately characterize the data evidence, and the model must account for the results obtained by the system. Model formulation and identification, estimation (using an estimator generating equation), encompassing, and model evaluation are considered. Numerical optimization is considered separately.

All these issues are addressed at various levels in Part III. Chapter 9 provides an introduction, with a more rigorous review in Chapter 11 (system modelling), Chapter 12 (cointegration analysis), and Chapter 13 (simultaneous equations modelling). Chapter 10 presents a brief summary of the matrix algebra required to understand the derivations in Chapters 11–13. Chapter 14 discusses numerical optimization and numerical accuracy. Although separate subjects, these are fundamental to a computer program such as PcGive. Finally, Chapter 15, which is in Part IV, lists all the output (both numerical and graphical) generated by PcGive. That chapter also repeats the econometric notation, and is to a large extent self-contained (if preceded by this chapter).

9.2 Introduction

Simultaneous equations models have been criticized from a number of viewpoints (see Sims, 1980, and Hendry, Neale and Srba, 1988, among others). Such criticisms arise in part because dynamic system modelling usually commences from (an assumed known) structural form of the process generating the data, from which the reduced form is derived (see, Judge, Griffiths, Hill, Lütkepohl and Lee, 1985, Chapter 14, for example). Such an approach raises numerous difficulties: in particular, by not first testing the validity of the reduced form, which constitutes the baseline for the test of over-identifying restrictions, the credibility of the structural parameter estimates is unclear. A more methodical and ordered approach to linear dynamic system modelling circumvents most of the extant criticisms (see Hendry and Mizon, 1993, and Hendry and Doornik, 1994).

The dynamic system is the maintained statistical model. Its initial specification is crucial to the success of the entire analysis since a simultaneous equations structure is a model of that system (see, for example, Spanos, 1986). Given linearity, the system is defined by the variables of interest, their distributions, their classification into modelled and non-modelled variables (although the latter may be absent, as in a vector autoregressive representation or VAR), and the lag polynomials applicable to every variable. Section 9.3 describes the theoretical formulation; §9.4 discusses the statistical system and the status of its variables; §9.5 considers the specification of the system dynamics to ensure that the residuals are innovation processes; then §9.6 considers system evaluation. At that stage, a congruent system is available against which any postulated econometric model can be evaluated. The step of mapping to a stationary, or non-integrated (I(0)) representation would follow §9.5 and is discussed in §9.7.

An econometric model imposes a structure on a statistical system to isolate autonomous relationships with parsimonious interpretations based on economic theory. Necessary conditions for a valid model are that the system adequately characterizes the data evidence (congruency), that its parameters are uniquely identified, and that the model accounts for the results obtained by the system (parsimonious encompassing). System congruency conditions are the focus of §9.3–§9.7; the latter are the subject of §9.8–§9.9. Thus, §9.8 considers model formulation and identification; §9.9 considers model evaluation by testing its parsimonious encompassing of the system.

This sequence of stages aims to structure the empirical modelling of small linear dynamic systems, and represents the steps needed to ensure valid parsimonious representations of the data generation process (DGP) within a general-to-specific modelling methodology: see Mizon (1977), Hendry (1987) and Pagan (1987). Moreover, the same stages are inherent in the working of PcGive. The statistical system must be formulated first (the selection of variables, their classification into modelled and non-modelled, the choice of lag polynomials, and any deterministic components such as constants and seasonals etc.). Then the system must be estimated, and evaluated for congruency (homoscedastic innovation errors; valid weak exogeneity of any conditioning variables for the parameters of interest; I(0) regressors, and constant parameters). Only then can a model of the system be formulated, checked for identification, estimated, and its parsimonious encompassing of the system investigated. The process of specification is in fact straightforward and quick, and is designed to avoid endless and directionless revisions of postulated models in the light of adverse diagnostic test findings.

9.3 Economic theoretical formulation

Starting from a general economic theoretical framework of intertemporal optimizing behaviour by rational agents, empirical research in economics is often faced with the issue of jointly modelling a number of potentially interdependent variables (denoted $\mathbf{y}_t$) as a function of a second set not to be modelled (denoted $\mathbf{z}_t$). The subject-matter theory specifies systems of relationships of the form:

$$\mathbf{B}(L)\boldsymbol{\xi}_t = \mathsf{E}\left[\boldsymbol{\Gamma}(L)\boldsymbol{\zeta}_t \mid \mathcal{I}_t\right] \tag{9.1}$$

where $(\boldsymbol{\xi}_t, \boldsymbol{\zeta}_t)$ are $(n \times 1)$ and $(q \times 1)$ vectors of the theoretical variables of interest for which $(\mathbf{y}_t, \mathbf{z}_t)$ will be taken as the observable correspondences, $\mathsf{E}[\cdot|\mathcal{I}_t]$ is the conditional expectations operator, and $\mathcal{I}_t$ denotes the information set available to agents at the start of decision time-period t. Also, L denotes the lag operator such that $L^h x_t = x_{t-h}$. The lag polynomial matrices $\mathbf{B}(\cdot)$ and $\boldsymbol{\Gamma}(\cdot)$ may involve leads (L^{-1} etc.), in which case the latent constructs become expectations of future variables. If only finite lags are involved, then $\mathbf{B}(L)$ and $\boldsymbol{\Gamma}(L)$ can be written as:

$$\mathbf{B}(L) = \sum_{j=0}^{h} \mathbf{B}_j L^j \text{ and } \boldsymbol{\Gamma}(L) = \sum_{j=0}^{h} \boldsymbol{\Gamma}_j L^j$$

where h is the maximum lag length (some of the elements of $\{\mathbf{B}_j, \boldsymbol{\Gamma}_j\}$ may be zero). It is often assumed that there are sufficient restrictions to identify the $\{\mathbf{B}_j, \boldsymbol{\Gamma}_j\}$, some of which may be zero with others normalized, and that these parameters are constant.

While the economic theory may appear to offer a complete specification of the elements of the system determining $\boldsymbol{\xi}_t$, its practical implementation confronts a number of serious difficulties as follows:

(1) Decision time and observation time-periods need not coincide, such that one decision period may equal N observation periods (N could be greater than or less than unity). Thus $\mathbf{B}(L)$ and $\boldsymbol{\Gamma}(L)$ may not correspond to the relevant empirical lag polynomials characterizing the agents' responses.

(2) The theory may be incomplete (for example, involve *ceteris paribus* conditions) and variables other than $(\boldsymbol{\xi}_t, \boldsymbol{\zeta}_t)$ may in fact be directly involved in the decision process. Thus, the theory system must be reinterpreted as marginalized with respect to such variables so that apparent cross restrictions on $\mathbf{B}(\cdot)$, $\boldsymbol{\Gamma}(\cdot)$ may be invalid, and even identification (in the sense of uniqueness) could fail.

(3) The contents of $\mathcal{I}_t$ could be empirically mis-specified since the economists' perception of the information set selected by agents need not coincide one-to-one with that actually used: it could be over- or under-inclusive in important aspects.
(4) How $\mathcal{I}_t$ enters the joint density (and thereby determines $\mathsf{E}[\cdot|\mathcal{I}_t]$) may not be as postulated, and hence the formulation may fail to characterize the actual behaviour of the agents.
(5) The assumption that $\boldsymbol{\xi}_t$ can be explained as a function of $\boldsymbol{\zeta}_t$ without modelling the latter may be inappropriate, and doubtless would be seen as such in a larger model. Even if the assumption is correct, it is insufficient to ensure that $\mathbf{z}_t$ need not be modelled empirically: an example is multi-step forecasting when past values of $\boldsymbol{\xi}_t$ influence $\boldsymbol{\zeta}_t$.
(6) The correspondence of $(\boldsymbol{\xi}_t, \boldsymbol{\zeta}_t)$ to $(\mathbf{y}_t, \mathbf{z}_t)$ may be tenuous and may itself be dynamic (for example, permanent income; choice of a 'money' magnitude etc.).
(7) Evolution, innovation, learning, regime shifts, and other forms of non-stationarity are not yet easily incorporated into intertemporal theoretical analyses but are crucial elements to model in any empirical study.

Thus, while any given economic theory potentially offers a useful initial framework, theory is not so much definitive as guiding. Hence, theory should not constitute a strait-jacket to empirical research in the sense that theory models should not simply be imposed on data. If an empirical counterpart to a theory is imposed on data, it will exclude many phenomena: it is valid to test such restrictions under the assumption that the theory is correct. However, for any inferences concerning $\mathbf{B}(\cdot)$ and $\mathbf{\Gamma}(\cdot)$ (and hence the underlying theory) to be sustainable, accurate estimates of the inferential uncertainty are required. This necessitates establishing both the innovation variance for $\mathbf{y}_t$ given the available information, and a set of constants or invariants $\boldsymbol{\theta}$ characterizing the data density, on which $\mathbf{B}(\cdot)$ and $\mathbf{\Gamma}(\cdot)$ therefore depend. In the present state of knowledge, modelling is inevitable if such objectives are to be achieved (see Hendry, Neale and Srba, 1988).

First, consider the case where $(\mathbf{y}_t, \mathbf{z}_t)$ are accurate measures of $(\boldsymbol{\xi}_t, \boldsymbol{\zeta}_t)$ respectively and $\mathbf{z}_t \in \mathcal{I}_t$ so that a conditional analysis is valid, and future expectations do not affect outcomes (this is a convenient simplification here, but is not necessary and may not coincide with agent behaviour in some markets). Thus, the counterpart of (9.1) in terms of observable variables becomes:

$$\mathsf{E}\left[\mathbf{y}_t \mid \mathbf{z}_t, \mathbf{X}_0, \mathbf{x}_1, \ldots, \mathbf{x}_{t-1}\right] = \mathbf{p}_0\mathbf{z}_t + \sum_{i=1}^{h} \mathbf{p}_i\mathbf{x}_{t-i} \tag{9.2}$$

where $\mathbf{x}_t' = (\mathbf{y}_t' : \mathbf{z}_t')$, and $\mathbf{X}_0$ denotes the set of initial conditions, with h being the longest lag. Only current and lagged values of observable variables enter this formulation, so that if it is a solved-out version of the theory system (for example, eliminating future values) its parameters $\boldsymbol{\phi}$ will be functions of the parameters in the marginal model for $\mathbf{z}_t$. Thus the constancy of ϕ will depend on the constancy of that marginal model; this point applies even more forcefully to closed (or VAR) representations. Of course, the marginal model for $\mathbf{z}_t$ may itself be studied for constancy, but any conclusions about its behaviour depend on precisely the same considerations as those currently being discussed. Equally, the constancy of the $\{\mathbf{p}_i\}$ could be ascertained directly, and if failure results (that is, the $\{\mathbf{p}_i\}$ are non-constant), a revised specification is clearly needed. The recursive procedures incorporated in PcGive offer a powerful tool for this task.

In the present setting, the observable system in (9.2) comprises the most unrestricted model to be entertained. If the $\{\mathbf{p}_i\}$ are empirically constant, then:

$$\mathbf{v}_t = \mathbf{y}_t - \mathsf{E}\left[\mathbf{y}_t \mid \mathbf{z}_t, \mathbf{x}_{t-1}, \ldots, \mathbf{x}_{t-h}\right] \tag{9.3}$$

is an innovation process against the available information, with variance $\mathsf{E}[\mathbf{v}_t\mathbf{v}_t'] = \mathbf{\Omega}_t$. Direct tests for $\{\mathbf{v}_t\}$ being homoscedastic and white noise are feasible, and the value of continued modelling requires both that such tests are applied and that satisfactory outcomes result. If so, the system is data-congruent and it seems worth developing a parsimonious model: Spanos (1986) refers to (9.3) as the statistical model, and a parsimonious, interpretable representation thereof as the econometric model. The main advantage of first formulating the statistical model is that later tests (e.g., tests of over-identifying restrictions) can be conducted against a valid background, so awkward circles of the kind arising in simple-to-general searches are avoided (see Hendry, 1979).

When writing a computer program like PcGive, the dichotomy of a system versus a model thereof (or of a statistical versus an econometric model) is essential, since every so-called structural model entails a reduced form which is a restriction of the system. If the former is deemed valid, the latter must be also, so tests of it are valid. As noted above, prior to specifying structural models, the program requires the specification of the data set $\mathbf{X}_T^1 = (\mathbf{x}_1 \ldots \mathbf{x}_T)$, the maximum lag h, and the status of modelled or non-modelled for the elements of $\mathbf{x}_t$. Together, these define the system. Estimators of the parameters of interest ϕ correspond to minimizing $|\mathbf{\Omega}|$ with respect to ϕ subject to various restrictions (that is, parsimonious interpretations of the $\{\mathbf{p}_i\}$).

In this framework, a test of over-identifying restrictions is equivalent to a test of whether the restricted reduced form (RRF) parsimoniously encompasses the unrestricted reduced form (URF) (see Hendry and Mizon, 1993). If this hypothesis is not rejected, the model constitutes a valid reduction of the system and as such is more interpretable, more robust and (being lower-dimensional) allows more powerful tests for mis-specification. The next issue is whether the theoretical model is consistent with the empirical model: this is testable in principle, but the practical difficulties are great for forward-looking or non-linear models and incomplete specifications of $\mathcal{I}_t$. Some considerations for expectations models versus feedback representations are discussed in Hendry (1988) and Favero and Hendry (1992).

Next, consider the case where $\mathbf{z}_t \notin \mathcal{I}_t$. Either a lag formulation could be used or, when a set $\mathbf{z}_t^*$ is available ($\mathbf{Z}_{t-h}^{t-k^*}$ in general), the system should be extended to incorporate these additional variables as instruments. Such variables could enter (9.1) directly, in which case the initial system needs reformulating, or enter only through affecting the marginal process for $\mathbf{z}_t$. It is a testable restriction that they matter only via the marginal model for $\mathbf{z}_t$, but to do so requires modelling $\{\mathbf{z}_t\}$.

Particular economic theory implementations cannot be discussed in the abstract, but readers doubtless have examplars in mind when consulting this book. Standard cases include highly aggregate macro-models; models of sectors (such as the monetary or labour sector); or small systems that commence by endogenizing all variables to allow tests of conditioning assumptions (such as when modelling consumers' expenditure).

9.4 The statistical system

The statistical system is the Haavelmo distribution defined by specifying the variables of interest, their status (modelled or not), their degree of integration, data transformations, the retained history of the process, and the sample period. As above, $\{\mathbf{x}_t\}$ denotes the complete vector of observable variables of interest suggested by previous research, economic theory and the objectives of the analysis, available over a sample period of size T. The statistical generating mechanism is denoted by $\mathsf{D_X}\left(\mathbf{X}_T^1|\mathbf{X}_0,\boldsymbol{\theta}\right)$, where $\mathbf{X}_0$ is the set of initial conditions and $\boldsymbol{\theta} \in \Theta \subseteq \mathbb{R}^N$ is the parameter vector in an N-dimensional parameter space Θ. Writing $\mathbf{X}_{t-1} = (\mathbf{X}_0\mathbf{x}_1 \ldots \mathbf{x}_{t-1}) = \left(\mathbf{X}_0 : \mathbf{X}_{t-1}^1\right)$, $\mathsf{D_X}(\cdot)$ is sequentially factorized as:

$$\mathsf{D_X}\left(\mathbf{X}_T^1 \mid \mathbf{X}_0,\boldsymbol{\theta}\right) = \prod_{t=1}^{T} \mathsf{D_x}\left(\mathbf{x}_t \mid \mathbf{X}_{t-1},\boldsymbol{\theta}\right), \tag{9.4}$$

where $\boldsymbol{\theta}$ allows for any necessary transient parameters.

Since $\mathbf{x}_t' = (\mathbf{y}_t' : \mathbf{z}_t')$, then $\mathbf{X}_T^{1\prime} = \left(\mathbf{Y}_T^{1\prime} : \mathbf{Z}_T^{1\prime}\right)$ where $\mathbf{y}_t$ is the $n \times 1$ vector of endogenous variables and $\mathbf{z}_t$ is the $q \times 1$ vector of variables which will not be modelled.[1] To treat $\mathbf{z}_t$ as a valid conditioning vector requires that $\mathbf{z}_t$ be weakly exogenous for the parameters of interest $\boldsymbol{\phi}$ (see Engle, Hendry and Richard, 1983). If so, inference in the conditional distribution of $\mathbf{y}_t$, given $\mathbf{z}_t$ and the history of the process, involves no loss of information relative to analyzing the joint distribution of $\mathbf{x}_t$. Map from $\boldsymbol{\theta} \mapsto \boldsymbol{\lambda} = \mathbf{f}(\boldsymbol{\theta}) \in \boldsymbol{\Lambda}$ where $\mathbf{f}(\cdot)$ is 1–1, then from (9.4):

$$\prod_{t=1}^{T} \mathsf{D_x}\left(\mathbf{x}_t|\mathbf{X}_{t-1},\boldsymbol{\theta}\right) = \prod_{t=1}^{T} \mathsf{D_{y|z}}\left(\mathbf{y}_t|\mathbf{z}_t,\mathbf{X}_{t-1},\boldsymbol{\lambda}_1\right) \mathsf{D_z}\left(\mathbf{z}_t,|\mathbf{X}_{t-1},\boldsymbol{\lambda}_2\right). \tag{9.5}$$

Thus, if $\boldsymbol{\phi}$ is a function of $\boldsymbol{\lambda}_1$ alone, and $\boldsymbol{\lambda}_1$ and $\boldsymbol{\lambda}_2$ are variation free, so that $(\boldsymbol{\lambda}_1 : \boldsymbol{\lambda}_2) \in \boldsymbol{\Lambda}_1 \times \boldsymbol{\Lambda}_2$, then $\mathbf{z}_t$ is weakly exogenous for $\boldsymbol{\phi}$. When the same parameters enter both

[1]The system may be closed as in a VAR, in which case there are no non-modelled variables $\mathbf{z}_t$, except possibly deterministic variables such as a constant, trend or seasonals.

$\boldsymbol{\lambda}_1$ and $\boldsymbol{\lambda}_2$, as with cross-equation restrictions linking the conditional and marginal models, then weak exogeneity is liable to be violated, leading to a loss of information from analyzing only the conditional distribution. Such information loss could entail just inefficiency, but could also entail a loss of structurality. This formulation is a direct application of the principles for reducing a process to a model thereof, and clarifies when reduction is valid.

If, in addition, $\mathbf{y}$ does not Granger cause $\mathbf{z}$ (see Granger, 1969), then the marginal distribution $\mathsf{D}_{\mathrm{z}}(\mathbf{z}_t|\mathbf{X}_{t-1}, \boldsymbol{\lambda}_2)$ can be simplified without loss to $\mathsf{D}_{\mathrm{z}}(\mathbf{z}_t|\ \mathbf{Z}_{t-1}, \boldsymbol{\lambda}_2)$, so that $\mathbf{z}_t$ is strongly exogenous for $\boldsymbol{\phi}$. This condition is needed to sustain conditional dynamic, or multi-period, forecasts and conditional dynamic simulation.

Finally, if $\mathbf{z}_t$ is weakly exogenous for $\boldsymbol{\phi}$, and $\boldsymbol{\lambda}_1$ is invariant to changes in $\boldsymbol{\lambda}_2$, then $\mathbf{z}_t$ is super exogenous for $\boldsymbol{\phi}$ (see Engle and Hendry, 1993).

Since we restrict attention to linear systems, the $\{\mathbf{x}_t\}$ will generally have been transformed from the original raw data such that linearity is a reasonable approximation. Consequently, we commence by selecting $\mathbf{y}_t$ and $\mathbf{z}_t$ and specifying the statistical structure as in (9.5). The econometric model then seeks to isolate the autonomous relationships with interpretable parameters, having an economic theory basis, while still remaining statistically consistent with the system.

9.5 System dynamics

Having assumed linearity, specified the menu comprising $\{\mathbf{x}_t\}$, and classified the variables into $\{\mathbf{y}_t\}$ and $\{\mathbf{z}_t\}$, the system formulation is complete when the degrees and roots of every lag polynomial are specified.[2] Let:

$$\mathbf{y}_t \mid \mathbf{z}_t, \mathbf{X}_{t-1} \sim \mathsf{N}_n \left[\mathbf{p}_0 \mathbf{z}_t + \sum_{i=1}^{h} \mathbf{p}_i \mathbf{x}_{t-i}, \boldsymbol{\Omega} \right], \tag{9.6}$$

so that the longest lag is h periods and the conditional distribution is normal. Then the conditional system of n linear equations for $t = 1, \ldots, T$ is:

$$\mathbf{y}_t = \sum_{i=1}^{m} \boldsymbol{\pi}_{1i} \mathbf{y}_{t-i} + \sum_{j=0}^{r} \boldsymbol{\pi}_{2j} \mathbf{z}_{t-j} + \mathbf{v}_t \text{ where } \mathbf{v}_t \sim \mathsf{N}_n [\mathbf{0}, \boldsymbol{\Omega}], \tag{9.7}$$

and $h = \max(r, m)$, noting that $\mathbf{p}_0 = \boldsymbol{\pi}_{20}$ and $\mathbf{p}_i = (\boldsymbol{\pi}_{1i} : \boldsymbol{\pi}_{2i})$ for $i = 1, \ldots, h$. A subset of the variables in $\mathbf{y}_t$ can be linked by identities but otherwise $\boldsymbol{\Omega}$ is symmetric, positive definite and unrestricted. Then (9.7) is the general, unrestricted, conditional dynamic system once r and m are specified. Let $\boldsymbol{\Pi} = (\boldsymbol{\pi}_{11} \ldots \boldsymbol{\pi}_{1m} \boldsymbol{\pi}_{20} \ldots \boldsymbol{\pi}_{2r})$, then $\boldsymbol{\Pi}$

[2]For estimation, models of the system need not be complete but must be fully specified (see Richard, 1984).

and $\boldsymbol{\Omega}$ are variation-free and are the parameters of interest in the sequential conditional distribution, though not necessarily the parameters of interest in the overall analysis.

At this stage, the main requirement is that the system in (9.7) should be a congruent representation of the data, since it will be the specification against which all other simplifications are tested, and hence is the baseline for encompassing: see Hendry and Richard (1982, 1989) and Mizon and Richard (1986). Congruency requires that:

(1) $\{\mathbf{v}_t\}$ is a homoscedastic innovation process against $\mathbf{X}_{t-1}$, which depends on the adequate specification of the lag structure (see Hendry, Pagan and Sargan, 1984);
(2) $\mathbf{z}_t$ is weakly exogenous for $(\boldsymbol{\Pi},\ \boldsymbol{\Omega})$ (see Engle, Hendry and Richard, 1983); and:
(3) $(\boldsymbol{\Pi},\ \boldsymbol{\Omega})$ is constant $\forall t$ (see Hendry and Richard, 1983).

Once the system is congruent, a structural model of that system can be developed. Although the system (9.7) corresponds to what is often called the unrestricted reduced form (URF), it is the initial formulation and not a derived representation based on a prior structural specification. This is an important difference, since if the system is mis-specified, owing to residual autocorrelation, parameter non-constancy, and so on, further restrictions on it will be invalid, and tests thereof will be against an invalid baseline. In the conventional approach, where the structural model is estimated first, tests of the structural over-identifying restrictions against the URF are conditional on untested assumptions about the validity of the latter. When the URF is itself a parsimonious specification, assumptions about its validity are less than fully plausible.

The selection of r and m is usually data-based, given a prior maximum lag length. Since (9.7) is a statistical model, parsimony is not essential at this stage, whereas ensuring that the $\{\mathbf{v}_t\}$ are innovations is crucial for later inferences. This argument supports commencing with an over-parametrized representation. Although the context is multivariate, lag selection is susceptible to the usual approaches (see, for example, Hendry, Pagan and Sargan, 1984).

The next issue for valid inference concerns the degree of integration of the time series in $\{\mathbf{x}_t\}$ since the correct critical values of tests are different between I(0) and I(1) or higher orders (for an overview, see Banerjee, Dolado, Galbraith and Hendry, 1993, Hendry, 1995, and Johansen, 1995b). Moreover, equilibrium correction mechanisms (ECMs) – which are isomorphic to cointegration in linear models – play a fundamental role in stabilizing economic behaviour and attaining long-run targets, as well as implementing insights from economic theory into dynamic statistical analyses, see §9.7.

9.6 System evaluation

If system residuals are not innovations, or parameters are statistically non-constant over time, then the distributions of likelihood ratio tests will not correspond to those conventionally assumed even after the transformation to I(0) variables. Restricting the parametrization by structural formulations of the system, without changing the conditioning or lag assumptions, cannot remove, but could camouflage, such problems. System evaluation seeks to reduce the chances of imposing restrictions on a system only to discover at a later stage that the framework cannot provide an adequate representation of the data.

There is a wide range of hypotheses to be investigated corresponding to the three basic information sets of past, present and future data, applied to the system as a whole rather than to single equations isolated from it. The modelling procedures and tests are vector analogues of those arising for single equations albeit that modelling a system is more difficult than modelling a single conditional relationship. System tests of congruency can be constructed for vector residual autocorrelation(for example, Lagrange Multiplier tests for dependence between $\mathbf{v}_t$ and $\mathbf{v}_{t-1}$), vector heteroscedasticity (for example, testing whether squared residuals depend on squared functions of conditioning variables), dynamic mis-specification (the significance of a longer lag $(\mathbf{y}_{t-m-1}, \mathbf{z}_{t-r-1})$), weak exogeneity (modelling $\mathbf{z}_t$ as a function of $(\mathbf{y}_{t-i}, \mathbf{z}_{t-i};\ i = 1, \ldots, h)$ and perhaps further lagged non-modelled variables, and testing cross-equation independence from the $\mathbf{y}_t$ system), and constancy (using recursive procedures). Weak exogeneity is also indirectly testable via super exogeneity tests which include tests of $(\mathbf{\Pi},\ \mathbf{\Omega})$ being constant. Some of the $\mathbf{z}_t$ could be dummy variables so that the corresponding parameters are transients. Normality is useful but not essential in a linear formulation, and is also testable. For example, the various constancy statistics from multivariate RLS match those from univariate RLS closely, so the analysis applies to, for example, break-point tests of one equation from the system or the system as a whole. The formulae for forecast statistics are also similar. Details of all the available tests in PcGive are presented in Chapter 11 for the system.

The weak exogeneity of $\mathbf{z}_t$ for the parameters of interest in the system remains important. Subject to a correct specification of the marginal system for $\mathbf{z}_t$, the errors on the conditional system could be tested for being uncorrelated with those in the marginal system. The difficulty lies in appropriately formulating the marginal system, especially when conditioning is desired because of anticipated non-constancy in the marginal process. Direct tests on the common presence of the cointegrating vectors in both marginal and conditional systems at least check for weak exogeneity of $\mathbf{z}_t$ for the long-run parameters (see Chapter 12).

9.7 The impact of I(1) on econometric modelling

At first sight, unit-root econometrics seems wholly different from stationary econometrics. On the statistical side, the limiting distributions of estimators and tests are functionals of Brownian motions, so the forms of analysis, the resulting distributions and the associated critical values of tests are usually different. On the conceptual side, the treatment of many 'problems' differs for integrated data. For example, collinearity problems may be owing to including in a relationship all the elements in a cointegrating combination (a 'problem' which cannot be solved by deleting variables); and measurement errors may be irrelevant (if I(0)) or even more serious than usual (if I(1) and not cointegrated). Parameter change may lead to confusing an I(1) process with an I(0) subject to shifts (see Hendry and Neale, 1991) and so on.

However, both the statistical and conceptual differences seem less marked on second sight. Many functionals of Brownian motions in fact have normal distributions (for a summary, see Banerjee and Hendry, 1992). Moreover, even with I(1) data, many tests have conventional distributions; and conditioning later tests on the I(1) decision for the number of cointegrating combinations allows them to be treated as having conventional distributions once variables are reduced to I(0) (see e.g. Johansen, 1992a). Further, I(0) and I(1) are more like the ends of a continuum than discrete entities (see Molinas, 1986): a root of nearly -1 on a moving-average error in a unit-root autoregression essentially cancels the latter, leaving a process which is empirically similar to white noise. Conversely, a stationary process with a root near unity may be better treated as if it were I(1) in samples of the size common in economics (see, for example, Campbell and Perron, 1991, for a survey). In practice, therefore, modelling decisions may sensibly be conditioned on the outcome of unit-root tests, even if theory tests remain open to question (as with tests for 'persistence' of shocks).

In cointegrated processes, weak exogeneity of the conditioning variables for the parameters of interest remains as vital as it has proved to be in stationary processes – even for the long-run parameters (see Johansen, 1992b, and Hendry, 1995). One necessary condition is the absence of cointegrating vectors in other equations, and system modelling seems advisable until weak exogeneity has been ascertained (see Hendry and Doornik, 1994, for further details).

On the positive side, a number of benefits are clear. The Granger representation theorem links cointegration to equilibrium correction mechanisms (ECM), so that ECMs do not necessarily violate rationality in an I(1) world. Thus, the links between economic theory or long-run equilibrium reasoning and data modelling have been placed on a sounder footing. Other problems appear in a new light. For example, a linear system is invariant under non-singular linear transforms, but usually its parameters are altered by such transforms. However, in I(1) processes, the cointegrating vector β is an invariant of a linear system. Further, β is invariant to seasonal adjustment by a diagonal scale-preserving seasonal filter (like X-11, see Ericsson, Hendry and Tran, 1994).

Conditional models of I(1) data essentially complete the circle to reinstate structural dynamic models as a viable research vehicle. Now it is possible to test for the existence of a long-run relation before devoting resources to modelling it. Weak exogeneity of a subset of the variables for the long-run parameters simplifies doing so by allowing contemporaneous conditioning. Once a long-run relation is established, then conditional on a reduction from I(1) to I(0), the analysis can proceed as a reduction of the system to a parsimonious and interpretable econometric model thereof. The tutorials in Part II follow this approach through all the steps of an empirical application.

9.8 The econometric model and its identification

The main criterion for the validity of the system is its congruence, since that is a necessary condition for efficient statistical estimation and inference. An econometric model is a restricted version of a congruent system which sustains an economic interpretation, consistent with the associated theory. All linear structural models of (9.7) can be obtained by premultiplying (9.7) by a non-singular matrix $\mathbf{B}$ which generates:

$$\mathbf{B}\mathbf{y}_t = \sum_{i=1}^{m} \mathbf{B}\boldsymbol{\pi}_{1i}\mathbf{y}_{t-i} + \sum_{j=0}^{r} \mathbf{B}\boldsymbol{\pi}_{2j}\mathbf{z}_{t-j} + \mathbf{B}\mathbf{v}_t. \tag{9.8}$$

Let $\mathbf{B}_i = -\mathbf{B}\boldsymbol{\pi}_{1i}$ for $i = 1, \ldots, m$ and $\mathbf{C}_j = -\mathbf{B}\boldsymbol{\pi}_{2j}$ for $j = 0, \ldots, r$ with $\mathbf{u}_t = \mathbf{B}\mathbf{v}_t$, then:

$$\sum_{i=0}^{m} \mathbf{B}_i\mathbf{y}_{t-i} + \sum_{j=0}^{r} \mathbf{C}_j\mathbf{z}_{t-j} = \mathbf{u}_t \quad \text{where } \mathbf{u}_t \sim \mathsf{IN}_n\left[\mathbf{0}, \boldsymbol{\Sigma}\right], \tag{9.9}$$

with $\boldsymbol{\Sigma} = \mathbf{B}\boldsymbol{\Omega}\mathbf{B}'$ and $\mathbf{B}_0 = \mathbf{B}$. Let $\mathbf{C} = (\mathbf{B}_1 \ldots \mathbf{B}_m\mathbf{C}_0 \ldots \mathbf{C}_r)$, with $\mathbf{A} = (\mathbf{B} : \mathbf{C})$ and $\mathbf{X} = (\mathbf{Y} : \mathbf{W})$ being the matrices of all the coefficients and all the observations respectively, partitioned by current endogenous and all other variables. We drop the sample subscripts on data matrices, and implicitly assume that the diagonal of $\mathbf{B}_0$ is normalized at unity to ensure a unique scaling in every equation: other normalizations are feasible. Further, the reformulation in I(0) space would have the same form, but in terms of I(0) variables: the notation $\mathbf{W}$ is intended to highlight that reformulation. Then (9.9) can be written in compact notation as:

$$\mathbf{B}\mathbf{Y}' + \mathbf{C}\mathbf{W}' = \mathbf{A}\mathbf{X}' = \mathbf{U}'. \tag{9.10}$$

When identities are present, the corresponding elements of $\{\mathbf{u}_t\}$ are precisely zero, so the model can be written as:

$$\mathbf{A}\mathbf{X}' = \begin{pmatrix} \mathbf{A}_1 \\ \mathbf{A}_2 \end{pmatrix} \mathbf{X}' = \begin{pmatrix} \mathbf{U}_1' \\ \mathbf{0} \end{pmatrix}, \tag{9.11}$$

where $n = n_1 + n_2$, for n_1 stochastic equations and n_2 identities. The elements of $\mathbf{A}_2$ must be known and do not need estimation. In what follows, we set $n_2 = 0$ for simplicity: the program handles identities as required.

However, without some restrictions, the coefficients in $\mathbf{A}$ in (9.11) will not be identified. The matrix $\mathbf{B}$ used to multiply the system to obtain the model could in turn be multiplied by an arbitrary non-singular matrix, $\mathbf{D}$ say, and still produce a linear model, but with different coefficients. To resolve such arbitrariness, we need to know the form of $\mathbf{A}$ in advance (or perhaps of $\boldsymbol{\Sigma}$), and it must be sufficiently restricted that the only admissible $\mathbf{D}$ matrix is $\mathbf{I}_{n_1}$. This issue of unique parametrization is further discussed in Chapter 13.

9.9 Simultaneous equations modelling

So far, we have assumed that the structural form of the DGP was known. Textbook presentations of simultaneous equations estimation usually treat $\mathbf{A}(\phi)$ as given, then derive the reduced form from this structure (for example, Judge, Griffiths, Hill, Lütkepohl and Lee, 1985, Chapter 14). However, since the reduced form has many more parameters than there are ϕs in the structure, such an approach is simple to general and so is open to all the difficulties discussed in Hendry, Neale and Srba (1988). Moreover, by not first testing the validity of the reduced form, which is the basis of the test of over-identifying restrictions used to validate the structural form, all inferences are doubtful (see Sims, 1980, and Hendry, 1987). Thus, in practice, the statistical system should be modelled from the data to determine its congruency before any structural interpretation can be attempted in terms of an econometric model of that system (as discussed in, for example, Spanos, 1986, 1989). Our approach, therefore, remains within the general $\rightarrow$ specific modelling methodology, extended to allow for the complications of multi-equations, cointegration and identification.

For the model to be a valid, congruent representation of the data, given that the system already is, the model must parsimoniously encompass the system (see Hendry and Richard, 1989). In the present context, that can be checked by a likelihood ratio test for over-identifying restrictions. Denote the concentrated likelihood function for the system with n_1 stochastic equations by ℓ and that for the complete model by ℓ_0. The test is computed by:

$$\xi\left(M - n_1^2\right) = 2\left(\widehat{\ell}_0 - \widehat{\ell}\right) \underset{a}{\sim} \chi^2\left(M - n_1^2\right)$$

for M *a priori* restrictions on $\mathbf{A}$. If $\xi\left(.\right)$ is significant, the model fails to encompass the system, so that particular implementation of the underlying theory should be rejected. To ensure that appropriate critical values are selected, the system must first be mapped to $\mathsf{I}(0)$ space.

There may be several models consistent with the identification restrictions, even if all are highly over-identified. In particular, this is true for just-identified models when $M = n_1^2$, so that $\xi\left(\cdot\right)$ is not computable. More generally, however, satisfying the test is insufficient to justify a model, especially if the system is itself not rigorously tested for congruency.

Consequently, the modelling approach described in detail in the tutorials first specifies the statistical dynamic system, assesses its congruency against the past (homoscedastic innovation errors), thereby ensuring an adequate lag length, then tests constancy. At present, such tests are only approximate when the data are $\mathsf{I}(1)$ but seem to provide reasonable guides in practice. Next, cointegration is investigated, thereby determining the degree of integration of the system *en route*. Once the cointegration rank and the number of unit roots have been determined, identified cointegration vectors can be considered, allowing useful tests of necessary conditions for weak exogeneity of some of the potential conditioning variables for the parameters of interest. The roles of deterministic variables and their presence/absence from the long run also can be investigated. Given that information, the system can be reduced to I(0) space in terms of differences and cointegrating combinations of the levels data using tests based on appropriate critical values.

Next, that system can be modelled. Depending on the outcomes of the weak exogeneity tests, conditional representations in terms of open systems may be feasible. These are unique by construction, but need not always represent agent behaviour. Simultaneous equations offer the possibility of jointly obtaining parsimonious and structural representations, so these merit careful consideration given the underlying theory. The final model can be checked for unique identification (which does not by itself preclude other observationally-equivalent representations, although regime shifts tend to make such an outcome unlikely). If dummies are needed to make any marginal processes constant, then super-exogeneity tests are feasible. Finally, the model can be tested for parsimonious encompassing of the system and its parsimony may allow more powerful tests of some hypothesis of interest, especially constancy. Forecasting exercises are then feasible and have some credibility (see Clements and Hendry, 1998b, for a more detailed analysis).

9.10 General to specific modelling of systems

Enforcing a system approach to simultaneous equations modelling necessitates a large modelling burden, primarily determined by the 'infoglut' of handling large numbers of variables, equations, and parameters. While PcGive is specifically designed to help attenuate that burden by its graphical presentation of information and its support of simplification procedures, it behoves us to consider the potential advantages of commencing from the unrestricted joint density of all the stochastic variables.

We presented a number of arguments for general to specific methods in Volume I (Hendry and Doornik, 2006), including developing directed search strategies; validly interpreting intermediate test outcomes by avoiding later potential contradictions; escaping the *non sequitur* of accepting the alternative hypothesis when a test rejects a null; determining the baseline innovation-error process on the available information; and circumventing the drawbacks of correcting flaws only to have to alter their interpretation later. These are powerful arguments for commencing an empirical econometric study from the most general model it is feasible to consider at the outset. Certainly, it is difficult to specify that general system when the sample may be small and heterogeneous, or the potential model class includes non-linear specifications. Nevertheless, tracking deliberate simplifying assumptions made at the commencement of an analysis can clarify later problems and potential directions for their resolution. This advice remains applicable even if a complete economic theory specification is available, since it can be embedded in a extended dynamic system that it should encompass when its claimed completeness is indeed correct.

In the limit, the joint density should comprise all relevant economic variables, but an important source of an investigator's value added is appropriate specifications of the sets of variables which necessitate joint modelling. We now develop some further, inter-related, reasons for commencing econometric analyses of economic time series from the joint density (see Hendry and Doornik, 1994).

9.10.1 The economy is a system

This is the most obvious reason for joint modelling, and was the basis for the advances in econometrics precipitated by Haavelmo (1944). Potentially all variables are endogenously determined by the economic mechanism, and these interact in many ways. In a Walrasian general-equilibrium setting, all variables influence each other in the long run (like a waterbed, which oscillates in all directions when disturbed anywhere). It may happen that some sectors or variables can be decoupled (i.e., the system is block decomposable), but that is an empirical matter. However, to make progress some simplifying assumptions will be essential, depending on the numbers of variables involved and the available sample size. Implicitly, all empirical analyses are based on reductions of the DGP from marginalizing with respect to all variables omitted from the system under study: the crucial issue is to retain as informative a set as possible.

9.10.2 To test marginalization

To check the validity of marginalizing with respect to any set of variates, their joint density must be modelled. Let $\mathbf{w}_t$ denote the vector of possibly relevant variables, and $\mathsf{D}_{\mathsf{W,X}}(\cdot)$ the joint density of all the variables characterized by the parameter $\psi \in \Psi$, then since:

$$\mathsf{D}_{\mathsf{W,X}}\left(\mathbf{W}_T^1, \mathbf{X}_T^1 \mid \mathbf{W}_0, \mathbf{X}_0, \psi\right) = \mathsf{D}_{\mathsf{W|X}}\left(\mathbf{W}_T^1 \mid \mathbf{X}_T^1, \mathbf{W}_0, \psi_1\right) \mathsf{D}_{\mathsf{X}}\left(\mathbf{X}_T^1 \mid \mathbf{X}_0, \psi_2\right) \tag{9.12}$$

the conditions for a fully efficient analysis from $\mathsf{D}_{\mathsf{X}}(\cdot)$ alone mirror those of weak exogeneity (see Engle, Hendry and Richard, 1983, and Ericsson, 1992) namely:

- the parameters of interest ϕ are a function of ψ_2 alone; and
- $(\psi_1, \psi_2) \in \Psi_1 \times \Psi_2$ (variation free).

In such a case, $\psi_2 = \boldsymbol{\theta}$ in (9.4), and there is no loss of relevant information about ϕ from analyzing the marginal density only. A necessary condition for the validity of such a reduction is that $\mathbf{W}_{t-1}^1$ does not Granger cause $\mathbf{x}_t$: this can only be tested from either $\mathsf{D}_{\mathsf{W,X}}(\cdot)$ or $\mathsf{D}_{\mathsf{W|X}}(\cdot)$.

9.10.3 Simultaneity

Simultaneity is a system property. Although individual-equation (limited information) methods exist, and the curse of dimensionality relative to data availability remains a serious limitation, computational problems no longer provide an excuse for avoiding system methods. Simultaneity is also a long-standing reason, dating from Haavelmo (1943), but a much disputed formulation in the history of econometrics (see Hendry and Morgan, 1995).

9.10.4 To test weak exogeneity

To test conditioning on a subset of stochastic variables (denoted $\{\mathbf{z}_t\} \subset \{\mathbf{x}_t\}$) rather paradoxically first requires modelling $\mathbf{z}_t$, then testing that the marginal density does not contain information relevant to the parameters of interest. For example, elements of ϕ (such as cointegration vectors) could occur in $\boldsymbol{\lambda}_2$ which would violate weak exogeneity, and could induce serious distortions of inference in $\mathsf{I}(1)$ systems (see below).

9.10.5 To check identification

The necessary and sufficient criterion for identification (in the sense of uniqueness) under linear restrictions on simultaneous systems is given by the rank condition (see Koopmans, 1950), which depends on the (unknown) values of the parameters in all equations. These other equations need to be specified to ensure the condition is met. PcGive checks generic identification within the system being modelled, by using non-zero random values for parameters, so global unidentification does not occur when that condition is satisfied.

9.10.6 Cointegration is a system property

The rank of the long-run system matrix can only be determined by considering the complete vector of variables $\mathbf{x}_t$, which necessitates modelling the joint density either explicitly (as in Johansen, 1988) or implicitly (as in Phillips, 1991). Similarly, determining the matrix of cointegrating vectors involves a system analysis. This requirement interacts with the issue of testing weak exogeneity, since if elements of the cointegrating vectors from the ith equation enter any other equation weak exogeneity for parameters of interest which include cointegrating vectors is violated. Tests on the structure of the feedback matrix provide information about cointegration links, are easily conducted, and have conventional (χ^2) distributions asymptotically when cointegration rank is preserved (see Johansen, 1992b, and Boswijk, 1992).

9.10.7 To test cross-equation dependencies

Cross-equation links include many forms of restrictions, cross-equation serial correlation and so on. Any test for system mis-specification logically requires system analysis. One important test is that of over-identifying restrictions, and is equivalent to a test of whether the restricted model parsimoniously encompasses the VAR (see Hendry and Mizon, 1993).

9.10.8 To test super exogeneity and invariance

In many economic processes, a VAR will not manifest constant parameters. This is because it is a derived, rather than a structural, representation so every equation involves functions of the more basic parameters of agents' decision rules. When one of the agents is a policy maker, or an agency of the central government, regime shifts are liable to have occurred, so a constant linear parametrization will be insufficient to capture the data behaviour. Thus, some dummy variables may be needed to make the system approximately constant in practice, especially in equations for policy variables (which the investigator may not wish to model). Conditioning on such variables without first testing for weak and super exogeneity runs the risk that the resulting model will not sustain policy analysis, and may be inadequate as a forecasting device when economic policy change occurs. Engle and Hendry (1993) develop constant-parameter representations of the policy processes, then test the irrelevance of the newly-created variables in the equations of interest. This is most usefully conducted in a system context, and a natural generalization of their test is the significance of the additional variables from the joint marginal model in the joint conditional model under analysis.

9.10.9 To conduct h-step forecasts

The system context has no effect on 1-step forecasts, and each equation could be used in isolation from the others. However, for h-step forecasting when $h \geq 2$ and the system is dynamic, then to predict $\Delta \mathbf{x}_{T+2}$, $\Delta \widehat{\mathbf{x}}_{T+1}$ must first be forecast, so the system context is of the essence.

We believe that any of these reasons by itself is sufficient justification for commencing an econometric analysis from the joint density to allow a sustainable analysis of any proposed empirical models. Together, they constitute a strong case for joint modelling, without resolving how general the starting point must be. Data limitations alone preclude beginning with more than a relatively small number of variables, and the illustration in the tutorials only involves 4 variables, but the issue is one of modelling principles. In particular, knowledge acquisition tends to be progressive and partial, rather than once-for-all crucial discoveries that permanently resolve a modelling problem by forging an empirical 'law'.

Chapter 10

Some Matrix Algebra

An essential element of multivariate analysis is concise notation using matrix algebra. In this section we shall summarize the matrix algebra required to understand Part III of this book. No proofs will be given. For a more thorough overview consult Magnus and Neudecker (1988), Dhrymes (1984), Rao (1973, Chapter 1) or Anderson (1984, Appendix A), among others.

First consider the four-equation model which generated the artificial data set as used in Volume I:

$$\begin{aligned}
\Delta c_t &= -0.9 + 0.4\,\Delta y_t + 0.15\,(y-c)_{t-1} - 0.9\,\Delta p_t + \epsilon_{1t} && (10.1)\\
\Delta y_t &= -75.0 + 0.3\,\Delta c_t + 0.25\,(q-y)_{t-1} + 0.25\,\Delta q_t + \epsilon_{2t} && (10.2)\\
\Delta p_t &= 0.3 + 0.7\,\Delta p_{t-1} + 0.08\,(q-1200)_{t-1} + \epsilon_{3t} && (10.3)\\
\Delta q_t &= 121.3 - 0.1\,q_{t-1} - 1.30\,\Delta p_{t-1} + \epsilon_{4t} && (10.4)
\end{aligned}$$

The relevant matrices are:

$$\begin{pmatrix} 1 & -0.4 & 0.9 & 0 \\ -0.3 & 1 & 0 & -0.25 \\ 0 & 0 & 1 & 0 \\ 0 & 0 & 0 & 1 \end{pmatrix}\begin{pmatrix} \Delta c_t \\ \Delta y_t \\ \Delta p_t \\ \Delta q_t \end{pmatrix} +$$

$$\begin{pmatrix} 0.9 & -0.15 & 0 & 0 & 0 \\ 75 & 0 & -0.25 & 0 & 0 \\ 95.7 & 0 & 0 & -0.08 & -0.7 \\ -121.3 & 0 & 0 & 0.1 & 1.3 \end{pmatrix}\begin{pmatrix} 1 \\ (y-c)_{t-1} \\ (q-y)_{t-1} \\ q_{t-1} \\ \Delta p_{t-1} \end{pmatrix} = \begin{pmatrix} u_{1t} \\ u_{2t} \\ u_{3t} \\ u_{4t} \end{pmatrix}. \qquad (10.5)$$

In matrix form the model can be expressed as:

$$\mathbf{B}\mathbf{y}_t + \mathbf{C}\mathbf{w}_t = \mathbf{u}_t,\ t = 1, \ldots, T, \qquad (10.6)$$

in which the matrices are written in bold face upper case and the vectors in bold face lower case. $\mathbf{B}$ is a (4×4) matrix, $\mathbf{C}$ is (4×5), $\mathbf{y}_t$ and $\mathbf{u}_t$ are (4×1) and $\mathbf{w}_t$ is

(5×1). The simultaneous system (10.6) can be expressed more concisely by merging all T equations. Take $\mathbf{y}_t$ for example:

$$\mathbf{Y}' = (\mathbf{y}_1 \cdots\cdots \mathbf{y}_T) = \begin{pmatrix} \Delta c_1 \cdots\cdots \Delta c_T \\ \Delta y_1 \cdots\cdots \Delta y_T \\ \Delta p_1 \cdots\cdots \Delta p_T \\ \Delta q_1 \cdots\cdots \Delta q_T \end{pmatrix}.$$

Using this notation the model becomes:

$$\mathbf{BY}' + \mathbf{CW}' = \mathbf{U}',$$

in which $\mathbf{Y}$ and $\mathbf{U}$ are $(T \times 4)$ and $\mathbf{W}$ is $(T \times 5)$. The matrices $\mathbf{B}$ and $\mathbf{C}$ are unchanged. Of course this is identical to:

$$\mathbf{YB}' + \mathbf{WC}' = \mathbf{U}.$$

To define the elementary operators on matrices we shall write $(a_{ij})_{m,n}$ for the $(m \times n)$ matrix $\mathbf{A}$ when this is convenient:

$$\mathbf{A} = (a_{ij})_{m,n} = \begin{pmatrix} a_{11} & \cdots & a_{1n} \\ \vdots & \ddots & \vdots \\ a_{m1} & \cdots & a_{mn} \end{pmatrix}.$$

- *addition,* $\mathbf{A}$ is $(m \times n)$, $\mathbf{B}$ is $(m \times n)$:

$$\mathbf{A} + \mathbf{B} = (a_{ij} + b_{ij})_{m,n}.$$

- *multiplication,* $\mathbf{A}$ is $(m \times n)$, $\mathbf{B}$ is $(n \times p)$, c is a scalar:

$$\mathbf{AB} = \left(\sum_{k=1}^{n} a_{ik} b_{kj} \right)_{m,p}, \quad c\mathbf{A} = (c a_{ij})_{m,n}.$$

- *Kronecker product,* $\mathbf{A}$ is $(m \times n)$, $\mathbf{B}$ is $(p \times q)$:

$$\mathbf{A} \otimes \mathbf{B} = (a_{ij}\mathbf{B})_{mp,nq}.$$

For example, with $\mathbf{\Omega} = (\omega_{ij})_{2,2}$, $\mathbf{S} = (s_{ij})_{2,2}$:

$$\mathbf{\Omega} \otimes \mathbf{S} = \begin{pmatrix} \omega_{11}s_{11} & \omega_{11}s_{12} & \omega_{12}s_{11} & \omega_{12}s_{12} \\ \omega_{11}s_{21} & \omega_{11}s_{22} & \omega_{12}s_{21} & \omega_{12}s_{22} \\ \omega_{21}s_{11} & \omega_{21}s_{12} & \omega_{22}s_{11} & \omega_{22}s_{12} \\ \omega_{21}s_{21} & \omega_{21}s_{22} & \omega_{22}s_{21} & \omega_{22}s_{22} \end{pmatrix}.$$

- *Hadamard product,* $\mathbf{A}$ is $(m \times n)$, $\mathbf{B}$ is $(m \times n)$:

$$\mathbf{A} \odot \mathbf{B} = (a_{ij} b_{ij})_{m,n}\,.$$

For example:

$$\mathbf{\Omega} \odot \mathbf{S} = \begin{pmatrix} \omega_{11} s_{11} & \omega_{12} s_{12} \\ \omega_{21} s_{21} & \omega_{22} s_{22} \end{pmatrix}.$$

- *transpose,* $\mathbf{A}$ is $(m \times n)$:

$$\mathbf{A}' = (a_{ji})_{n,m}\,.$$

- *determinant,* $\mathbf{A}$ is $(n \times n)$:

$$|\mathbf{A}| = \sum (-1)^{c(j_1,\ldots,j_n)} \prod_{i=1}^{n} a_{ij_i}$$

where the summation is over all permutations $(j_1, \ldots, j_n)$ of the set of integers $(1, \ldots, n)$, and $c(j_1, \ldots, j_n)$ is the number of transpositions required to change $(1, \ldots, n)$ into $(j_1, \ldots, j_n)$. In the 2×2 case, the set $(1, 2)$ can be transposed once into $(2, 1)$, so $|\mathbf{\Omega}| = (-1)^0 \omega_{11}\omega_{22} + (-1)^1 \omega_{12}\omega_{21}$.
- *trace,* $\mathbf{A}$ is $(n \times n)$:

$$\mathrm{tr}\mathbf{A} = \sum_{i=1}^{n} a_{ii}.$$

- *rank,* $\mathbf{A}$ is $(m \times n)$: the rank of $\mathbf{A}$ is the number of linearly independent columns (or rows, row rank always equals column rank) in $\mathbf{A}$, $\mathrm{r}(\mathbf{A}) \leq \min(m, n)$. If $\mathbf{A}$ is $(n \times n)$ and of full rank then:

$$\mathrm{r}(\mathbf{A}) = n.$$

- *symmetric matrix,* $\mathbf{A}$ is $(n \times n)$: $\mathbf{A}$ is symmetric if:

$$\mathbf{A}' = \mathbf{A}.$$

- *matrix inverse,* $\mathbf{A}$ is $(n \times n)$ and of full rank (non-singular, which is equivalent to $|\mathbf{A}| \neq 0$) then $\mathbf{A}^{-1}$ is the unique $(n \times n)$ matrix such that:

$$\mathbf{A}\mathbf{A}^{-1} = \mathbf{I}_n.$$

This implies that $\mathbf{A}^{-1}\mathbf{A} = \mathbf{I}_n$; $\mathbf{I}_n$ is the $(n \times n)$ identity matrix:

$$\mathbf{I}_n = \begin{pmatrix} 1 & 0 & \cdots & 0 \\ 0 & 1 & \cdots & 0 \\ \vdots & \vdots & \ddots & \vdots \\ 0 & 0 & \cdots & 1 \end{pmatrix}.$$

- *orthogonal matrix*, $\mathbf{A}$ is $(n \times n)$: $\mathbf{A}$ is orthogonal if:

$$\mathbf{A}'\mathbf{A} = \mathbf{I}_n.$$

Then also $\mathbf{A}\mathbf{A}' = \mathbf{I}_n$; further: $\mathrm{r}(\mathbf{A}) = n$, $\mathbf{A}' = \mathbf{A}^{-1}$.

- *orthogonal complement*, $\mathbf{A}$ is $(m \times n)$, $m > n$ and $\mathrm{r}(\mathbf{A}) = n$, define the orthogonal complement $\mathbf{A}_\perp$ as the $(m \times (m-n))$ matrix such that: $\mathbf{A}'\mathbf{A}_\perp = \mathbf{0}$ with $\mathrm{r}(\mathbf{A}_\perp) = m - n$ and $\mathrm{r}(\mathbf{A} : \mathbf{A}_\perp) = m$. $\mathbf{A}_\perp$ spans the *null space* of $\mathbf{A}$; $\mathrm{r}(\mathbf{A}_\perp)$ is called the *nullity* of $\mathbf{A}$.
- *idempotent matrix*, $\mathbf{A}$ is $(n \times n)$: $\mathbf{A}$ is idempotent if:

$$\mathbf{A}\mathbf{A} = \mathbf{A}.$$

An example is the projection matrix $\mathbf{M}_X = \mathbf{I}_T - \mathbf{X}\left(\mathbf{X}'\mathbf{X}\right)^{-1}\mathbf{X}'$.

- *vectorization*, $\mathbf{A}$ is $(m \times n)$:

$$\mathrm{vec}\mathbf{A} = \begin{pmatrix} a_{11} \\ \vdots \\ a_{m1} \\ \vdots \\ a_{1n} \\ \vdots \\ a_{mn} \end{pmatrix},$$

which is an $(mn \times 1)$ vector consisting of the stacked columns of $\mathbf{A}$. Transposing the vectorized form of the $\mathbf{B}'$ matrix of (10.5) gives:

$$(\mathrm{vec}\,(\mathbf{B}'))' = (1\ \ -0.4\ 0.9\ 0\ \ -0.3\ 1\ 0\ \ -0.25\ 0\ 0\ 1\ 0\ 0\ 0\ 0\ 1)\,.$$

This is the order we wish to have the model coefficients in: stacked by equation. We use $\mathrm{vec}(\mathbf{B}') \equiv \mathrm{vec}\mathbf{B}'$. With $\mathbf{a}$ an $(n \times 1)$ vector: $\mathrm{vec}(\mathbf{a}) = \mathbf{a}$.
If $\mathbf{A}$ is $(n \times n)$ and symmetric, we can use the vech operator to vectorize the unique elements, thus ignoring the elements above the diagonal:

$$\mathrm{vech}\mathbf{A} = \begin{pmatrix} a_{11} \\ \vdots \\ a_{n1} \\ a_{22} \\ \vdots \\ a_{n2} \\ \vdots \\ a_{nn} \end{pmatrix},$$

which is a $(\frac{1}{2}n(n+1) \times 1)$ vector.

- *unrestricted elements,* when deriving simultaneous equations estimators, it is often convenient to restrict attention to the parameters that are to be estimated and ignore the remaining parameters. $(\cdot)^u$ selects the unrestricted elements of a vector, or crosses out rows and columns of a matrix, thus reducing the dimensionality. $(\cdot)^{v_u}$ transposes and vectorizes a matrix, stores the elements in a column vector, and selects the unrestricted elements. In the $\mathbf{B}$ matrix of (10.5), the 0s and 1s are restrictions, the remainder are parameters, so:

$$\mathbf{B}^{v_u} = (\mathrm{vec}\,(\mathbf{B}'))^u = \begin{pmatrix} -0.4 \\ 0.9 \\ -0.3 \\ -0.25 \end{pmatrix}.$$

- *diagonalization,* $\mathbf{A}$ is $(n \times n)$:

$$\mathrm{dg}\mathbf{A} = \begin{pmatrix} a_{11} & 0 & \cdots & 0 \\ 0 & a_{22} & \cdots & 0 \\ \vdots & \vdots & \ddots & \vdots \\ 0 & 0 & \cdots & a_{nn} \end{pmatrix} = \mathrm{diag}\,(a_{11}, a_{22}, \ldots, a_{nn})\,.$$

- *positive definite,* $\mathbf{A}$ is $(n \times n)$ and symmetric: $\mathbf{A}$ is positive definite if $\mathbf{x}'\mathbf{A}\mathbf{x} > 0$ for all $(n \times 1)$ vectors $\mathbf{x} \neq \mathbf{0}$, positive semi-definite if $\mathbf{x}'\mathbf{A}\mathbf{x} \geq 0$ for all $\mathbf{x} \neq \mathbf{0}$, and negative definite if $\mathbf{x}'\mathbf{A}\mathbf{x} < 0$ for all $\mathbf{x} \neq \mathbf{0}$.
- *eigenvalues and eigenvectors,* $\mathbf{A}$ is $(n \times n)$: the eigenvalues of $\mathbf{A}$ are the roots of the characteristic equation:

$$|\mathbf{A} - \lambda\mathbf{I}_n| = 0.$$

If λ_i is an eigenvalue of $\mathbf{A}$, then $\mathbf{x}_i \neq \mathbf{0}$ is an eigenvector of $\mathbf{A}$ if it satisfies:

$$(\mathbf{A} - \lambda_i\mathbf{I}_n)\,\mathbf{x}_i = \mathbf{0}.$$

- *Choleski decomposition,* $\mathbf{A}$ is $(n \times n)$ and symmetric positive definite, then:

$$\mathbf{A} = \mathbf{L}\mathbf{L}',$$

where $\mathbf{L}$ is a unique lower-triangular matrix with positive diagonal elements.
- *singular value decomposition,* decomposes an $(m \times n)$ matrix $\mathbf{A}$, $m \geq n$ and $\mathrm{r}(\mathbf{A}) = r > 0$, into:

$$\mathbf{A} = \mathbf{U}\mathbf{W}\mathbf{V}',$$

with:

$\mathbf{U}$ is $(m \times r)$ and $\mathbf{U}'\mathbf{U} = \mathbf{I}_r$,
$\mathbf{W}$ is $(r \times r)$ and diagonal, with non-negative diagonal elements,
$\mathbf{V}$ is $(n \times r)$ and $\mathbf{V}'\mathbf{V} = \mathbf{I}_r$.

This can be used to find the orthogonal complement of $\mathbf{A}$. Assume $\mathrm{r}(\mathbf{A}) = n$ and compute the singular value decomposition of the $(m \times m)$ matrix $\mathbf{B} = (\mathbf{A} : \mathbf{0})$. The last $m - n$ diagonal elements of $\mathbf{W}$ will be zero. Corresponding to that are the last $m - n$ columns of $\mathbf{U}$ which form $\mathbf{A}_\perp$:

$$\mathbf{B} = (\mathbf{A} : \mathbf{0}) = \mathbf{U}\mathbf{W}\mathbf{V}' = (\mathbf{U}_1 : \mathbf{U}_2) \begin{pmatrix} \mathbf{W}_1 & \mathbf{0} \\ \mathbf{0} & \mathbf{0} \end{pmatrix} \begin{pmatrix} \mathbf{V}_1' \\ \mathbf{V}_2' \end{pmatrix}.$$

Here $\mathbf{U}$, $\mathbf{V}$ and $\mathbf{W}$ are $(m \times m)$ matrices; $\mathbf{U}_2'\mathbf{U}_1 = \mathbf{0}$ so that $\mathbf{U}_2'\mathbf{A} = \mathbf{U}_2'\mathbf{U}_1\mathbf{W}_1\mathbf{V}_1' = \mathbf{0}$ and $\mathrm{r}(\mathbf{A} : \mathbf{U}_2) = m$ as $\mathbf{U}_2'\mathbf{U}_2 = \mathbf{I}_{(m-n)}$.

- *differentiation*, define $f(\cdot) : \mathbb{R}^m \mapsto \mathbb{R}$ then:

$$\nabla f = \frac{\partial f(\mathbf{a})}{\partial \mathbf{a}} = \begin{pmatrix} \frac{\partial f(\mathbf{a})}{\partial a_1} \\ \vdots \\ \frac{\partial f(\mathbf{a})}{\partial a_m} \end{pmatrix}, \quad \nabla^2 f = \frac{\partial^2 f(\mathbf{a})}{\partial \mathbf{a} \partial \mathbf{a}'} = \left(\frac{\partial^2 f(\mathbf{a})}{\partial a_i \partial a_j} \right)_{m,m}.$$

If $f(\cdot)$ is a log-likelihood function we shall write $\mathbf{q}(\cdot)$ for the first derivative (or score), and $\mathbf{H}(\cdot)$ for the second derivative (or *Hessian*) matrix.
For $f(\cdot) : \mathbb{R}^{m \times n} \mapsto \mathbb{R}$ we define:

$$\frac{\partial f(\mathbf{A})}{\partial \mathbf{A}} = \left(\frac{\partial f(\mathbf{A})}{\partial a_{ij}} \right)_{m,n}.$$

- *Jacobian matrix*, for a vector function $\mathbf{f}(\cdot) : \mathbb{R}^m \mapsto \mathbb{R}^n$ we define the $(n \times m)$ Jacobian matrix $\mathbf{J}$:

$$\frac{\partial \mathbf{f}(\mathbf{a})}{\partial \mathbf{a}'} = \begin{pmatrix} \frac{\partial f_1(\mathbf{a})}{\partial a_1} & \cdots & \frac{\partial f_1(\mathbf{a})}{\partial a_m} \\ \vdots & & \vdots \\ \frac{\partial f_n(\mathbf{a})}{\partial a_1} & \cdots & \frac{\partial f_n(\mathbf{a})}{\partial a_m} \end{pmatrix} = \begin{pmatrix} (\nabla f_1)' \\ \vdots \\ (\nabla f_m)' \end{pmatrix} = (\nabla \mathbf{f})'.$$

The transpose of the Jacobian is called the gradient, and corresponds to the $\mathbf{q}(\cdot)$ above for $n = 1$ (so in that case the Jacobian is $(1 \times m)$ and the score $(n \times 1)$). The Jacobian is the absolute value of the determinant of $\mathbf{J}$ when $m = n$: $||\mathbf{J}||$.
Normally we wish to compute the Jacobian matrix for a transformation of a coefficient matrix: $\boldsymbol{\Psi} = \mathbf{F}(\boldsymbol{\Pi}')$ where $\mathbf{F}$ is a matrix function $\mathbf{F}(\cdot) : \mathbb{R}^{m \times n} \mapsto \mathbb{R}^{p \times q}$:

$$\mathbf{J} = \frac{\partial \mathrm{vec} \boldsymbol{\Psi}}{\partial (\mathrm{vec} \boldsymbol{\Pi}')'},$$

with $\boldsymbol{\Pi}$ $(n \times m)$ and $\boldsymbol{\Psi}$ $(p \times q)$ so that $\mathbf{J}$ is $(pq \times mn)$.

Some useful relations (c is scalar, λ_i are eigenvalues of $\mathbf{A}$):

- product, determinant, trace, rank

$$(\mathbf{AB})' = \mathbf{B}'\mathbf{A}'$$
$$(\mathbf{AB})^{-1} = \mathbf{B}^{-1}\mathbf{A}^{-1}, \text{ if } \mathbf{A}, \mathbf{B} \text{ non-singular}$$
$$(\mathbf{A}^{-1})' = (\mathbf{A}')^{-1}$$
$$|\mathbf{AB}| = |\mathbf{A}|\,|\mathbf{B}|\,, \mathbf{A}, \mathbf{B} \text{ are } (n \times n)$$
$$|\mathbf{A}'| = |\mathbf{A}|$$
$$|c\mathbf{A}| = c^n\,|\mathbf{A}|\,, \mathbf{A} \text{ is } (n \times n)$$
$$\left|\mathbf{A}^{-1}\right| = |\mathbf{A}|^{-1}$$
$$\text{tr}(\mathbf{AB}) = \text{tr}(\mathbf{BA})$$
$$\text{tr}(\mathbf{A} + \mathbf{B}) = \text{tr}\mathbf{A} + \text{tr}\mathbf{B}$$
$$\text{tr}\mathbf{A} = \sum \lambda_i, \mathbf{A} \text{ is } (n \times n)$$
$$|\mathbf{A}| = \prod \lambda_i, \mathbf{A} \text{ is } (n \times n)$$

if $\mathbf{A}$ $(n \times n)$, symmetric with p roots $\lambda_i \neq 0$ and $n - p$ roots $\lambda_i = 0$, then $\text{r}(\mathbf{A}) = p$.

- Kronecker, vec

$$(\mathbf{A} \otimes \mathbf{B})' = \mathbf{A}' \otimes \mathbf{B}'$$
$$(\mathbf{A} \otimes \mathbf{B})^{-1} = \mathbf{A}^{-1} \otimes \mathbf{B}^{-1}, \text{ if } \mathbf{A}, \mathbf{B} \text{ non-singular}$$
$$|\mathbf{A} \otimes \mathbf{B}| = |\mathbf{A}|^m\,|\mathbf{B}|^n\,, \mathbf{A} \text{ is } (n \times n) \text{ and } \mathbf{B} \text{ is } (m \times m)$$
$$(\mathbf{A} \otimes \mathbf{B})(\mathbf{C} \otimes \mathbf{D}) = \mathbf{AC} \otimes \mathbf{BD}$$
$$c \otimes \mathbf{A} = c\mathbf{A} = \mathbf{A}c = \mathbf{A} \otimes c$$
$$\text{tr}(\mathbf{A} \otimes \mathbf{B}) = \text{tr}\mathbf{A}\text{tr}\mathbf{B}$$
$$(\text{vec}\mathbf{A})'\text{vec}\mathbf{B} = \text{tr}(\mathbf{A}'\mathbf{B}), \mathbf{A}, \mathbf{B} \text{ both } (m \times n)$$
$$\text{vec}(\mathbf{a}') = \text{vec}(\mathbf{a}) = \mathbf{a}, \mathbf{a} \text{ is } (n \times 1)$$
$$\text{vec}(\mathbf{ABC}) = (\mathbf{C}' \otimes \mathbf{A})\text{vec}\mathbf{B}, \text{ if } \mathbf{ABC} \text{ defined}$$
$$\text{tr}(\mathbf{ABCD}) = (\text{vec}\mathbf{D}')'(\mathbf{C}' \otimes \mathbf{A})\text{vec}\mathbf{B} = (\text{vec}\mathbf{D})'(\mathbf{A} \otimes \mathbf{C}')\text{vec}\mathbf{B}'$$

since $\text{vec}\mathbf{B}' \equiv \text{vec}(\mathbf{B}')$

- differentiation

$$\frac{\partial \log|\mathbf{A}|}{\partial \mathbf{A}} = \mathbf{A}'^{-1} \text{ if } \mathbf{A} \text{ asymmetric}$$
$$\frac{\partial \log|\mathbf{A}|}{\partial \mathbf{A}} = 2\mathbf{A}^{-1} - \text{dg}\left(\mathbf{A}^{-1}\right) \text{ if } \mathbf{A} \text{ symmetric}$$
$$\frac{\partial \text{tr}(\mathbf{BA})}{\partial \mathbf{B}} = \mathbf{A}' \text{ if } \mathbf{B} \text{ asymmetric}$$
$$\frac{\partial \text{tr}(\mathbf{BA})}{\partial \mathbf{B}} = \mathbf{A} + \mathbf{A}' - \text{dg}\mathbf{A} \text{ if } \mathbf{B} \text{ symmetric}$$

$$\frac{\partial \mathbf{g}(\mathbf{f}(\mathbf{a}))}{\partial \mathbf{a}'} = \frac{\partial \mathbf{g}(\mathbf{b})}{\partial \mathbf{b}'}\frac{\partial \mathbf{f}(\mathbf{a})}{\partial \mathbf{a}'}$$

$$\text{with } \mathbf{f}(\cdot) : \mathbb{R}^m \mapsto \mathbb{R}^n,\ \mathbf{g}(\cdot) : \mathbb{R}^n \mapsto \mathbb{R}^p,\ \mathbf{b} = \mathbf{f}(\mathbf{a})$$

$$\frac{\partial \text{vec}(\mathbf{ABC})}{\partial (\text{vec}\mathbf{B})'} = \mathbf{C}' \otimes \mathbf{A}$$

$$\frac{\partial \text{vec}\left(\mathbf{A}^{-1}\right)}{\partial (\text{vec}\mathbf{A})'} = -\mathbf{A}^{-1\prime} \otimes \mathbf{A}^{-1}$$

- Jacobian matrix

$$\mathsf{V}\left[\text{vec}\,\mathbf{F}\left(\widehat{\mathbf{\Pi}}'\right)\right] = \mathbf{J}\mathsf{V}\left[\text{vec}\widehat{\mathbf{\Pi}}'\right]\mathbf{J}',$$

where $\mathbf{J}$ is the Jacobian matrix. This relation is only approximately valid, unless $\mathbf{F}(\cdot)$ is linear. Here $\mathsf{V}[\mathbf{x}]$ denotes the (co)variance matrix of the vector $\mathbf{x}$:

$$\mathsf{V}[\mathbf{x}] = \mathsf{E}\left[(\mathbf{x} - \mathsf{E}[\mathbf{x}])(\mathbf{x} - \mathsf{E}[\mathbf{x}])'\right],$$

and $\mathsf{E}[\cdot]$ is the expected value.

- partitioned matrices

Let $\mathbf{F} = \begin{pmatrix} \mathbf{A} & \mathbf{C} \\ \mathbf{B} & \mathbf{D} \end{pmatrix}$ be non-singular. If $\mathbf{A}$ and $\mathbf{H} = \mathbf{D} - \mathbf{BA}^{-1}\mathbf{C}$ are non-singular then:

$$\mathbf{F}^{-1} = \begin{pmatrix} \mathbf{A}^{-1} + \mathbf{A}^{-1}\mathbf{CH}^{-1}\mathbf{BA}^{-1} & -\mathbf{A}^{-1}\mathbf{CH}^{-1} \\ -\mathbf{H}^{-1}\mathbf{BA}^{-1} & \mathbf{H}^{-1} \end{pmatrix}.$$

If $\mathbf{D}$ and $\mathbf{G} = \mathbf{A} - \mathbf{CD}^{-1}\mathbf{B}$ are non-singular then:

$$\mathbf{F}^{-1} = \begin{pmatrix} \mathbf{G}^{-1} & -\mathbf{G}^{-1}\mathbf{CD}^{-1} \\ -\mathbf{D}^{-1}\mathbf{BG}^{-1} & \mathbf{D}^{-1} + \mathbf{D}^{-1}\mathbf{BG}^{-1}\mathbf{CD}^{-1} \end{pmatrix}.$$

If $\mathbf{A}$ is non-singular:

$$|\mathbf{F}| = \left|\mathbf{D} - \mathbf{BA}^{-1}\mathbf{C}\right| |\mathbf{A}|.$$

If $\mathbf{D}$ is non-singular:

$$|\mathbf{F}| = \left|\mathbf{A} - \mathbf{CD}^{-1}\mathbf{B}\right| |\mathbf{D}|.$$

Chapter 11

Econometric Analysis of the System

11.1 System estimation

As discussed in Chapter 9, the modelling process in PcGive starts with the statistical system, which is the maintained hypothesis against which further reductions can be tested. We assume in this chapter that all the variables in the system have been reduced to I(0), that the conditions for valid weak exogeneity of the $\mathbf{z}_t$ for the parameters of interest in the conditional system are satisfied, and write the system as:

$$\mathbf{y}_t = \boldsymbol{\Pi}\mathbf{w}_t + \mathbf{v}_t, \quad t = 1, \ldots, T, \tag{11.1}$$

with

$$\mathsf{E}\left[\mathbf{v}_t\right] = \mathbf{0} \text{ and } \mathsf{E}\left[\mathbf{v}_t\mathbf{v}_t'\right] = \boldsymbol{\Omega}, \tag{11.2}$$

where $\mathbf{w}$ here contains $\mathbf{z}$, r lags of $\mathbf{z}$ and m lags of $\mathbf{y}$:

$$\mathbf{w}_t' = \left(\mathbf{y}_{t-1}', \ldots, \mathbf{y}_{t-m}', \mathbf{z}_t', \ldots, \mathbf{z}_{t-r}'\right).$$

As in Chapter 9, we take $\mathbf{y}_t$ as an $(n \times 1)$ vector and $\mathbf{z}_t$ as $(q \times 1)$.

As an example of a system, consider the parsimonious unrestricted reduced form corresponding to the model which generated the artificial data set (see Chapter 10):

$$\begin{pmatrix} \Delta c_t \\ \Delta y_t \\ \Delta p_t \\ \Delta q_t \end{pmatrix} = \begin{pmatrix} \pi_{11} & \pi_{12} & \pi_{13} & \pi_{14} & \pi_{15} \\ \pi_{21} & \pi_{22} & \pi_{23} & \pi_{24} & \pi_{25} \\ \pi_{31} & \pi_{32} & \pi_{33} & \pi_{34} & \pi_{35} \\ \pi_{41} & \pi_{42} & \pi_{43} & \pi_{44} & \pi_{45} \end{pmatrix} \begin{pmatrix} \Delta p_{t-1} \\ 1 \\ (y-c)_{t-1} \\ (q-y)_{t-1} \\ q_{t-1} \end{pmatrix} + \begin{pmatrix} v_{1t} \\ v_{2t} \\ v_{3t} \\ v_{4t} \end{pmatrix}. \tag{11.3}$$

The system (11.1) can be written more compactly by using $\mathbf{Y}' = (\mathbf{y}_1\, \mathbf{y}_2 \ldots \mathbf{y}_T)$, and $\mathbf{W}'$, $\mathbf{V}'$ correspondingly:

$$\mathbf{Y}' = \boldsymbol{\Pi}\mathbf{W}' + \mathbf{V}', \tag{11.4}$$

in which $\mathbf{Y}'$ is $(n \times T)$, $\mathbf{W}'$ is $(k \times T)$ and $\boldsymbol{\Pi}$ is $(n \times k)$, with $k = nm + (r+1)q$ (assuming no lags have been dropped altogether, as in the example of equation (11.3)).

This is simply the multivariate linear regression model since there is a common set of regressors in each equation. Formulae for parameter and equation standard errors, test statistics etc. are generalized analogues of those in ordinary least squares (OLS), as in single equation modelling. Anderson (1984) contains an extensive discussion of the multivariate linear regression model, also see Spanos (1986). If $q = 0$ (no **z**s) the system is a vector autoregression (VAR): see, for example, Lütkepohl (1991) or Ooms (1994).

The multivariate least squares estimates of the coefficients and residual covariance are:

$$\widehat{\mathbf{\Pi}}' = \left(\mathbf{W}'\mathbf{W}\right)^{-1}\mathbf{W}'\mathbf{Y} \text{ and } \widetilde{\mathbf{\Omega}} = \widehat{\mathbf{V}}'\widehat{\mathbf{V}}/\left(T-k\right), \tag{11.5}$$

where the residuals are defined by:

$$\widehat{\mathbf{V}} = \mathbf{Y} - \mathbf{W}\widehat{\mathbf{\Pi}}' = \mathbf{M}_W\mathbf{Y}. \tag{11.6}$$

$\mathbf{M}_W$ is the symmetric idempotent projection matrix which annihilates $\mathbf{W}$:

$$\mathbf{M}_W = \mathbf{I}_T - \mathbf{W}(\mathbf{W}'\mathbf{W})^{-1}\mathbf{W}' = \mathbf{I}_T - \mathbf{Q}_W, \tag{11.7}$$

$\mathbf{M}_W\mathbf{W} = \mathbf{0}$, and $\mathbf{M}_W\mathbf{M}_W = \mathbf{M}_W$.

To derive the variance of the estimated coefficients, we need:

$$\mathsf{V}\left[\text{vec}\widehat{\mathbf{\Pi}}'\right] = \mathsf{E}\left[\text{vec}\left(\widehat{\mathbf{\Pi}}' - \mathbf{\Pi}'\right)\left(\text{vec}\left(\widehat{\mathbf{\Pi}}' - \mathbf{\Pi}'\right)\right)'\right]. \tag{11.8}$$

Note that vec$\mathbf{\Pi}'$ is an $(nk \times 1)$ column vector of coefficients, stacked by equation. In dynamic models, this calculation is intractable, and an asymptotic approximation is used as follows. It is convenient to consider the transpose of (11.4) in vectorized form, with $\boldsymbol{\pi} = \text{vec}\mathbf{\Pi}'$, $\mathbf{y} = \text{vec}\mathbf{Y}$ and $\mathbf{v} = \text{vec}\mathbf{V}$:

$$\mathbf{y} = (\mathbf{I}_n \otimes \mathbf{W})\boldsymbol{\pi} + \mathbf{v}. \tag{11.9}$$

So:

$$\widehat{\boldsymbol{\pi}} = \left((\mathbf{I}_n \otimes \mathbf{W})'(\mathbf{I}_n \otimes \mathbf{W})\right)^{-1}(\mathbf{I}_n \otimes \mathbf{W})'\mathbf{y} = \left(\mathbf{I}_n \otimes (\mathbf{W}'\mathbf{W})^{-1}\mathbf{W}'\right)\mathbf{y} \tag{11.10}$$

and:

$$\widehat{\boldsymbol{\pi}} - \boldsymbol{\pi} = \left(\mathbf{I}_n \otimes (\mathbf{W}'\mathbf{W})^{-1}\mathbf{W}'\right)\mathbf{v}. \tag{11.11}$$

In the case of fixed $\mathbf{W}$, direct evaluation yield:

$$\begin{aligned}\mathsf{E}\left[(\widehat{\boldsymbol{\pi}} - \boldsymbol{\pi})(\widehat{\boldsymbol{\pi}} - \boldsymbol{\pi})'\right] &= \left(\mathbf{I}_n \otimes (\mathbf{W}'\mathbf{W})^{-1}\mathbf{W}'\right)(\mathbf{\Omega} \otimes \mathbf{I}_n)\left(\mathbf{I}_n \otimes \mathbf{W}(\mathbf{W}'\mathbf{W})^{-1}\right) \\ &= \mathbf{\Omega} \otimes (\mathbf{W}'\mathbf{W})^{-1}.\end{aligned} \tag{11.12}$$

A corresponding formula holds asymptotically (when suitably scaled by T) in $\mathsf{I}(0)$ dynamic processes:

$$\sqrt{T}\left(\widehat{\boldsymbol{\pi}}-\boldsymbol{\pi}\right) \xrightarrow{D} \mathsf{N}_{n^2}\left[\mathbf{0}, \boldsymbol{\Omega}\otimes\mathbf{S}_W^{-1}\right] \text{ where } \mathbf{S}_W = \underset{T\to\infty}{\text{plim}}\, T^{-1}\mathbf{W}'\mathbf{W}. \tag{11.13}$$

The estimated variance matrix of the coefficients is:

$$\widetilde{\mathsf{V}\left[\text{vec}\widehat{\boldsymbol{\Pi}}'\right]} = \widetilde{\boldsymbol{\Omega}}\otimes\left(\mathbf{W}'\mathbf{W}\right)^{-1} \tag{11.14}$$

The variance matrix of coefficients derived from $\boldsymbol{\Pi}$, $\boldsymbol{\Psi} = \mathbf{f}\left(\boldsymbol{\Pi}'\right)$, has the general form:

$$\mathsf{V}\left[\text{vec}\,\mathbf{f}\left(\widehat{\boldsymbol{\Pi}}'\right)\right] = \mathsf{V}\left[\text{vec}\widehat{\boldsymbol{\Psi}}\right] \simeq \mathbf{J}'\mathsf{V}\left[\text{vec}\widehat{\boldsymbol{\Pi}}'\right]\mathbf{J} \tag{11.15}$$

where $\mathbf{J}$ is the Jacobian matrix of the transformation $\boldsymbol{\Psi} = \mathbf{f}\left(\boldsymbol{\Pi}'\right)$:

$$\mathbf{J} = \frac{\partial \text{vec}\boldsymbol{\Psi}}{\partial\left(\text{vec}\boldsymbol{\Pi}'\right)'}. \tag{11.16}$$

This approximation is asymptotically valid in that from (11.13), when $\boldsymbol{\psi} = \text{vec}\boldsymbol{\Psi}$:

$$\sqrt{T}\left(\widehat{\boldsymbol{\psi}}-\boldsymbol{\psi}\right) \xrightarrow{D} \mathsf{N}_{ns}\left[\mathbf{0}, \mathbf{J}\left(\boldsymbol{\Omega}\otimes\mathbf{S}_W^{-1}\right)\mathbf{J}'\right].$$

With $\widehat{\boldsymbol{\Pi}}$ an $(n\times k)$ matrix and $\widehat{\boldsymbol{\Psi}}$ an $(s\times n)$ matrix, $\mathbf{J}$ will be $(ns\times nk)$.

11.2 Maximum likelihood estimation

Under the assumptions that (11.1) is the DGP, $\mathbf{v}_t \sim \mathsf{IN}_n[\mathbf{0}, \boldsymbol{\Omega}]$, and that all the coefficient matrices are constant, the log-likelihood function $\ell\left(\boldsymbol{\Pi}, \boldsymbol{\Omega}|\mathbf{Y}, \mathbf{W}\right)$ depends on the multivariate normal distribution:

$$\begin{aligned} \ell\left(\boldsymbol{\Pi}, \boldsymbol{\Omega} \mid \mathbf{Y}, \mathbf{W}\right) &= -\tfrac{Tn}{2}\log 2\pi - \tfrac{T}{2}\log|\boldsymbol{\Omega}| - \tfrac{1}{2}\sum_{t=1}^{T}\mathbf{v}_t'\boldsymbol{\Omega}^{-1}\mathbf{v}_t \\ &= K - \tfrac{T}{2}\log|\boldsymbol{\Omega}| - \tfrac{1}{2}\text{tr}\left(\boldsymbol{\Omega}^{-1}\mathbf{V}'\mathbf{V}\right) \\ &= K + \tfrac{T}{2}\log\left|\boldsymbol{\Omega}^{-1}\right| - \tfrac{1}{2}\text{tr}\left(\boldsymbol{\Omega}^{-1}\mathbf{V}'\mathbf{V}\right). \end{aligned} \tag{11.17}$$

The sample is denoted $t = 1, \ldots, T$ after creating all necessary lags.

We first concentrate $\ell\left(\cdot\right)$ with respect to $\boldsymbol{\Omega}$, which involves differentiating (11.17) with respect to $\boldsymbol{\Omega}^{-1}$ and equating that to $\mathbf{0}$. Taking account of its symmetry (that is, $\omega_{ij} = \omega_{ji}$) we find:

$$2\mathbf{V}'\mathbf{V} - \text{dg}\left(\mathbf{V}'\mathbf{V}\right) = 2T\boldsymbol{\Omega} - T\text{dg}\left(\boldsymbol{\Omega}\right), \tag{11.18}$$

evaluated at $\mathbf{\Omega} = \mathbf{\Omega}_c$, yielding:

$$\mathbf{\Omega}_c = T^{-1}\sum_{t=1}^{T} \mathbf{v}_t\mathbf{v}_t' = T^{-1}\mathbf{V}'\mathbf{V}. \tag{11.19}$$

This is a rather natural result, given that $\mathsf{E}[T^{-1}\mathbf{V}'\mathbf{V}] = \mathbf{\Omega}$. The resulting concentrated log-likelihood function (CLF) $\ell_c(\mathbf{\Pi}|\mathbf{Y},\mathbf{W};\mathbf{\Omega})$ is:

$$\begin{aligned} \ell_c(\mathbf{\Pi} \mid \mathbf{Y},\mathbf{W};\mathbf{\Omega}) &= K - \tfrac{T}{2}\log|\mathbf{V}'\mathbf{V}| + \tfrac{Tn\log T}{2} - \tfrac{Tn}{2} \\ &= K^* - \tfrac{T}{2}\log\left|(\mathbf{Y}' - \mathbf{\Pi}\mathbf{W}')(\mathbf{Y} - \mathbf{W}\mathbf{\Pi}')\right|. \end{aligned} \tag{11.20}$$

We know the minimizer of $(\mathbf{Y}' - \mathbf{\Pi}\mathbf{W}')(\mathbf{Y} - \mathbf{W}\mathbf{\Pi}')$ from least-squares theory, and find the maximum likelihood estimates:

$$\widehat{\mathbf{\Pi}}' = (\mathbf{W}'\mathbf{W})^{-1}\mathbf{W}'\mathbf{Y} \text{ and } \widehat{\mathbf{\Omega}} = T^{-1}\widehat{\mathbf{V}}'\widehat{\mathbf{V}}, \tag{11.21}$$

The attained maximum of $\ell(\cdot)$ is:

$$\widehat{\ell} = K_c - \frac{T}{2}\log\left|\widehat{\mathbf{\Omega}}\right| \tag{11.22}$$

with:

$$K_c = \frac{-Tn}{2}(1 + \log 2\pi). \tag{11.23}$$

Note that $\widehat{\mathbf{\Omega}}$ is scaled by T, whereas $\widetilde{\mathbf{\Omega}}$ is scaled by $T - k$. This convention is adopted throughout the book.

11.3 Recursive estimation

Recursive least squares (RLS) is OLS where coefficients are estimated sequentially, and is a powerful tool for investigating parameter constancy. The sample starts from a minimal number of observations, and statistics are recalculated adding observations one at a time. The multivariate version of RLS is analogous to univariate RLS, and involves little additional computation since the formulae for updating the regressor second-moment matrix are identical owing to the common regressors. Write $\mathbf{W}_t' = (\mathbf{w}_1 \ldots \mathbf{w}_t)$. The parameter estimates up to t are:

$$\widehat{\mathbf{\Pi}}_t' = (\mathbf{W}_t'\mathbf{W}_t)^{-1}\mathbf{W}_t'\mathbf{Y}_t \text{ and } \widetilde{\mathbf{\Omega}}_t = \widehat{\mathbf{V}}_t'\widehat{\mathbf{V}}_t/(t-k). \tag{11.24}$$

If the sample is increased by one observation, we can avoid inverting the second moment matrix by using the following rank-one updating formula for the inverse:

$$(\mathbf{W}_{t+1}'\mathbf{W}_{t+1})^{-1} = (\mathbf{W}_t'\mathbf{W}_t)^{-1} - \frac{\boldsymbol{\lambda}_{t+1}\boldsymbol{\lambda}_{t+1}'}{1 + \mathbf{w}_{t+1}'\boldsymbol{\lambda}_{t+1}} \tag{11.25}$$

where:

$$\boldsymbol{\lambda}_{t+1} = \left(\mathbf{W}_t'\mathbf{W}_t\right)^{-1}\mathbf{w}_{t+1}.$$

From this, $\widehat{\boldsymbol{\Pi}}_{t+1}$ can be calculated by application of (11.24). To update $\widetilde{\boldsymbol{\Omega}}_t$, we define the innovations $\boldsymbol{\nu}_t$ and the standardized innovations (or recursive residuals, see Harvey, 1990) $\mathbf{s}_t$:

$$\boldsymbol{\nu}_t = \mathbf{y}_t - \widehat{\boldsymbol{\Pi}}_{t-1}\mathbf{w}_t,\ \ \mathbf{s}_t = \frac{\boldsymbol{\nu}_t}{\sqrt{1+\mathbf{w}_t'\boldsymbol{\lambda}_t}}. \tag{11.26}$$

Successive innovations are independent, $\mathsf{E}[\boldsymbol{\nu}_t\boldsymbol{\nu}_{t+1}'] = 0$. Now (see, for example, Hendry, 1995):

$$\widehat{\mathbf{V}}_{t+1}'\widehat{\mathbf{V}}_{t+1} = \widehat{\mathbf{V}}_t'\widehat{\mathbf{V}}_t + \mathbf{s}_{t+1}\mathbf{s}_{t+1}', \tag{11.27}$$

from which $\widetilde{\boldsymbol{\Omega}}_{t+1}$ and $\widehat{\boldsymbol{\Omega}}_{t+1}$ can be derived. The 1-step residuals at $t+1$ are $\mathbf{y}_{t+1} - \widehat{\boldsymbol{\Pi}}_{t+1}\mathbf{w}_{t+1}$. Sequences of parameter constancy tests are readily computed and their use for investigating parameter constancy is discussed in §11.8.1.

11.4 Unrestricted variables

If any variables (such as, for example, the constant, seasonal shift factors or trend) are included unrestrictedly in all equations, the likelihood function can be concentrated with respect to these. The stochastic part of the system is then rewritten as:

$$\mathbf{Y}' = \boldsymbol{\Pi}\mathbf{W}' + \mathbf{D}\mathbf{S}' + \mathbf{V}' \tag{11.28}$$

where $\mathbf{D}$ is the $(n \times s)$ of coefficients of the unrestricted variables, and $\mathbf{S}$ is the $T \times s$ matrix of observations on these variables (where, for example, $s = 1$ if only a constant term is partialled out). The log-likelihood for (11.28) is:

$$\begin{aligned}
&\ell\left(\boldsymbol{\Pi},\mathbf{D},\boldsymbol{\Omega} \mid \mathbf{Y},\mathbf{W},\mathbf{S}\right)\\
&= K + \tfrac{T}{2}\log\left|\boldsymbol{\Omega}^{-1}\right| - \tfrac{1}{2}\mathrm{tr}\left(\boldsymbol{\Omega}^{-1}(\mathbf{Y}' - \boldsymbol{\Pi}\mathbf{W}' - \mathbf{D}\mathbf{S}')\left(\mathbf{Y} - \mathbf{W}\boldsymbol{\Pi}' - \mathbf{S}\mathbf{D}'\right)\right)\\
&= K + \tfrac{T}{2}\log\left|\boldsymbol{\Omega}^{-1}\right|\\
&\quad -\tfrac{1}{2}\mathrm{tr}\left(\boldsymbol{\Omega}^{-1}\left\{\left(\mathbf{Y}' - \boldsymbol{\Pi}\mathbf{W}'\right)\left(\mathbf{Y} - \mathbf{W}\boldsymbol{\Pi}'\right) - 2\mathbf{Y}'\mathbf{S}\mathbf{D}' + 2\boldsymbol{\Pi}\mathbf{W}'\mathbf{S}\mathbf{D}' + \mathbf{D}\mathbf{S}'\mathbf{S}\mathbf{D}'\right\}\right).
\end{aligned} \tag{11.29}$$

Therefore, since $\mathbf{D}$ is unrestricted:

$$\frac{\partial\ell\left(\cdot\right)}{\partial\mathbf{D}} = \tfrac{1}{2}\,\boldsymbol{\Omega}^{-1}\left(2\mathbf{Y}'\mathbf{S} - 2\boldsymbol{\Pi}\mathbf{W}'\mathbf{S} - 2\mathbf{D}\mathbf{S}'\mathbf{S}\right). \tag{11.30}$$

Equating the derivative to zero yields the solution $\mathbf{D}_c'$ as a function of $\boldsymbol{\Pi}'$:

$$\mathbf{D}_c' = \left(\mathbf{S}'\mathbf{S}\right)^{-1}\mathbf{S}'\left(\mathbf{Y} - \mathbf{W}\boldsymbol{\Pi}'\right) = \mathbf{P}_Y' - \mathbf{P}_W'\boldsymbol{\Pi}'. \tag{11.31}$$

and in turn the maximum likelihood estimator of $\mathbf{D}'$ is:

$$\widehat{\mathbf{D}}' = \mathbf{P}'_Y - \mathbf{P}'_W \widehat{\mathbf{\Pi}}'. \tag{11.32}$$

$\mathbf{P}'_W, \mathbf{P}'_Y$ are the 'prior coefficients' from regressing $\mathbf{W}$ on $\mathbf{S}$ and $\mathbf{Y}$ on $\mathbf{S}$ respectively. Although $\mathbf{\Pi}$ is not known at the time $\mathbf{D}$ is eliminated, the effect of (11.31) is to remove $\mathbf{S}$ from (11.28) and replace the original data by deviations from the 'seasonal' means. Using (11.7), we let $\check{\mathbf{Y}} = \mathbf{M}_S\mathbf{Y}$ and $\check{\mathbf{W}} = \mathbf{M}_S\mathbf{W}$ denote the 'deseasonalized' data (that is, the residuals from the least-squares regressions of $\mathbf{Y}$ and $\mathbf{W}$ on $\mathbf{S}$; we shall also refer to these as the data after 'partialling out' $\mathbf{S}$).

The CLF is:

$$\ell_c\left(\mathbf{\Pi}, \mathbf{\Omega} \mid \mathbf{Y}, \mathbf{W}, \mathbf{S}; \mathbf{D}\right) = K + \frac{T}{2}\log\left|\mathbf{\Omega}^{-1}\right| - \tfrac{1}{2}\operatorname{tr}\left(\mathbf{\Omega}^{-1}\left(\check{\mathbf{Y}}' - \mathbf{\Pi}\check{\mathbf{W}}'\right)\left(\check{\mathbf{Y}} - \check{\mathbf{W}}\mathbf{\Pi}'\right)\right) \tag{11.33}$$

Now $\mathbf{\Pi}$ can be estimated using:

$$\check{\mathbf{Y}}' = \mathbf{\Pi}\check{\mathbf{W}}' + \check{\mathbf{V}}'. \tag{11.34}$$

The formula for the variance matrix of $\widehat{\mathbf{D}}$ after obtaining $\widehat{\mathbf{\Pi}}$ is derived in Hendry (1971). Using the Jacobian matrix:

$$\mathbf{J}_S = -\left(\mathbf{I}_n \otimes \mathbf{P}'_W\right), \tag{11.35}$$

it is given as:

$$\widetilde{\mathsf{V}\left[\text{vec}\widehat{\mathbf{D}}'\right]} = \widetilde{\mathbf{\Omega}} \otimes \left(\mathbf{S}'\mathbf{S}\right)^{-1} + \widehat{\mathbf{J}}_S \widetilde{\mathsf{V}\left[\text{vec}\widehat{\mathbf{\Pi}}'\right]} \widehat{\mathbf{J}}'_S \tag{11.36}$$

with:

$$\widetilde{\mathsf{V}\left[\text{vec}\widehat{\mathbf{\Pi}}'\right]} = \widetilde{\mathbf{\Omega}} \otimes \left(\check{\mathbf{W}}'\check{\mathbf{W}}\right)^{-1}. \tag{11.37}$$

Thus, the model can be stated throughout in terms of deseasonalized data $\check{\mathbf{Y}}$, $\check{\mathbf{W}}$, and multivariate least squares applied to the smaller specification.

11.5 Forecasting

Forecasting may be done 1-step ahead or h-steps ahead. The former are *ex post* (or static): any lagged information required to form forecasts is based on observed values. The latter are *ex ante* (or dynamic) and will reuse forecasts from previous period(s) if required. Consider the simple 1-equation system:

$$y_t = \pi_1 y_{t-1} + \pi_2 y_{t-2} + \pi_3 z_t + v_t$$

estimated over $t = 1, \ldots, T$; z_t is not modelled. Assuming a forecast horizon of $H = 3$, we find:

	static forecast	dynamic forecast
$T+1$	$\widehat{y}_{T+1} = \widehat{\pi}_1 y_T + \widehat{\pi}_2 y_{T-1} + \widehat{\pi}_3 z_{T+1}$	$\widehat{y}_{T+1} = \widehat{\pi}_1 y_T + \widehat{\pi}_2 y_{T-1} + \widehat{\pi}_3 z_{T+1}$
$T+2$	$\widehat{y}_{T+2} = \widehat{\pi}_1 y_{T+1} + \widehat{\pi}_2 y_T + \widehat{\pi}_3 z_{T+2}$	$\widehat{y}_{T+2} = \widehat{\pi}_1 \widehat{y}_{T+1} + \widehat{\pi}_2 y_T + \widehat{\pi}_3 z_{T+2}$
$T+3$	$\widehat{y}_{T+3} = \widehat{\pi}_1 y_{T+2} + \widehat{\pi}_2 y_{T+1} + \widehat{\pi}_3 z_{T+3}$	$\widehat{y}_{T+3} = \widehat{\pi}_1 \widehat{y}_{T+2} + \widehat{\pi}_2 \widehat{y}_{T+1} + \widehat{\pi}_3 z_{T+3}$

(11.38)

Both types of forecast require data for $t = 1, \ldots, T$ to obtain the coefficient estimates. Beyond that, static forecasts require z for $t = T+1, \ldots, T+H$ and y up to $T+H-1$, whereas dynamic forecasts only need z for $t = T+1, \ldots, T+H$. In both types of forecast, the parameter estimates in PcGive are not updated over the forecast period. This would be possible in principle for static forecasts, and would then mimic an operational procedure where a system was re-estimated each period on the maximum data prior to forecasting. However, given the unrealistic assumption that the future z are known, we prefer to think of static forecasts as delivering information about parameter constancy, and therefore use the usual (rather than the recursive) residuals.

To distinguish the two types of forecast we let $\widehat{y}_{T+i,h}$ denote the h-step forecast made for period $T+i$ $(i \geq h)$ and based on parameter estimation up to T. The h-step forecasts use actual values for lagged ys which go further back than h periods. An extreme case is 1-step forecasts, $\widehat{y}_{T+h,1}$ $(h = 1, \ldots, H)$, which always use actual values for lagged ys. Dynamic forecasts, $\widehat{y}_{T+h,h}$ $(h = 1, \ldots, H)$, are at the other end of the spectrum: they never use actual values beyond T. In addition to these two cases it is possible to define intermediate (h) step forecasts. Using the new notation and dropping the zs:

	1-step	2-step	3-step
$T+1$	$\widehat{y}_{T+1,1}$	$-$	$-$
$T+2$	$\widehat{y}_{T+2,1}$	$\widehat{y}_{T+2,2} = \widehat{\pi}_1 \widehat{y}_{T+1,1} + \widehat{\pi}_2 y_T$	$-$
$T+3$	$\widehat{y}_{T+3,1}$	$\widehat{y}_{T+3,2} = \widehat{\pi}_1 \widehat{y}_{T+2,1} + \widehat{\pi}_2 y_{T+1}$	$\widehat{y}_{T+3,3} = \widehat{\pi}_1 \widehat{y}_{T+2,2} + \widehat{\pi}_2 \widehat{y}_{T+1,1}$
$\vdots$	$\vdots$	$\vdots$	$\vdots$
$T+i$	$\widehat{y}_{T+i,1}$	$\widehat{y}_{T+i,2} = \widehat{\pi}_1 \widehat{y}_{T+i-1,1} + \widehat{\pi}_2 y_{T+i-2}$	$\widehat{y}_{T+i,3} = \widehat{\pi}_1 \widehat{y}_{T+i-1,2} + \widehat{\pi}_2 \widehat{y}_{T+i-2,1}$

(11.39)

In this terminology, the static forecasts are equivalent to the 1-step forecasts, whereas the dynamic forecasts are the sequence of $1, 2, \ldots, H$ step forecasts.

The innovations defined in (11.26) can be seen as 1-step forecast errors, where the parameter estimates are updated after each step. From (11.41) below, the variance matrix of the 1-step forecast error vector in the notation of (11.26) is $\mathbf{\Omega}\,(1 + \mathbf{w}_t' \boldsymbol{\lambda}_t)$.

11.5.1 Static forecasting

To test for predictive failure, 1-step forecast errors $\mathbf{e}_{T+i,1} = \mathbf{y}_{T+i} - \widehat{\mathbf{y}}_{T+i,1}$ are calculated as:

$$
\begin{aligned}
\mathbf{e}_{T+i,1} &= \mathbf{\Pi w}_{T+i} + \mathbf{v}_{T+i} - \widehat{\mathbf{\Pi}}\mathbf{w}_{T+i} \\
&= \left(\mathbf{\Pi} - \widehat{\mathbf{\Pi}}\right)\mathbf{w}_{T+i} + \mathbf{v}_{T+i} \\
\mathbf{e}'_{T+i,1} &= \mathbf{w}'_{T+i}\left(\mathbf{\Pi} - \widehat{\mathbf{\Pi}}\right)' + \mathbf{v}'_{T+i} \\
\text{vec}\left(\mathbf{e}'_{T+i,1}\right) = \mathbf{e}_{T+i,1} &= \left(\mathbf{I}_n \otimes \mathbf{w}'_{T+i}\right)\text{vec}\left(\mathbf{\Pi}' - \widehat{\mathbf{\Pi}}'\right) + \mathbf{v}_{T+i}
\end{aligned}
\tag{11.40}
$$

Note that $\mathbf{e}_t$ is $(n \times 1)$ and that $\mathbf{I}_n \otimes \mathbf{w}'_{T+i}$ is $(n \times nk)$. To a first approximation, $\widehat{\mathbf{\Pi}}$ is an unbiased estimator of $\mathbf{\Pi}$ for forecasting purposes (see Clements and Hendry, 1998b), so $\mathsf{E}[\mathbf{e}_{T+i,1}] \simeq \mathbf{0}$ and:

$$
\begin{aligned}
\mathsf{V}\left[\mathbf{e}_{T+i,1}\right] &= \mathbf{\Omega} + \left(\mathbf{I}_n \otimes \mathbf{w}'_{T+i}\right)\mathsf{V}\left[\text{vec}\widehat{\mathbf{\Pi}}'\right]\left(\mathbf{I}_n \otimes \mathbf{w}_{T+i}\right) \\
&= \mathbf{\Omega} + \mathbf{\Omega} \otimes \mathbf{w}'_{T+i}\left(\mathbf{W}'\mathbf{W}\right)^{-1}\mathbf{w}_{T+i} \\
&= \mathbf{\Omega}\left(1 + \mathbf{w}'_{T+i}\left(\mathbf{W}'\mathbf{W}\right)^{-1}\mathbf{w}_{T+i}\right) \\
&= \mathbf{\Psi}_{T+i},
\end{aligned}
\tag{11.41}
$$

so that:

$$
\mathbf{e}_{T+i,1} \,\widetilde{app}\, \mathsf{IN}_n\left[\mathbf{0}, \mathbf{\Psi}_{T+i}\right], \tag{11.42}
$$

where $\mathbf{\Psi}_{T+i}$ reflects both innovation and parameter uncertainty (also see Chong and Hendry, 1986 and Clements and Hendry, 1994). The parameter uncertainty is of order T^{-1} and tends to be small relative to $\mathbf{\Omega}$. However, the derivation assumes constant parameters and homoscedastic innovation errors over the forecast period, which may be invalid assumptions in practice – see Clements and Hendry (1998b) on the general issue of forecasting under conditions of parameter change.

To derive forecast accuracy and constancy tests we require the full variance matrix of all forecast errors. Transposing the error vector of (11.40), and stacking the H rows on top of each other we may write (11.40) as:

$$
\mathbf{E} = \mathbf{W}_H\left(\mathbf{\Pi} - \widehat{\mathbf{\Pi}}\right)' + \mathbf{V}_H. \tag{11.43}
$$

$\mathbf{E}$ is the $(H \times n)$ matrix of 1-step forecast errors, $\mathbf{W}_H$ is the $(H \times k)$ matrix of data for the forecast period $T+1, \ldots, T+H$. Proceeding in similar fashion:

$$
\mathbf{e} = \text{vec}\mathbf{E} = \left(\mathbf{I}_H \otimes \mathbf{W}_H\right)\text{vec}\left(\mathbf{\Pi}' - \widehat{\mathbf{\Pi}}'\right) + \text{vec}\mathbf{V}_H. \tag{11.44}
$$

So again $\mathsf{E}[\mathbf{e}] = \mathbf{0}$, and:

$$\mathsf{E}[\mathbf{e}\mathbf{e}'] = \mathbf{\Omega} \otimes \left(\mathbf{I}_H + \mathbf{W}_H \left(\mathbf{W}'\mathbf{W}\right)^{-1} \mathbf{W}_H'\right) = \mathbf{\Psi}. \tag{11.45}$$

Under the null of no parameter change, tests can be based on the following approximate test statistics over a forecast horizon of H periods:

$$\begin{aligned} \xi_1 &= \mathbf{e}'\left(\widetilde{\mathbf{\Omega}} \otimes \mathbf{I}_H\right)^{-1}\mathbf{e} = \textstyle\sum_{i=1}^{H} \mathbf{e}_{T+i}'\widetilde{\mathbf{\Omega}}^{-1}\mathbf{e}_{T+i} && \widetilde{app}\ \chi^2(nH) \\ \xi_2 &= \textstyle\sum_{i=1}^{H} \mathbf{e}_{T+i}'\widetilde{\mathbf{\Psi}}_{T+i}^{-1}\mathbf{e}_{T+i} && \widetilde{app}\ \chi^2(nH) \\ \xi_3 &= \mathbf{e}'\widetilde{\mathbf{\Psi}}^{-1}\mathbf{e} && \widetilde{app}\ \chi^2(nH) \\ \eta_i &= (nH)^{-1}\xi_i,\ i=1,2,3 && \widetilde{app}\ \mathsf{F}(nH, T-k) \end{aligned} \tag{11.46}$$

The first test arises from ξ_2 when $\widetilde{\mathbf{\Psi}}_{T+i} = \widetilde{\mathbf{\Omega}}_H$ is used, thus ignoring the parameter uncertainty. This implies $\xi_1 \geq \xi_2$. The η_i are the F equivalents of ξ_i and are expected to have better small-sample properties. The form of ξ_3 as given in (11.46) requires an $(nH \times nH)$ matrix, and is computationally inconvenient. Analogous to the procedure used in single equation modelling, the test may be rewritten as:

$$\begin{aligned} \xi_3 &= \operatorname{tr}\left(\widetilde{\mathbf{\Omega}}^{-1}\mathbf{E}'\left(\mathbf{I}_H + \mathbf{W}_H\left(\mathbf{W}'\mathbf{W}\right)^{-1}\mathbf{W}_H'\right)^{-1}\mathbf{E}\right) \\ &= \operatorname{tr}\left(\widetilde{\mathbf{\Omega}}^{-1}\mathbf{E}'\left(\mathbf{I}_H - \mathbf{W}_H\left(\mathbf{W}'\mathbf{W} + \mathbf{W}_H'\mathbf{W}_H\right)^{-1}\mathbf{W}_H'\right)\mathbf{E}\right) \end{aligned} \tag{11.47}$$

The first line involves inversion of an $(H \times H)$ matrix, whereas the inversion in the second expression is $(k \times k)$. Single equation output, which has $n = 1$, reports ξ_1 and η_3.

11.5.2 Dynamic forecasting

To derive expressions for dynamic forecasts, we need to take the lag structure of $\mathbf{y}$ into account. Consider a simple system with one lag of the dependent variable:

$$\mathbf{y}_t = \boldsymbol{\pi}_1\mathbf{y}_{t-1} + \boldsymbol{\pi}_2\mathbf{z}_t + \mathbf{v}_t \tag{11.48}$$

Using backward substitution for any h $(h = 1, \ldots, H)$ commencing at T we find:

$$\begin{aligned} \mathbf{y}_{T+h} &= \boldsymbol{\pi}_1\mathbf{y}_{T+h-1} + \boldsymbol{\pi}_2\mathbf{z}_{T+h} + \mathbf{v}_{T+h} \\ &= \boldsymbol{\pi}_1\left(\mathbf{y}_{T+h-2} + \boldsymbol{\pi}_2\mathbf{z}_{T+h-1} + \mathbf{v}_{T+h-1}\right) + \boldsymbol{\pi}_2\mathbf{z}_{T+h} + \mathbf{v}_{T+h} \\ &= \boldsymbol{\pi}_1^h\mathbf{y}_T + \sum_{j=0}^{h-1}\boldsymbol{\pi}_1^j\boldsymbol{\pi}_2\mathbf{z}_{T+h-j} + \sum_{j=0}^{h-1}\boldsymbol{\pi}_1^j\mathbf{v}_{T+h-j}. \end{aligned} \tag{11.49}$$

The forecast at h is:

$$\widehat{\mathbf{y}}_{T+h,h} = \widehat{\boldsymbol{\pi}}_1^h \mathbf{y}_T + \sum_{j=0}^{h-1} \widehat{\boldsymbol{\pi}}_1^j \widehat{\boldsymbol{\pi}}_2 \mathbf{z}_{T+h-j}, \tag{11.50}$$

so that the forecast error at h is:

$$\begin{aligned}\mathbf{e}_{T+h,h} &= \mathbf{y}_{T+h} - \widehat{\mathbf{y}}_{T+h,h} \\ &= (\boldsymbol{\pi}_1^h - \widehat{\boldsymbol{\pi}}_1^h)\mathbf{y}_T + \sum_{j=0}^{h-1}(\boldsymbol{\pi}_1^j \boldsymbol{\pi}_2 - \widehat{\boldsymbol{\pi}}_1^j \widehat{\boldsymbol{\pi}}_2)\mathbf{z}_{T+h-j} + \sum_{j=0}^{h-1} \boldsymbol{\pi}_1^j \mathbf{v}_{T+h-j}.\end{aligned} \tag{11.51}$$

When the parameter uncertainty is negligible, the forecast error is:

$$\mathbf{e}_{T+h,h} = \sum_{j=0}^{h-1} \boldsymbol{\pi}_1^j \mathbf{v}_{T+h-j} \tag{11.52}$$

with variance:

$$\mathsf{V}\left[\mathbf{e}_{T+h,h}\right] = \mathsf{E}\left[\sum_{i=0}^{h-1}\sum_{j=0}^{h-1} \boldsymbol{\pi}_1^i \mathbf{v}_{T+h-i} \mathbf{v}_{T+h-j}' \boldsymbol{\pi}_1^{j\prime}\right] = \sum_{j=0}^{h-1} \boldsymbol{\pi}_1^j \boldsymbol{\Omega} \boldsymbol{\pi}_1^{j\prime} \tag{11.53}$$

since $\mathsf{E}\left[\mathbf{v}_i \mathbf{v}_j'\right] = \mathbf{0}$ for $i \neq j$; $\mathsf{E}\left[\mathbf{v}_i \mathbf{v}_i'\right] = \boldsymbol{\Omega}$. The next section takes parameter uncertainty into account.

With m lags of the dependent variable we may still use expression (11.53) by writing the system:

$$\mathbf{y}_t = \sum_{i=1}^{m} \boldsymbol{\pi}_i \mathbf{y}_{t-i} + \sum_{j=0}^{r} \boldsymbol{\pi}_{m+1+j} \mathbf{z}_{t-j} + \mathbf{v}_t \tag{11.54}$$

in *companion form*:

$$\begin{pmatrix} \mathbf{y}_t \\ \mathbf{y}_{t-1} \\ \vdots \\ \mathbf{y}_{t-m+1} \end{pmatrix} = \begin{pmatrix} \boldsymbol{\pi}_1 & \boldsymbol{\pi}_2 & \cdots & \boldsymbol{\pi}_{m-1} & \boldsymbol{\pi}_m \\ \mathbf{I}_n & \mathbf{0} & \cdots & \mathbf{0} & \mathbf{0} \\ \mathbf{0} & \mathbf{I}_n & \cdots & \mathbf{0} & \mathbf{0} \\ \vdots & \vdots & \ddots & \vdots & \vdots \\ \mathbf{0} & \mathbf{0} & \cdots & \mathbf{I}_n & \mathbf{0} \end{pmatrix} \begin{pmatrix} \mathbf{y}_{t-1} \\ \mathbf{y}_{t-2} \\ \vdots \\ \mathbf{y}_{t-m} \end{pmatrix}$$

$$+ \begin{pmatrix} \boldsymbol{\pi}_{m+1} & \cdots & \boldsymbol{\pi}_{m+1+r} \\ \mathbf{0} & \cdots & \mathbf{0} \\ \vdots & \ddots & \vdots \\ \mathbf{0} & \cdots & \mathbf{0} \end{pmatrix} \begin{pmatrix} \mathbf{z}_t \\ \vdots \\ \mathbf{z}_{t-r} \end{pmatrix} + \begin{pmatrix} \mathbf{v}_t \\ \mathbf{0} \\ \vdots \\ \mathbf{0} \end{pmatrix}$$

or more briefly:

$$\mathbf{y}_t^* = \mathbf{D}\mathbf{y}_{t-1}^* + \mathbf{E}\mathbf{z}_t^* + \mathbf{v}_t^*. \tag{11.55}$$

With the companion matrix, $\mathbf{D}$, of dimension $(nm \times nm)$, taking the place of $\boldsymbol{\pi}_1$ in (11.53), the variance of the forecast error $\mathbf{e}_{T+h,h}^* = \mathbf{y}_{T+h}^* - \widehat{\mathbf{y}}_{T+h,h}^*$ becomes:

$$\mathsf{V}\left[\mathbf{e}_{T+h,h}^*\right] = \sum_{j=0}^{h-1} \mathbf{D}^j \mho \mathbf{D}^{j\prime}, \quad \mho = \begin{pmatrix} \boldsymbol{\Omega} & \mathbf{0} & \cdots \\ \mathbf{0} & \mathbf{0} & \cdots \\ \vdots & \vdots & \ddots \end{pmatrix}. \tag{11.56}$$

The relevant part of this expression is the $(n \times n)$ top-left block.

The system must characterize the economy as accurately in the forecast period as it did over the estimation sample if the forecast errors are to be from the same distribution as that assumed in (11.55) (ignoring the sampling variation owing to estimating $\mathbf{D}$). This is a strong requirement, and seems unlikely to be met unless $\mathbf{D}$ is constant within sample: the further condition that $\mathbf{D}$ is invariant to any regime changes out-of-sample is not considered here. Even if $\mathbf{D}$ is both constant and invariant, $\mathsf{V}[\mathbf{y}_{T+h,h}^* - \widehat{\mathbf{y}}_{T+h,h}^*]$ will generally increase with h, often quite rapidly, and the forecast errors will be heteroscedastic and serially correlated, so care is required in interpreting forecast errors. Clements and Hendry (1998a) give forecast error variances for the whole sequence of forecasts. Clements and Hendry (1999) discuss forecasting with non-stationary series.

Finally, we may wish to compute h-step forecasts, where $h \leq H$ is a fixed number, rather than running from 1 to H as in dynamic forecasting. Using the companion form (11.55):

$$\begin{aligned} \widehat{\mathbf{y}}_{T+i,h}^* &= \widehat{\mathbf{D}}\widehat{\mathbf{y}}_{T+i-1,h-1}^* + \widehat{\mathbf{E}}\mathbf{z}_{T+i}^* \\ &= \widehat{\mathbf{D}}^h \mathbf{y}_{T+i-h}^* + \sum_{j=0}^{h-1} \widehat{\mathbf{D}}^j \widehat{\mathbf{E}}\mathbf{z}_{T+i-j}^*, \quad i = h, \ldots, H. \end{aligned} \tag{11.57}$$

Again we ignore the parameter uncertainty in computing the error variance of the h-step forecast errors, so that we may use (11.56): when h is fixed the variance is constant.

11.5.3 Dynamic forecasting: parameter uncertainty

Equation (11.53) ignored the parameter uncertainty in forming dynamic forecasts. The static forecast standard errors of (11.41) take this into account, and we shall now derive this component for dynamic forecasts in a similar way, which corresponds to Schmidt (1974). It is assumed that the system has been mapped to an I(0) representation, and there are no unrestricted variables.

Rewrite the dynamic forecast at $T + h$ as:

$$\widehat{\mathbf{y}}_{T+h,h} = \widehat{\boldsymbol{\pi}}_1^h \mathbf{y}_T + \sum_{j=1}^{h} \widehat{\boldsymbol{\pi}}_1^{h-j} \widehat{\boldsymbol{\pi}}_2 \mathbf{z}_{T+j} = \widehat{\mathbf{A}}_h \mathbf{W}_h, \tag{11.58}$$

where

$$\widehat{\mathbf{A}}_h = \left(\widehat{\boldsymbol{\pi}}_1^h, \widehat{\boldsymbol{\pi}}_1^{h-1}\widehat{\boldsymbol{\pi}}_2, \widehat{\boldsymbol{\pi}}_1^{h-2}\widehat{\boldsymbol{\pi}}_2, \ldots, \widehat{\boldsymbol{\pi}}_2\right), \tag{11.59}$$

and

$$\mathbf{W}_h = \left(\mathbf{y}_T', \mathbf{z}_{T+1}', \mathbf{z}_{T+2}', \ldots, \mathbf{z}_{T+h}'\right)'. \tag{11.60}$$

The matrix $\widehat{\mathbf{A}}_h$ is $(n \times r)$ and $\mathbf{W}_h$ is $(r \times 1)$ where $r = n + hq$ when $\mathbf{z}$ is $(q \times 1)$. Note that $\mathbf{y}_T$ still belongs to the estimation sample, and is known when forecasting. Write $\mathbf{y}_{T+h,h}$ for the forecasts when the parameters are known:

$$\mathbf{y}_{T+h,h} = \boldsymbol{\pi}_1^h \mathbf{y}_T + \sum_{j=1}^{h} \boldsymbol{\pi}_1^{h-j} \boldsymbol{\pi}_2 \mathbf{z}_{T+j} = \mathbf{A}_h \mathbf{W}_h. \tag{11.61}$$

Then the parameter uncertainty component of the forecast errors is:

$$\mathbf{p} = \mathbf{y}_{T+h,h} - \widehat{\mathbf{y}}_{T+h,h} = \left(\mathbf{A}_h - \widehat{\mathbf{A}}_h\right) \mathbf{W}_h, \tag{11.62}$$

from which we can derive:

$$\text{vec}(\mathbf{p}) = \mathbf{p} = (\mathbf{W}_h' \otimes \mathbf{I}_n) \, \text{vec}\left(\mathbf{A}_h - \widehat{\mathbf{A}}_h\right), \tag{11.63}$$

so that

$$\widetilde{\mathsf{V}[\mathbf{p}]} \approx (\mathbf{W}_h' \otimes \mathbf{I}_n) \, \widehat{\mathbf{J}} \widetilde{\mathsf{V}\left[\text{vec}\widehat{\boldsymbol{\Pi}}\right]} \widehat{\mathbf{J}}' \left(\mathbf{W}_h \otimes \mathbf{I}_n\right), \tag{11.64}$$

where

$$\mathbf{J} = \frac{\partial \text{vec} \mathbf{A}_h}{\partial \left(\text{vec}\boldsymbol{\Pi}\right)'}. \tag{11.65}$$

Using

$$\frac{\partial \text{vec}\left(\boldsymbol{\pi}^h\right)}{\partial \left(\text{vec}\boldsymbol{\pi}\right)'} = \sum_{i=0}^{h-1} \left(\boldsymbol{\pi}'\right)^{h-1-i} \otimes \boldsymbol{\pi}^i \tag{11.66}$$

the $(nr \times nk)$ Jacobian matrix can be found:

$$\mathbf{J} = \begin{pmatrix} \left(\frac{\partial \text{vec}\boldsymbol{\pi}_1^h}{\partial \left(\text{vec}\boldsymbol{\pi}_1\right)'}\right)_{n^2 \times n^2} & \left(\frac{\partial \text{vec}\boldsymbol{\pi}_1^h}{\partial \left(\text{vec}\boldsymbol{\pi}_2\right)'}\right)_{n^2 \times nq} \\ \left(\frac{\partial \text{vec}\boldsymbol{\pi}_1^{h-1}\boldsymbol{\pi}_2}{\partial \left(\text{vec}\boldsymbol{\pi}_1\right)'}\right)_{nq \times n^2} & \left(\frac{\partial \text{vec}\boldsymbol{\pi}_1^{h-1}\boldsymbol{\pi}_2}{\partial \left(\text{vec}\boldsymbol{\pi}_2\right)'}\right)_{nq \times nq} \\ \vdots & \vdots \\ \left(\frac{\partial \text{vec}\boldsymbol{\pi}_2}{\partial \left(\text{vec}\boldsymbol{\pi}_1\right)'}\right)_{nq \times n^2} & \left(\frac{\partial \text{vec}\boldsymbol{\pi}_2}{\partial \left(\text{vec}\boldsymbol{\pi}_2\right)'}\right)_{nq \times nq} \end{pmatrix}, \tag{11.67}$$

$$\mathbf{J} = (\mathbf{J}_1 : \mathbf{J}_2) = \begin{pmatrix} \sum_{i=0}^{h-1} (\boldsymbol{\pi}_1')^{h-1-i} \otimes \boldsymbol{\pi}_1^i & \mathbf{0} \\ \sum_{i=0}^{h-2} \boldsymbol{\pi}_2' (\boldsymbol{\pi}_1')^{h-2-i} \otimes \boldsymbol{\pi}_1^i & \mathbf{I}_q \otimes \boldsymbol{\pi}_1^{h-1} \\ \vdots & \vdots \\ \boldsymbol{\pi}_2' \otimes \mathbf{I}_n & \mathbf{I}_q \otimes \boldsymbol{\pi}_1 \\ \mathbf{0} & \mathbf{I}_q \otimes \mathbf{I}_n \end{pmatrix}. \tag{11.68}$$

As Calzolari (1987) points out, the $\mathbf{J}$ matrix can be quite massive, for example for $n = 5$, $q = 20$, $h = 10$ the matrix is (1025×125). However, we are not interested in $\mathbf{J}$ per se, but in $(\mathbf{W}_h' \otimes \mathbf{I}_n)\mathbf{J}$ and find using:

$$(\mathbf{W}_h' \otimes \mathbf{I}_n) = \left(\mathbf{y}_T' \otimes \mathbf{I}_n : \mathbf{z}_{T+1}' \otimes \mathbf{I}_n : \cdots : \mathbf{z}_{T+h}' \otimes \mathbf{I}_n\right) \tag{11.69}$$

the following expression:

$$\begin{aligned} (\mathbf{W}_h' \otimes \mathbf{I}_n)\,\mathbf{J}_1 &= \sum_{i=0}^{h-1} \mathbf{y}_T' (\boldsymbol{\pi}_1')^{h-1-i} \otimes \boldsymbol{\pi}_1^i + \sum_{j=1}^{h-1} \sum_{i=0}^{h-1-j} \mathbf{z}_{T+j}' \boldsymbol{\pi}_2' (\boldsymbol{\pi}_1')^{h-1-j-i} \otimes \boldsymbol{\pi}_1^i, \\ (\mathbf{W}_h' \otimes \mathbf{I}_n)\,\mathbf{J}_2 &= \sum_{j=1}^{h} \mathbf{z}_{T+j}' \otimes \boldsymbol{\pi}_1^{h-j} = \sum_{i=0}^{h-1} \mathbf{z}_{T+h-i}' \otimes \boldsymbol{\pi}_1^i. \end{aligned} \tag{11.70}$$

Hence, we see that the results in Schmidt (1974) do not require computation of $\mathbf{J}$.

Reordering the double summation and using (11.61) yields for the first part of (11.70):

$$\begin{aligned} (\mathbf{W}_h' \otimes \mathbf{I}_n)\,\mathbf{J}_1 &= \sum_{i=0}^{h-1} \mathbf{y}_T' (\boldsymbol{\pi}_1')^{h-1-i} \otimes \boldsymbol{\pi}_1^i + \sum_{i=0}^{h-2} \sum_{j=1}^{h-1-i} \mathbf{z}_{T+j}' \boldsymbol{\pi}_2' (\boldsymbol{\pi}_1')^{h-1-j-i} \otimes \boldsymbol{\pi}_1^i \\ &= \sum_{i=0}^{h-1} \mathbf{y}_{T+h-1-i,h-1-i}' \otimes \boldsymbol{\pi}_1^i \end{aligned} \tag{11.71}$$

Combining $\mathbf{J}_1$ and $\mathbf{J}_2$, and writing $\mathbf{b}_{T+h-i}' = \left(\mathbf{y}_{T+h-1-i,h-1-i}' : \mathbf{z}_{T+h-i}'\right)$, $\mathbf{b}_T' = \left(\mathbf{y}_T' : \mathbf{z}_{T+1}'\right)$:

$$(\mathbf{W}_h' \otimes \mathbf{I}_n)\,\mathbf{J} = \sum_{i=0}^{h-1} \mathbf{b}_{T+h-i}' \otimes \boldsymbol{\pi}_1^i. \tag{11.72}$$

This is computationally more convenient than (11.70).

To express the Jacobian in terms of $\mathsf{V}[\mathrm{vec}\widehat{\mathbf{\Pi}}']$, rather than $\mathsf{V}[\mathrm{vec}\widehat{\mathbf{\Pi}}]$, requires column reordering. The asymptotic variance of $\mathbf{p}$ is then estimated by:

$$\widetilde{\mathsf{V}[\mathbf{p}]} \approx \left(\sum_{i=0}^{h-1} \widehat{\boldsymbol{\pi}}_1^i \otimes \widehat{\mathbf{b}}_{T+h-i}'\right) \widetilde{\mathsf{V}\left[\mathrm{vec}\widehat{\mathbf{\Pi}}'\right]} \left(\sum_{i=0}^{h-1} \widehat{\boldsymbol{\pi}}_1^i \otimes \widehat{\mathbf{b}}_{T+h-i}'\right)', \tag{11.73}$$

which corresponds to the result in Calzolari (1987). When more than one lag of the dependent variable is used, π_1 should be replaced by the companion matrix $\mathbf{D}$, but $\widehat{\mathbf{b}}_{T+h-i}$ remains unchanged.

The formulae can be derived somewhat differently, bringing out more clearly the terms which are omitted in the approximation. Write:

$$\widehat{\pi}_1 = \pi_1 + \boldsymbol{\delta}, \tag{11.74}$$

so that, ignoring higher order terms in $\boldsymbol{\delta}$:

$$\begin{aligned} \widehat{\pi}_1^h &= (\pi_1 + \boldsymbol{\delta})^h \\ &\approx \pi_1^h + \sum_{i=0}^{h-1} \pi_1^i \boldsymbol{\delta} \pi_1^{h-1-i} \\ &= \pi_1^h + \sum_{i=0}^{h-1} \pi_1^i (\widehat{\pi}_1 - \pi_1) \pi_1^{h-1-i}. \end{aligned} \tag{11.75}$$

In a closed system, this would lead to:

$$\widetilde{\mathsf{V}[\mathbf{p}]} \approx \left(\sum_{i=0}^{h-1} \mathbf{y}_T' (\widehat{\pi}_1')^{h-1-i} \otimes \widehat{\pi}_1^i \right) \mathsf{V}\left[\widetilde{\mathrm{vec}\widehat{\boldsymbol{\Pi}}}\right] \left(\sum_{i=0}^{h-1} \mathbf{y}_T' (\widehat{\pi}_1')^{h-1-i} \otimes \widehat{\pi}_1^i \right)', \tag{11.76}$$

which corresponds to the first component in (11.70).

Next, consider the part arising from non-modelled variables, for $j = 1, \ldots, h-1$:

$$\begin{aligned} \widehat{\pi}_1^j \widehat{\pi}_2 - \pi_1^j \pi_2 &= \pi_1^j (\widehat{\pi}_2 - \pi_2) + \left(\widehat{\pi}_1^j - \pi_1^j\right) \pi_2 - \left(\pi_1^j - \widehat{\pi}_1^j\right) (\widehat{\pi}_2 - \pi_2) \\ &\approx \pi_1^j (\widehat{\pi}_2 - \pi_2) + \left(\widehat{\pi}_1^j - \pi_1^j\right) \pi_2 \\ &\approx \pi_1^j (\widehat{\pi}_2 - \pi_2) + \sum_{i=0}^{j-1} \pi_1^i (\widehat{\pi}_1 - \pi_1) \pi_1^{j-1-i} \pi_2. \end{aligned} \tag{11.77}$$

The first approximation ignores $(\pi_1^j - \widehat{\pi}_1^j)(\widehat{\pi}_2 - \pi_2)$, then (11.75) is used. Combining (11.75) and (11.77) gives:

$$\begin{aligned} \mathbf{p} &= \left(\pi_1^h - \widehat{\pi}_1^h\right) \mathbf{y}_T + \sum_{j=1}^{h} \left(\pi_1^{h-j} \pi_2 - \widehat{\pi}_1^{h-j} \widehat{\pi}_2\right) \mathbf{z}_{T+j} \\ &\approx \sum_{i=0}^{h-1} \pi_1^i (\pi_1 - \widehat{\pi}_1) \pi_1^{h-1-i} \mathbf{y}_T + (\pi_2 - \widehat{\pi}_2) \mathbf{z}_{T+h} + \\ &\quad \sum_{j=1}^{h} \left(\pi_1^{h-j} (\pi_2 - \widehat{\pi}_2) + \sum_{i=0}^{h-j-1} \pi_1^i (\pi_1 - \widehat{\pi}_1) \pi_1^{h-j-1-i} \pi_2 \right) \mathbf{z}_{T+j} \\ &= \sum_{i=0}^{h-1} \pi_1^i (\pi_1 - \widehat{\pi}_1) \pi_1^{h-1-i} \mathbf{y}_T + \sum_{i=0}^{h-1} \pi_1^i (\pi_2 - \widehat{\pi}_2) \mathbf{z}_{T+h-i} \\ &\quad + \sum_{j=1}^{h-1} \sum_{i=0}^{h-j-1} \pi_1^i (\pi_1 - \widehat{\pi}_1) \pi_1^{h-j-1-i} \pi_2 \mathbf{z}_{T+j}, \end{aligned}$$

which leads directly to (11.70).

When the system is in I(1) space, it can be expressed as an I(0) model augmented with I(1) linear combinations of variables (essentially 'nonsense regressions'). The standard errors of the latter are not well defined (see, for example, Phillips, 1986, and Banerjee, Dolado, Galbraith and Hendry, 1993). Moreover, the approximation in (11.75) may be poor, in that unit roots are generally underestimated. When the system is properly estimated in I(0) space, forecasts and their standard errors for levels can be obtained by augmenting the system with identities of the form

$$\mathbf{y}_T \equiv \mathbf{y}_{T-1} + \Delta \mathbf{y}_T.$$

Unit roots are estimated, and the resulting (explosive) confidence bands reflect the cumulative uncertainty.

11.5.4 Dynamic simulation and impulse response analysis

A concept closely related to dynamic forecasting is dynamic simulation. Dynamic simulation values are obtained by computing dynamic forecasts from a starting point within the estimation sample. Commencing from period M as initial conditions:

$$\widehat{\mathbf{s}}_t = \sum_{i=1}^{m} \widehat{\boldsymbol{\pi}}_i \widehat{\mathbf{s}}_{t-i} + \sum_{j=0}^{r} \widehat{\boldsymbol{\pi}}_{j+m+1} \mathbf{z}_{t-j} \quad \text{for } t = M+1, \ldots, M+H \leq T, \tag{11.78}$$

where $\widehat{\mathbf{s}}_{t-i} = \mathbf{y}_{t-i}$ for $t - i \leq M$.

Dynamic simulation uses actual values of the non-modelled variables, but the simulated values of the ys. It can be seen as conditional dynamic forecasting within the estimation sample. However, the forecast error-variance formulae do not apply. As Chong and Hendry (1986) argue, dynamic simulation is not a valid method of model selection or model evaluation. To quote: 'In fact, what dynamic simulation tracking accuracy mainly reflects is the extent to which the *explanation of the data is attributed to non-modelled variables*.' However, dynamic simulation could be useful to investigate theory consistency or data admissibility. In addition, it can help elucidate the dynamic properties of the model. This information is also available through the eigenvalues of the companion matrix: roots outside or on the unit circle entail an unstable system with explosive behaviour. In that case, (11.56) will diverge as the forecast horizon increases towards infinity.

Impulse response analysis is similar to dynamic simulation, but focuses on the dynamics of the endogenous variables only:

$$\widehat{\boldsymbol{\imath}}_t = \sum_{i=1}^{m} \widehat{\boldsymbol{\pi}}_i \widehat{\boldsymbol{\imath}}_{t-i} \quad \text{for } t = 2, \ldots, H < \infty, \tag{11.79}$$

where $\widehat{\boldsymbol{\imath}}_t = \mathbf{0}$ for $t \leq 0$ and $\widehat{\boldsymbol{\imath}}_1 = \mathbf{i}_1$. Various forms are commonly used for the initial values $\mathbf{i}_1$. A simple form is to take all but one values zero, which can be set to unity, or the residual standard error of that equation. This effectively gives powers of the companion matrix. Then the matrix of $\{\widehat{\imath}_t\}$ with $\mathbf{I}_n$ as a basis shows the system equivalent of the moving-average representation. Alternatively, initial values can be taken from the orthogonalized system: see Lütkepohl (1991).

11.6 Dynamic analysis

Consider the system (11.1), and rewrite it slightly as (cf. equation 11.54):

$$\mathbf{y}_t = \sum_{i=1}^{m} \boldsymbol{\pi}_i \mathbf{y}_{t-i} + \sum_{j=0}^{r} \boldsymbol{\Gamma}_j \mathbf{z}_{t-j} + \mathbf{v}_t, \quad \mathbf{v}_t \sim \mathsf{IN}_n \left[\mathbf{0}, \boldsymbol{\Omega}\right], \tag{11.80}$$

with $\mathbf{y}_t$ $(n \times 1)$ and $\mathbf{z}_t$ $(q \times 1)$, $\boldsymbol{\Pi} = (\boldsymbol{\pi}_1 \cdots \boldsymbol{\pi}_m, \boldsymbol{\Gamma}_0 \cdots \boldsymbol{\Gamma}_r)$. Write this as:

$$\left(\mathbf{I} - \boldsymbol{\pi}\left(L\right)\right) \mathbf{y}_t = \mathbf{B}(L)\mathbf{y}_t = \boldsymbol{\Gamma}\left(L\right) \mathbf{z}_t + \mathbf{v}_t, \tag{11.81}$$

where $\mathbf{B}\left(L\right)$ and $\boldsymbol{\Gamma}\left(L\right)$ are matrix lag polynomials of order m and r respectively.[1] L is the lag operator:

$$L^i \mathbf{x}_t = \mathbf{x}_{t-i},$$

and a matrix lag polynomial of order m is:

$$\mathbf{B}\left(L\right) = \mathbf{B}_0 + \mathbf{B}_1 L^1 + \cdots + \mathbf{B}_m L^m.$$

So $\mathbf{B}_0 = \mathbf{I}_n$, $\mathbf{B}_1 = -\boldsymbol{\pi}_1$, $\mathbf{B}_2 = -\boldsymbol{\pi}_2$, etc. Also $\boldsymbol{\pi}(1) = \boldsymbol{\pi}_1 + \cdots + \boldsymbol{\pi}_m$, with m the longest lag on the endogenous variable(s), and $\boldsymbol{\Gamma}(1) = \boldsymbol{\Gamma}_0 + \cdots + \boldsymbol{\Gamma}_r$, with r the longest lag on any non-modelled variable. The lag polynomial $\mathbf{B}\left(L\right)$ is invertible if all solutions z_i to $|\mathbf{B}\left(z\right)| = 0$ lie outside the unit circle (the modulus of all $\lambda_i = 1/z_i$ is less than unity), in which case, the inverse can be written as:

$$\mathbf{B}\left(L\right)^{-1} = \sum_{i=0}^{\infty} \mathbf{G}_i L^i.$$

$\mathbf{P}_0 = -\mathbf{B}(1) = \boldsymbol{\pi}(1) - \mathbf{I}_n$ can be inverted only if it is of rank $p = n$, in which case, for $q > 0$, $\mathbf{y}$ and $\mathbf{z}$ are cointegrated. If $p < n$, only a subset of the ys and zs are cointegrated: see Chapter 12. If $\mathbf{P}_0$ is invertible, and the variables are I(0), we can write the static long-run solution as:

$$\mathsf{E}\left[\mathbf{y}_t\right] = -\mathbf{P}_0^{-1} \boldsymbol{\Gamma}\left(1\right) \mathsf{E}\left[\mathbf{z}_t\right]. \tag{11.82}$$

Let $\mathbf{u}_t = -\mathbf{P}_0^{-1}\mathbf{v}_t$, then the covariance matrix of $\{\mathbf{u}_t\}$ is the long-run covariance matrix of $\{\mathbf{y}_t\}$, namely:

$$\mathsf{V}\left[\mathbf{u}_t\right] = \mathbf{P}_0^{-1} \boldsymbol{\Omega} \mathbf{P}_0^{-1\prime} \tag{11.83}$$

[1]Note that this use of $\mathbf{B}$ and $\boldsymbol{\Gamma}$ is different from that in §9.3.

If $q = 0$, the system is closed (that is, a VAR), and (11.82) is not defined. However, $\mathbf{P}_0$ can still be calculated, in which case, p characterizes the number of cointegrating vectors linking the ys (again see Chapter 12).

The unconditional covariance matrix $\mathbf{\Phi}_y$ of $\mathbf{y}_t$ can be derived from the companion form (11.55):

$$\begin{aligned}\mathbf{\Phi}_y^* &= \mathsf{V}\left[\mathbf{y}_t^*\right] \\ &= \mathsf{E}\left[\left(\mathbf{D}\mathbf{y}_{t-1}^* + \mathbf{v}_t^*\right)\left(\mathbf{y}_{t-1}^{*\prime}\mathbf{D}' + \mathbf{v}_t^{*\prime}\right)\right] \\ &= \mathbf{D}\mathsf{E}\left[\mathbf{y}_{t-1}^*\mathbf{y}_{t-1}^{*\prime}\right]\mathbf{D}' + \mathsf{E}\left[\mathbf{v}_t^*\mathbf{v}_t^{*\prime}\right] \\ &= \mathbf{D}\mathbf{\Phi}_y^*\mathbf{D}' + \mho\end{aligned} \tag{11.84}$$

using the stationarity of $\mathbf{v}_t$, and with $\mho$ as in (11.56). $\mathbf{\Phi}_y$ is the $(n \times n)$ top left block of $\mathbf{\Phi}_y^*$:

$$\mathbf{\Phi}_y = \boldsymbol{\pi}(1)\mathbf{\Phi}_y\boldsymbol{\pi}(1)' + \mathbf{\Omega}. \tag{11.85}$$

Then, using vectorization:

$$\mathrm{vec}\mathbf{\Phi}_y = \left(\boldsymbol{\pi}(1) \otimes \boldsymbol{\pi}(1)\right)\mathrm{vec}\mathbf{\Phi}_y + \mathrm{vec}\mathbf{\Omega}, \tag{11.86}$$

so that:

$$\mathrm{vec}\mathbf{\Phi}_y = \left(\mathbf{I} - \boldsymbol{\pi}(1) \otimes \boldsymbol{\pi}(1)\right)^{-1}\mathrm{vec}\mathbf{\Omega}. \tag{11.87}$$

The estimated static long-run solution is:

$$\widehat{\mathbf{y}} = -\widehat{\mathbf{P}}_0^{-1}\widehat{\mathbf{\Gamma}}\left(1\right)\mathbf{z}. \tag{11.88}$$

The variance of $\widehat{\mathbf{P}} = -\widehat{\mathbf{P}}_0^{-1}\widehat{\mathbf{\Gamma}}\left(1\right)$ is most easily derived in two steps. Changing notation slightly, we write $\mathbf{P} = -\mathbf{B}^{-1}\mathbf{C}$, $\mathbf{A} = (\mathbf{B} : \mathbf{C}) = (\mathbf{P}_0 : \mathbf{\Gamma}\left(1\right))$.[2] With $\mathbf{R}$ summing the two parts of $\mathbf{\Pi}$ (defined below equation (11.80)), so $\mathbf{A} = \mathbf{\Pi}\mathbf{R}$, we have:

$$\mathsf{V}\left[\mathrm{vec}\widehat{\mathbf{A}}'\right] = \mathbf{H}\mathsf{V}\left[\mathrm{vec}\widehat{\mathbf{\Pi}}'\right]\mathbf{H}' \quad \text{where} \quad \mathbf{H} = \left(\mathbf{I}_n \otimes \mathbf{R}'\right) \tag{11.89}$$

$\mathbf{R}$ is $(k \times (n+q))$ so that $\mathbf{H}$ is $(n(n+q) \times nk)$; remember that $\mathbf{P}$ is $(n \times q)$. The Jacobian matrix of the transformation in (11.88) based on $\mathbf{A}$ can now be written as:

$$\begin{aligned}\mathbf{J} = \frac{\partial\mathrm{vec}\mathbf{P}'}{\partial\left(\mathrm{vec}\mathbf{A}'\right)'} &= \left(\frac{\partial\mathrm{vec}\mathbf{P}'}{\partial\left(\mathrm{vec}\mathbf{B}'\right)'} : \frac{\partial\mathrm{vec}\mathbf{P}'}{\partial\left(\mathrm{vec}\mathbf{C}'\right)'}\right)\mathbf{K}' \\ &= \left(\left(\mathbf{I}_q \otimes -\mathbf{C}'\right)\left(-\mathbf{B}^{-1} \otimes \mathbf{B}^{-1\prime}\right) : -\mathbf{B}^{-1} \otimes \mathbf{I}_q\right)\mathbf{K}' \\ &= \left(-\mathbf{B}^{-1} \otimes \mathbf{P}' : -\mathbf{B}^{-1} \otimes \mathbf{I}_q\right)\mathbf{K}' \\ &= -\mathbf{B}^{-1} \otimes \left(\mathbf{P}' : \mathbf{I}_q\right).\end{aligned} \tag{11.90}$$

[2] Here the use of $\mathbf{B}$ and $\mathbf{C}$ is different from, but analogous to, that in Chapter 13.

The $(nq \times n(n+q))$ matrix $\mathbf{J}$ does not have its elements in the right order to allow partitioning. However, $\mathbf{JK}$ does, when $\mathbf{K}$ is the $(n(n+q) \times n(n+q))$ matrix which permutes columns of $\mathbf{J}$, so that for each row, we first take the derivatives with respect to elements of $\mathbf{B}$, and then with respect to elements of $\mathbf{C}$. As $\mathbf{K}$ is orthogonal, $\mathbf{K}^{-1} = \mathbf{K}'$. When moving from line 3 to line 4 in (11.90), $\mathbf{K}'$ drops out again, as the same column reordering is required to collect the partitioned component on the right-hand side.

The variance of the static long-run coefficients may now be computed as:

$$\widetilde{\mathsf{V}\left[\mathrm{vec}\widehat{\mathbf{P}}'\right]} = \widehat{\mathbf{J}}\widehat{\mathbf{H}}\widetilde{\mathsf{V}\left[\mathrm{vec}\widehat{\mathbf{\Pi}}'\right]}\widehat{\mathbf{H}}'\widehat{\mathbf{J}}'. \tag{11.91}$$

This is a multivariate extension of the results derived by Bårdsen (1989).

Returning to the companion form (11.55), we find by back substitution that $\mathbf{y}_t$ consists of the accumulation of past $\mathbf{z}$s and errors:

$$\mathbf{y}_t^* = \sum_{i=0}^{\infty} \mathbf{D}^i \mathbf{E} \mathbf{z}_{t-i}^* + \sum_{i=0}^{\infty} \mathbf{D}^i \mathbf{v}_{t-i}^*. \tag{11.92}$$

A dynamically stable system requires $\mathbf{D}^i \rightarrow \mathbf{0}$ as $i \rightarrow \infty$, which implies that all eigenvalues of $\mathbf{D}$ must lie inside the unit circle. When the system is closed ($q = 0$), under stationarity, the unconditional variance of $\mathbf{y}_t^*$ is also given by:

$$\mathsf{V}\left[\mathbf{y}_t^*\right] = \sum_{i=0}^{\infty} \mathbf{D}^i \mho \mathbf{D}^{i\prime}. \tag{11.93}$$

When $\{\mathbf{z}_t\}$ is strongly exogenous and stationary, (11.93) applies to the variance of $\mathbf{y}_t^*$ around its long-run mean.

11.7 Test types

Various test principles are commonly used in econometrics and the three main ones are Wald (W), Lagrange multiplier (LM, also called score test) and likelihood ratio (LR) tests (for a thorough discussion of these tests, and testing in general, see Hendry, 1995, and Godfrey, 1988, and the references cited therein). For example, the Chow (1960) test for parameter constancy in a single equation is derivable from all three principles, whereas the test of over-identifying restrictions is LR, most of the mis-specification tests are LM, and tests for non-linear parameter restrictions are Wald tests. In each instance, the choice of test type tends to reflect computational ease. Under the relevant null hypothesis and for local alternatives, the three test types are asymptotically equivalent in stationary systems; however, if equations are mis-specified in other ways than that under test, or the sample size is small, different inferences can result.

With a k vector of parameters $\boldsymbol{\theta} \in \Theta \subset \mathbb{R}^k$ and corresponding likelihood function $\mathsf{L}(\boldsymbol{\theta}|\cdot)$ we assume that the regularity conditions hold, so that the limiting distribution of the MLE $\widehat{\boldsymbol{\theta}}$ is:

$$\sqrt{T}\left(\widehat{\boldsymbol{\theta}} - \boldsymbol{\theta}_p\right) \xrightarrow{D} \mathsf{N}_k\left[\mathbf{0}, \boldsymbol{\Sigma}\right], \tag{11.94}$$

where $\boldsymbol{\theta}_p$ denotes the population value of $\boldsymbol{\theta}$, and $\boldsymbol{\Sigma}$ is the variance-covariance matrix of the limiting distribution. In finite samples, we approximate the distribution in (11.94) by:

$$\widehat{\boldsymbol{\theta}} \underset{app}{\sim} \mathsf{N}_k\left[\boldsymbol{\theta}_p, T^{-1}\boldsymbol{\Sigma}\right]. \tag{11.95}$$

The general problem is formulated as follows. The maintained hypothesis H_m: $\boldsymbol{\theta} \in \Theta$ defines the statistical model within which all testing will take place. We wish to know which of two hypotheses holds within H_m, the null hypothesis denoted by H_0 or the alternative hypothesis H_1. Thus, we wish to test the r restrictions imposed by H_0:

$$\mathsf{H}_0\colon \boldsymbol{\theta} = \boldsymbol{\theta}_0 \text{ or } \boldsymbol{\theta} \in \Theta_0 \quad \text{versus} \quad \mathsf{H}_1\colon \boldsymbol{\theta} \neq \boldsymbol{\theta}_0 \text{ or } \boldsymbol{\theta} \notin \Theta_0.$$

The likelihood ratio λ is given by:

$$0 \leq \lambda = \frac{\max_{\boldsymbol{\theta}\in\Theta_0} \mathsf{L}(\boldsymbol{\theta})}{\max_{\boldsymbol{\theta}\in\Theta} \mathsf{L}(\boldsymbol{\theta})} \leq 1. \tag{11.96}$$

If H_m is true and the regularity conditions hold, the likelihood ratio test is:

$$-2\log\widehat{\lambda} = 2\ell\left(\widehat{\boldsymbol{\theta}}\right) - 2\ell\left(\widehat{\boldsymbol{\theta}}_0\right) \xrightarrow{D} \chi^2(r) \tag{11.97}$$

when H_0 holds and imposes r restrictions and $\ell(\cdot) = \log \mathsf{L}(\cdot)$.

Writing the r restrictions implied by the null hypothesis as:

$$\mathsf{H}_0\colon \mathbf{f}(\boldsymbol{\theta}) = \mathbf{0} \tag{11.98}$$

where $\mathbf{f}\colon \Theta \mapsto \Theta_0$, the Wald test of hypothesis (11.98) is expressed as:

$$\widehat{\mathsf{w}} = \mathbf{f}(\widehat{\boldsymbol{\theta}})' \left(\mathbf{J}(\widehat{\boldsymbol{\theta}})\widehat{\mathsf{V}[\widehat{\boldsymbol{\theta}}]}\mathbf{J}'(\widehat{\boldsymbol{\theta}})\right)^{-1} \mathbf{f}(\widehat{\boldsymbol{\theta}}) \xrightarrow[\mathsf{H}_0]{D} \chi^2(r) \tag{11.99}$$

where $\mathbf{J}$ is the Jacobian matrix of the transformation: $\mathbf{J}(\boldsymbol{\theta}) = \partial\mathbf{f}(\boldsymbol{\theta})/\partial\boldsymbol{\theta}'$.

The Lagrange multiplier (or efficient score) test may be expressed as:

$$\mathbf{q}\left(\widehat{\boldsymbol{\theta}}_0\right) \widehat{\mathsf{V}[\widehat{\boldsymbol{\theta}}_0]}\mathbf{q}'\left(\widehat{\boldsymbol{\theta}}_0\right) \xrightarrow[\mathsf{H}_0]{D} \chi^2(r), \tag{11.100}$$

in which the score and variance of the unrestricted model are evaluated at the restricted parameters. With respect to the last two expressions, we may point out three consistent estimators of the asymptotic variance of the MLEs under the maintained being a congruent model:

$$
\begin{aligned}
\mathsf{V}_1\widehat{[\widehat{\boldsymbol{\theta}}]} &= \mathcal{I}\left(\widehat{\boldsymbol{\theta}}\right)^{-1}, \\
\mathsf{V}_2\widehat{[\widehat{\boldsymbol{\theta}}]} &= -\mathbf{H}\left(\widehat{\boldsymbol{\theta}}\right)^{-1}, \\
\mathsf{V}_3\widehat{[\widehat{\boldsymbol{\theta}}]} &= \left(\sum_{t=1}^{T}\mathbf{q}_t\left(\widehat{\boldsymbol{\theta}}\right)\mathbf{q}_t'\left(\widehat{\boldsymbol{\theta}}\right)\right)^{-1}.
\end{aligned}
\tag{11.101}
$$

$\mathcal{I}$ is the information matrix, $\mathsf{E}[\sum_{t=1}^{T}\mathbf{q}_t(\boldsymbol{\theta})\mathbf{q}_t'(\boldsymbol{\theta})]$; the second form involves the Hessian matrix $\mathbf{H}$, $\partial^2\ell/\partial\boldsymbol{\theta}\partial\boldsymbol{\theta}'$; the third form is based on the sample outer product of the gradients (OPG).

The LR test requires estimation of both the unrestricted and the restricted model; the W test requires estimation of the unrestricted model, whereas the LM test only requires estimation of the restricted model.

11.8 Specification tests

The objective of specification testing in PcGive is to simplify the specification of the system at hand. As the unrestricted system has already been estimated, the most convenient candidates for test types are LR and W.

An obvious example of a specification test is testing whether a group of variables can be omitted from the system, that is, testing whether columns of $\boldsymbol{\Pi}$ are significantly different from zero. With the system expressed as in (11.4) and taken to be congruent,

$$
\mathbf{Y}' = \boldsymbol{\Pi}\mathbf{W}' + \mathbf{V}', \tag{11.102}
$$

and partitioning the coefficients as $\boldsymbol{\Pi} = (\boldsymbol{\Pi}_1 : \boldsymbol{\Pi}_2)$ and $\mathbf{W}$ accordingly, we may write this test as:

$$
\mathsf{H}_0 : \boldsymbol{\Pi}_2 = \mathbf{0} \text{ versus } \mathsf{H}_1 : \boldsymbol{\Pi}_2 \neq \mathbf{0} \text{ with } \mathsf{H}_m \text{ as in (11.102).} \tag{11.103}
$$

$\boldsymbol{\Pi}$ is $(n \times k)$, $\boldsymbol{\Pi}_i$ is $(n \times k_i)$, so that $k = k_1 + k_2$. The likelihood ratio follows from Section [11.2]:

$$
\widehat{\lambda} = \frac{\mathsf{L}_0\left(\widehat{\boldsymbol{\Pi}}_1 : \mathbf{0}\right)}{\mathsf{L}\left(\widehat{\boldsymbol{\Pi}}\right)} = \frac{K_c\left|\widehat{\boldsymbol{\Omega}}_0\right|^{-T/2}}{K_c\left|\widehat{\boldsymbol{\Omega}}\right|^{-T/2}} = \left(\left|\widehat{\boldsymbol{\Omega}}\right|\left|\widehat{\boldsymbol{\Omega}}_0\right|^{-1}\right)^{T/2}. \tag{11.104}
$$

$T\widehat{\boldsymbol{\Omega}}_0 = \widehat{\mathbf{V}}_0'\widehat{\mathbf{V}}_0 = \mathbf{Y}'\mathbf{M}_{W_1}\mathbf{Y}$, $\widehat{\mathbf{V}}_0$ are the residuals from regressing $\mathbf{Y}$ on $\mathbf{W}_1$, whereas $\widehat{\boldsymbol{\Omega}}$ comes from the unrestricted system (11.102). Minus twice the logarithm of (11.104) is asymptotically $\chi^2(nk_2)$ distributed under the null hypothesis. Anderson (1984, Section 8.4) and Rao (1973, Section 8b.2) derive the exact distribution of $\lambda^{2/T}$ for fixed $\mathbf{W}$; Anderson gives small-sample correction factors for the χ^2 test.

The restriction imposed by H_0 in (11.103) may be expressed as:

$$\mathbf{\Pi R} = (\mathbf{\Pi}_1 : \mathbf{\Pi}_2)\begin{pmatrix} \mathbf{0} \\ \mathbf{I}_{k_2} \end{pmatrix} = \mathbf{0}, \tag{11.105}$$

in which $\mathbf{R}$ is $(k \times k_2)$. The Jacobian matrix of this transformation is $\mathbf{J} = \mathbf{I}_n \otimes \mathbf{R}'$, so that the Wald test may be written as:

$$\begin{aligned} \widehat{\mathsf{w}} &= \left(\mathrm{vec}\left(\widehat{\mathbf{\Pi}}\mathbf{R}\right)\right)'\left\{\widehat{\mathbf{\Omega}}^{-1} \otimes \left(\mathbf{R}'\left(\mathbf{W}'\mathbf{W}\right)^{-1}\mathbf{R}\right)^{-1}\right\}\mathrm{vec}\left(\widehat{\mathbf{\Pi}}\mathbf{R}\right) \\ &= \mathrm{tr}\left\{\left(\left(\mathbf{W}'\mathbf{W}\right)^{22}\right)^{-1}\widehat{\mathbf{\Pi}}_2'\widehat{\mathbf{\Omega}}^{-1}\widehat{\mathbf{\Pi}}_2\right\}, \end{aligned} \tag{11.106}$$

where $(\mathbf{W}'\mathbf{W})^{22}$ is the relevant block of $(\mathbf{W}'\mathbf{W})^{-1}$. $\widehat{\mathsf{w}}$ has an asymptotic $\chi^2(nk_2)$ distribution. When testing one column of $\mathbf{\Pi}$ (that is, the significance of one variable), the trace is taken of a scalar expression. In this case, the test statistic $\widehat{\mathsf{w}}$ is an instance of the Hotelling T^2 statistic, and is distributed as (assuming normality and fixed regressors):

$$\widehat{\mathsf{w}}\frac{T-k}{Tn} \sim \mathsf{F}(n, T-k). \tag{11.107}$$

Expressions (11.104) and (11.106) are more similar than they might seem at first sight. From §11.4, we know that $\widehat{\mathbf{V}}' = \mathbf{Y}'\mathbf{M}_{W_1} - \widehat{\mathbf{\Pi}}_2\mathbf{W}_2'\mathbf{M}_{W_1}$, so:

$$\widehat{\mathbf{V}}'\widehat{\mathbf{V}} = \mathbf{Y}'\mathbf{M}_{W_1}\mathbf{Y} - \widehat{\mathbf{\Pi}}_2\mathbf{W}_2'\mathbf{M}_{W_1}\mathbf{W}_2\widehat{\mathbf{\Pi}}_2'$$

follows. Using partitioned inversion, (11.106) can be written as:

$$\widehat{\mathsf{w}}/T = \mathrm{tr}\left(\widehat{\mathbf{\Pi}}_2\mathbf{W}_2'\mathbf{M}_{W_1}\mathbf{W}_2\widehat{\mathbf{\Pi}}_2'\widehat{\mathbf{\Omega}}^{-1}/T\right) = \mathrm{tr}\left(\left(\widehat{\mathbf{\Omega}}_0 - \widehat{\mathbf{\Omega}}\right)\widehat{\mathbf{\Omega}}^{-1}\right). \tag{11.108}$$

$\widehat{\mathsf{w}}/T$ is known as the Lawley–Hotelling trace criterion.

R^2-type measures of goodness of fit, as reported by PcGive, are based on LM and LR. The LM-test of (11.103) is:

$$\widehat{\mathsf{lm}}/T = \mathrm{tr}\left(\left(\widehat{\mathbf{\Omega}}_0 - \widehat{\mathbf{\Omega}}\right)\widehat{\mathbf{\Omega}}_0^{-1}\right), \tag{11.109}$$

(Anderson calls this the Bartlett–Nanda–Pillai trace criterion), so that we may define:

$$\begin{aligned} \mathsf{R}_r^2 &= 1 - \left|\widehat{\mathbf{\Omega}}\right|\left|\widehat{\mathbf{\Omega}}_0\right|^{-1} \\ \mathsf{R}_m^2 &= 1 - \tfrac{1}{n}\mathrm{tr}\left(\widehat{\mathbf{\Omega}}\widehat{\mathbf{\Omega}}_0^{-1}\right). \end{aligned} \tag{11.110}$$

In a one-equation system ($n = 1$), these two measures are identical, but they only correspond to the traditional R^2 if the constant term is the only variable excluded in the specification test.

Following Rao (1952), as described in Rao (1973, Section 8c.5) or Anderson (1984, Section 8.5.4), we may define an F-approximation for likelihood-ratio based tests of (11.103) as:

$$\frac{1-\left(1-\mathsf{R}_r^2\right)^{1/s}}{\left(1-\mathsf{R}_r^2\right)^{1/s}}\cdot\frac{Ns-q}{nk_2} \underset{app}{\sim} \mathsf{F}\left(nk_2, Ns-q\right), \tag{11.111}$$

with:

$$s=\sqrt{\frac{n^2k_2^2-4}{n^2+k_2^2-5}},\ q=\ \tfrac{1}{2}\ nk_2-1,\ N=T-k_1-k_2-\ \tfrac{1}{2}\ (n-k_2+1) \tag{11.112}$$

and:

k_1	number of regressors in restricted system	
k_2	number of regressors involved in test	
n	dimension of unrestricted system	(11.113)
T	number of observations in unrestricted system	
$T-k_1-k_2$	degrees of freedom in unrestricted system	

This F-approximation is exact for fixed regressors when $k_2 \leq 2$ or $n \leq 2$.

The following table gives the degrees of freedom of Rao's F-approximation for $T = 100$, $k = 20$:

k_2	$n=1$	$n=2$	$n=3$	$n=4$
1	$1,80$	$2,79$	$3,78$	$4,77$
2	$2,80$	$4,158$	$6,156$	$8,154$
3	$3,80$	$6,158$	$9,189.98$	$12,204.01$
4	$4,80$	$8,158$	$12,206.66$	$16,235.88$
5	$5,80$	$10,158$	$15,215.73$	$20,256.33$
6	$6,80$	$12,158$	$18,221.10$	$24,269.83$
7	$7,80$	$14,158$	$21,224.52$	$28,279.05$
8	$8,80$	$16,158$	$24,226.82$	$32,285.56$
9	$9,80$	$18,158$	$27,228.44$	$36,290.29$
10	$10,80$	$20,158$	$30,229.62$	$40,293.83$

The first two columns and the first two rows correspond to exact F-distributions (assuming fixed regressors and stationarity). Testing the significance of k_2 regressors in a single equation system is $\mathsf{F}(k_2, T-k)$; (11.114) below does not follow from Rao's F-approximation, although it is the same distribution. Testing the significance of one regressor in an n-equation system is $\mathsf{F}(n, T-k+1-n)$.

Testing for significance within a single equation of the n equation system proceeds as in the univariate case. This derives from the fact that $T\widehat{\boldsymbol{\Omega}}$ and $\boldsymbol{\Pi}$ are independent with respectively a Wishart and a normal distribution. To test whether k_2 coefficients in equation i are zero:

$$\frac{RSS_0 - RSS}{RSS} \cdot \frac{T-k}{k_2} \sim \mathsf{F}\left(k_2, T-k\right), \tag{11.114}$$

where RSS and RSS_0 are the ith diagonal element of $T\widehat{\boldsymbol{\Omega}}$ and $T\widehat{\boldsymbol{\Omega}}_0$ respectively. Also, the t-test may be used to test the significance of a single coefficient in an equation:

$$\frac{\widehat{\Pi}_{ij} - 0}{\sqrt{\widetilde{\sigma}^2 \left(\mathbf{W}'\mathbf{W}\right)^{-1}_{jj}}} \sim \mathsf{t}\left(T-k\right), \tag{11.115}$$

where $\widetilde{\sigma}^2$ is the ith diagonal element of $\widetilde{\boldsymbol{\Omega}}$.

11.8.1 Parameter constancy tests

Parameter constancy tests for a one-off break at T_1, $T = T_1 + T_2$, as introduced by Chow (1960), may be described within the framework of this section. First, consider the prediction test where T_2 observations are added to the T_1 we already have. The Chow test may be expressed as a test for significance of $\mathbf{D}$ in:

$$\mathbf{Y}' = \boldsymbol{\Pi}\mathbf{W}' + \mathbf{D}\mathbf{S}' + \mathbf{V}', \tag{11.116}$$

where $\mathbf{S}$ consists of dummies removing the influence of the last T_2 observations (see Salkever, 1976). The parameter constancy test is H_0: $\mathbf{D} = \mathbf{0}$. This test is more conveniently done through two separate regressions: for the first T_1 observations (yielding $\widehat{\boldsymbol{\Omega}}_{T_1}$; this is the unrestricted system, as it has all the dummies in it); and for all observations, yielding $\widehat{\boldsymbol{\Omega}}_T$. The first term has to be corrected for the sample size, so that the F-test may be based on:

$$\mathsf{R}^2_r = 1 - \left(\frac{T_1}{T}\right)^n \left|\widehat{\boldsymbol{\Omega}}_{T_1}\right| \left(\left|\widehat{\boldsymbol{\Omega}}_T\right|\right)^{-1}. \tag{11.117}$$

The Wald test of H_0: $\mathbf{D} = \mathbf{0}$ is identical to the parameter-constancy test ξ_3 of (11.46). That equation gives an F-version with a degrees-of-freedom correction which is different from the LR-derived F-test based on (11.117).

When testing within a single equation (a row of $\mathbf{D}$), the familiar F-test arises:

$$\frac{RSS_T - RSS_{T_1}}{RSS_{T_1}} \cdot \frac{T_1 - k}{T_2} \sim \mathsf{F}\left(T_2, T_1 - k\right). \tag{11.118}$$

Now RSS_T and RSS_{T_1} are the ith diagonal element of $T\widehat{\boldsymbol{\Omega}}_T$ and $T_1\widehat{\boldsymbol{\Omega}}_{T_1}$. This is approximate in dynamic models. After recursive estimation, these tests are computed for every possible break-point (although the distribution only holds for a one-off, known break-point). If T_2 is large enough, an analysis-of-covariance type test may be computed, by fitting the system three times, over T_1, T_2 and T, and performing a likelihood ratio test (see, for example, Pesaran, Smith and Yeo, 1985):

$$2\left(\widehat{\ell}_{T_1}+\widehat{\ell}_{T_2}-\widehat{\ell}_T\right)\underset{app}{\sim}\chi^2\left(nk-\ \tfrac{1}{2}\ n\left(n+1\right)\right). \qquad (11.119)$$

11.9 Mis-specification tests

Mis-specification tests check whether the system is deficient in the direction of more general specifications, such as systems incorporating heteroscedasticity, serial correlation, etc. The model should have constant parameters and residuals which are homoscedastic innovations, in order to allow us to perform specification tests. Note that rejection of the null hypothesis should not lead to automatic acceptance of the alternative hypothesis, as the tests could have power against other deficiencies. Hendry (1995) discusses these issues and the issue of multiple testing.

Mis-specification testing starts after system specification and estimation, so it can be no surprise that most tests encountered are derived as LM tests.

Diagnostic testing in PcGive is performed at two levels: individual equations and the system as a whole. Individual-equation diagnostics take the residuals of each equation of the system in turn, and treat them as if they are from a single equation. Usually this means that they are only valid if the remaining equations are problem-free. We first consider single equation statistics.

11.9.1 Single equation tests

To simplify notation, write a single equation of the system (11.1) as:

$$y_t=\boldsymbol{\pi}'\mathbf{w}_t+v_t. \qquad (11.120)$$

In (11.120), the $(k\times 1)$ vector π is the transpose of a row of $\mathbf{\Pi}$ of (11.1) and $\mathsf{E}[v_t^2]=\sigma^2$. Many tests take the form of:

$$T\mathsf{R}^2 \qquad (11.121)$$

for an auxiliary regression, so that they are asymptotically distributed as $\chi^2\left(s\right)$ under their nulls, and hence have the usual additive property for independent $\chi^2 s$. In addition, following Harvey (1990) and Kiviet (1986), F-approximations of the form

$$\frac{\mathsf{R}^2}{1-\mathsf{R}^2}\cdot\frac{T-k-s}{s}\sim\mathsf{F}\left(s,T-k-s\right) \qquad (11.122)$$

are calculated because they may be better behaved in small samples. We can relate these to the Lagrange multiplier and Wald tests of (11.109) and (11.108) by writing $\widehat{\sigma}^2 = \sum \widehat{v}_t^2/T$ and $\widehat{\sigma}_0^2 = \sum(y_t - \bar{y})^2/T$, giving:

$$\mathsf{R}^2 = \left(\widehat{\sigma}_0^2\right)^{-1}\left(\widehat{\sigma}_0^2 - \widehat{\sigma}^2\right) \text{ and } \frac{\mathsf{R}^2}{1-\mathsf{R}^2} = \left(\widehat{\sigma}^2\right)^{-1}\left(\widehat{\sigma}_0^2 - \widehat{\sigma}^2\right). \qquad (11.123)$$

11.9.1.1 Portmanteau statistic

This is a degrees-of-freedom corrected version of the Box and Pierce (1970) statistic (it is sometimes called Ljung–Box or Q*-statistic), designed as a goodness-of-fit test in stationary autoregressive moving-average models. It is only a valid test in a single equation with no exogenous variables. An appropriate test for residual autocorrelation is provided by the LM test below. The statistic calculated is:

$$\mathsf{LB}(s) = T^2 \sum_{j=1}^{s} \frac{\mathsf{r}_j^2}{T-j}, \qquad (11.124)$$

where s is the length of the correlogram and r_j is the jth coefficient of residual autocorrelation:

$$\mathsf{r}_j^* = \frac{\sum_{t=j+1}^{T} \widehat{v}_t \widehat{v}_{t-j}}{\sum_{t=1}^{T} \widehat{v}_t^2}. \qquad (11.125)$$

Under the assumptions of the test, $\mathsf{LB}(s)$ is asymptotically distributed as $\chi^2(s-k)$, with k being the lag length in an autoregressive model. The degrees-of-freedom correction in (11.124) is not exactly identical to that in Ljung and Box (1978), who use $T(T+2)$ instead of T^2, but chosen to coincide with the vector analogue below.

11.9.1.2 LM test for autocorrelated residuals

A Lagrange-multiplier test for serial correlation uses the formulation:

$$v_t = \sum_{i=r}^{s} \alpha_i v_{t-i} + \epsilon_t, \quad 1 \le r \le s \qquad (11.126)$$

with $\epsilon_t \sim \mathsf{IID}[0, \sigma^2]$. This test is done through the auxiliary regression of the residuals on the original variables and lagged residuals (missing lagged residuals at the start of the sample are replaced by zero, so no observations are lost). Then the significance of all regressors in this regression is tested through the $\chi^2(s-r+1)$ and F-statistic, based on R^2. The null hypothesis is no autocorrelation, which would be rejected if the test statistic is too high. This LM test is valid for systems with lagged dependent variables, whereas neither the Durbin–Watson nor residual correlogram based tests are valid in that case.

11.9.1.3 LM test for autocorrelated squared residuals

In the linear ARCH model (autoregressive conditional heteroscedasticity, see Engle, 1982) the variance is specified as:

$$\sigma_t^2 = \mathsf{E}\left[v_t^2 \mid v_{t-1}, \ldots, v_{t-s}\right] = c + \sum_{i=1}^{s} \gamma_i v_{t-i}^2. \tag{11.127}$$

An LM-test for the hypothesis $\boldsymbol{\gamma} = (\gamma_1, \ldots, \gamma_s)' = \mathbf{0}$, called the ARCH test, may be obtained as $T\mathsf{R}^2$ from the regression of $\widehat{v}_t^2$ on a constant and $\widehat{v}_{t-1}^2$ to $\widehat{v}_{t-s}^2$. This test is asymptotically distributed as $\chi^2(s)$ on H_0: $\boldsymbol{\gamma} = \mathbf{0}$. The F-form (11.122) may also be computed. Engle, Hendry and Trumbull (1985) investigate the small-sample properties of this test.

11.9.1.4 Test for normality

Let μ, σ^2 denote the mean and variance of v, and write $\mu_i = \mathsf{E}[v-\mu]^i$, so that $\sigma^2 = \mu_2$. The skewness and kurtosis are defined as:

$$\sqrt{\beta_1} = \frac{\mu_3}{\mu_2^{3/2}} \text{ and } \beta_2 = \frac{\mu_4}{\mu_2^2}. \tag{11.128}$$

Sample counterparts are defined by:

$$\bar{v} = \frac{1}{T}\sum_{i=1}^{T} v_i, \quad m_i = \frac{1}{T}\sum_{i=1}^{T}\left(v_i - \bar{v}\right)^i, \quad \sqrt{b_1} = \frac{m_3}{m_2^{3/2}} \text{ and } b_2 = \frac{m_4}{m_2^2}. \tag{11.129}$$

A normal variate will have $\sqrt{\beta_1} = 0$ and $\beta_2 = 3$. Bowman and Shenton (1975) consider the test:

$$\frac{T\left(\sqrt{b_1}\right)^2}{6} + \frac{T\left(b_2 - 3\right)^2}{24} \;\widetilde{a}\; \chi^2(2) \tag{11.130}$$

unsuitable unless used in very large samples. The statistics $\sqrt{b_1}$ and b_2 are not independently distributed, and the sample kurtosis especially approaches normality very slowly. The test reported by PcGive is fully described in Doornik and Hansen (1994). It derives from Shenton and Bowman (1977), who give b_2 (conditional on $b_2 > 1 + b_1$) a gamma distribution, and D'Agostino (1970), who approximates the distribution of $\sqrt{b_1}$ by the Johnson S_u system. Let z_1 and z_2 denote the transformed skewness and kurtosis, where the transformation creates statistics which are much closer to standard normal. The test statistic is:

$$\mathsf{e}_2 = z_1^2 + z_2^2 \;\widetilde{app}\; \chi^2(2). \tag{11.131}$$

Table 11.1 compares (11.131) with its asymptotic form (11.130). It gives the rejection frequencies under the null of normality, using $\chi^2(2)$ critical values. The experiments are based on 10 000 replications and common random numbers.

Table 11.1 Empirical size of normality tests.

	nominal probabilities of e_2				nominal probabilities of (11.130)			
T	20%	10%	5%	1%	20%	10%	5%	1%
50	0.1734	0.0869	0.0450	0.0113	0.0939	0.0547	0.0346	0.0175
100	0.1771	0.0922	0.0484	0.0111	0.1258	0.0637	0.0391	0.0183
150	0.1845	0.0937	0.0495	0.0131	0.1456	0.0703	0.0449	0.0188
250	0.1889	0.0948	0.0498	0.0133	0.1583	0.0788	0.0460	0.0180

11.9.1.5 Test for heteroscedasticity

This test is based on White (1980), and involves an auxiliary regression of $\{\widehat{v}_t^2\}$ on a constant, the original regressors $\{w_{it}\}$, and all their squares $\{w_{it}^2\}$. The null is unconditional homoscedasticity, and the alternative is that the variance of the $\{v_t\}$ process depends on $\mathbf{w}_t$ and on the $\{w_{it}^2\}$. Assuming that the auxiliary regression has $1+s$ regressors, the two statistics are distributed as $\chi^2(s)$ and $\mathsf{F}(s, T-s-1-k)$. If one of the $\{w_{it}\}$ is the constant term, and no other variables are redundant when squared, $s=(k-1)^2$. Redundant variables are automatically omitted from the regression, and s is adjusted accordingly.

11.9.2 Vector tests

During development of PcGive 8 (in 1992) tests were implemented which operate on the system as a whole. Whenever the vector tests are implemented through an auxiliary multivariate regression, we define extensions of the χ^2 and F-statistics of (11.121) and (11.122). The first is an LM test in the auxiliary system, defined in terms of (11.110):

$$Tn\mathsf{R}_m^2 \underset{app}{\sim} \chi^2(sn). \tag{11.132}$$

The second uses the F-approximation of (11.111). In addition to computational simplicity, this gives the vector tests of PcGive the attractive property of reducing to the single equation tests in a one-equation system.

11.9.2.1 Vector portmanteau statistic

This is the multivariate equivalent of the single equation portmanteau statistic, and is a valid asymptotic test only in a VAR. The portmanteau statistic uses a small-sample correction. Define:

$$\widehat{\mathbf{C}}_{rs} = \frac{1}{T}\sum_{t=1}^{T} \widehat{\mathbf{v}}_{t-r}\widehat{\mathbf{v}}_{t-s}', \quad \text{with } \widehat{\mathbf{v}}_i = \mathbf{0} \text{ for } i \le 0. \tag{11.133}$$

Then $\widehat{\mathbf{C}}_{00} = \widehat{\boldsymbol{\Omega}}$. The vector Box–Pierce statistic is:

$$\mathsf{BP}(s) = T \sum_{j=1}^{s} \mathrm{tr}\left(\widehat{\mathbf{C}}_{0j}' \widehat{\mathbf{C}}_{00}^{-1} \widehat{\mathbf{C}}_{0j} \widehat{\mathbf{C}}_{00}^{-1}\right), \tag{11.134}$$

whereas the vector portmanteau equals:

$$\mathsf{LB}(s) = T^2 \sum_{j=1}^{s} \frac{1}{T-j} \mathrm{tr}\left(\widehat{\mathbf{C}}_{0j}' \widehat{\mathbf{C}}_{00}^{-1} \widehat{\mathbf{C}}_{0j} \widehat{\mathbf{C}}_{00}^{-1}\right). \tag{11.135}$$

See Hosking (1980) or Lütkepohl (1991). Under the assumptions of the test (one of them being that s is large: $s = O(T^{1/2})$), with s the chosen lag length and m the lag length of the n dependent variables, both statistics are asymptotically $\chi^2(n^2(s-m))$. The multivariate LB statistic is the only statistic in PcGive that does not reduce to its univariate counterpart in a one-equation system. This would require $\widehat{\mathbf{C}}_{jj}^{-1}$ instead of $\widehat{\mathbf{C}}_{00}^{-1}$ as the last term in (11.135). The actual implementation is computationally simpler.

11.9.2.2 Vector error autocorrelation test

For lags $r \ldots s$ with $1 \le r \le s$, this tests the null hypothesis:

$$\mathsf{H}_0\colon \mathbf{R}_r = \cdots = \mathbf{R}_s = \mathbf{0} \tag{11.136}$$

in the augmented system with vector autoregressive errors:

$$\mathbf{Y}' = \boldsymbol{\Pi}\mathbf{W}' + \mathbf{V}' \quad \text{where} \quad \mathbf{V}' = \sum_{i=r}^{s} \mathbf{R}_i \mathbf{V}_i' + \mathbf{E}'. \tag{11.137}$$

It is implemented through the auxiliary system:

$$\mathbf{Y}' = \boldsymbol{\Pi}\mathbf{W}' + \mathbf{R}_r \widehat{\mathbf{V}}_r' + \cdots + \mathbf{R}_s \widehat{\mathbf{V}}_s' + \mathbf{E}'. \tag{11.138}$$

Lagged residuals are partialled out from the original regressors, and the original system is re-estimated using the new regressors, providing a Lagrange-multiplier test based on comparing the likelihoods for H_0 and H_1: $\mathbf{R}_r \neq \mathbf{0}, \ldots, \mathbf{R}_s \neq \mathbf{0}$. The LM form of the χ^2 test will be asymptotically $\chi^2\left((s-r+1)\,n^2\right)$ distributed. For a discussion, see Godfrey (1988). The F-approximation is also computed. Simulations on this test are reported in Doornik (1996), showing that the F-approximation behaves considerably better in small samples than the χ^2 form, without loss of power.

11.9.2.3 Vector normality test

First standardize the residuals of each equation. Call the new residuals $\mathbf{r}_t$, with $\mathbf{R}' = (\mathbf{r}_1 \ldots \mathbf{r}_T)$. So $\mathbf{C} = T^{-1}\mathbf{R}'\mathbf{R}$ is the correlation matrix. Following Doornik and Hansen (1994), we define the transformed residuals:

$$\mathbf{e}_t = \mathbf{E}\boldsymbol{\Lambda}^{-1/2}\mathbf{E}'\left(\mathbf{r}_t - \overline{\mathbf{r}}\right) \tag{11.139}$$

with $\boldsymbol{\Lambda} = \text{diag}(\lambda_1, \ldots, \lambda_n)$ the matrix with the eigenvalues of $\mathbf{C}$ on the diagonal. The columns of $\mathbf{E}$ are the corresponding eigenvectors, such that $\mathbf{E}'\mathbf{E} = \mathbf{I}_n$ and $\boldsymbol{\Lambda} = \mathbf{E}'\mathbf{C}\mathbf{E}$. Equation (11.139) transforms residuals $\mathbf{r}_t \sim \mathsf{IN}_n[\mathbf{0}, \mathbf{C}]$ into independent normal: $\mathbf{e}_t \sim \mathsf{IN}_n[\mathbf{0}, \mathbf{I}]$. We may now compute univariate skewness and kurtosis of each transformed residual. Defining $\mathbf{b}_1' = (\sqrt{b_{11}}, \ldots, \sqrt{b_{1n}})$, $\mathbf{b}_2' = (b_{21}, \ldots, b_{2n})$, the test statistic:

$$\frac{T\mathbf{b}_1'\mathbf{b}_1}{6} + \frac{T(\mathbf{b}_2 - 3\boldsymbol{\iota})'(\mathbf{b}_2 - 3\boldsymbol{\iota})}{24} \;\widetilde{\scriptstyle a}\; \chi^2(2n). \tag{11.140}$$

will again require large samples. The reported statistic is:

$$\mathsf{e}_{2n} = \mathbf{z}_1'\mathbf{z}_1 + \mathbf{z}_2'\mathbf{z}_2 \;\widetilde{\scriptstyle app}\; \chi^2(2n), \tag{11.141}$$

where $\mathbf{z}_1' = (z_{11}, \ldots, z_{1p})$ and $\mathbf{z}_2' = (z_{21}, \ldots, z_{2p})$ are determined as in (11.131). So, after transformation to standard normals, the univariate test is applied to each dimension. The transformation involved in (11.139) is the square root of $\mathbf{C}$. An alternative would be to use Choleski decomposition, but then the subsequent test would not be invariant to reordering of equations.

11.9.2.4 Vector heteroscedasticity test (using squares)

The test implemented by PcGive amounts to a multivariate regression of all error variances and covariances on the original regressors and their squares. Consider, for example, a two-equation system with a constant and z_t as regressors. In this case the auxiliary regression would be:

$$\begin{pmatrix} \widehat{v}_{11}^2 & \cdots & \widehat{v}_{T1}^2 \\ \widehat{v}_{12}^2 & \cdots & \widehat{v}_{T2}^2 \\ \widehat{v}_{11}\widehat{v}_{12} & \cdots & \widehat{v}_{T1}\widehat{v}_{T2} \end{pmatrix} = \begin{pmatrix} \omega_1^2 \\ \omega_2^2 \\ \omega_{12} \end{pmatrix} + \begin{pmatrix} \beta_{11} & \beta_{12} \\ \beta_{21} & \beta_{22} \\ \beta_{31} & \beta_{32} \end{pmatrix} \begin{pmatrix} z_1 & \cdots & z_T \\ z_1^2 & \cdots & z_T^2 \end{pmatrix} + \boldsymbol{\epsilon}. \tag{11.142}$$

The vector heteroscedasticity test checks the significance of the βs in the auxiliary system (11.142). Two statistics may be computed. The first is the LM test for $\boldsymbol{\beta} = \mathbf{0}$, which is $\chi^2(sn(n+1)/2)$, where s is the number of non-redundant added regressors (collinear regressors are automatically removed). Doornik (1996) shows that this test is identical to the Kelejian (1982) procedure using a common regressor set. The second statistic is the F-approximation. Unlike the vector autocorrelation test, there is not so much benefit of using the F-approximation. In general, this test tends to underreject.

11.9.2.5 Vector heteroscedasticity test (using squares and cross-products)

This test is similar to the heteroscedasticity test, but now both squares and cross-products of the regressors are included in the auxiliary regression. Again, the null hypothesis is no heteroscedasticity (the name 'functional form' was used in version 8 of PcGive).

This concludes the discussion of the system statistics based on assuming that the data are I(0). We now consider the issues of unit roots and cointegration.

Chapter 12

Cointegration Analysis

12.1 Introduction

This chapter gives a summary introduction to cointegration analysis as implemented in PcGive. There is a vast literature on unit roots and cointegration analysis. The main reference for the current chapter is Johansen (1995b). For more expository overviews, we recommend Doornik, Hendry and Nielsen (1998) and Hendry and Juselius (2001)

12.2 Equilibrium correction models

In the dynamic analysis of the system (see §11.6), we referred to the rank of the long-run matrix as determining the number of cointegrating vectors. In this chapter, we shall discuss how to estimate this rank. The original system contains n endogenous variables $\mathbf{y}$ and q non-modelled variables $\mathbf{z}$:

$$\mathbf{y}_t = \sum_{i=1}^{m} \boldsymbol{\pi}_i \mathbf{y}_{t-i} + \sum_{j=0}^{r} \boldsymbol{\Gamma}_j \mathbf{z}_{t-j} + \mathbf{v}_t, \mathbf{v}_t \sim \mathsf{IN}_n \left[\mathbf{0}, \boldsymbol{\Omega}\right], \tag{12.1}$$

so $\mathbf{y}_t$ is $n \times 1$ and $\mathbf{z}_t$ is $q \times 1$. Introducing lag-polynomials, this system is written as:

$$\left(\mathbf{I}_n - \boldsymbol{\pi}\left(L\right)\right) \mathbf{y}_t = \boldsymbol{\Gamma}\left(L\right) \mathbf{z}_t + \mathbf{v}_t, \tag{12.2}$$

with $\mathbf{P}_0 = \boldsymbol{\pi}\left(1\right) - \mathbf{I}_n$, the matrix of long-run responses.

In much of this chapter, we shall assume that no variables are known to be weakly exogenous for $(\boldsymbol{\Pi}, \boldsymbol{\Omega})$, and work with a fully endogenized system ($q = 0$, that is, the VAR):

$$\mathbf{y}_t = \sum_{i=1}^{m} \boldsymbol{\pi}_i \mathbf{y}_{t-i} + \mathbf{v}_t \;\text{ where }\; \mathbf{v}_t \sim \mathsf{IN}_n \left[\mathbf{0}, \boldsymbol{\Omega}\right]. \tag{12.3}$$

All non-singular transformations of (12.3) are isomorphic, and in particular retain an equivalent basic innovation process. When the data $\{\mathbf{y}_t\}$ are $\mathsf{I}(1)$, a useful reformulation of the system is to *equilibrium-correction form* (see Hendry, Pagan and Sargan,

1984, Engle and Granger, 1987, Johansen, 1988, Boswijk, 1992 and Banerjee, Dolado, Galbraith and Hendry, 1993):

$$\Delta \mathbf{y}_t = \sum_{i=1}^{m-1} \boldsymbol{\delta}_i \Delta \mathbf{y}_{t-i} + \mathbf{P}_0 \mathbf{y}_{t-1} + \mathbf{v}_t, \tag{12.4}$$

which has the same innovation process $\{\mathbf{v}_t\}$.[1] The transformations imply that $(\boldsymbol{\pi}_1, \boldsymbol{\pi}_2, \boldsymbol{\pi}_3, \ldots, \boldsymbol{\pi}_m) = (\mathbf{P}_0 + \boldsymbol{\delta}_1 + \mathbf{I}_n, \boldsymbol{\delta}_2 - \boldsymbol{\delta}_1, \boldsymbol{\delta}_3 - \boldsymbol{\delta}_2, \ldots, -\boldsymbol{\delta}_{m-1}) = (\gamma_1 + \mathbf{I}_n, \gamma_2 - \gamma_1, \gamma_3 - \gamma_2, \ldots, \mathbf{P}_0 - \gamma_{m-1})$.

No restrictions are imposed by the transformation in (12.4). However, when $\mathbf{y}_t$ is I(1), then $\Delta \mathbf{y}_t$ is I(0) and the system specification is balanced only if $\mathbf{P}_0 \mathbf{y}_{t-1}$ is I(0). Clearly $\mathbf{P}_0$ cannot be full rank in such a state of nature since that would contradict the assumption that $\mathbf{y}_t$ was I(1), so let rank$(\mathbf{P}_0) = p < n$. Then $\mathbf{P}_0 = \boldsymbol{\alpha}\boldsymbol{\beta}'$ where $\boldsymbol{\alpha}$ and $\boldsymbol{\beta}$ are $n \times p$ matrices of rank p, and $\boldsymbol{\beta}'\mathbf{y}_t$ must comprise p cointegrating I(0) relations inducing the restricted I(0) representation:

$$\Delta \mathbf{y}_t = \sum_{i=1}^{m-1} \boldsymbol{\delta}_i \Delta \mathbf{y}_{t-i} + \boldsymbol{\alpha} \left(\boldsymbol{\beta}' \mathbf{y}_{t-1}\right) + \mathbf{v}_t. \tag{12.5}$$

To ensure that $\mathbf{y}_t$ is not I(2), a further requirement is that:

$$\text{rank}\left(\boldsymbol{\alpha}'_{\perp} \boldsymbol{\Gamma} \boldsymbol{\beta}_{\perp}\right) = n - p \text{ when } \boldsymbol{\Gamma} = \mathbf{I}_n - \sum_{i=1}^{m-1} \boldsymbol{\delta}_i. \tag{12.6}$$

$\boldsymbol{\Gamma}$ is the long-run matrix of the differenced model; $\boldsymbol{\alpha}_{\perp}$ and $\boldsymbol{\beta}_{\perp}$ are orthogonal complements of $\boldsymbol{\alpha}$ and $\boldsymbol{\beta}$ respectively (see Chapter 10, which also shows how to compute the orthogonal complement). Should the analysis commence in I(2) space, then $\boldsymbol{\alpha}'_{\perp} \boldsymbol{\Gamma} \boldsymbol{\beta}_{\perp}$ is also reduced rank, so some linear combinations first cointegrate from I(2) to I(1), and then others (perhaps with I(1) differences of I(2) variables) cointegrate to I(0). Thus, both I(2) and I(1) impose reduced-rank restrictions on the initial formulation in (12.3), and the former imposes restrictions on (12.5). See §12.5 for a further discussion.

The rank of $\mathbf{P}_0$ is estimated using the maximum likelihood method proposed by Johansen (1988), described in the next section.

The representation of a cointegrated process in (12.3) above is via an autoregression. There is also a moving-average representation of $\mathbf{y}_t$, obtained by inverting the VAR (see Banerjee, Dolado, Galbraith and Hendry, 1993, and Johansen, 1995b):

$$\mathbf{y}_t = \mathbf{y}_0 + \mathbf{C}(1)\boldsymbol{\mu} t + \mathbf{C}(1) \sum_{i=1}^{t} \mathbf{v}_i + \mathbf{C}^* (L) \mathbf{v}_t.$$

[1] In the early cointegration literature, the convention was to write: $\Delta \mathbf{y}_t = \sum_{i=1}^{m-1} \gamma_i \Delta \mathbf{y}_{t-i} + \mathbf{P}_0 \mathbf{y}_{t-m} + \mathbf{v}_t$, and: $(\boldsymbol{\pi}_1, \boldsymbol{\pi}_2, \boldsymbol{\pi}_3, \ldots, \boldsymbol{\pi}_m) = (\gamma_1 + \mathbf{I}_n, \gamma_2 - \gamma_1, \gamma_3 - \gamma_2, \ldots, \mathbf{P}_0 - \gamma_{m-1})$.

Then $\mathbf{C}(1)$ is the moving-average impact matrix. It is computed from:

$$\mathbf{C}(1) = \boldsymbol{\beta}_{\perp} \left(\boldsymbol{\alpha}_{\perp}'\boldsymbol{\Gamma}\boldsymbol{\beta}_{\perp}\right)^{-1} \boldsymbol{\alpha}_{\perp}'$$

where

$$\text{rank}\left(\boldsymbol{\alpha}_{\perp}'\boldsymbol{\Gamma}\boldsymbol{\beta}_{\perp}\right) = n - p$$

as above.

12.3 Estimating the cointegrating rank

Since the $\{\Delta\mathbf{y}_{t-i}\}$ on the left-hand side of (12.4) enter with unrestricted coefficients, we may concentrate these out as in §11.4: regress $\Delta\mathbf{y}_t$ and $\mathbf{y}_{t-1}$ on $\{\Delta\mathbf{y}_{t-i}\}$, giving residuals $\mathbf{r}_{0t}$, $\mathbf{r}_{1t}$ respectively (both $(n \times 1)$ vectors) for $t = 1, \ldots, T$. Writing $\mathbf{R}_i' = (\mathbf{r}_{i1}\ \mathbf{r}_{i2} \cdots \mathbf{r}_{iT})$ for $i = 0, 1$, the concentrated system is:

$$\mathbf{R}_0' = \mathbf{P}_0\mathbf{R}_1' + \mathbf{V}'. \tag{12.7}$$

From §11.2, we may find the concentrated likelihood function of the system (12.7) as:

$$\begin{aligned} \ell_c(\mathbf{P}_0) &= K_c - \tfrac{T}{2}\log\left|T^{-1}\left(\mathbf{R}_0' - \mathbf{P}_0\mathbf{R}_1'\right)\left(\mathbf{R}_0 - \mathbf{R}_1\mathbf{P}_0'\right)\right| \\ &= K_c - \tfrac{T}{2}\log\left|\mathbf{S}_{00} - \mathbf{P}_0\mathbf{S}_{10} - \mathbf{S}_{01}\mathbf{P}_0' + \mathbf{P}_0\mathbf{S}_{11}\mathbf{P}_0'\right|. \end{aligned} \tag{12.8}$$

In the last line, we introduced $\mathbf{S}_{ij} = T^{-1}\mathbf{R}_i'\mathbf{R}_j$ for $i, j = 0, 1$. If $\mathbf{P}_0$ were unrestricted, we would maximize the CLF by minimizing the sum of squares, and find:

$$\widehat{\mathbf{P}}_0 = \mathbf{S}_{01}\left(\mathbf{S}_{11}\right)^{-1}. \tag{12.9}$$

We may impose the reduced-rank restriction by writing $\mathbf{P}_0 = \boldsymbol{\alpha}\boldsymbol{\beta}'$, where $\boldsymbol{\alpha}$ is an $(n \times p)$ and $\boldsymbol{\beta}'$ is a $(p \times n)$ matrix, and concentrate $\ell_c(\boldsymbol{\alpha}, \boldsymbol{\beta})$ with respect to $\boldsymbol{\alpha}$:

$$\frac{\partial \ell_c(\boldsymbol{\alpha}, \boldsymbol{\beta})}{\partial \boldsymbol{\alpha}}_{\rfloor \boldsymbol{\alpha}_c} = \mathbf{0}, \tag{12.10}$$

which implies that:

$$\boldsymbol{\alpha}_c(\boldsymbol{\beta}) = \mathbf{S}_{01}\boldsymbol{\beta}\left(\boldsymbol{\beta}'\mathbf{S}_{11}\boldsymbol{\beta}\right)^{-1}. \tag{12.11}$$

Substituting the expression for $\boldsymbol{\alpha}$ back into (12.8) yields the final CLF $\ell_c^*(\boldsymbol{\beta})$:

$$\ell_c^*(\boldsymbol{\beta}) = K_c - \frac{T}{2}\log\left|\mathbf{S}_{00} - \mathbf{S}_{01}\boldsymbol{\beta}\left(\boldsymbol{\beta}'\mathbf{S}_{11}\boldsymbol{\beta}\right)^{-1}\boldsymbol{\beta}'\mathbf{S}_{10}\right|. \tag{12.12}$$

Differentiating $\ell_c^*(\boldsymbol{\beta})$ with respect to $\boldsymbol{\beta}$ uses the same algebra as the limited-information maximum likelihood estimator for simultaneous equations (LIML). The determinant in (12.12) is (using the determinantal relation for partitioned matrices):

$$\left|\mathbf{S}_{00}\right|\left|\boldsymbol{\beta}'\mathbf{S}_{11}\boldsymbol{\beta}\right|^{-1}\left|\boldsymbol{\beta}'\left(\mathbf{S}_{11} - \mathbf{S}_{10}\mathbf{S}_{00}^{-1}\mathbf{S}_{01}\right)\boldsymbol{\beta}\right|. \tag{12.13}$$

Since $|\mathbf{S}_{00}|$ is a constant relative to $\boldsymbol{\beta}$, maximizing $\ell_c^*(\boldsymbol{\beta})$ with respect to $\boldsymbol{\beta}$ entails minimizing the generalized variance ratio, which is:

$$\frac{\left|\boldsymbol{\beta}'\left(\mathbf{S}_{11}-\mathbf{S}_{10}\mathbf{S}_{00}^{-1}\mathbf{S}_{01}\right)\boldsymbol{\beta}\right|}{\left|\boldsymbol{\beta}'\mathbf{S}_{11}\boldsymbol{\beta}\right|}. \tag{12.14}$$

This is a ratio of determinants of quadratic forms, such that the denominator matrix exceeds the numerator by a non-negative definite matrix. A normalization is needed on $\boldsymbol{\beta}$ to select a unique outcome, and we use $\boldsymbol{\beta}'\mathbf{S}_{11}\boldsymbol{\beta}=\mathbf{I}_p$. The MLE therefore requires minimizing:

$$\left|\boldsymbol{\beta}'\left(\mathbf{S}_{11}-\mathbf{S}_{10}\mathbf{S}_{00}^{-1}\mathbf{S}_{01}\right)\boldsymbol{\beta}\right| \quad \text{subject to} \quad \boldsymbol{\beta}'\mathbf{S}_{11}\boldsymbol{\beta}=\mathbf{I}_p, \tag{12.15}$$

so we must solve:[2]

$$\left|\lambda\mathbf{S}_{11}-\mathbf{S}_{10}\mathbf{S}_{00}^{-1}\mathbf{S}_{01}\right|=0 \tag{12.16}$$

for the p largest eigenvalues $1>\widehat{\lambda}_1>\cdots>\widehat{\lambda}_p>\cdots>\widehat{\lambda}_n>0$. The corresponding eigenvectors are found from:

$$\left(\widehat{\lambda}_i\mathbf{S}_{11}-\mathbf{S}_{10}\mathbf{S}_{00}^{-1}\mathbf{S}_{01}\right)\widehat{\boldsymbol{\beta}}_i=\mathbf{0}, \tag{12.17}$$

subject to $\widehat{\boldsymbol{\beta}}_i'\mathbf{S}_{11}\widehat{\boldsymbol{\beta}}_i=1$ and $\widehat{\boldsymbol{\beta}}_i'\mathbf{S}_{11}\widehat{\boldsymbol{\beta}}_j=0$ for $i\neq j$. Selecting the p largest eigenvalues, with corresponding eigenvector matrix $\widehat{\boldsymbol{\beta}}$, corresponds to imposing a cointegrating rank of p. From (12.15) and (12.17) we find the restricted likelihood to be proportional to:

$$\left|\widehat{\boldsymbol{\beta}}'\left(\mathbf{S}_{11}-\mathbf{S}_{10}\mathbf{S}_{00}^{-1}\mathbf{S}_{01}\right)\widehat{\boldsymbol{\beta}}\right|=\left|\mathbf{I}_p-\widehat{\boldsymbol{\Lambda}}_p\right|=\prod_{i=1}^{p}\left(1-\widehat{\lambda}_i\right), \tag{12.18}$$

where $\widehat{\boldsymbol{\Lambda}}_p$ is the $(p\times p)$ diagonal matrix of eigenvalues. Consequently, from (12.12) and (12.13):

$$\ell_c^*\left(\widehat{\boldsymbol{\beta}}\right)=K_c-\frac{T}{2}\log|\mathbf{S}_{00}|-\frac{T}{2}\sum_{i=1}^{p}\log\left(1-\widehat{\lambda}_i\right) \tag{12.19}$$

corresponding to the p largest eigenvalues.

When $\mathbf{P}_0$ is estimated unrestrictedly, the maximum of the likelihood is:

$$\ell_c^*\left(\widehat{\boldsymbol{\beta}}_0\right)=K_c-\frac{T}{2}\log|\mathbf{S}_{00}|-\frac{T}{2}\sum_{i=1}^{n}\log\left(1-\widehat{\lambda}_i\right), \tag{12.20}$$

where $\widehat{\boldsymbol{\beta}}_0$ denotes the $(n\times n)$ matrix of eigenvectors.

---

[2]This is a generalized eigenvalue problem which can be transformed to the standard eigenvalue problem by writing $\mathbf{S}_{11}=\mathbf{L}\mathbf{L}'$. Let $\boldsymbol{\gamma}=\mathbf{L}'\boldsymbol{\beta}$, then (12.15) may be written as: $|\boldsymbol{\gamma}'(\mathbf{I}_p-\mathbf{L}^{-1}\mathbf{S}_{10}\mathbf{S}_{00}^{-1}\mathbf{S}_{01}\mathbf{L}'^{-1})\boldsymbol{\gamma}|$ subject to $\boldsymbol{\gamma}'\boldsymbol{\gamma}=\mathbf{I}_p$.

The hypothesis that there are $0 \leq p < n$ cointegrating vectors yields (12.19), so tests can be based on twice the difference of (12.19) and (12.20):

$$\eta_p = -T \sum_{i=p+1}^{n} \log\left(1 - \widehat{\lambda}_i\right) \quad \text{for} \quad p = 0, 1, \ldots, n-1. \tag{12.21}$$

The distribution of the η_p test, derived under the hypothesis that there are p cointegrating vectors, is a functional of $n - p$ dimensional Brownian motion. Testing proceeds by the sequence $\eta_0, \eta_1, \ldots, \eta_{n-1}$. Then p is selected as the first insignificant statistic η_p, or zero if η_0 is not significant. This is the *trace statistic* for H_p within H_n, akin to a vector Dickey–Fuller test.

Tests of the hypothesis of p cointegrating vectors within H_{p+1} (that is, testing if there are p when at most $p+1$ exist) can be based on the $(p+1)^{st}$ eigenvalue using:

$$\xi_p = -T \log\left(1 - \widehat{\lambda}_{p+1}\right), \tag{12.22}$$

called the *maximum eigenvalue statistic*. Again ξ_p has a distribution that is a functional of vector Brownian motion.

The sequence of trace tests leads to a consistent test procedure, but no such result is available for the maximum eigenvalue test. Therefore current practice is to only consider the former. Critical values for the trace tests have been tabulated by *inter alia* Johansen (1988), Johansen and Juselius (1990), Osterwald-Lenum (1992), and Doornik (1998). The p-values which are reported in PcGive are based on the approximations to the asymptotic distributions derived by Doornik (1998).

The solution to the unrestricted system is (12.20), with coefficient estimates $\widehat{\boldsymbol{\alpha}}_0$, $\widehat{\boldsymbol{\beta}}_0$ where $\widehat{\boldsymbol{\beta}}_0$ is the full $(n \times n)$ matrix of orthogonalized eigenvectors (the coefficients in the equilibrium-correction mechanisms), and $\widehat{\boldsymbol{\alpha}}_0$ the $(n \times n)$ matrix of feedback coefficients on the ECMs (the 'loadings') which may be found from (12.11): $\widehat{\boldsymbol{\alpha}}_0 = \mathbf{S}_{01}\widehat{\boldsymbol{\beta}}_0$. The unrestricted long-run matrix is $\widehat{\mathbf{P}}_0 = \widehat{\boldsymbol{\alpha}}_0\widehat{\boldsymbol{\beta}}_0'$. If, on the basis of the test procedure, it is decided to accept a rank of p, $0 < p < n$, the solution is (12.19), with loadings $\widehat{\boldsymbol{\alpha}}$ (the first p columns of $\widehat{\boldsymbol{\alpha}}$) and coefficients $\widehat{\boldsymbol{\beta}}$ (the first p columns of $\widehat{\boldsymbol{\beta}}_0$). The reduced rank long-run matrix will be $\widehat{\boldsymbol{\alpha}}\widehat{\boldsymbol{\beta}}'$, and $\widehat{\boldsymbol{\beta}}'\mathbf{y}_{t-1}$ are the equilibrium-correction terms (this follows from Granger's representation theorem: see, for example, Banerjee, Dolado, Galbraith and Hendry, 1993).

12.4 Deterministic terms and restricted variables

The above results are presented for the simplest model to clarify the analysis. One natural extension is the presence of intercepts in equations. Under the null of no cointegrating vectors, non-zero intercepts would generate trends. However, in equations with equilibrium corrections, two possibilities arise, namely, the intercept only enters the equilibrium correction (to adjust its mean value), or it enters as an autonomous growth factor in the equation.

Let us reintroduce the $(q \times 1)$ variable $\mathbf{z}_t$ to indicate the additional variables in the system. Usually $\mathbf{z}_t$ contains variables such as the constant, trend or centred seasonals. The second possibility implies that $\mathbf{z}_t$ enters unrestricted, and it is concentrated out together with the $\{\Delta \mathbf{y}_{t-i}\}$, leaving the procedure otherwise unaltered; denote these q_u variables by $\mathbf{z}_t^u$. The first possibility means that some zs are restricted to enter the cointegrating space, which now becomes $\boldsymbol{\beta}'(\mathbf{y}_{t-1} : \mathbf{z}_t^r)$, so that $\boldsymbol{\beta}'$ is now $(p \times (n + q_r))$. Then $\mathbf{S}_{01}$ and $\mathbf{S}_{11}$ change accordingly, but otherwise the analysis of the previous section goes through unaltered, adding q_r eigenvalues of zero. It is important to note that *the distributions of the tests are affected by the presence of (un)restricted* $\mathbf{z}_t$.

In practice, how the deterministic components are treated has an important impact on the statistics and careful thought should be given at the outset as to whether or not z_t can be restricted to the cointegrating space. If one component is a trend, such restriction is essential when there are unit roots unless a quadratic trend in levels is anticipated (although the inclusion may be an attempt to induce similarity in the associated tests: see Kiviet and Phillips, 1992). Because of its importance, this issue featured extensively in the tutorials, see §§4.2, 4.6, §5.3. Three models for the deterministic components merit consideration when determining the rank of cointegration space rank. These can be described by the dependence of the expected values of $\mathbf{y}$ and $\boldsymbol{\beta}'\mathbf{y}$ on functions of time t:

Hypothesis	$\mathbf{y}$	$\boldsymbol{\beta}'\mathbf{y}$	*Constant*	*Trend*
$\mathsf{H}_l(p)$	linear	linear	unrestricted	restricted
$\mathsf{H}_c(p)$	constant	constant	restricted	not present
$\mathsf{H}_z(p)$	zero	zero	not present	not present

12.5 The $\mathsf{I}(2)$ analysis

Tests in $\mathsf{I}(2)$ models combine testing the rank of $\mathbf{P}_0$ in:

$$\Delta^2 \mathbf{y}_t = \mathbf{P}_0 \mathbf{y}_{t-1} - \boldsymbol{\Gamma} \Delta \mathbf{y}_{t-1} + \boldsymbol{\Phi} \mathbf{q}_t + \mathbf{v}_t, \quad t = 1, \ldots, T, \tag{12.23}$$

with a reduced rank condition on $\boldsymbol{\Gamma}$.

The equivalent of $\mathsf{H}_l(p)$ is discussed in Rahbek, Kongsted and Jørgensen (1999) This is the trend-stationary model which precludes a quadratic trend but allows for a linear trend in the levels:

$$\Delta^2 \mathbf{y}_t = \mathbf{P}_0 \left(\mathbf{y}_{t-1} - \boldsymbol{\mu} - \boldsymbol{\tau}(t-1) \right) + \boldsymbol{\Gamma} \left(\Delta \mathbf{y}_{t-1} - \boldsymbol{\tau} \right) + \mathbf{v}_t. \tag{12.24}$$

In the $\mathsf{I}(2)$ model presented in (12.23) there are two reduced rank matrices. The first is $\mathbf{P}_0 = \boldsymbol{\alpha}\boldsymbol{\beta}'$, where $\boldsymbol{\alpha}$ and $\boldsymbol{\beta}$ are $n \times p$ matrices as before. Next, define the $n \times (n-p)$

matrix $\boldsymbol{\alpha}_\perp$ so that $\boldsymbol{\alpha}_\perp'\boldsymbol{\alpha}_\perp = \mathbf{I}_{n-p}$ and $\alpha_\perp'\alpha = 0$. The second reduced rank condition is:

$$\boldsymbol{\alpha}_\perp'\boldsymbol{\Gamma}\boldsymbol{\beta}_\perp = \boldsymbol{\xi}'\boldsymbol{\eta}, \tag{12.25}$$

where $\boldsymbol{\xi}$ and $\boldsymbol{\eta}$ are $(n-p) \times s$ matrices.

The statistical analysis follows the two-step procedure proposed by Johansen (1995c):

(1) In the first step, $\Delta\mathbf{y}_{t-1}$ and a constant enter unrestrictedly in an $\mathsf{I}(1)$ analysis of $\Delta^2\mathbf{y}_t$ on $\mathbf{y}_{t-1}$ with a restricted trend. This gives $\widehat{\boldsymbol{\alpha}}$ and $\widehat{\boldsymbol{\beta}}$ for each rank p, and corresponding orthogonal complements.

(2) The second step is a reduced rank analysis of $\widehat{\boldsymbol{\alpha}}_\perp'\Delta^2\mathbf{y}_t$ on $(\widehat{\boldsymbol{\beta}}_\perp'\widehat{\boldsymbol{\beta}}_\perp)^{-1}\widehat{\boldsymbol{\beta}}_\perp'\Delta\mathbf{y}_{t-1}$ with restricted constant and the differenced linear combinations of $\mathsf{I}(2)$ variables from the first step entered unrestrictedly.

The first step of the procedure involves testing the rank of $\mathbf{P}_0$, leaving $\boldsymbol{\Gamma}$ unrestricted. The test statistic is denoted by $\mathsf{Q}(p)$. This step amounts to testing the number of $\mathsf{I}(2)$ components. The second step then tests for the number of $\mathsf{I}(1)$ components remaining, and is denoted by $\mathsf{Q}(p,s)$. The test statistic of interest is $\mathsf{S}(p,s) = \mathsf{Q}(p) + \mathsf{Q}(p,s)$.

The hypotheses involved are:

- $\mathsf{Q}(p)$ tests whether $\text{rank}(\mathbf{P}_0) \leq p$ given that $\text{rank}(\mathbf{P}_0) \leq n$: $\mathsf{H}(p)|\mathsf{H}(n)$. When there are no $\mathsf{I}(2)$ relations: $n-p-s=0$, and $\mathsf{Q}(p)$ equals $\mathsf{T}(p)$, the trace test in the $\mathsf{I}(1)$ case.
- $\mathsf{Q}(p,s)$ tests whether $\text{rank}(\mathbf{P}_0) \leq p$ and there are $\leq n-p-s$ $\mathsf{I}(2)$ components given that $\text{rank}(\mathbf{P}_0) \leq n$ and there are $\leq n-p$ components which are $\mathsf{I}(2)$.
- $\mathsf{S}(p,s)$ tests whether $\text{rank}(\mathbf{P}_0) \leq p$ and there are $\leq n-p-s$ $\mathsf{I}(2)$ components given that $\text{rank}(\mathbf{P}_0) \leq n$. When there are no $\mathsf{I}(2)$ relations: $\mathsf{S}(p, n-p) = \mathsf{Q}(p) = \mathsf{T}(p)$.

As for the $\mathsf{I}(1)$ tests, 5 cases may be distinguished, although we rule out the cases without a constant term, and with a quadratic trend:

	Constant	Trend	Model, $\Delta^2\mathbf{y}_t =$
H_l	unrestricted	restricted	$\mathbf{P}_0(\mathbf{y}_{t-1} - \boldsymbol{\mu} - \boldsymbol{\tau}(t-1)) + \boldsymbol{\Gamma}(\Delta\mathbf{y}_{t-1} - \boldsymbol{\tau}) + \mathbf{v}_t,$
H_{lc}	unrestricted	none	$\mathbf{P}_0(\mathbf{y}_{t-1} - \mu) + \boldsymbol{\Gamma}(\Delta\mathbf{y}_{t-1} - \tau) + \mathbf{v}_t,$
H_c	restricted	none	$\mathbf{P}_0(\mathbf{y}_{t-1} - \boldsymbol{\mu}) + \boldsymbol{\Gamma}\Delta\mathbf{y}_{t-1} + \mathbf{v}_t.$

The theory for H_l is developed in Rahbek, Kongsted and Jørgensen (1999), H_{lc} and H_c are tabulated in Paruolo (1996). Models H_z and H_{ql} are omitted here; the former is tabulated in Johansen (1995c), the latter in Paruolo (1996). Doornik (1998) provides distributional approximations for H_l, H_{lc}, and H_c, which are used in PcGive.

12.6 Numerically stable estimation

From the perspective of numerical analysis, it is not recommended to use equation (12.16) as it stands. The computations can become numerically unstable, and in some rare cases we have eigenvalues that are far outside the $(0, 1)$ interval (in which they should fall theoretically). Doornik (1995a) found that a singular value decomposition based implementation avoids these pitfalls. A full discussion of the numerical aspects of cointegration analysis is in Doornik and O'Brien (2002); PcGive uses their Algorithm 4.

12.7 Recursive estimation

Recursive estimation of the cointegrating space requires solving the eigenvalue problem (12.16) for each sample size $t = M, \ldots, T$. A choice has to be made between doing the whole procedure recursively, or fixing the short-run dynamics at their full sample values (hence recursively solving from (12.7) onwards). Hansen and Johansen (1992) call the former the Z-representation and the latter the R-representation. Both representations have been implemented in PcGive.

12.8 Testing restrictions on $\boldsymbol{\alpha}$ and $\boldsymbol{\beta}$

12.8.1 Introduction

Having accepted H_p: cointegrating rank $= p$, we may test further restrictions on $\boldsymbol{\alpha}$ and $\boldsymbol{\beta}$. Over time, we have seen the development of procedures for testing a range of hypotheses. Initially, these were imposing the same restrictions on each vector, but now they are primarily concerned with identifying cointegrating vectors and testing for long-run weak exogeneity.

Table 12.1 gives a summary of various hypotheses on the cointegrating space with references to their development and application. As one moves down the table, the complexity of the implementation increases.

H_g, which allows for general restrictions is the richest and encompasses the other test statistics. However, it is also the hardest to compute. Computation of H_a to H_c involves a modified eigenproblem, whereas the other test procedures use iterative methods. The hypothesis on $\boldsymbol{\alpha}$ of type H_a can be combined with restrictions on $\boldsymbol{\beta}$ without substantial change to the methods; but often it is more interesting to test exclusion restrictions on the $\boldsymbol{\alpha}$ matrix.

In the remainder, we shall first discuss several types of restriction separately, and then combine the tests on $\boldsymbol{\alpha}$ and $\boldsymbol{\beta}$. Finally the more general procedures are discussed. Because all tests in this section are conditional on H_p, they are in I(0) space, and likelihood ratio test statistics have conventional χ^2 distributions (asymptotically). Detailed descriptions of the mathematics of the tests have been omitted.

Table 12.1 Summary of restrictions on cointegrating space.

	hypothesis	reference
H_a	$\boldsymbol{\alpha} = \mathbf{A}_1\boldsymbol{\theta}_1$	Johansen (1991), Johansen and Juselius (1990)
H_b	$\boldsymbol{\beta}_2 = \mathbf{H}_2\boldsymbol{\phi}_2$	Johansen (1988, 1991) Johansen and Juselius (1990)
H_c	$\boldsymbol{\beta}_3 = (\mathbf{H}_3 : \boldsymbol{\phi}_3)$	Johansen and Juselius (1992)
H_d	$\boldsymbol{\beta}_4 = (\mathbf{H}_4\boldsymbol{\varphi} : \boldsymbol{\psi})$	Johansen and Juselius (1992)
H_e	$\boldsymbol{\beta}_5 = (\mathbf{H}_1\boldsymbol{\varphi}_1 \ldots \mathbf{H}_p\boldsymbol{\varphi}_p)$	Johansen (1995a), Johansen and Juselius (1994)
H_f	$\text{vec}\boldsymbol{\beta}_6 = \mathbf{H}\boldsymbol{\varphi} + h$, $\text{vec}\boldsymbol{\alpha}_6' = \mathbf{G}\boldsymbol{\theta}$	Boswijk (1995)
H_g	$\boldsymbol{\beta}_7 = \mathbf{f}_\beta(\boldsymbol{\theta}), \boldsymbol{\alpha} = \mathbf{f}_\alpha(\boldsymbol{\theta})$	Doornik (1995b), Hendry and Doornik (1994), Boswijk and Doornik (2004)

12.8.2 Restrictions on $\boldsymbol{\alpha}$, H_a: $\boldsymbol{\alpha}_1 = \mathbf{A}_1\boldsymbol{\theta}_1$

Suppose that we have a VAR of three equations, $\mathbf{y} = (y_1, y_2, y_3)'$, so $\mathbf{P}_0$ is (3×3). Then we could (for example) test that none of the cointegrating vectors enters the first equation (believing that the cointegrating rank is 2: $\boldsymbol{\alpha}$ and $\boldsymbol{\beta}$ are (3×2)). This restricts the $\boldsymbol{\alpha}$ matrix and is expressed as $\boldsymbol{\alpha}_r = \mathbf{A}\boldsymbol{\theta}$:

$$\mathbf{A} = \begin{pmatrix} 0 & 0 \\ 1 & 0 \\ 0 & 1 \end{pmatrix}, \quad \boldsymbol{\theta} = \begin{pmatrix} \theta_{11} & \theta_{12} \\ \theta_{21} & \theta_{22} \end{pmatrix}, \quad \mathbf{A}\boldsymbol{\theta} = \begin{pmatrix} 0 & 0 \\ \theta_{11} & \theta_{12} \\ \theta_{21} & \theta_{22} \end{pmatrix}. \tag{12.26}$$

This choice of $\mathbf{A}$ implies a selected cointegrating rank ≤ 2. If this restriction is rejected, Δy_1 is not weakly exogenous for $\boldsymbol{\alpha}$ and $\boldsymbol{\beta}$ (the distribution of Δy_1 given lagged $\Delta y_1, \Delta y_2, \Delta y_3$ contains elements of $\boldsymbol{\alpha}$ and $\boldsymbol{\beta}$).

12.8.3 Restrictions on $\boldsymbol{\beta}$, H_b: $\boldsymbol{\beta}_2 = \mathbf{H}_2\boldsymbol{\phi}_2$

The first hypothesis on $\boldsymbol{\beta}$, $\boldsymbol{\beta} = \mathbf{H}\boldsymbol{\phi}$, allows us to impose linear restrictions linking coefficients in the cointegrating vectors. Suppose we wish to test that the first two variables enter the cointegrating vector with opposite sign. Assuming $p = 2$, the unrestricted vectors are:

$$\boldsymbol{\beta}'\mathbf{y} = \begin{pmatrix} \beta_{11}y_1 + \beta_{21}y_2 + \beta_{31}y_3 \\ \beta_{12}y_1 + \beta_{22}y_2 + \beta_{32}y_3 \end{pmatrix}. \tag{12.27}$$

We can impose $\beta_{21} = -\beta_{11}$, $\beta_{22} = -\beta_{12}$:

$$\mathbf{H} = \begin{pmatrix} 1 & 0 \\ -1 & 0 \\ 0 & 1 \end{pmatrix}, \quad \boldsymbol{\phi} = \begin{pmatrix} \phi_{11} & \phi_{12} \\ \phi_{21} & \phi_{22} \end{pmatrix}, \quad \boldsymbol{\phi}'\mathbf{H}' = \begin{pmatrix} \phi_{11} & -\phi_{11} & \phi_{21} \\ \phi_{12} & -\phi_{12} & \phi_{22} \end{pmatrix}. \tag{12.28}$$

This $\mathbf{H}$ implies a selected cointegrating rank ≤ 2.

12.8.4 Restrictions on $\boldsymbol{\beta}$, H_c: $\boldsymbol{\beta}_3 = (\mathbf{H}_3 : \boldsymbol{\phi}_3)$

The second hypothesis on $\boldsymbol{\beta}$ allows us to impose known cointegrating vectors. Consider that the first vector is $y_1 - y_2 - y_3$. Again assuming $p = 2$, the $\mathbf{H}$ matrix is:

$$\mathbf{H} = \begin{pmatrix} 1 \\ -1 \\ -1 \end{pmatrix}, \quad \boldsymbol{\phi} = \begin{pmatrix} \phi_{11} \\ \phi_{21} \\ \phi_{31} \end{pmatrix}, \quad (\mathbf{H} : \boldsymbol{\phi})' = \begin{pmatrix} 1 & -1 & -1 \\ \phi_{11} & \phi_{21} & \phi_{31} \end{pmatrix}. \tag{12.29}$$

12.8.5 Combining restrictions on $\boldsymbol{\alpha}$ and $\boldsymbol{\beta}$

The combination of tests on $\boldsymbol{\alpha}$ and $\boldsymbol{\beta}$ is explained more easily if we see that all tests start with a second moment matrix, which is transformed:

$$\begin{pmatrix} \mathbf{S}_{11} & \mathbf{S}_{12} \\ \mathbf{S}_{21} & \mathbf{S}_{22} \end{pmatrix} \longrightarrow \begin{pmatrix} \mathbf{S}_{11.1} & \mathbf{S}_{12.1} \\ \mathbf{S}_{21.1} & \mathbf{S}_{22.1} \end{pmatrix}, \tag{12.30}$$

and then solve the eigenproblem:

$$\left|\lambda \mathbf{S}_{22.1} - \mathbf{S}_{21.1}\mathbf{S}_{11.1}^{-1}\mathbf{S}_{12.1}\right| = 0. \tag{12.31}$$

The test on $\boldsymbol{\alpha}$ effectively reduces the dimension of the $\mathbf{S}_{11}$ part, the test on $\boldsymbol{\beta}$ that of the $\mathbf{S}_{22}$ part. So combining H_a with either H_b or H_c works by first transforming according to H_a, then replacing $\mathbf{S}_{00}$, $\mathbf{S}_{01}$, $\mathbf{S}_{11}$, $\mathbf{S}_{10}$ by $\mathbf{S}_{aa.b}$, $\mathbf{S}_{a1.b}$, $\mathbf{S}_{1a.b}$, $\mathbf{S}_{11.b}$. Next H_b or H_c are implemented, and the resulting eigenvalue problem may be solved. From this $\widehat{\boldsymbol{\beta}}$ may be derived as in the previous two sections.

12.8.6 Testing more general restrictions

The appeal of the aforementioned tests is that they all have a general eigenproblem as their solution. The drawback, however, is that the tests require separate implementation, while not exhausting all interesting hypotheses. The primary interest here is in restrictions of the form $\boldsymbol{\beta}_i = \mathbf{H}_i\boldsymbol{\phi}_i$, $i = 1, \ldots, p$, perhaps combined with restrictions on $\boldsymbol{\alpha}$: $\boldsymbol{\alpha}_i = \mathbf{A}_i\boldsymbol{\psi}_i$. It is crucial to check that the set of restrictions yields uniquely identified $\boldsymbol{\beta}_i$: see Johansen (1995a). These tests are all in I(0) space and correspond to

LR tests, so the easiest implementation is direct maximization of the likelihood function allowing for general restrictions (possibly non-linear). This is done sequentially using a numerical optimization procedure outlined below.

Again assume a cointegrating rank p. The hypothesis is expressed as:

$$\mathsf{H}_g\text{: } \{\boldsymbol{\alpha} = \mathbf{f}(\boldsymbol{\alpha}^u)\} \cap \{\boldsymbol{\beta} = \mathbf{f}(\boldsymbol{\beta}^u)\}, \tag{12.32}$$

where $\boldsymbol{\alpha}$ and $\boldsymbol{\beta}$ are expressed as a function of the unrestricted elements $\boldsymbol{\alpha}^u$, $\boldsymbol{\beta}^u$. The function in (12.32) may be non-linear, and even link $\boldsymbol{\alpha}$ and $\boldsymbol{\beta}$. Consider an example with $n = 4, p = 2$:

$$\boldsymbol{\alpha} = \begin{pmatrix} \theta_0 & \theta_1 \\ \theta_2 & \theta_3 \\ \theta_4 & \theta_5 \\ \theta_6 & \theta_7 \end{pmatrix}, \quad \boldsymbol{\beta}' = \begin{pmatrix} \theta_8 & \theta_9 & \theta_{10} & \theta_{11} \\ \theta_{12} & \theta_{13} & \theta_{14} & \theta_{15} \end{pmatrix}. \tag{12.33}$$

A possible restriction we may wish to test is $\theta_6 = 0, \theta_7 = 0, \theta_{10} = \theta_{11}, \theta_{14} = \theta_{15}$. Another could be $\theta_6\theta_{11} + \theta_7\theta_{15} = 0$; this type of restriction is considered by Hunter (1992) and Mosconi and Giannini (1992) (also see Toda and Phillips, 1993, who note the need for care in testing when some parameters vanish from the hypothesis when others are zero).

12.9 Estimation under general restrictions

PcGive can estimate restrictions of the type H_e, H_f and H_g. The log-likelihood being maximized is:

$$\ell_c(\boldsymbol{\alpha}^u, \boldsymbol{\beta}^u) \propto -\log\left|(\mathbf{I}_n : -\boldsymbol{\alpha}\boldsymbol{\beta}') \begin{pmatrix} \mathbf{S}_{00} & \mathbf{S}_{01} \\ \mathbf{S}_{10} & \mathbf{S}_{11} \end{pmatrix} \begin{pmatrix} \mathbf{I}_n \\ -\boldsymbol{\beta}\boldsymbol{\alpha}' \end{pmatrix}\right|.$$

There are various reasons why this is a difficult optimization problem: it may happen that not all parameters are identified, it could be that normalization is on coefficients which are actually not well identified, and when switching, the resulting function can be very flat, leading to slow progress. The current implementation has been tuned over quite a few years, and is hopefully robust in most practical settings.

Input of restrictions is not in the form of H matrices, but in the form of explicit relations. These restrictions are then analyzed as follows:

(1) Analytical differentiation at two random points is used to check for linearity. If linear this yields the $\mathbf{F}$ and $\mathbf{f}$ matrices:

$$\left[(\text{vec}\boldsymbol{\alpha}')' : (\text{vec}\boldsymbol{\beta})'\right]' = \mathbf{F}\boldsymbol{\phi} + \mathbf{f}.$$

(2) Next, it is checked whether the restrictions on $\boldsymbol{\alpha}$ and $\boldsymbol{\beta}$ are *variation free*, i.e. whether $\mathbf{F}$ is block diagonal. If so, this yields the $\mathbf{G}$, $\mathbf{g}$, $\mathbf{H}$ and $\mathbf{h}$ matrices:

$$\text{vec}\boldsymbol{\beta} = \mathbf{H}\boldsymbol{\varphi} + \mathbf{h}, \quad \text{vec}\boldsymbol{\alpha}' = \mathbf{G}\boldsymbol{\theta} + \mathbf{g}.$$

(3) The $\boldsymbol{\alpha}$ restrictions are *homogeneous* when $\mathbf{g}$ is zero.
(4) The $\boldsymbol{\beta}$ restrictions are *scale-homogeneous* when all non-zero elements in $\mathbf{h}$ have a corresponding row of zeros in $\mathbf{H}$ (i.e. each normalization is directly in terms of a β_i and does not involve any ϕs).
(5) The absence of cross-equation restrictions on $\boldsymbol{\beta}$ implies that $\mathbf{H}$ is block diagonal.
(6) The restrictions on $\boldsymbol{\alpha}$ are *simple* if they consist of exclusion restrictions only.
(7) *Scale removal*
When the $\boldsymbol{\alpha}$ restrictions are homogeneous and simple, the $\boldsymbol{\beta}$ restrictions scale-homogeneous, and the joint restrictions are linear and variation free PcGive implements scale removal. When a normalizing restriction is imposed on each equation, the restrictions can be written in various ways. For example, the restriction $\boldsymbol{\beta}' = (1, 0, -1, 1)$ can be written as:

$$(\beta_1 = 1, \ \beta_2 = 0, \ \beta_3 = -1, \ \beta_4 = 1),$$

or as:

$$(\beta_1 = \phi, \ \beta_2 = 0, \ \beta_3 = -\phi, \ \beta_4 = \phi),$$

in combination with the normalization $\phi = 1$. Thus, PcGive is able to rewrite the equality restrictions on $\boldsymbol{\beta}$, which makes the switching more robust and much faster.

The currently available implemented estimation methods are as follows:

- Switching (scaled linear)
This method alternates between $\boldsymbol{\alpha}|\boldsymbol{\beta}$ and $\boldsymbol{\beta}|\boldsymbol{\alpha}$. Each of these is a restricted linear regression problem which can be solved explicitly, as discussed in Boswijk (1995). The scaled variant removes the normalization prior to estimation, and then reimposes it afterwards.
- Switching (linear)
This method is similar to the previous one, but here the restrictions did not allow scale removal. It requires linear and variation-free restrictions.
- Switching
In PcGive version 8, non-linear switching was the only available method. The principle is the same as in linear switching, but with each maximization step performed using non-linear optimization (BFGS, see Chapter 14). When the restrictions are linear, this is somewhat less efficient. With non-linear restrictions, the previous methods are not available.

All these methods may suffer from slow convergence, or even failure of convergence (when some parameters diverge to very large or to very small values, or both happen).

The starting values are derived from the unrestricted cointegration analysis, followed by two steps:

(1) beta switching
Occasionally, the rank of the initial $\boldsymbol{\beta}_0$ matrix is less than p (this happens when the restrictions on different vectors are linearly dependent). In that case the beta switching method is applied to obtain full rank starting values. This method switches between restricted cointegrating vectors, keeping all but one fixed. At each step, this requires solution of a generalized eigenproblem, after the matrices have been deflated using the fixed vectors. Beta switching was suggested by Johansen (1995a), and is available when $\boldsymbol{\alpha}$ is unrestricted, and the $\boldsymbol{\beta}$ restrictions are linear, within equation, and homogeneous (after the normalization has been removed).

(2) Gauss–Newton warm-up
The Gauss–Newton/quasi-Newton method is applied simultaneously to all the unknown parameters in both $\boldsymbol{\alpha}$ and $\boldsymbol{\beta}$ as long as this improves the log-likelihood by at least 1.5%. When the restrictions are not identifying, the Hessian matrix in the Gauss–Newton is singular, and the generalized inverse is used.

A first requirement for convergence is that the relative increase in the likelihood is less than $0.001\epsilon_1$. Then strong convergence (see §14.3.6) leads to termination, as does four successive occurrences of weak convergence.

12.10 Identification

Deriving the degrees of freedom involved in these test is not straightforward, especially when $\boldsymbol{\alpha}$ restrictions are involved. For example, version 8.0 of PcGive would not always get it correct. When beta switching is allowed, the global method of Johansen (1995a) could be used. This will not work for more general restrictions, and the generic identification check of Doornik (1995b) is used instead, see Boswijk and Doornik (2004). This involves checking the rank of the Jacobian matrix of $\mathbf{P}_0(\boldsymbol{\theta}) = \boldsymbol{\alpha}(\boldsymbol{\theta})\boldsymbol{\beta}(\boldsymbol{\theta})'$ with respect to $\boldsymbol{\theta}$ at a randomly selected parameter value $\boldsymbol{\theta}^*$.

It is important to bear in mind that the following situations may occur:

- some cointegrating vectors are identified, but others are not;
- although restrictions have been imposed, these are just rotations, not affecting the likelihood at all;
- restrictions have been imposed, but no identification achieved.

It is easy to illustrate the inherent complexity of counting restrictions. For simplicity, we assume that the identifying restrictions are imposed on $\boldsymbol{\beta}$. In the unrestricted case of rank p, there are np parameters in $\boldsymbol{\alpha}$ and $np - p^2$ in $\boldsymbol{\beta}$. Restrictions on $\boldsymbol{\beta}$ are only binding if they cannot be 'absorbed' by the $\boldsymbol{\alpha}$s, and vice versa. This is most easily seen for rank n: restricting $\boldsymbol{\beta}' = \mathbf{I}_n$ results in $\widehat{\boldsymbol{\alpha}} = \widehat{\mathbf{P}}_0$, whereas imposing $\boldsymbol{\alpha} = \mathbf{I}_n$ gives $\widehat{\boldsymbol{\beta}}' = \widehat{\mathbf{P}}_0$. But setting $\boldsymbol{\alpha} = \mathbf{0}$ imposes n^2 restrictions (which, of course, violate cointegration).

Restrictions of the form $\theta_8 = 0$, or $\theta_8 = 0$ and $\theta_9 = 1$ in example (12.33) are not binding, because we may choose $\mathbf{L}$ such that $\theta_8 = \theta_{13} = 0$, $\theta_9 = \theta_{12} = 1$. However, imposing $\theta_8 = \theta_9 = 0$ would be binding, as it would require a singular $\mathbf{L}$; instead it involves one restriction, because only one of the zeros can be absorbed by a non-singular $\mathbf{L}$. The hypothesis $\theta_{10} = \theta_{11}$, $\theta_{14} = \theta_{15}$ equates two columns of $\boldsymbol{\beta}'$, one of which can be absorbed, resulting in two restrictions. This explains the number of restrictions involved in H_b, which amounts to fixing $(n - s)$ columns of p elements each. Fixing a row of $\boldsymbol{\beta}'$, as does H_c, constrains only $n - p$ parameters, as the first p may be absorbed by $\mathbf{L}$ (provided it can be done with a non-singular $\mathbf{L}$).

Further examples on the identification of the cointegrating vectors are given in Chapter 5.

Finally, some forms of constraint on $\boldsymbol{\alpha}$ and $\boldsymbol{\beta}$ can induce a failure of identification of the other under the null, in which case the tests need not have χ^2 distributions (see, for example, Toda and Phillips, 1993).

Chapter 13

Econometric Analysis of the Simultaneous Equations Model

13.1 The econometric model

The main criterion for the validity of the system:

$$\mathbf{y}_t = \boldsymbol{\Pi}\mathbf{w}_t + \mathbf{v}_t, \quad \mathbf{v}_t \sim \mathsf{IN}_n\left[\mathbf{0}, \boldsymbol{\Omega}\right], \quad t = 1, \ldots, T, \tag{13.1}$$

is its congruence, since that is a necessary condition for efficient statistical estimation and inference. Chapter 11 established notation and discussed the econometric techniques for estimation and evaluation of (13.1). An econometric model is a restricted version of a congruent system which sustains an economic interpretation, consistent with the associated theory. All linear structural models of (13.1) can be obtained by premultiplying (13.1) by a non-singular $(n \times n)$ matrix $\mathbf{B}$ which generates:

$$\mathbf{B}\mathbf{y}_t + \mathbf{C}\mathbf{w}_t = \mathbf{u}_t, \quad \mathbf{u}_t \sim \mathsf{IN}_n\left[\mathbf{0}, \boldsymbol{\Sigma}\right], \quad t = 1, \ldots, T, \tag{13.2}$$

with $\mathbf{u}_t = \mathbf{B}\mathbf{v}_t$, $\boldsymbol{\Sigma} = \mathbf{B}\boldsymbol{\Omega}\mathbf{B}'$ and $\mathbf{C} = -\mathbf{B}\boldsymbol{\Pi}$. We implicitly assume that the diagonal of $\mathbf{B}$ is normalized at unity to ensure a unique scaling in every equation: other normalizations are feasible. Further, the reformulation in I(0) space would have the same form. Then (13.2) can be written in compact notation as:

$$\mathbf{B}\mathbf{Y}' + \mathbf{C}\mathbf{W}' = \mathbf{A}\mathbf{X}' = \mathbf{U}'. \tag{13.3}$$

So $\mathbf{A} = (\mathbf{B} : \mathbf{C})$ and $\mathbf{X} = (\mathbf{Y} : \mathbf{W})$: these are $(n \times (n+k))$ and $(T \times (n+k))$ matrices respectively.

We shall require the matrices $\mathbf{R}$ and $\mathbf{Q}$:

$$\mathbf{R} = (\mathbf{I}_n : -\boldsymbol{\Pi}), \quad \mathbf{Q}' = (\boldsymbol{\Pi}' : \mathbf{I}_k).$$

This allows us to express the system (13.1) in matrix form as $\mathbf{R}\mathbf{X}' = \mathbf{V}'$. Comparing with $\mathbf{A}\mathbf{X}' = \mathbf{U}'$, we have $\mathbf{B}\mathbf{R} = \mathbf{A}$. This is usually expressed as $\mathbf{B}\boldsymbol{\Pi} + \mathbf{C} = \mathbf{0}$, but a more convenient form is obtained by $\mathbf{A}\mathbf{Q} = \mathbf{0}$.

When identities are present, the corresponding elements of $\{\mathbf{u}_t\}$ are precisely zero, so the model can be written as:

$$\mathbf{AX}' = \begin{pmatrix} \mathbf{A}_1 \\ \mathbf{A}_2 \end{pmatrix} \mathbf{X}' = \begin{pmatrix} \mathbf{U}_1' \\ \mathbf{0} \end{pmatrix}, \tag{13.4}$$

where $n = n_1 + n_2$, for n_1 stochastic equations and n_2 identities. The elements of $\mathbf{A}_2$ must be known, so do not need estimation. In much of what follows, we set $n_2 = 0$ for simplicity: however, the program handles identities by finding the value of $\mathbf{A}_2$ once the 'menu' of variables in each identity is known.

Given the system formulation, the model depends on the mapping between the unknown coefficients in the matrix $\mathbf{A}$ and the parameters of interest ϕ. This mapping can be written in many different notations: the one that follows is natural in a computer programming context, and is that used in PcGive, namely $\phi = \mathbf{A}^{v_u}$. First we stack the rows of $\mathbf{A}$ as a vector (each row of $\mathbf{A}$ corresponds to an equation). From this vector, we select only unrestricted elements. Other than the elements of ϕ and the normalization that the diagonals of $\mathbf{B}$ are unity, the remaining elements of $\mathbf{A}$ are zero. Thus, $(\cdot)^{v_u}$ codes where in $\mathbf{A}$ the unrestricted elements occur and selects them in the right order. An example is given in Chapter 10.

13.2 Identification

Without some restrictions, the coefficients in $\mathbf{A}$ in (13.4) will not be identified. The matrix $\mathbf{B}$ used to multiply the system to obtain the model could in turn be multiplied by an arbitrary non-singular matrix, $\mathbf{D}$ say, and still produce a linear model, but with different coefficients. To resolve such arbitrariness, we need to know the form of $\mathbf{A}$ in advance, and it must be sufficiently restricted that the only admissible $\mathbf{D}$ matrix is $\mathbf{I}_n$. The *order condition* for identification concerns the number of unrestricted coefficients in $\mathbf{A}$. Since $\mathbf{\Pi}$ is $n \times k$, no more than k regressors can enter any equation, and no more than $n \times k$ unknowns in total can enter $\mathbf{A}$, where $k = n \times m + q \times (r+1)$ (m is the number of lags on $\mathbf{y}_t$, q is the number of variables in $\mathbf{z}_t$ and the model includes $\mathbf{z}_t, \ldots, \mathbf{z}_{t-r}$). This condition is easily checked by just counting the number of unrestricted elements of $\mathbf{A}$. However, to ensure that no equation can be obtained as a linear combination of other equations, these elements need to be located in the appropriate positions. This requires the exclusion of some variables and the inclusion of others in every equation. Since $\mathbf{Q}$ is the conditional expectation matrix of $\mathbf{x}_t$ given $\mathbf{w}_t$:

$$\mathsf{E}\left[\mathbf{x}_t \mid \mathbf{w}_t\right] = \mathsf{E}\left[\begin{pmatrix} \mathbf{y}_t \\ \mathbf{w}_t \end{pmatrix} \mid \mathbf{w}_t\right] = \begin{pmatrix} \mathbf{\Pi} \\ \mathbf{I}_k \end{pmatrix} \mathbf{w}_t = \mathbf{Q}\mathbf{w}_t, \tag{13.5}$$

it is unique, so that the identification of $\mathbf{A}$ rests on being able to uniquely solve for $\mathbf{A}$ from $\mathbf{AQ} = \mathbf{0}$. The order condition ensures a sufficient number of equations, and the *rank condition* that these equations are linearly independent. A rank condition can only be determined on a probability-one basis: if a variable is included in an equation, then its associated coefficient a_{ij} in the matrix $\mathbf{A}$ is assumed to be non-zero ($1+\delta$, where δ is a uniform random number), although in practice an estimate may be zero or there may exist linear combinations of coefficients that are collinear and hence lower the rank. An implication of this analysis is that any linear system like (13.1) can be interpreted as the unrestricted solved, or reduced, form of a just-identified structural econometric model (see Hendry and Mizon, 1993).

13.3 The estimator generating equation

Estimation methods in PcGive are summarized by the estimator generating equation (EGE) based on Hendry (1976); for general discussions of simultaneous equations estimation, see, for example, Judge, Griffiths, Hill, Lütkepohl and Lee (1985, Chapter 15), Spanos (1986, Chapter 25), or Hendry (1995, Chapter 11). Consider the system of n structural simultaneous equations in (13.2), written as:

$$\mathbf{B}\mathbf{y}_t + \mathbf{C}\mathbf{w}_t = \mathbf{A}\mathbf{x}_t = \mathbf{u}_t \quad \text{with} \quad \mathbf{u}_t \sim \mathsf{IN}_n\left[\mathbf{0}, \mathbf{\Sigma}\right]. \tag{13.6}$$

There are n endogenous variables $\mathbf{y}_t$ and k weakly exogenous or lagged variables $\mathbf{w}_t$ where the parameters of interest ϕ in (13.6) are assumed to be identified and $|\mathbf{B}| \neq 0$. In this section, we will only consider models in which $\mathbf{A}$ is a linear function of ϕ.

In fact, (13.6) is a useful way to view the claims of econometrics: a stochastic vector $\mathbf{x}_t$, multiplied by the correct constant matrix $\mathbf{A}$, is asserted to be a homoscedastic, normally distributed white-noise process $\mathbf{u}_t$. Expressed in that form, the claim is ambitious, and although $\mathbf{x}_t$ is a carefully selected vector, the claim does yield insight into econometrics as filtering data through a matrix $\mathbf{A}$ to produce an unpredictable component $\mathbf{u}_t \sim \mathsf{IN}_n[\mathbf{0}, \mathbf{\Sigma}]$. Large macro-econometric models are generally non-linear in both variables and parameters, so are only approximated by (13.6), but in practice linearity seems a reasonable first approximation.

The statistical structure of (13.6) is expressed in (13.5) through the conditional expectation:

$$\mathsf{E}\left[\mathbf{x}_t \mid \mathbf{w}_t\right] = \mathbf{Q}\mathbf{w}_t \tag{13.7}$$

and we now interpret $\mathbf{\Pi}$ as $-\mathbf{B}^{-1}\mathbf{C}$, so that:

$$\mathbf{y}_t \mid \mathbf{w}_t \sim \mathsf{N}_n\left[\mathbf{\Pi}\mathbf{w}_t, \mathbf{\Omega}\right] \quad \text{with} \quad \mathbf{\Omega} = \mathbf{B}^{-1}\mathbf{\Sigma}\mathbf{B}'^{-1}. \tag{13.8}$$

These relationships are the inverse of those associated with (13.2). Whenever confusion is likely, we shall write $\mathbf{\Pi}_u$, $\mathbf{\Omega}_u$ for the unrestricted reduced form coefficients (obtained by multivariate least squares), and $\mathbf{\Pi}_r$, $\mathbf{\Omega}_r$ for the restricted reduced-form coefficients, obtained out of $\mathbf{B}$, $\mathbf{C}$, $\mathbf{\Sigma}$ from the simultaneous equations model (which itself is derived from the URF by imposing (over-)identifying restrictions).

The likelihood function is that of the multivariate normal distribution dependent on $(\mathbf{\Pi}, \mathbf{\Omega}) = f(\phi, \mathbf{\Sigma})$, namely $\ell(\mathbf{\Pi}, \mathbf{\Omega})$. We wish to maximize $\ell(\cdot)$ with respect to ϕ, so first map to $\ell(\phi, \mathbf{\Sigma})$. Then ϕ corresponds to $\boldsymbol{\theta}_1$ and $\mathbf{\Sigma}$ corresponds to $\boldsymbol{\theta}_2$ in $\ell(\boldsymbol{\theta}_1, \boldsymbol{\theta}_2)$. However, $\mathbf{Q}$ will also be part of $\boldsymbol{\theta}_2$ (see Hendry, 1976). Consider the condition:

$$\mathsf{E}\left[\mathbf{w}_t \mathbf{u}_t'\right] = \mathbf{0} \tag{13.9}$$

entailed by the fact that the $\mathbf{w}_t$ are the conditioning variables, and so are uncorrelated with the $\mathbf{u}_t$. Since (13.7) implies that $\mathbf{Q}\mathbf{w}_t$ (the best predictor of $\mathbf{x}_t$ given $\mathbf{w}_t$) is also uncorrelated with $\mathbf{u}_t$:

$$\mathsf{E}\left[\mathbf{Q}\mathbf{w}_t \mathbf{u}_t'\right] = \mathbf{0}. \tag{13.10}$$

But $\mathbf{u}_t' = \mathbf{x}_t' \mathbf{A}_t'$, so (13.10) becomes:

$$\mathsf{E}\left[\mathbf{Q}\mathbf{w}_t \mathbf{x}_t' \mathbf{A}'\right] = \mathbf{0}. \tag{13.11}$$

However, $\mathbf{u}_t$ is generally heteroscedastic across equations (it is assumed homoscedastic over time), and its variance-covariance matrix is $\mathbf{\Sigma}$, so to obtain a suitably-weighted function of $\mathbf{u}_t$, postmultiply $\mathbf{u}_t$ by $\mathbf{\Sigma}^{-1}$:

$$\mathsf{E}\left[\mathbf{Q}\mathbf{w}_t \mathbf{x}_t' \mathbf{A}' \mathbf{\Sigma}^{-1}\right] = \mathbf{0}. \tag{13.12}$$

Finally (13.12) has to hold for all t. Thus, sum over the sample, and transpose the result for convenience, to obtain the EGE:

$$\mathsf{E}\left[\mathbf{\Sigma}^{-1} \mathbf{A} \mathbf{X}' \mathbf{W} \mathbf{Q}'\right] = \mathbf{0}. \tag{13.13}$$

Dropping the expectations operator, (13.13) is in fact the conditional score equation $\mathbf{q}_1(\boldsymbol{\theta}_1 | \boldsymbol{\theta}_2)$, where $\boldsymbol{\theta}_1$ corresponds to $\mathbf{A}(\phi)$ and $\boldsymbol{\theta}_2$ to $(\mathbf{\Sigma}, \mathbf{Q})$. All known linear simultaneous equations estimation methods are generated by special cases of (13.13).

The next section gives a formal derivation.

13.4 Maximum likelihood estimation

13.4.1 Linear parameters

Starting from the log-likelihood (11.17) and substituting $\mathbf{\Omega}^{-1} = \mathbf{B}' \mathbf{\Sigma}^{-1} \mathbf{B}$ and $\mathbf{\Pi} = -\mathbf{B}^{-1} \mathbf{C}$:

$$\begin{aligned} \ell(\mathbf{\Pi}, \mathbf{\Omega} \mid \mathbf{X}) &= K + \tfrac{T}{2} \log \left|\mathbf{\Omega}^{-1}\right| - \tfrac{1}{2} \operatorname{tr}\left(\mathbf{\Omega}^{-1} \mathbf{V}' \mathbf{V}\right) \\ &= K + \tfrac{T}{2} \log \left|\mathbf{\Sigma}^{-1}\right| + T \log \|\mathbf{B}\| - \tfrac{1}{2} \operatorname{tr}\left(\mathbf{\Sigma}^{-1} \mathbf{U}' \mathbf{U}\right) \end{aligned} \tag{13.14}$$

where $\|\mathbf{B}\|$ is the modulus of $|\mathbf{B}|$ and the last right-hand term can also be written as:

$$-\tfrac{1}{2} \operatorname{tr}\left(\mathbf{\Sigma}^{-1} \left(\mathbf{B}\mathbf{Y}' + \mathbf{C}\mathbf{W}'\right)\left(\mathbf{Y}\mathbf{B} + \mathbf{W}\mathbf{C}\right)\right) = -\tfrac{1}{2} \operatorname{tr}\left(\mathbf{\Sigma}^{-1} \mathbf{A} \mathbf{X}' \mathbf{X} \mathbf{A}'\right),$$

If $\mathbf{B}$ is not square, as in an incompletely-specified system with fewer than n equations, the term $\frac{T}{2}\log|\mathbf{B}'\mathbf{\Sigma}^{-1}\mathbf{B}|$ is retained in place of the two middle right-hand terms in (13.14).

Concentrating with respect to $\mathbf{\Sigma}$ requires differentiating (13.14) with respect to $\mathbf{\Sigma}^{-1}$, which yields $\mathbf{\Sigma}_c = T^{-1}\mathbf{U}'\mathbf{U} = T^{-1}\mathbf{A}\mathbf{X}'\mathbf{X}\mathbf{A}'$ (see the derivation of (11.18) above), and the resulting concentrated likelihood function (CLF):

$$\ell_c\left(\mathbf{A}\left(\boldsymbol{\phi}\right) \mid \mathbf{X};\mathbf{\Sigma}\right) = K_c - \frac{T}{2}\log\left|T^{-1}\mathbf{A}\mathbf{X}'\mathbf{X}\mathbf{A}'\right| + T\log||\mathbf{B}||. \tag{13.15}$$

The constant K_c is given in (11.23).

We first proceed as if we are interested in $\mathbf{A}$ rather than $\boldsymbol{\phi}$, and differentiate the log-likelihood $\ell_c\left(\mathbf{B},\mathbf{C}|\mathbf{X};\mathbf{\Sigma}\right)$ with respect to $\mathbf{B}$ and $\mathbf{C}$, evaluating the outcome at $\mathbf{\Sigma}_c = T^{-1}\mathbf{A}\mathbf{X}'\mathbf{X}\mathbf{A}'$:

$$\frac{\partial\ell_c}{\partial\mathbf{B}} = T\mathbf{B}'^{-1} - \mathbf{\Sigma}_c^{-1}\mathbf{U}'\mathbf{Y} \tag{13.16}$$

and:

$$\frac{\partial\ell_c}{\partial\mathbf{C}} = -\mathbf{\Sigma}_c^{-1}\mathbf{U}'\mathbf{W}. \tag{13.17}$$

The trick to solving these two equations together was discovered by Durbin (presented in 1963, published as Durbin, 1988). From the function for $\mathbf{\Sigma}_c$ at the first step, we have:

$$\mathbf{\Sigma}_c = T^{-1}\mathbf{A}\mathbf{X}'\mathbf{X}\mathbf{A}', \tag{13.18}$$

which on premultiplication of both sides by $\mathbf{\Sigma}_c^{-1}$ and postmultiplication of both sides by $T\mathbf{B}'^{-1}$ implies that:

$$T\mathbf{B}'^{-1} = \mathbf{\Sigma}_c^{-1}\mathbf{A}\mathbf{X}'\mathbf{X}\mathbf{R}' \tag{13.19}$$

since $\mathbf{R} = \mathbf{B}^{-1}\mathbf{A} = (\mathbf{I}_n : -\mathbf{\Pi})$ and hence $\mathbf{X}\mathbf{R}' = \left(\mathbf{Y} - \mathbf{W}\mathbf{\Pi}'\right) = \mathbf{V}$ is the matrix of reduced-form errors. Thus, in (13.19), since $\mathbf{A}\mathbf{X}' = \mathbf{U}'$:

$$T\mathbf{B}'^{-1} - \mathbf{\Sigma}_c^{-1}\mathbf{U}'\mathbf{Y} = \mathbf{\Sigma}_c^{-1}\mathbf{U}'\mathbf{X}\mathbf{R}' - \mathbf{\Sigma}_c^{-1}\mathbf{U}'\mathbf{Y} = -\mathbf{\Sigma}_c^{-1}\mathbf{U}'\mathbf{W}\mathbf{\Pi}'. \tag{13.20}$$

Combining the two derivatives in (13.16) and (13.17) using (13.20):

$$\left.\frac{\partial\ell_c}{\partial\mathbf{A}}\right\rfloor_{\mathbf{\Sigma}_c,\mathbf{Q}_c} = -\left(\mathbf{\Sigma}_c^{-1}\mathbf{U}'\mathbf{W}\mathbf{\Pi}_c' : \mathbf{\Sigma}_c^{-1}\mathbf{U}'\mathbf{W}\right) = -\mathbf{\Sigma}_c^{-1}\mathbf{A}\mathbf{X}'\mathbf{W}\mathbf{Q}_c' \tag{13.21}$$

which is the EGE discussed in (13.13) above. With the selection operator explicitly present:

$$\left(\frac{\partial\ell_c}{\partial\mathbf{A}}\right)^{v_u} = \frac{\partial\ell_c}{\partial\left(\mathbf{A}^{v_u}\right)} = \frac{\partial\ell_c}{\partial\boldsymbol{\phi}} = \mathbf{q}_1^c\left(\boldsymbol{\phi}\right) \tag{13.22}$$

we find $\widehat{\boldsymbol{\phi}}$ as the solution to:

$$\mathbf{q}_1^c\left(\boldsymbol{\phi}\right)\rfloor_{\mathbf{\Sigma}_c,\mathbf{Q}_c} = -\left(\mathbf{\Sigma}^{-1}\mathbf{A}\mathbf{X}'\mathbf{W}\mathbf{Q}'\right)^{v_u}_{\rfloor\mathbf{\Sigma}_c,\mathbf{Q}_c} = \mathbf{0}. \tag{13.23}$$

The variance of $\widehat{\phi}$ depends on $-T^{-1}$ times the inverse Hessian:

$$-T^{-1}\frac{\partial^2 \ell_c}{\partial\phi\partial\phi'}_{\rfloor \boldsymbol{\Sigma}_c,\mathbf{Q}_c} = \frac{\partial}{\partial\phi'}\left(\boldsymbol{\Sigma}^{-1}\left[T^{-1}\mathbf{U}'\mathbf{W}\right]\mathbf{Q}'\right)^{v_u}_{\rfloor \boldsymbol{\Sigma}_c,\mathbf{Q}_c} \tag{13.24}$$

which must take account of the dependence of $\mathbf{Q}_c$ and $\boldsymbol{\Sigma}_c$ on ϕ. However, the central term in $\mathbf{q}_1^c(\phi)$ is $\left[T^{-1}\mathbf{U}'\mathbf{W}\right]$ which has an expectation, and a probability limit, of zero, so the effects of changing ϕ on $\boldsymbol{\Sigma}_c$ and $\mathbf{Q}_c$ are negligible asymptotically, since the resulting terms are multiplied by a term that vanishes. The only non-negligible derivative asymptotically is that owing to $\mathbf{A}^{v_u}$, which is an identity matrix. Further, $\text{plim}\, T^{-1}\mathbf{X}'\mathbf{W} = \text{plim}\ T^{-1}\mathbf{Q}\mathbf{W}'\mathbf{W}$, since $\text{plim}\, T^{-1}\mathbf{U}'\mathbf{W} = \mathbf{0}$. Thus, the asymptotic variance $\mathsf{AV}[\cdot]$ of $\sqrt{T}(\widehat{\phi}-\phi)$ is (here $(\cdot)^u$ simply crosses out unwanted rows and columns):

$$\mathsf{AV}\left[\sqrt{T}\left(\widehat{\phi}-\phi\right)\right] = \left(\left(\boldsymbol{\Sigma}^{-1}\otimes\mathbf{Q}\mathbf{S}_W\mathbf{Q}'\right)^u\right)^{-1} \quad \text{where } \mathbf{S}_W = \underset{T\to\infty}{\text{plim}}\ T^{-1}\mathbf{W}'\mathbf{W}. \tag{13.25}$$

Consequently, it does not matter for asymptotic efficiency what estimates of $\boldsymbol{\Sigma}_c^{-1}$ or $\mathbf{Q}_c$ are used in evaluating the EGE, providing they converge to their population values. In fact, even inappropriate $\widehat{\mathbf{Q}}$ or $\widehat{\boldsymbol{\Sigma}}^{-1}$ will suffice for consistent estimates of $\mathbf{A}$ in (13.21) if they converge to non-zero, finite values $\mathbf{Q}^*$ and $\boldsymbol{\Sigma}^{*-1}$ since such choices cannot affect the fact that $\mathbf{w}_t$ is uncorrelated with $\mathbf{u}_t$. There is an infinite number of estimators that we can get by choosing different $\widehat{\mathbf{Q}}$ and $\widehat{\boldsymbol{\Sigma}}$.

13.4.2 Non-linear parameters

Reconsider the model in (13.6):

$$\mathbf{A}(\phi)\,\mathbf{x}_t = \mathbf{u}_t \sim \mathsf{IN}_n\left[\mathbf{0},\boldsymbol{\Sigma}\right]. \tag{13.26}$$

The log-likelihood is given by (13.21), namely:

$$\ell(\phi,\boldsymbol{\Sigma}) = K + \frac{T}{2}\log\left|\boldsymbol{\Sigma}^{-1}\right| + T\log\|\mathbf{B}(\phi)\| - \ \tfrac{1}{2}\,\text{tr}\left(\boldsymbol{\Sigma}^{-1}\mathbf{A}(\phi)\,\mathbf{X}'\mathbf{X}\mathbf{A}(\phi)'\right). \tag{13.27}$$

The score equation cannot now be written generally, since the mapping from $\mathbf{A}$ to ϕ could cross-relate many elements, but it remains similar to that obtained above. Differentiate $\ell(\cdot)$ with respect to ϕ_i and equate to zero for a maximum:

$$\frac{\partial\ell}{\partial\phi_i} = \text{tr}\left(T\mathbf{B}(\phi)'^{-1}\frac{\partial\mathbf{B}(\phi)}{\partial\phi_i} - \boldsymbol{\Sigma}^{-1}\mathbf{A}(\phi)\,\mathbf{X}'\mathbf{X}\frac{\partial\mathbf{A}(\phi)'}{\partial\phi_i}\right). \tag{13.28}$$

Further, as in (13.19) (omitting the conditioning on the maximizing functions for $\boldsymbol{\Sigma}$ etc.):

$$T\mathbf{B}(\phi)'^{-1} = \boldsymbol{\Sigma}^{-1}\mathbf{A}(\phi)\,\mathbf{X}'\left(\mathbf{Y}-\mathbf{W}\boldsymbol{\Pi}'\right). \tag{13.29}$$

Thus, we obtain an expression similar to that of the previous EGE:

$$\mathrm{tr}\left(\boldsymbol{\Sigma}^{-1}\mathbf{A}\left(\phi\right)\mathbf{X}'\mathbf{W}\mathbf{Q}'\mathbf{J}_i\right)=\mathbf{0} \quad \text{where } \mathbf{J}_i=\frac{\partial\mathbf{A}\left(\phi\right)'}{\partial\phi_i} \text{ for } i=1,\ldots,p. \tag{13.30}$$

The earlier analysis of linear parameters set $\mathbf{J}_i$ equal to a matrix that was zero except for unity in the position associated with the relevant parameter. Thus, the same analysis goes through, but both the symbols and the solution are somewhat more awkward.

13.5 Estimators in PcGive

As an example of the EGE, consider two-stage least squares (2SLS), which is just a special case of instrumental variables (IV). In 2SLS, the variance-covariance matrix is ignored by setting $\widehat{\boldsymbol{\Sigma}}^{-1}=\mathbf{I}_n$, which is certainly inconsistent and potentially could be very different from $\boldsymbol{\Sigma}$ in general. But because $\boldsymbol{\Sigma}$ is part of $\boldsymbol{\theta}_2$, that inconsistency does not affect the consistency of $\boldsymbol{\theta}_1$ as long as $\widehat{\boldsymbol{\Sigma}}$ converges (as it does here). Next, 2SLS estimates $\mathbf{Q}$ by regression:

$$\widehat{\mathbf{Q}}'=\left(\mathbf{W}'\mathbf{W}\right)^{-1}\mathbf{W}'\mathbf{X}, \tag{13.31}$$

which is often called the first stage of 2SLS. The predicted $\mathbf{X}$ is given by:

$$\widehat{\mathbf{X}}=\widehat{\mathbf{Q}}\mathbf{W}. \tag{13.32}$$

Solve the EGE expression (13.21) for $\mathbf{A}$ using (13.31) and $\boldsymbol{\Sigma}=\mathbf{I}_n$ to obtain:

$$\left(\mathbf{A}\mathbf{X}'\mathbf{W}\left(\mathbf{W}'\mathbf{W}\right)^{-1}\mathbf{W}'\mathbf{X}\right)^{v_u}=\mathbf{0}, \tag{13.33}$$

which is 2SLS applied simultaneously to every equation. The asymptotic distribution of 2SLS can be established directly, but is easily obtained from EGE theory. Writing (13.33) as $(\mathbf{A}\mathbf{X}'\mathbf{W}\widehat{\mathbf{Q}}')=(\mathbf{U}'\mathbf{W}\widehat{\mathbf{Q}}')=\mathbf{0}$, 2SLS is consistent and has an asymptotic variance matrix given by $\sigma_{ii}(\mathbf{Q}\mathbf{S}_W\mathbf{Q}')^{-1}$ for the ith equation.

Next, we examine the full-information maximum likelihood (FIML) estimator, which requires $\widehat{\boldsymbol{\theta}}_2$ and bases $\widehat{\boldsymbol{\theta}}_1$ explicitly on $\mathbf{h}(\widehat{\boldsymbol{\theta}}_2)$, the entailed function from the CLF. However, $\widehat{\boldsymbol{\theta}}_2$ requires $\widehat{\mathbf{Q}}$ which requires $\widehat{\boldsymbol{\Pi}}$, which requires $\widehat{\mathbf{B}}$ and $\widehat{\mathbf{C}}$, which obviously require $\widehat{\mathbf{A}}$. Likewise, $\widehat{\boldsymbol{\Sigma}}$ is quadratic in $\mathbf{A}$, because:

$$\widehat{\boldsymbol{\Sigma}}=T^{-1}\widehat{\mathbf{A}}\mathbf{X}'\mathbf{X}\widehat{\mathbf{A}}'. \tag{13.34}$$

Therefore, both $\mathbf{Q}$ and $\boldsymbol{\Sigma}$ are complicated non-linear functions of $\mathbf{A}$, and we have to solve the whole EGE expression (13.21) for $\widehat{\mathbf{A}}=(\widehat{\mathbf{B}}:\widehat{\mathbf{C}})$ simultaneously:

$$\left(\left(T^{-1}\mathbf{A}\mathbf{X}'\mathbf{X}\mathbf{A}'\right)^{-1}\mathbf{A}\mathbf{X}'\mathbf{W}\left(-\mathbf{C}'\mathbf{B}'^{-1}:\mathbf{I}_k\right)\right)^{v_u}=\mathbf{0}. \tag{13.35}$$

Trying to solve that highly non-linear problem slowed the progress of econometrics in the 1940s, because FIML seemed too complicated to apply with existing computers. As a result, econometrics somewhat digressed to inventing methods that were easier to compute, and have since transpired to be other EGE solutions. The revolution in computer power has rendered most of these short-cut solutions otiose.

We now summarize all the estimators available in PcGive, beginning with an overview of all their acronyms:

- Single-equation OLS (1SLS);
- Two-stage least squares (2SLS);
- Three-stage least squares (3SLS);
- Limited-information instrumental variables (LIVE);
- Full-information instrumental variables (FIVE);
- Full-information maximum likelihood (FIML);
- Constrained FIML (CFIML);
- Limited-information maximum likelihood (LIML);
- Seemingly unrelated regression equations (SURE).

The maximum likelihood methods (FIML and CFIML) are available recursively. OLS is, of course, inconsistent in a simultaneous system, both in the statistical sense of converging to an inappropriate parameter, and logically in that endogenous variables in one equation are treated conditionally in another. However, for large systems with little interdependence or small samples, it is often used. The general estimation formulation is based on the EGE, from which all estimators are derived. For 2SLS, 3SLS, LIVE and FIVE, the EGE can be solved analytically, taking $\mathbf{\Sigma}_{in}$ and $\mathbf{\Pi}_{in}$ as input and yielding $\mathbf{\Sigma}_{out}$, $\mathbf{A}_{out}$ (and hence $\mathbf{\Omega}_{out}$, $\mathbf{\Pi}_{out}$) as output. A more formal statement of the estimation methods supported by PcGive (other than 1SLS) is given in Table 13.1.

Table 13.1 Model estimation methods.

		Input $\widetilde{\mathbf{\Sigma}}$	Input $\widehat{\mathbf{\Pi}}$	Output $\widetilde{\mathbf{\Sigma}}$	Output $\widehat{\mathbf{\Pi}}$
0	system (URF)	n/a	n/a	$\mathbf{\Sigma}_{URF}$	$\mathbf{\Pi}_{URF}$
1	2SLS	$\mathbf{I}_n$	$\mathbf{\Pi}_{URF}$	$\mathbf{\Sigma}_{2SLS}$	$\mathbf{\Pi}_{2SLS}$
2	3SLS	$\mathbf{\Sigma}_{2SLS}$	$\mathbf{\Pi}_{URF}$	$\mathbf{\Sigma}_{3SLS}$	$\mathbf{\Pi}_{3SLS}$
3	LIVE	$\mathbf{I}_n$	$\mathbf{\Pi}_{2SLS}$	$\mathbf{\Sigma}_{LIVE}$	$\mathbf{\Pi}_{LIVE}$
4a	FIVE after 2SLS	$\mathbf{\Sigma}_{2SLS}$	$\mathbf{\Pi}_{2SLS}$	$\mathbf{\Sigma}_{FIVE1}$	$\mathbf{\Pi}_{FIVE1}$
4b	FIVE after 3SLS	$\mathbf{\Sigma}_{3SLS}$	$\mathbf{\Pi}_{3SLS}$	$\mathbf{\Sigma}_{FIVE2}$	$\mathbf{\Pi}_{FIVE2}$
4c	FIVE after LIVE	$\mathbf{\Sigma}_{LIVE}$	$\mathbf{\Pi}_{LIVE}$	$\mathbf{\Sigma}_{FIVE3}$	$\mathbf{\Pi}_{FIVE3}$
5	FIML solves $\mathbf{\Sigma}$ and $\mathbf{A}$ as mutually consistent functions of ϕ.				
6	CFIML is FIML with constraints on the parameters.				
◦	LIML: as FIML with other equations in reduced form.				
◦	SURE: formulate the equations and apply 3SLS.				

Table 13.2 Model coefficient variances.

		$\widetilde{\mathsf{V}[\widehat{\phi}]}$	$\widehat{\mathbf{\Pi}}$ used in $\mathbf{Q}$
0.	system (URF)	$\mathbf{\Omega}_{URF} \otimes (\mathbf{W}'\mathbf{W})^{-1}$	n/a
1.	2SLS	$\left(\left([\mathrm{dg}\mathbf{\Sigma}_{2SLS}]^{-1} \otimes \mathbf{QW}'\mathbf{WQ}'\right)^u\right)^{-1}$	$\mathbf{\Pi}_{URF}$
2.	3SLS	$\left(\left(\mathbf{\Sigma}_{2SLS}^{-1} \otimes \mathbf{QW}'\mathbf{WQ}'\right)^u\right)^{-1}$	$\mathbf{\Pi}_{URF}$
3.	LIVE	$\left(\left(\mathbf{\Sigma}_{LIVE}^{-1} \otimes \mathbf{QW}'\mathbf{WQ}'\right)^u\right)^{-1}$	$\mathbf{\Pi}_{LIVE}$
4a.	FIVE after 2SLS	$\left(\left(\mathbf{\Sigma}_{FIVE1}^{-1} \otimes \mathbf{QW}'\mathbf{WQ}'\right)^u\right)^{-1}$	$\mathbf{\Pi}_{FIVE1}$
4b.	FIVE after 3SLS	$\left(\left(\mathbf{\Sigma}_{FIVE2}^{-1} \otimes \mathbf{QW}'\mathbf{WQ}'\right)^u\right)^{-1}$	$\mathbf{\Pi}_{FIVE2}$
4c.	FIVE after LIVE	$\left(\left(\mathbf{\Sigma}_{FIVE3}^{-1} \otimes \mathbf{QW}'\mathbf{WQ}'\right)^u\right)^{-1}$	$\mathbf{\Pi}_{FIVE3}$
5.	FIML	$\left(\left(\mathbf{\Sigma}_{FIML}^{-1} \otimes \mathbf{QW}'\mathbf{WQ}'\right)^u\right)^{-1}$	$\mathbf{\Pi}_{FIML}$
6.	CFIML uses $\mathbf{J}\widetilde{\mathsf{V}[\widehat{\phi}]}\mathbf{J}'$ with $\mathbf{J}$ computed analytically.		

It is not sensible to compute a lower after a higher method (for example 2 after 5) although this option is allowed. FIML and CFIML are non-linear estimation methods and require numerical optimization. CFIML requires prior estimation of FIML, together with a specification of the constraints. Recursive implementation of FIML and CFIML require iterative optimization at every sample point, so can take a long time to calculate.

The estimated variance of $\mathbf{u}_t$ is:

$$\widetilde{\mathbf{\Sigma}} = \frac{\widehat{\mathbf{A}}_1\mathbf{X}'\mathbf{X}\widehat{\mathbf{A}}_1'}{T-c} = \frac{\widehat{\mathbf{U}}_1'\widehat{\mathbf{U}}_1}{T-c}. \tag{13.36}$$

A degrees of freedom correction, c, is used which equals the average number of parameters per equation (rounded towards 0); this would be k for the system. The estimated parameter variances as computed by PcGive are given in Table 13.2.

13.6 Recursive estimation

A brute force method of recursive estimation is simply repeating the estimation procedure for each sample size. Computationally, this is not as efficient as the method employed for the system (see §11.3), but numerically, it is more stable than the rank-one updating technique for the inverse employed for RLS. The naive brute force method is used by PcGive for recursive estimation of FIML, albeit with some time-saving devices (the coefficients and Hessian approximation of the previous step are reused in the next). Often this method is surprisingly fast.

System parameter constancy tests are readily computed from the recursive likelihood, as described in §11.8.1. As discussed there, this amounts to removing observations using dummy variables. Single-equation constancy tests are not a direct product of the recursive estimation: successive innovations are not independent. Even though they can be reconstructed as $\mathbf{V}_{t+1}'\mathbf{V}_{t+1} - \mathbf{V}_t'\mathbf{V}_t$, we do not end up with independent Wishart distributed variates from which to construct the single equation tests in the same way as for the system. In the model it is possible that $RSS_T - RSS_{T_1}$ is negative (cf. equation (11.118)). A dummy variable method is still possible: omit the dummy variable from equation i for the period of interest.

13.7 Computing FIML

FIML and CFIML estimation all require *numerical optimization* to maximize the likelihood $\log \mathsf{L}(\boldsymbol{\theta}) = \ell(\boldsymbol{\theta})$ as a non-linear function of $\boldsymbol{\theta}$. PcGive maximization algorithms are based on the Newton scheme. These are discussed in detail in Chapter 14, but we now note their form:

$$\boldsymbol{\theta}_{i+1} = \boldsymbol{\theta}_i + s_i \mathbf{Q}_i^{-1} \mathbf{q}_i \tag{13.37}$$

with

- $\boldsymbol{\theta}_i$ parameter value at iteration i;
- s_i step length, normally unity;
- $\mathbf{Q}_i$ symmetric positive-definite matrix (at iteration i);
- $\mathbf{q}_i$ first derivative of the log-likelihood (at iteration i) (the score vector);
- $\boldsymbol{\delta}_i = \boldsymbol{\theta}_i - \boldsymbol{\theta}_{i-1}$ is the change in the parameters;

PcGive uses the quasi-Newton method developed by Broyden, Fletcher, Goldfarb, Shanno (BFGS) to update $\mathbf{K} = \mathbf{Q}^{-1}$ directly:

(1) BFGS with analytical first derivatives;
The derivatives are calculated analytically (FIML and CFIML). For CFIML, this method computes $(\partial\ell(\boldsymbol{\phi})/\partial\phi_i)$ together with analytical derivatives of the parameter constraints $(\partial\boldsymbol{\phi}/\partial\theta_i)$. This is the preferred method and the only one allowed for recursive FIML and CFIML.

(2) BFGS with numerical first derivatives.
Uses numerical derivatives to compute $\partial\ell\left(\boldsymbol{\phi}\left(\boldsymbol{\theta}\right)\right)/\partial\theta_i$. The numerical scores are less accurate than analytical scores, and usually more costly to obtain.

Starting values are determined as follows. Immediately after a system estimation, the starting values are $\boldsymbol{\theta}_0 = \boldsymbol{\theta}_{2SLS}$. If the model has been estimated before, the most recent parameters are used (2SLS or 3SLS provide excellent starting values). $\mathbf{K}$ is initialized to $\mathbf{I}_n$ every time the optimization process starts. So if the process is aborted (for example, by pressing `Esc`) and then restarted, the approximate Hessian is reset to $\mathbf{I}_n$.

Recursive FIML and CFIML is computed backwards: starting from the full sample values for $\boldsymbol{\theta}$ and $\mathbf{K}$, one observation at a time is dropped. At each sample size, the previous values at convergence are used to start with.

Owing to numerical problems, it is possible (especially close to the maximum) that the calculated $\boldsymbol{\delta}_i$ does not yield a higher likelihood. Then an $s_i \in [0,1]$ yielding a higher function value is determined by a line search. Theoretically, since the direction is upward, such an s_i should exist; however numerically it might be impossible to find one. When using BFGS with numerical derivatives, it often pays to scale the data so that the initial gradients are of the same order of magnitude.

The *convergence* decision is based on two tests. The first uses likelihood elasticities $(\partial\ell/\partial\log\boldsymbol{\theta})$:

$$\begin{aligned} |q_{i,j}\theta_{i,j}| &\leq \epsilon \quad \text{for all } j \text{ when } \theta_{i,j} \neq 0, \\ |q_{i,j}| &\leq \epsilon \quad \text{for all } j \text{ with } \theta_{i,j} = 0. \end{aligned} \tag{13.38}$$

The second is based on the one-step-ahead relative change in the parameter values:

$$\begin{aligned} |\delta_{i+1,j}| &\leq 10\epsilon\,|\theta_{i,j}| \quad \text{for all } j \text{ with } \theta_{i,j} \neq 0, \\ |\delta_{i+1,j}| &\leq 10\epsilon \quad \text{for all } j \text{ when } \theta_{i,j} = 0. \end{aligned} \tag{13.39}$$

13.8 Restricted reduced form

From any selected estimator, the MLE of the restricted reduced form is:

$$\widehat{\boldsymbol{\Pi}} = -\widehat{\mathbf{B}}^{-1}\widehat{\mathbf{C}}. \tag{13.40}$$

The covariance matrix of the restricted reduced-form residuals for the subset of stochastic equations is obtained by letting:

$$\mathbf{B}^{-1} = \begin{pmatrix} \mathbf{B}^{11} & \mathbf{B}^{12} \\ \mathbf{B}^{21} & \mathbf{B}^{22} \end{pmatrix}, \tag{13.41}$$

where $\mathbf{B}^{11}$ is $n_1 \times n_1$ and so on. Then:

$$\widetilde{\boldsymbol{\Omega}} = \begin{pmatrix} \mathbf{B}^{11} \\ \mathbf{B}^{21} \end{pmatrix} \widetilde{\boldsymbol{\Sigma}} \left(\mathbf{B}^{11\prime} : \mathbf{B}^{21\prime}\right), \tag{13.42}$$

and $\boldsymbol{\Omega}_{11} = \mathbf{B}^{11}\boldsymbol{\Sigma}\mathbf{B}^{11\prime}$ is the part corresponding to the stochastic equations.

The variance-covariance matrix of the restricted reduced-form coefficients is:

$$\widetilde{\mathsf{V}\left[\text{vec}\widehat{\boldsymbol{\Pi}}'\right]} = \widehat{\mathbf{J}}\widetilde{\mathsf{V}\left[\widehat{\boldsymbol{\phi}}\right]}\widehat{\mathbf{J}}' \quad \text{where } \mathbf{J} = \frac{\partial \text{vec}\boldsymbol{\Pi}'}{\left(\partial\widehat{\boldsymbol{\phi}}\right)'} = \left(-\mathbf{B}^{-1} \otimes (\boldsymbol{\Pi}' : \mathbf{I}_k)\right)^u. \tag{13.43}$$

In $\mathbf{J}$, we choose only those columns corresponding to unrestricted elements in $\mathbf{A}$. The derivation of $\mathbf{J}$ is the same as in (11.90). The estimated variances of the elements of $\widehat{\phi}$ are given in Table 13.2.

13.9 Unrestricted variables

Variables that are included unrestrictedly in all equations of the model, such as dummy variables for the constant term, seasonal shift factors, or trend, can be concentrated out of the likelihood function. This reduces the dimensionality of the parameter vector, and enhances numerical optimization. The stochastic part of the model is written as:

$$\mathbf{A}_1\mathbf{X}' + \mathbf{D}\mathbf{S}' = \mathbf{U}', \tag{13.44}$$

where $\mathbf{D}$ is the $n_1 \times s$ unrestricted matrix of coefficients of the unrestricted variables and $\mathbf{S}$ is the $T \times s$ matrix of observations on these seasonal dummies. Then (see Hendry, 1971):

$$\begin{aligned}\ell(\mathbf{A}_1, \mathbf{\Sigma} \mid \mathbf{X}, \mathbf{S}) = \quad & K + T\log\|\mathbf{B}\| - \tfrac{T}{2}\log|\mathbf{\Sigma}| \\ & -\tfrac{1}{2}\mathrm{tr}\left(\mathbf{\Sigma}^{-1}\left(\mathbf{A}_1\mathbf{X}'\mathbf{X}\mathbf{A}_1' + 2\mathbf{A}_1\mathbf{X}'\mathbf{S}\mathbf{D}' + \mathbf{D}\mathbf{S}'\mathbf{S}\mathbf{D}'\right)\right).\end{aligned} \tag{13.45}$$

Since $\mathbf{D}$ is unrestricted, maximizing $\ell(\cdot)$ with respect to $\mathbf{D}$ yields:

$$\widehat{\mathbf{D}}' = \left(\mathbf{S}'\mathbf{S}\right)^{-1}\mathbf{S}'\mathbf{X}\widehat{\mathbf{A}}_1'. \tag{13.46}$$

Let $\check{\mathbf{X}} = \left(\mathbf{I}_T - \mathbf{S}\left(\mathbf{S}'\mathbf{S}\right)^{-1}\mathbf{S}'\right)\mathbf{X} = \mathbf{M}_S\mathbf{X}$, namely the residuals from the least-squares regression of $\mathbf{X}$ on $\mathbf{S}$, denote the 'deseasonalized' data, then the concentrated likelihood function is:

$$\ell_c(\mathbf{A}_1, \mathbf{\Sigma} \mid \mathbf{X}, \mathbf{S}; \mathbf{D}) = K_c + T\log\|\mathbf{B}\| - \frac{T}{2}\log|\mathbf{\Sigma}| - \tfrac{1}{2}\mathrm{tr}\left(\mathbf{\Sigma}^{-1}\mathbf{A}_1\check{\mathbf{X}}'\check{\mathbf{X}}\mathbf{A}_1'\right). \tag{13.47}$$

From (13.46), the variance-covariance matrix of the $\widehat{\mathbf{D}}$ coefficients is:

$$\mathsf{V}\left[\widetilde{\mathrm{vec}\widehat{\mathbf{D}}'}\right] = \widetilde{\mathbf{\Sigma}} \otimes \left(\mathbf{S}'\mathbf{S}\right)^{-1} + \widehat{\mathbf{J}}_S\mathsf{V}\left[\widetilde{\widehat{\phi}}\right]\widehat{\mathbf{J}}_S' \text{ where } \mathbf{J}_S = \left(\mathbf{I}_{n_1} \otimes \left(\mathbf{S}'\mathbf{S}\right)^{-1}\mathbf{S}'\mathbf{X}\right)^u \tag{13.48}$$

which is similar to (11.36) for the system.

13.10 Derived statistics

When the model encompasses the system, other derived statistics can usefully highlight the properties of the estimated model. Such statistics include forecast tests, static long run, etc. The results for forecasting and dynamic analysis derived for the system (sections §11.5 and §11.6) carry over after replacing $\mathbf{\Pi}_u$, $\mathbf{\Omega}_u$ by $\mathbf{\Pi}_r$, $\mathbf{\Omega}_r$. The forecast error variance for a single step ahead is:

$$\widetilde{\mathsf{V}[\mathbf{e}_{T+i,1}]} = \widetilde{\mathbf{\Omega}}_r + \left(\mathbf{I}_n \otimes \mathbf{w}'_{T+i}\right) \widehat{\mathbf{J}} \widetilde{\mathsf{V}\left[\widehat{\boldsymbol{\phi}}\right]} \widehat{\mathbf{J}}' \left(\mathbf{I}_n \otimes \mathbf{w}_{T+i}\right), \tag{13.49}$$

where $\mathbf{J}$ is given in (13.43).

The same holds to a large extent for mis-specification tests: the residuals involved in the tests are the RRF residuals. This is straightforward for the portmanteau statistic and the normality test. For both heteroscedasticitytests, the model is treated as if it were a system, albeit with coefficients $\mathbf{\Pi}_r$, $\mathbf{\Omega}_r$. This implies that these tests are likely to reject if the test for over-identifying restrictions fails. The vector error autocorrelation test re-estimates the model after the lagged structural residuals are partialled out from the original regressors, using the auxiliary system:

$$\mathbf{B}\mathbf{Y}' + \mathbf{C}\mathbf{W}' - \mathbf{R}_r\widehat{\mathbf{U}}'_r - \cdots - \mathbf{R}_s\widehat{\mathbf{U}}'_s = \mathbf{E}'. \tag{13.50}$$

This involves recourse to numerical optimization for tests in models estimated by FIML or CFIML.

Tests at the level of the model may have more power to reject owing to the (often much) smaller number of free parameters estimated.

13.10.1 General restrictions

PcGive allows you to test general restrictions on parameters. Restrictions are entered in the constraints editor.

Given the estimated coefficients $\hat{\boldsymbol{\theta}}$, and their covariance matrix $\widetilde{\mathsf{V}[\hat{\boldsymbol{\theta}}]}$, we can test for (non-) linear restrictions of the form:

$$\mathbf{f}(\boldsymbol{\theta}) = \mathbf{0}; \tag{13.51}$$

A Wald test is reported, which has a $\chi^2(r)$ distribution, where r is the number of restrictions (that is, equations entered in the restrictions editor). The null hypothesis is rejected if we observe a significant test statistic.

For example, the two restrictions implied by the long-run solution of:

$$Ya = \beta_0 Ya_1 + \beta_1 Yb + \beta_2 Yb_1 + \beta_3 Yc + \mu \tag{13.52}$$

are expressed as:

$$\begin{aligned} (\beta_1 + \beta_2)/(1 - \beta_0) &= 0; \\ \beta_3/(1 - \beta_0) &= 0; \end{aligned} \tag{13.53}$$

which has to be fed into PcGive as (since coefficient numbering starts at 0):

```
(&1 + &2) / (1 - &0) = 0;
      &3  / (1 - &0) = 0;
```

13.11 Progress

The Progress command reports on the progress made during a general-to-simple modelling strategy (the Progress dialog can be used to exclude systems/models from the default model nesting sequence).

PcGive keeps a record of the sequence of systems, and for the most recent system the sequence of models (which could be empty). It will report the likelihood-ratio tests indicating the progress in system modelling, the progress in model modelling, and the tests of over-identifying restrictions of all models in the system.

In the following discussion, *model* refers to both model and system. A more recent model (Model 2) is nested in an older (Model 1) if:

(1) Model 2 is derived from a parameter restriction on Model 1.

This entails:

(2) Model 2 is estimated over the same period.
(3) Model 2 has fewer coefficients than Model 1.
(4) Model 2 has a lower likelihood than Model 1.

But not necessarily:

(5) Both models have the same dependent variable, and the set of explanatory variables of Model 2 is a subset of that of Model 1.

PcGive will offer you a default nesting sequence based on (2), (3), (4) and (5), but since it cannot decide on (1) itself, you will have the opportunity to change this nesting sequence. However, model sequences that do not satisfy (2), (3) or (4) will always be deleted.

Consider, for example, Model 2:

$$\Delta Ya_t = \mu + \gamma \Delta Yb_t \tag{13.54}$$

which is nested in Model 1:

$$Ya_t = \beta_0 + \beta_1 Ya_{t-1} + \beta_2 Yb_t + \beta_3 Yb_{t_1} \tag{13.55}$$

through two restrictions: $\beta_1 = 1$ and $\beta_3 = -\beta_2$. This nesting doesn't satisfy point (5), and hence is not recognized by PcGive. You can mark Model 2 for inclusion in the progress report.

Chapter 14

Numerical Optimization and Numerical Accuracy

14.1 Introduction to numerical optimization

Any approach to estimation and inference implicitly assumes that it is feasible to obtain a maximum likelihood estimator (MLE) in situations of interest. For any fixed set of data and a given model specification, the log-likelihood function $\ell(\cdot)$ depends only on the parameters $\boldsymbol{\theta}$ of the model. Consequently, obtaining the MLE entails locating the value $\widehat{\boldsymbol{\theta}}$ of $\boldsymbol{\theta}$ which maximizes $\ell(\boldsymbol{\theta})$, and this is a numerical, not a statistical, problem – a matter of computational technique – which could be considered peripheral to econometrics.

However, optimization algorithms differ dramatically in their speeds of locating $\widehat{\boldsymbol{\theta}}$, and hence their computational costs. A statistical technique that needed (say) ten hours of computer time could not expect routine application if a closely similar statistical method required only one second on the same computer. Moreover, algorithms have different computer memory requirements, and certain methods may be too inefficient in their memory requirements for the available computers. Next, some algorithms are far more robust than others, that is, are much more likely to obtain $\widehat{\boldsymbol{\theta}}$ and not fail for mysterious reasons in the calculation process. While all of these points are in the province of numerical analysis and computing, in order to implement new methods, econometricians need to be aware of the problems involved in optimization.

There is also an intimate connection between the statistical and the numerical aspects of estimation. Methods of maximizing $\ell(\boldsymbol{\theta})$ yield insight into the statistical properties of $\widehat{\boldsymbol{\theta}}$. Some algorithms only calculate an approximation to $\widehat{\boldsymbol{\theta}}$, say $\widetilde{\boldsymbol{\theta}}$, but if they consist of well-defined rules that always yield unique values of $\widetilde{\boldsymbol{\theta}}$ from given data, then $\widetilde{\boldsymbol{\theta}}$ is an estimator of $\boldsymbol{\theta}$ with statistical properties that may be similar to those of $\widehat{\boldsymbol{\theta}}$ – but also may be very different. Thus, computing the maximum of $\ell(\boldsymbol{\theta})$ only approximately can have statistical implications: the discussion of the estimator-generating equation in Chapter 13 showed that different estimators can be reinterpreted as alternative numerical methods for approximating the maximum of $\ell(\boldsymbol{\theta})$.

There is a vast literature on non-linear optimization techniques (see, among many others, Fletcher, 1987, Gill, Murray and Wright, 1981, Cramer, 1986, Quandt, 1983 and Thisted, 1988). Note that many texts on optimization focus on minimization, rather than maximization, but of course $\max \ell(\boldsymbol{\theta}) = -\min\{-\ell(\boldsymbol{\theta})\}$.

14.2 Maximizing likelihood functions

A first approach to obtaining the MLE $\widehat{\boldsymbol{\theta}}$ from $\ell(\boldsymbol{\theta})$ is to consider solving the score equations, assuming the relevant partial derivatives exist:

$$\nabla \ell(\boldsymbol{\theta}) = \frac{\partial \ell(\boldsymbol{\theta})}{\partial \boldsymbol{\theta}} = \mathbf{q}(\boldsymbol{\theta}). \tag{14.1}$$

Then $\mathbf{q}(\widehat{\boldsymbol{\theta}}) = \mathbf{0}$ defines the necessary conditions for a local maximum of $\ell(\boldsymbol{\theta})$ at $\widehat{\boldsymbol{\theta}}$. A sufficient condition is that:

$$\nabla^2 \ell(\boldsymbol{\theta}) = \frac{\partial^2 \ell(\boldsymbol{\theta})}{\partial \boldsymbol{\theta} \partial \boldsymbol{\theta}'} = \frac{\partial \mathbf{q}(\boldsymbol{\theta})'}{\partial \boldsymbol{\theta}} = \mathbf{H}(\boldsymbol{\theta}) = -\mathbf{Q}(\boldsymbol{\theta}) \tag{14.2}$$

also exists, and is negative definite at $\widehat{\boldsymbol{\theta}}$ (minimization would require positive definiteness). If the Hessian matrix $\mathbf{H}(\cdot)$ is negative definite for all parameter values, the likelihood is concave, and hence has a unique maximum; if not, there could be local optima or singularities. When the score $\mathbf{q}(\boldsymbol{\theta})$ is a set of equations that is linear in $\boldsymbol{\theta}$, (14.1) can be solved explicitly for $\widehat{\boldsymbol{\theta}}$. In such a situation, it is easy to implement the estimator without recourse to numerical optimization. To maximize $\ell(\cdot)$ as a non-linear function of its parameters requires numerical optimization techniques.

14.2.1 Direct search methods

A more prosaic approach views the matter as one of hill climbing. A useful analogy is to consider the likelihood function $\ell(\boldsymbol{\theta})$ as a two-dimensional hill as in Figure 14.1. This is a well-behaved function: it is continuous, differentiable and has a unique maximum. To maximize $\ell(\cdot)$, we need to climb to the top of the hill. Start somewhere on the hill, say at θ_1, and take a step of length δ. The step will go either down the hill or up the hill: in computing terms, move some distance δ each way and compute the functions $\ell_1 = \ell(\theta_1)$ and $\ell_2 = \ell(\theta_1 + \delta)$. Depending on $\ell_1 \geq \ell_2$ or $\ell_2 \geq \ell_1$, we discover in which direction to continue: here $+\delta$ as $\ell_2 \geq \ell_1$ ($-\delta$ otherwise). Take a second step of δ in the appropriate direction, compute $\ell(\theta_1 + 2\delta)$ and repeat until we go downhill again, and have overshot the maximum, at $\theta_1 + k\delta$, say. The maximum will be inside the bracket $[\theta_1 + (k-1)\delta, \theta_1 + k\delta]$. Take a step of $\delta/2$ back, compute the function, and fit a quadratic through the three points. Select θ_2 which maximizes the quadratic as the approximation to the value maximizing the function, reduce the step-length δ, and recommence from θ_2. This is a simple method for finding maxima without derivatives.

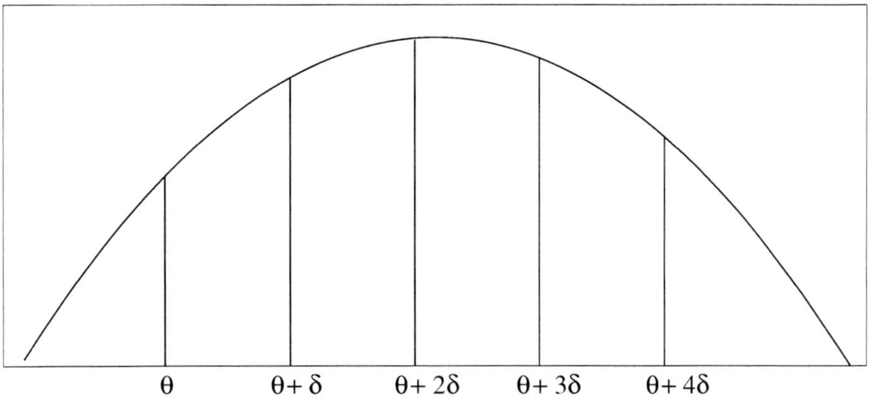

Figure 14.1 Two-dimensional hill.

We can extend this approach to the case of climbing a three-dimensional hill, applying exactly the same principles as above, but using two-dimensional iso-likelihood contours to represent a three-dimensional hill as in Figure 14.2.

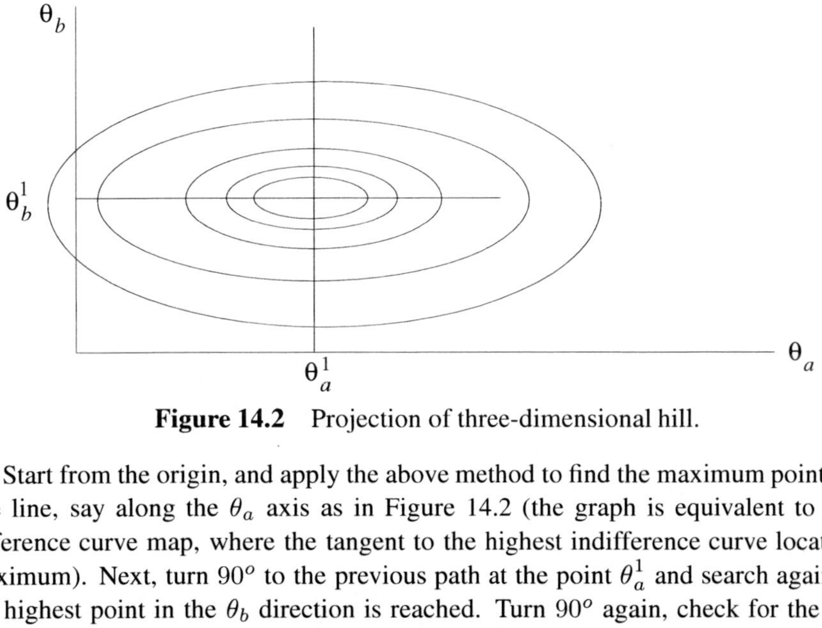

Figure 14.2 Projection of three-dimensional hill.

Start from the origin, and apply the above method to find the maximum point along one line, say along the θ_a axis as in Figure 14.2 (the graph is equivalent to an indifference curve map, where the tangent to the highest indifference curve locates the maximum). Next, turn 90° to the previous path at the point θ_a^1 and search again until the highest point in the θ_b direction is reached. Turn 90° again, check for the uphill direction and climb, and keep iterating the procedure. In this way, we will finally get to the top of the hill.

We can of course extend this approach to situations with more than three dimensions, but expensively, since it is not a very intelligent method. A better method would be to utilize the information that accrues as we climb the hill. After changing direction once and finding the highest point for the second time, we find that we could have done much better by taking the direction corresponding to the hypotenuse instead of walking along the two sides of the hill. The average progress along the first two directions corresponds to a better path than either alone, and is known as the direction of total progress (see Figure 14.3). We could get from the second path on to the direction of total progress and climb either vertically or horizontally until the highest position. Then we can find the second direction of total progress and use that, providing a better method of climbing to the top of the hill.

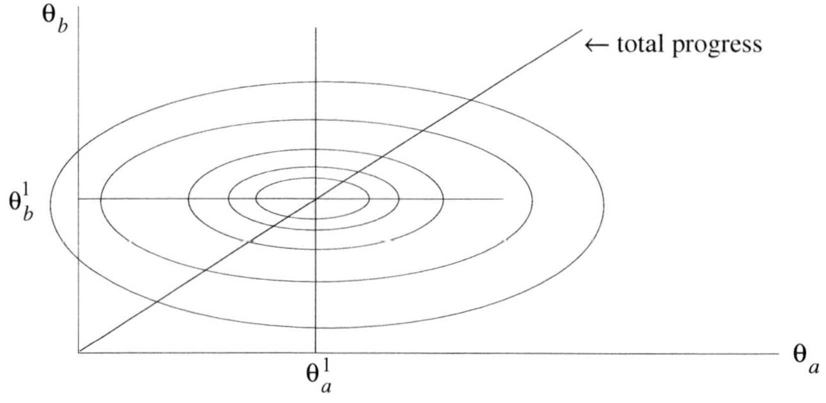

Figure 14.3 Direction of total progress.

This method (called conjugate directions) makes use of a Euclidean theorem: the line joining any two parallel tangent points of two concentric ellipses goes through their centre. So if a bivariate likelihood surface is elliptical, and we find one tangent of an iso-likelihood ellipse, then another tangent to a higher contour and follow the direction of total progress, we will get straight to the maximum of the likelihood.

A second way of climbing a hill is to exploit information at the starting point about the steepness of the slope: if the gradient is known, it seems worth trying to climb along the direction of steepest ascent. In many cases, the method progresses rapidly and beats the previous methods. However, there are a couple of *caveats*. First, the slope of a hill is not necessarily uniform, and a gradient method might be poor if the slope changes too much. Secondly, in the starting neighbourhood, the slope might be too flat or even point in the wrong direction. However, the obvious solution to that problem is to provide decent initial values. An EGE will often do so for FIML. For example, 2SLS initial values are an excellent set from which to commence FIML, and 3SLS are even better yet do not require iterative solution.

14.2.2 Newton type methods

We saw above that $\mathbf{q}(\widehat{\boldsymbol{\theta}}) = \mathbf{0}$ defines the necessary condition for a local maximum of $\ell(\boldsymbol{\theta})$ at $\widehat{\boldsymbol{\theta}}$, whereas a sufficient condition is that the negated Hessian matrix, $\mathbf{Q}(\boldsymbol{\theta}) = -\mathbf{H}(\boldsymbol{\theta})$, is positive definite at $\widehat{\boldsymbol{\theta}}$. When $\mathbf{q}(\boldsymbol{\theta})$ is a set of equations that are linear in $\boldsymbol{\theta}$, then $\mathbf{q}(\widehat{\boldsymbol{\theta}}) = \mathbf{0}$ can be solved explicitly for $\widehat{\boldsymbol{\theta}}$, as in the multiple regression model. More generally, $\mathbf{q}(\boldsymbol{\theta})$ is non-linear, yielding a problem of locating $\widehat{\boldsymbol{\theta}}$ which is no more tractable than maximizing $\ell(\boldsymbol{\theta})$. Thus, we consider iterative approaches in which a sequence of values of $\boldsymbol{\theta}$ (denoted $\boldsymbol{\theta}_i$ at the ith iteration) is obtained approximating $\mathbf{q}(\boldsymbol{\theta}_i) = \mathbf{0}$, and corresponding to non-decreasing values of the criterion function $\ell(\cdot)$, so $\ell(\boldsymbol{\theta}_{i+1}) \geq \ell(\boldsymbol{\theta}_i)$:

$$\boldsymbol{\theta}_{i+1} = \mathbf{h}(\boldsymbol{\theta}_i) \quad \text{for } i = 1, 2, \ldots, I \leq N \tag{14.3}$$

where N is a terminal maximum number of steps, from an initial value $\boldsymbol{\theta}_0$ (such as 2SLS). A convergence criterion is used to terminate the iteration, such as $\mathbf{q}(\boldsymbol{\theta}_{i+1}) \simeq \mathbf{0}$ or $|\ell(\boldsymbol{\theta}_{i+1}) - \ell(\boldsymbol{\theta}_i)| \leq \epsilon$. If convergence does not occur, try using a looser convergence criterion. These implementation-specific aspects are discussed below.

There is no optimal choice for $\mathbf{h}(\cdot)$, since optimization methods differ in their robustness, in the time taken to calculate successive values of $\boldsymbol{\theta}_i$, in the number of iterations required to achieve any given accuracy level (which may differ between problems), and in the effort needed to write a computer program to calculate $\mathbf{h}(\cdot)$. Moreover, an algorithm that performs excellently for a small number of parameters may be hopeless for a large number. The direct search methods just discussed only require $\ell(\cdot)$ to be programmed, and are robust but often require a large number of iterations.

Expand $\mathbf{q}(\widehat{\boldsymbol{\theta}}) = \mathbf{0}$ in a first-order Taylor's series:

$$\mathbf{q}\left(\widehat{\boldsymbol{\theta}}\right) \simeq \mathbf{q}(\boldsymbol{\theta}_1) + \mathbf{H}(\boldsymbol{\theta}_1)(\boldsymbol{\theta} - \boldsymbol{\theta}_1) = \mathbf{0}, \tag{14.4}$$

written as the iterative rule:

$$\boldsymbol{\theta}_{i+1} = \boldsymbol{\theta}_i - \mathbf{H}(\boldsymbol{\theta}_i)^{-1}\mathbf{q}(\boldsymbol{\theta}_i), \tag{14.5}$$

or alternatively:

$$\begin{array}{ll} \text{solve} & \mathbf{Q}(\boldsymbol{\theta}_i)\boldsymbol{\delta}_i = \mathbf{q}(\boldsymbol{\theta}_i) \quad \text{for } \boldsymbol{\delta}_i, \\ \text{set} & \boldsymbol{\theta}_{i+1} = \boldsymbol{\theta}_i + \boldsymbol{\delta}_i. \end{array} \tag{14.6}$$

The gradient, $\mathbf{q}(\boldsymbol{\theta}_i)$, determines the direction of the step to be taken, and $\mathbf{Q}(\boldsymbol{\theta}_i)^{-1}$ modifies the size of the step which determines the metric: this algorithm is the Newton–Raphson technique, or *Newton's method*. Even when the direction is uphill, it is possible to overstep the maximum in that direction. In that case, it is essential to add a line search to determine a step length $s_i \in [0, 1]$:

$$\boldsymbol{\theta}_{i+1} = \boldsymbol{\theta}_i + s_i\boldsymbol{\delta}_i, \tag{14.7}$$

where s_i is chosen to ensure that $\ell(\boldsymbol{\theta}_{i+1}) \geq \ell(\boldsymbol{\theta}_i)$.

Replacing the matrix $\mathbf{Q}(\cdot)$ by the unit matrix $\mathbf{I}_k$ is known as the method of *steepest ascent* (steepest descent when minimizing) since the step is in the direction of the gradient vector $\mathbf{q}(\cdot)$ – and so is useful only if $\boldsymbol{\theta}$ is sensibly scaled. Using $\mathbf{Q}_\mu(\cdot) = \mathbf{Q}(\cdot) + \mu\mathbf{I}_k$ (where $\mu > 0$ is chosen to ensure that $\mathbf{Q}_\mu(\cdot)$ is positive definite) is known as *quadratic hill climbing* (see Goldfeld and Quandt, 1972) or as the Levenberg–Marquardt method: note that $\mathbf{Q}_\mu(\cdot)$ varies between $\mathbf{Q}(\cdot)$ (Newton–Raphson) and $\mathbf{I}_k$ (steepest ascent) as μ increases from zero.

When we maximize a log-likelihood function and look back to the variance estimates given in (11.101), two additional methods suggest themselves. Of these, $\mathbf{Q} = -\mathbf{H}(\boldsymbol{\theta})$ is Newton's method discussed above. The method of scoring replaces $\mathbf{Q}(\cdot)$ by the information matrix $\mathcal{I} = \mathsf{E}[\mathbf{Q}(\cdot)]$; and the method which uses the outer product of the gradients is sometimes called the method of Berndt, Hall, Hall and Hausman (see e.g., Berndt, Hall, Hall and Hausman, 1974).

An important class of methods are the so-called variable metric or *quasi-Newton* methods. These approximate the matrix $\mathbf{Q}(\boldsymbol{\theta}_i)^{-1}$ by a symmetric positive definite matrix $\mathbf{K}_i$ which is updated at every iteration but converges on $\mathbf{Q}(\cdot)^{-1}$. The two most commonly used are the Davidon–Fletcher–Powell approach (DFP), and the Broyden–Fletcher–Goldfarb–Shanno (BFGS) update, where the latter is generally the preferred quasi-Newton method. Advantages of quasi-Newton methods over Newton–Raphson are that $\mathbf{K}_i$ is guaranteed to be positive definite, and only first derivatives are required. In the Newton–Raphson case, there could be parameter values for which the Hessian matrix is not negative definite. However, if the Hessian is negative definite for all parameter values, and not too costly to derive (in terms of derivation, programming time, and computational time), it tends to outperform the quasi-Newton methods.

Let $\mathbf{d} = s_i\boldsymbol{\delta}_i = \boldsymbol{\theta}_i - \boldsymbol{\theta}_{i-1}$ and $\mathbf{g} = \mathbf{q}(\boldsymbol{\theta}_i) - \mathbf{q}(\boldsymbol{\theta}_{i-1})$, then the BFGS update is:

$$\mathbf{K}_{i+1} = \mathbf{K}_i + \left(1 + \frac{\mathbf{g}'\mathbf{K}_i\mathbf{g}}{\mathbf{d}'\mathbf{g}}\right)\frac{\mathbf{d}\mathbf{d}'}{\mathbf{d}'\mathbf{g}} - \frac{\mathbf{d}\mathbf{g}'\mathbf{K}_i + \mathbf{K}_i\mathbf{g}\mathbf{d}'}{\mathbf{d}'\mathbf{g}}. \tag{14.8}$$

This satisfies the quasi-Newton condition $\mathbf{K}_{i+1}\mathbf{g} = \mathbf{d}$, and possesses the properties of hereditary symmetry ($\mathbf{K}_{i+1}$ is symmetric if $\mathbf{K}_i$ is), hereditary positive definiteness, and super-linear convergence. There is a close correspondence between the logic underlying the earlier RLS procedure for recursive (rank-one) updating of the inverse second-moment matrix as the sample size increases, and the BFGS method for sequential updating of the inverse Hessian approximation by rank-two updates as the number of iterations increases.

14.2.3 Derivative-free methods

When the analytic formula for $\mathbf{q}(\boldsymbol{\theta})$ cannot be obtained, so that only function values are available, the choice is between a conjugate-directions method and a quasi-Newton method using finite differences. BFGS using a numerical approximation to $\mathbf{q}(\cdot)$ based on finite difference approximations seems to outperform derivative-free algorithms in many situations while providing an equal degree of flexibility in the choice of parameters in $\ell(\cdot)$. The numerical derivatives are calculated using:

$$\frac{\ell(\boldsymbol{\theta}+\epsilon\boldsymbol{\iota})-\ell(\boldsymbol{\theta}-\delta\epsilon\boldsymbol{\iota})}{\mu} \simeq \frac{\partial\ell(\boldsymbol{\theta})}{\partial(\boldsymbol{\iota}'\boldsymbol{\theta})} \tag{14.9}$$

where $\boldsymbol{\iota}$ is a unit vector (for example, $(1\ 0\ldots0)'$ for the first element of $\boldsymbol{\theta}$), ϵ is a suitably chosen step length, and δ is either zero (forward difference) or unity (central difference) depending on the accuracy required at the given stage of the iteration. Thus, ϵ represents a compromise between round-off error (cancellation of leading digits when subtracting nearly equal numbers), and truncation error (ignoring terms of higher order than ϵ in the approximation). Although PcGive chooses ϵ carefully, there may be situations where the numerical derivative performs poorly.

It is worth noting that numerical values of second derivatives can be computed in a corresponding way using:

$$\frac{\ell(\boldsymbol{\theta}+\epsilon_1\boldsymbol{\iota}_1+\epsilon_2\boldsymbol{\iota}_2)+\ell(\boldsymbol{\theta}-\epsilon_1\boldsymbol{\iota}_1-\epsilon_2\boldsymbol{\iota}_2)-\ell(\boldsymbol{\theta}-\epsilon_1\boldsymbol{\iota}_1+\epsilon_2\boldsymbol{\iota}_2)-\ell(\boldsymbol{\theta}+\epsilon_1\boldsymbol{\iota}_1-\epsilon_2\boldsymbol{\iota}_2)}{4\epsilon_1\epsilon_2} \tag{14.10}$$

where $\boldsymbol{\iota}_1$ or $\boldsymbol{\iota}_2$ is zero except for unity in the ith or j^{th} position. When computed from the MLE $\widehat{\boldsymbol{\theta}}$, (14.10) yields a reasonably good approximation to $\mathbf{Q}(\widehat{\boldsymbol{\theta}})$ for use in calculating the covariance matrix of $\widehat{\boldsymbol{\theta}}$.

14.2.4 Conclusion

The present state of the art in numerical optimization, and the computational speeds of modern computers are such that large estimation problems can be solved quickly and cheaply. Many estimators which were once described as 'computationally burdensome' or complex are now as easy to use as OLS but are considerably more informative. Thus, the complexity of the appropriate estimator is no longer a serious constraint, although it is simple to invent large, highly non-linear problems which would be prohibitively expensive to solve.

14.3 Practical optimization

The discussion of numerical optimization above is rather abstract. Practical aspects such as choice of convergence criteria, line search algorithm, and potential problems are discussed in this section, with reference to the actual implementation in PcGive.

14.3.1 Maximization methods

PcGive maximizes the likelihood $\ell(\boldsymbol{\phi}(\boldsymbol{\theta}))$ as an unconstrained non-linear function of $\boldsymbol{\theta}$ using a Newton scheme:

$$\boldsymbol{\theta}_{i+1} = \boldsymbol{\theta}_i + s_i \mathbf{Q}(\boldsymbol{\theta}_i)^{-1} \mathbf{q}(\boldsymbol{\theta}_i) \tag{14.11}$$

where BFGS is used to update $\mathbf{Q}^{-1}$ directly. Two methods are available:

(1) *BFGS with analytical first derivatives*
The derivatives $\partial\ell/\partial\theta_i$ are calculated analytically. If the form of these derivatives is not known, this method employs a mixture of analytical $(\partial\ell(\boldsymbol{\phi})/\partial\phi_i)$ and numerical $(\partial\boldsymbol{\phi}/\partial\theta_i)$ derivatives. The numerical part, which corresponds to the Jacobian of the transformation, is computed by a central finite difference approximation. Where possible (as in CFIML and restricted cointegration analysis), the Jacobian matrix is computed analytically.

(2) *BFGS with numerical first derivatives*
This method uses central finite difference approximations to the derivatives $\partial\ell/\partial\theta_i$. It is slower than using analytical first derivatives, but the only method available if the analytical scores are unknown.

14.3.2 Line search

It is possible (especially close to the maximum) that the calculated parameter update $\boldsymbol{\delta}_i = \mathbf{Q}(\boldsymbol{\theta}_i)^{-1} \mathbf{q}(\boldsymbol{\theta}_i)$ does not yield a higher likelihood. Then an $s_i \in [0, 1]$ yielding a higher function value is determined by a line search. Theoretically, since the direction is upward, such an s_i should exist; however, numerically it might be impossible to find one. The line search implemented in PcGive is linear. It is only invoked when the step is not upwards, and keeps halving s_i until a better value is found. If that fails, the procedure aborts, either with weak convergence, or a failure to improve in the line search.

14.3.3 Starting values

Immediately after a system estimation, the starting values are $\boldsymbol{\theta}_0 = \boldsymbol{\theta}_{3SLS}$, which provide excellent starting values). $\mathbf{H}$ is initialized to $\mathbf{I}_k$.

14.3.4 Recursive estimation

Recursive estimation works as follows: starting values for $\boldsymbol{\theta}$ and $\mathbf{H}$ for the first estimation (M observations) are the full sample values (T observations); then at each sample size, the previous values for $\boldsymbol{\theta}$ and $\mathbf{H}$ at convergence are used to start with. Often only four steps are required, making recursive application of the optimization process very efficient relative to the size of the problem.

14.3.5 Convergence

The convergence decision is based on two tests. The first is based on likelihood elasticities $(\partial\ell/\partial\log|\theta_j|)$, writing $\boldsymbol{\theta}_i = (\theta_{i,j})$, $\mathbf{q}(\boldsymbol{\theta}_i) = (q_{i,j})$, $\boldsymbol{\delta}_i = (\delta_{i,j})$:

$$\left|q_{i,j}\left(k^{-2}+\theta_{i,j}\right)\right| \leq \epsilon_1 \qquad \text{for all } j=1,\ldots,k, \tag{14.12}$$

where k is the number of parameters being estimated. The k^{-2} is added in case parameters are very close to zero.

The second is based on the one-step ahead relative change in the parameter values:

$$|\delta_{i+1,j}| \leq 10\epsilon \left|\left(k^{-2}+\theta_{i,j}\right)\right| \qquad \text{for all } j=1,\ldots,k. \tag{14.13}$$

If convergence fails, it is possible to retry using a larger convergence criterion if you still want output. However, this could also be a result of model mis-specification or underidentification.

14.3.6 End of iteration process

The status of the iterative process is contained in the following messages:

(1) *Press Estimate to start iterating*
No attempt to maximize has been taken yet.

(2) *Strong convergence*
Both convergence tests (14.12) and (14.13) were passed, using tolerance ϵ_1.

(3) *Weak convergence*
The step length s_i has become too small. The convergence test (14.12) was passed, using tolerance ϵ_2.

(4) *No convergence (maximum no of iterations reached)*
The maximum number can be increased and the search resumed from the previous best values; the Hessian is reset to the identity matrix when restarting.

(5) *No convergence (no improvement in line search)*
The step length s_i has become too small. The convergence test (14.12) was not passed, using tolerance ϵ_2.

(6) *No convergence (function evaluation failed)*
This is rare in FIML, but could occur in other estimation problems. It indicates that the program failed to compute the function value at the current parameter values. The cause could be a singular matrix, or illegal argument to a function such as $\log(\cdot)$.

The chosen default values for the tolerances are:

$$\epsilon_1 = 10^{-4},\ \epsilon_2 = 5\times 10^{-3}. \tag{14.14}$$

14.3.7 Process control

When the maximization fails, or for teaching purposes, you wish to experiment with the maximization procedure, you can:

(1) set the initial values of the parameters;
(2) set the maximum number of iterations;
(3) write iteration output;
(4) change the convergence tolerance;
(5) choose the maximization algorithm;
(6) plot a grid of the log-likelihood for each parameter, see Figures 7.3, 7.4 and the next section for some examples. A grid may reveal potential multiple optima. See the next section for an example.

Options (1), (5) and (6) are mainly for teaching optimization. The multiple grid facility is especially useful for this purpose.

14.4 Numerical accuracy

Any computer program that performs numerical calculations is faced with the problem of (loss of) numerical accuracy. It seems a slightly neglected area in econometric computations, which to some extent could be owing to a perception that the gradual and steady increase in computational power went hand in hand with improvements in accuracy. This, however, is not true. At the level of software interaction with hardware, the major (and virtually the only) change has been the shift from single precision (4-byte) floating point computation to double precision (8-byte). Not many modern computer programs have problems with the Longley (1967) data set, which severely tests single precision implementations. Of course, there has been a gradual improvement in the understanding of numerical stability of various methods, but this must be offset against the increasing complexity of the calculations involved.

Loss of numerical accuracy is not a problem, provided we know when it occurs and to what extent. Computations are done with finite precision, so it is always possible to design a problem with analytical solution which fails numerically. Unfortunately, most calculations are too complex to precisely understand to what extent accuracy is lost. So it is important to implement the most accurate methods, and increase understanding of the methods used. The nature of economic data will force us to throw away many correct digits, but only at the end of the computations.

Real numbers are represented as *floating point* numbers, consisting of a sign, a mantissa, and an exponent. A finite number of bytes is used to store a floating point number, so only a finite set can be represented on the computer. The main storage size in PcGive is 8 bytes, which gives about 15 significant digits. Two sources of error result. The first is the *representation error*: most numbers can only be approximated on a computer. The second is *rounding error*. Consider the *machine precision* ϵ_m: this is the smallest number that can be added to one such that the result is different from one:

$$\epsilon_m = \underset{\epsilon}{\text{argmin}}\,(1 + \epsilon \neq 1)\,.$$

So an extreme example of rounding error would be $(1 + \epsilon_m/10) - 1$, where the answer would be 0, rather than $\epsilon_m/10$. In PcGive: $\epsilon_m \approx 2.2 \times 10^{-16}$.

Due to the accumulation of rounding errors, it is possible that mathematically-equivalent formulae can have very different numerical behaviour. For example, computing $\mathsf{V}[x]$ as $\frac{1}{T}\sum x_i^2 - \bar{x}^2$ is much less stable than $\frac{1}{T}\sum (x_i - \bar{x})^2$. In the first case, we potentially subtract two quite similar numbers, resulting in cancellation of significant digits. A similar cancellation could occur in the computation of inner products (a very common operation, as it is part of matrix multiplication). To keep the danger of cancellation to a minimum, PcGive accumulates these in 10-byte reals. PcGive allows the constant term to be entered unrestricted in the system. This corresponds to taking deviations from the mean, and hence to the second variance formula.

An interesting example of harmless numerical inaccuracies is in the case of a grid plot of an autoregressive parameter based on the concentrated likelihood function of an AR(k) model. Rounding errors make the likelihood function appear non-smooth (not differentiable). This tends to occur in models with many lags of the dependent variable and a high autoregressive order. It also occurs in an AR(1) model of the Longley data set, see Figure 14.4, which is a grid of 2000 steps between -1 and 0, (ignoring the warning that numerical accuracy is endangered).

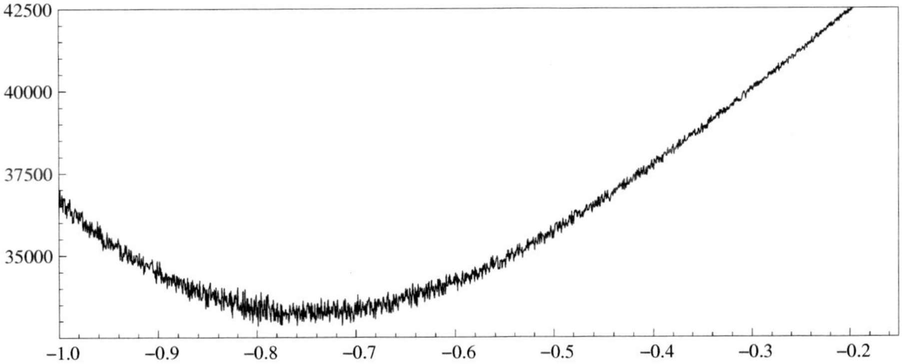

Figure 14.4 AR(1) grid of Longley data.

It is important to distinguish numerical accuracy from other problems that may occur. Multicollinearity, for example, is first and foremost a statistical problem. A certain parametrization of a model might make the estimates of one or more parameters statistically imprecise (see the concept of 'micronumerosity' playfully introduced by Goldberger in Kiefer, 1989). This imprecision could be changed (or moved) by altering the specification of the model, for example by linear or orthogonal transforms of the variables. Multicollinearity could induce numerical instability, leading to loss of significant digits in some or all results.

Another example is the determination of the optimum of a non-linear function that is not concave. Here it is possible to end up in a local optimum. This is clearly not a problem of numerical stability, but inherent in non-linear optimization techniques. A good example is provided by Klein model I. Figure 14.5 provides a grid plot of the FIML likelihood function for each parameter, centred around the maximum found with the 2SLS estimates as a starting point.

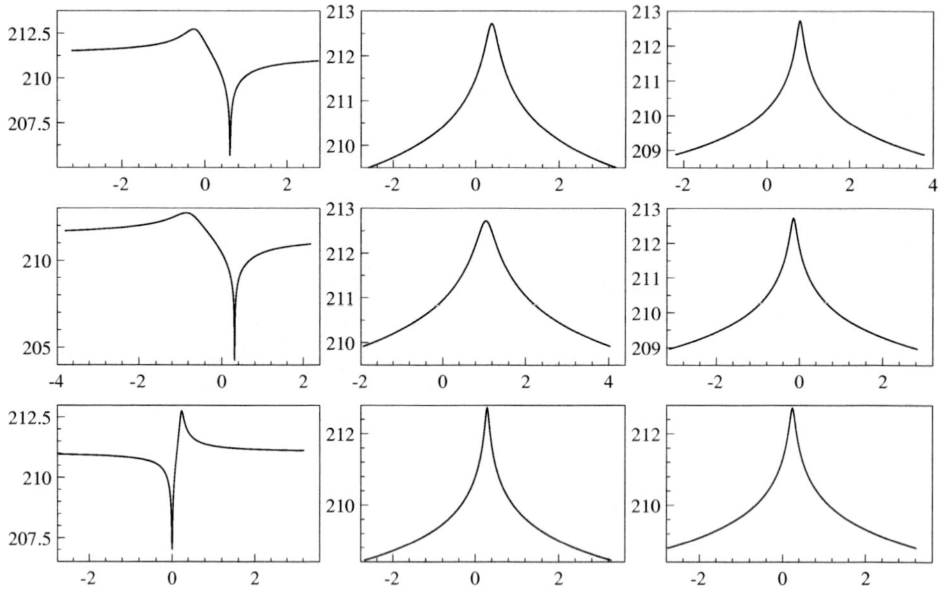

Figure 14.5 Likelihood grid of Klein model I.

These grids are of a different type from the AR grid. In the former all parameters but one are kept fixed, whereas the AR grid actually graphs the concentrated likelihood. In the case of one autoregressive parameter, the correct optimum may be read off the graph, as is the case in the AR grid plot above.

Part IV

The Statistical Output of Multiple Equation Models

Chapter 15

Unrestricted System

15.1 Introduction

This part explains the statistics computed and reported by PcGive for dynamic systems (this chapter), cointegration tests (§15.7.1), cointegrated VAR analysis (Chapter 16), and model analysis (Chapter 17).

A brief summary of the underlying mathematics is given in this chapter, but for a comprehensive overview the reader is referred to Chapters 11–13. The order is similar to that in the computer program. We first briefly describe system formulation in §15.2 to establish notation, then system estimation in §15.3, followed by estimation output §15.4 and graphic evaluation in §15.5, and dynamic analysis and I(1) and I(2) cointegration tests in §15.7. Section 15.8 considers testing, both at the single equation level as well as at the system level. Sections 15.7.1–16.0.1 discuss estimating the cointegrating space, related graphs and tests of restrictions on the space. Finally §15.9 considers the progress made during system and model development.

15.2 System formulation

In PcGive, a linear system, often called the *unrestricted reduced form* (URF), takes the form:

$$\mathbf{y}_t = \sum_{i=1}^{m} \boldsymbol{\pi}_i \mathbf{y}_{t-i} + \sum_{j=0}^{r} \boldsymbol{\pi}_{m+j+1} \mathbf{z}_{t-j} + \mathbf{v}_t \text{ for } t = 1, \ldots, T, \tag{15.1}$$

where $\mathbf{y}_t$, $\mathbf{z}_t$ are respectively $n \times 1$ and $q \times 1$ vectors of observations at time t on the endogenous and non-modelled variables. The $\{\boldsymbol{\pi}_i\}$ are unrestricted, except perhaps for columns of zeros, which would exclude certain $\mathbf{y}_{t-i}$ or $\mathbf{z}_{t-j}$ from the system. Hence each equation in the system has the same variables on the right-hand side. The orders m and r of the lag polynomial matrices for $\mathbf{y}$ and $\mathbf{z}$ should be specified so as to ensure that $\{\mathbf{v}_t\}$ is an innovation process against the available information when the $\{\boldsymbol{\pi}_i\}$ matrices are constant over t. Given a data set $\mathbf{x}_t$, then $\mathbf{y}_t$ is defined as the vector of endogenous variables and $(\mathbf{z}_t \ldots \mathbf{z}_{t-r})$ must be set as non-modelled (so they need to be at least weakly exogenous for the $\{\boldsymbol{\pi}_i\}$). A system in PcGive is formulated by:

(1) which variables $\mathbf{y}_t, \mathbf{z}_t$ are involved;
(2) the orders m, r of the *lag polynomials*;
(3) classification of the ys into *endogenous* variables and *identity (endogenous)* variables;
(4) any *non-modelled* variable may be classified as *restricted* or as *unrestricted* (Constant, Seasonals and Trend are labelled as such by default). The latter variables are separately estimated in FIML and CFIML to reduce the dimensionality of the parameter space. Their coefficients are estimated from a prior regression as described in §11.4.

A *vector autoregression* (VAR) arises when there are no z variables in the statistical system (15.1) ($q = 0$, but there could be a constant, seasonals or trend) and all y have the same lag length (no columns of $\boldsymbol{\pi}$ are zero).

Integrated systems can be transformed to *equilibrium correction form*, where all endogenous variables and their lags are transformed to differences, apart from the first lag:

$$\Delta \mathbf{y}_t = \sum_{i=1}^{m-1} \boldsymbol{\delta}_i \Delta \mathbf{y}_{t-i} + \mathbf{P}_0 \mathbf{y}_{t-1} + \sum_{j=0}^{r} \boldsymbol{\pi}_{m+j+1} \mathbf{z}_{t-j} + \mathbf{v}_t \quad \text{for} \quad t = 1, \ldots, T. \tag{15.2}$$

Returning to the notation of (15.1), a more compact way of writing the system is:

$$\mathbf{y}_t = \boldsymbol{\Pi} \mathbf{w}_t + \mathbf{v}_t, \tag{15.3}$$

where $\mathbf{w}$ contains $\mathbf{z}$, lags of $\mathbf{z}$, and lags of $\mathbf{y}$: $\mathbf{w}_t' = \left(\mathbf{y}_{t-1}', \ldots, \mathbf{y}_{t-m}', \mathbf{z}_t', \ldots, \mathbf{z}_{t-r}'\right)$. This can be further condensed by writing $\mathbf{Y}' = (\mathbf{y}_1\ \mathbf{y}_2 \ldots \mathbf{y}_T)$, and $\mathbf{W}'$, $\mathbf{V}'$ correspondingly:

$$\mathbf{Y}' = \boldsymbol{\Pi} \mathbf{W}' + \mathbf{V}', \tag{15.4}$$

in which $\mathbf{Y}'$ is $(n \times T)$, $\mathbf{W}'$ is $(k \times T)$ and $\boldsymbol{\Pi}$ is $(n \times k)$.

15.3 System estimation

Since the $\{\boldsymbol{\pi}_i\}$ are unrestricted (except perhaps for excluding elements from $\mathbf{w}_t$) the system (15.1) can be estimated by multivariate least squares, either directly (OLS) or recursively (often denoted RLS). These estimators are straightforward multivariate extensions of the single equation methods. Analogously, estimation of (15.1) requires $\mathbf{v}_t \sim \mathsf{ID}_n(\mathbf{0}, \boldsymbol{\Omega})$, where $\boldsymbol{\Omega}$ is constant over time. However, $\boldsymbol{\Omega}$ may be singular owing to identities linking elements of $\mathbf{x}_t$, and these are handled by estimating only the subset of equations corresponding to stochastic endogenous variables. If $\mathbf{v}_t \sim \mathsf{IN}_n[\mathbf{0}, \boldsymbol{\Omega}]$, OLS coincides with MLE, and estimation of (15.1) is discussed in Chapter 11; for notation, we note that the estimated coefficients are:

$$\widehat{\mathbf{\Pi}}' = (\mathbf{W}'\mathbf{W})^{-1}\mathbf{W}'\mathbf{Y}, \tag{15.5}$$

with residuals:

$$\widehat{\mathbf{V}}' = \mathbf{Y}' - \widehat{\mathbf{\Pi}}\mathbf{W}' \tag{15.6}$$

and estimated covariance matrix:

$$\widehat{\mathsf{V}\left[\text{vec}\widehat{\mathbf{\Pi}}'\right]} = \widetilde{\mathbf{\Omega}} \otimes (\mathbf{W}'\mathbf{W})^{-1}, \tag{15.7}$$

where:

$$\widetilde{\mathbf{\Omega}} = \widehat{\mathbf{V}}'\widehat{\mathbf{V}}/\left(T-k\right). \tag{15.8}$$

In the likelihood-based statistics, we shall scale by T:

$$\widehat{\mathbf{\Omega}} = \widehat{\mathbf{V}}'\widehat{\mathbf{V}}/T. \tag{15.9}$$

15.4 System output

A listing of the system output now follows. Items marked with a * are only printed on request, either automatically through settings in the Options dialog, or by using Further Output.

15.4.1 Equation output

(1) *URF coefficients and standard errors*

The coefficients $\widehat{\mathbf{\Pi}}$, and their standard errors $\sqrt{(\widehat{\mathsf{V}[\text{vec}\widehat{\mathbf{\Pi}}']})_{ii}}$. Any variables marked as unrestricted appear here too.

(2) t-*value and* t-*probability*

These statistics are conventionally calculated to determine whether individual coefficients are significantly different from zero:

$$\text{t-value} = \frac{\widehat{\pi}_{ij}}{\mathsf{SE}\left[\widehat{\pi}_{ij}\right]} \tag{15.10}$$

where the null hypothesis H_0 is $\pi_{ij} = 0$. The null hypothesis is rejected if the probability of getting a value at least as large is less than 5% (or any other chosen significance level). This probability is given as:

$$\text{t-prob} = 1 - \text{Prob}\left(|\tau| \leq |\text{t-value}|\right), \tag{15.11}$$

in which τ has a Student t-distribution with $T-k$ degrees of freedom.

When H_0 is true (and the model is otherwise correctly specified), a Student t-distribution is used since the sample size is often small, and we only have an estimate of the parameter's standard error: however, as the sample size increases, τ tends to a standard normal distribution under H_0. Large values of t reject H_0; but, in many situations, H_0 may be of little interest to test. Also, selecting variables in a model according to their t-values implies that the usual (Neyman-Pearson) justification for testing is not valid (see Judge, Griffiths, Hill, Lütkepohl and Lee, 1985, for example).

(3) *Equation standard error ($\widetilde{\sigma}$) and residual sum of squares (RSS)*
The square root of the residual variance for each equation:

$$\sqrt{\widetilde{\mathbf{\Omega}}_{ii}} \text{ for } i = 1, \ldots n. \tag{15.12}$$

The RSS is $(T-k)\,\widetilde{\mathbf{\Omega}}_{ii}$, that is, the diagonal elements of $\widehat{\mathbf{V}}'\widehat{\mathbf{V}}$.

15.4.2 Summary statistics

The log-likelihood value is (including the constant K_c):

$$\widehat{\ell} = -\frac{T}{2}\log\left|\widehat{\mathbf{\Omega}}\right| - \frac{Tn}{2}\left(1+\log 2\pi\right). \tag{15.13}$$

Then ℓ constitutes the highest attainable likelihood value in the class (15.4) (unless either the set of variables or the lag structure is altered), and hence is the statistical baseline against which simplifications can be tested. In textbook econometrics, (15.4) is called the unrestricted reduced form (URF) and is usually derived from a structural representation. Here, the process is reversed: the statistical system (15.4) is first specified and tested for being a congruent representation; only then is a structural (parsimonious) interpretation sought. If, for example, (15.4) is not congruent, then (15.13) is not a valid baseline, and subsequent tests will not have appropriate distributions. In particular, any just-identified structural representation has the same likelihood value as (15.4), and hence will be invalid if (15.4) is invalid: the 'validity' of imposing further restrictions via a model is hardly of interest.

Define $\check{\mathbf{Y}}$ as $\mathbf{Y}$ after removing the effects of the unrestricted variables, and let:

$$\widehat{\mathbf{\Omega}}_0 = \left(\check{\mathbf{Y}}'\check{\mathbf{Y}}/T\right)^{-1}. \tag{15.14}$$

PcGive reports:

(1) the log-likelihood (15.13);
(2) $-\frac{T}{2}\log|\widehat{\mathbf{\Omega}}|$;
(3) $|\widehat{\mathbf{\Omega}}|$;
(4) T, the number of observations used in the estimation, and nk, the number of parameters in all equations;

(5) $\log|\check{\mathbf{Y}}'\check{\mathbf{Y}}/T| = \log|\widehat{\mathbf{\Omega}}_0|$.

Various measures of the *goodness of fit* of a system can be calculated. The two reported by PcGive are:

(1) R^2(LR)
Reports $\mathsf{R}^2_r = 1-|\widehat{\mathbf{\Omega}}||\widehat{\mathbf{\Omega}}_0|$, which is an R^2 based on the likelihood-ratio principle. For a single equation system this statistic is identical to:

(2) R^2(LM)
Reports $\mathsf{R}^2_m = 1 - \frac{1}{n}\mathrm{tr}(\widehat{\mathbf{\Omega}}\widehat{\mathbf{\Omega}}_0)$, which derives from the Lagrange Multiplier principle.

Note that these are relative to the unrestricted variables. Both measures coincide with the traditional R^2 in a single equation, provided that the constant is the only unrestricted variable.

15.4.3 F-tests

Significance at 5% is marked with a *, at 1% with **. Reported are:

(1) F-*tests against unrestricted regressors*
This uses Rao's F-approximation (see §11.8) to test the significance of R^2_r, which amounts to testing the null hypothesis that all coefficients are zero, except those on the unrestricted variables. In a single-equation system, with only the constant unrestricted, this is identical to the reported F-statistic.

(2) F-*tests on retained regressors*
F-tests are shown for the significance of each column of $\widehat{\mathbf{\Pi}}$ together with their probability values (inside square brackets) under the null hypothesis that the corresponding column of coefficients is zero. So these test whether the variable at hand is significant in the system. The statistics are $\mathsf{F}(n, T-k+1-n)$.

Further F-tests of general to specific system modelling are available through the progress report: see §15.9.

15.4.4 Correlations

- *Correlation of URF Residuals*
  A typical element of this matrix is:

$$\mathsf{c}_{ij} = \frac{\widetilde{\mathbf{\Omega}}_{ij}}{\sqrt{\widetilde{\mathbf{\Omega}}_{ii}}\sqrt{\widetilde{\mathbf{\Omega}}_{jj}}}. \tag{15.15}$$

  The diagonal reports the *standard deviations* of the URF residuals
- *Correlation of actual and fitted*
  Prints the correlation between y_{it} and $\widehat{y}_{it}$ for each equation $i = 1, \ldots, n$.

15.4.5 1-step (*ex post*) forecast analysis

This is only reported when observations are withheld for static forecasting when the sample size is selected.

The 1-step forecast errors (from $T+1$ to $T+H$) are defined as:

$$\mathbf{e}_{T+i} = \mathbf{y}_{T+i} - \widehat{\mathbf{\Pi}}\mathbf{w}_{T+i} = \left(\mathbf{\Pi} - \widehat{\mathbf{\Pi}}\right)\mathbf{w}_{T+i} + \mathbf{v}_{T+i} \tag{15.16}$$

with estimated variance

$$\widetilde{\mathsf{V}[\mathbf{e}_{T+i}]} = \widetilde{\mathbf{\Omega}}\left(1 + \mathbf{w}'_{T+i}\left(\mathbf{W}'\mathbf{W}\right)^{-1}\mathbf{w}_{T+i}\right) = \widetilde{\mathbf{\Psi}}_{T+i}. \tag{15.17}$$

The forecast error variance matrix for a single step-ahead forecast is made up of a term for coefficient uncertainty and a term for innovation errors, as discussed in §11.5. Three types of parameter constancy tests are reported, in each case as a $\chi^2(nH)$ for n equations and H forecasts and an $\mathsf{F}(nH, T-k)$ statistic:

(1) *using* $\mathbf{\Omega}$.
This is an index of numerical parameter constancy, ignoring both parameter uncertainty and intercorrelation between forecasts errors at different time periods. It corresponds to ξ_1 and η_1 of (11.46).

(2) *using* $\mathsf{V}[\mathbf{e}]$.
This test is similar to (a), but takes parameter uncertainty into account, corresponding to ξ_2 and η_2 of (11.46).

(3) *using* $\mathsf{V}[\mathbf{E}]$.
Here, $\mathsf{V}[\mathbf{E}]$ is the full variance matrix of all forecast errors $\mathbf{E}$, which takes both parameter uncertainty and inter-correlations between forecast errors into account. This test is ξ_3 and η_3 of (11.46).

15.4.6 *Information criteria

The four statistics reported are the Schwarz criterion (SC), the Hannan–Quinn criterion (HQ), the Final Prediction Error (FPE) and the Akaike criterion (AIC). These can be defined as:

$$\begin{aligned}
\mathsf{SC} &= \log\left|\widehat{\mathbf{\Omega}}\right| + k\log(T)T^{-1}, \\
\mathsf{HQ} &= \log\left|\widehat{\mathbf{\Omega}}\right| + 2k\log(\log(T))T^{-1}, \\
\mathsf{AIC} &= \log\left|\widehat{\mathbf{\Omega}}\right| + 2kT^{-1}, \\
\mathsf{FPE} &= (T+k)\left|\widehat{\mathbf{\Omega}}\right| / (T-k).
\end{aligned} \tag{15.18}$$

Or, in terms of the log-likelihood:

$$\begin{aligned}\mathsf{SC} &= \left(-2\widehat{\ell} + k\log T\right)T^{-1}, \\ \mathsf{HQ} &= \left(-2\widehat{\ell} + 2k\log\log T\right)T^{-1}, \\ \mathsf{AIC} &= \left(-2\widehat{\ell} + 2k\right)T^{-1}, \\ \mathsf{FPE} &= -\tfrac{T+k}{T-k}\tfrac{2}{T}\widehat{\ell}.\end{aligned} \tag{15.19}$$

When using Further Output will first report (15.18) followed by (15.19). In the latter, the constant is included in the likelihood, resulting in different outcomes. In all other cases, PcGive will only report the values based on (15.19). For a discussion of the use of these and related scalar measures to choose between alternative models in a class, see Judge, Griffiths, Hill, Lütkepohl and Lee (1985) or Lütkepohl (1991).

15.4.7 *Correlation matrix of regressors

This reports the sample means and sample standard deviations of the selected variables, followed by the correlation matrix.

15.4.8 *Covariance matrix of estimated parameters

The $k \times k$ variance-covariance matrix of the estimated parameters. Along the diagonal, we have the variance of each estimated coefficient, and off the diagonal, the covariances.

15.4.9 *Static (1-step) forecasts

Reports the individual forecasts with forecast error standard errors. If the actual values are available, the forecast error and t-value are also printed.

Additional statistics are reported if more than two forecast errors are available:

(1) *Mean of the forecast errors*;
(2) *Standard deviation of the forecast errors*;
(3) *Forecast tests, single chi*^{2} $(\cdot)$
These are the individual test statistics underlying ξ_1 and ξ_2 above, for $i = 1, \ldots, H$:

$$\begin{aligned}&\text{using } \boldsymbol{\Omega} && \mathbf{e}_{T+i}'\widetilde{\boldsymbol{\Omega}}^{-1}\mathbf{e}_{T+i}, \\ &\text{using } \mathsf{V}[\mathbf{e}] && \mathbf{e}_{T+i}'\widetilde{\boldsymbol{\Psi}}_{T+i}^{-1}\mathbf{e}_{T+i},\end{aligned} \tag{15.20}$$

this time distributed as $\chi^2(n)$. They can also be viewed graphically.
(4) Root Mean Square Error:

$$\text{RMSE} = \left[\frac{1}{H}\sum_{t=1}^{H}(y_t - f_t)^2\right]^{1/2},$$

where the forecast horizon is H, y_t the actual values, and f_t the forecasts.

(5) Mean Absolute Percentage Error:

$$\text{MAPE} = \frac{100}{H} \sum_{t=1}^{H} \left| \frac{y_t - f_t}{y_t} \right|.$$

RMSE and MAPE are measures of forecast accuracy, see, e.g. Makridakis, Wheelwright and Hyndman (1998, Ch. 2). Note that the MAPE can be infinity if any $y_t = 0$, and is different when the model is reformulated in differences. For more information see Clements and Hendry (1998a).

15.5 Graphic analysis

Graphic analysis focuses on graphical inspection of individual equations. Let y_t, $\widehat{y}_t$ denote respectively the actual (that is, observed) values and the fitted values of the selected equation, with residuals $\widehat{v}_t = y_t - \widehat{y}_t$, $t = 1, \ldots, T$. If H observations are retained for forecasting, then $\widehat{y}_{T+1}, \ldots, \widehat{y}_{T+H}$ are the 1-step forecasts.

Many different types of graph are available:

(1) *Actual and fitted values*
This is a graph showing the fitted ($\widehat{y}_t$) and actual values (y_t) of the dependent variable over time, including the forecast period.

(2) *Cross-plot of actual and fitted*
$\widehat{y}_t$ against y_t, including the forecast period.

(3) *Residuals (scaled)*
($\widehat{v}_t / \widetilde{\sigma}$), where $\widetilde{\sigma}^2$ is the estimated equation error variance, plotted over $t = 1, \ldots, T + H$.

(4) *Forecasts and outcomes*
The 1-step forecasts can be plotted in a graph over time: y_t and $\widehat{y}_t$, $t = T + 1, \ldots, T + H$, are shown with error bars of $\pm 2\mathsf{SE}\,(e_t)$, and centred on $\widehat{y}_t$ (that is, an approximate 95% confidence interval for the 1-step forecast). Corresponding to (15.16) the forecast errors are $e_t = y_t - \widehat{y}_t$ and $\mathsf{SE}\,[e_t]$ is derived from (15.17). The error bars can be replaced by bands, set in Options, and the number of pre-forecast observations can be selected.

(5) *Residual density and histogram*
Plots the histogram of the standardized residuals, the estimated density $\widehat{f_{\mathsf{v}}(\cdot)}$ and a normal distribution with the same mean and variance (more details are in the OxMetrics book).

(6) *Residual correlogram (ACF)*
This plots the series $\{\mathsf{r}_j\}$ where r_j is the correlation coefficient between $\widehat{v}_t$ and $\widehat{v}_{t-j}$. The length of the correlogram is specified by the user, leading to a Figure

that shows $(\mathsf{r}_1, \mathsf{r}_2, \ldots, \mathsf{r}_s)$ plotted against $(1, 2, \ldots, s)$ where for any j:

$$\mathsf{r}_j = \frac{\sum_{t=j+1}^{T} (v_t - \bar{v}_0)(v_{t-j} - \bar{v}_j)}{\sum_{t=j}^{T} (v_t - \bar{v})^2}, \tag{15.21}$$

where $\bar{v}$ is the sample mean of v_t.

(7) *Partial correlogram (PACF)*
This plots the Partial autocorrrelation function (see the OxMetrics book).

(8) *Forecasts Chow tests*
These are the Chow tests using $\mathsf{V}[\mathsf{e}]$ of (15.20), available from $T+1$ to $T+H$, together with a fixed 5% critical value from $\chi^2(n)$. These are not scaled by their critical values, unlike the graphs in recursive graphics.

(9) *Residuals (unscaled)*
$(\hat{v}_t)$ over t;

(10) *Residual spectrum*
This plots the estimated spectral density (see the OxMetrics book) using $\hat{v}_t$ as the x_t variable.

(11) *Residual QQ plot against N(0,1)*
Shows a QQ plot of the residuals.

(12) *Residual density optionally with Histogram*
The histogram of the scaled residuals and the non-parametrically estimated density $\widehat{f_{\mathsf{v}}(\cdot)}$ are graphed using the settings described in the OxMetrics book.

(13) *Residual distribution (normal quantiles)*
Plots the distribution based on the non-parametrically estimated density.

(14) *Residual cross-plots*
Let $\widehat{v}_{it}$, $\widehat{v}_{jt}$ denote the residuals of equation i and j. This graph shows the cross-plot of $\widehat{v}_{it}$ against $\widehat{v}_{jt}$ for all marked equations $(i \neq j)$, over $t = 1, \ldots, T+H$.

The residuals can be saved to the database for further inspection.

15.6 Recursive graphics

When recursive OLS (RLS) is selected, the $\mathbf{\Pi}$ matrix is estimated at each t $(1 \leq M \leq t \leq T)$ where M is user-selected. Unlike previous versions, there is no requirement that $k \leq M$. So OLS is used for observations $1 \ldots M-1$, RLS for $M \ldots T$. The calculations proceed exactly as for the single equation case since the formulae for updating are unaffected by $\mathbf{Y}$ being a matrix rather than a vector. Indeed, the relative cost over single equation RLS falls; but the huge number of statistics $(nk(T-M+1)$ coefficients alone) cannot be stored in PcGive. Consequently, the graphical output omits coefficients and their t-values. Otherwise the output is similar to that in single equations, but now available for each equation in the system. In addition, system graphs are available, either of the log likelihood, or of the system Chow tests. At each t, system estimates are available, for example coefficients $\mathbf{\Pi}_t$ and residuals $\mathbf{v}_t = \mathbf{y}_t - \mathbf{\Pi}_t \mathbf{w}_t$. Unrestricted variables have their coefficients fixed at the full sample values. Define $\mathbf{V}_t'$ as $(\mathbf{v}_1 \mathbf{v}_2 \ldots \mathbf{v}_t)$ and let y_t, v_t, $\mathbf{w}_t$ denote the endogenous variable, residuals and regressors of equation i at time t.

The following graphs are available for the system (the information can be printed on request):

(1) *Residual sum of squares*
The residual sum of squares RSS_t for equation i is the ith diagonal element of $\widehat{\mathbf{V}}_t'\widehat{\mathbf{V}}_t$ for $t = M, \ldots, T$.

(2) *1-Step Residuals* $\pm 2\widetilde{\sigma}$ for equation i at each t:
The 1-step residuals $\widehat{v}_t$ are shown bordered by $0 \pm 2\widetilde{\sigma}_t$ over $M, \ldots, T$. Points outside the 2-standard-error region are either outliers or are associated with coefficient changes.

(3) *Log-likelihood/T*

$$\widehat{l}_t = - \tfrac{1}{2} \log \left| \frac{t}{T} \widehat{\mathbf{\Omega}}_t \right| = - \tfrac{1}{2} \log \left| T^{-1} \widehat{\mathbf{V}}_t' \widehat{\mathbf{V}}_t \right|, \ t = M, \ldots, T. \qquad (15.22)$$

Per definition: $\widehat{l}_t \geq \widehat{l}_{t+1}$. This follows from the fact that both can be derived from a system estimated up to $t+1$, where $\widehat{l}_t$ obtains from the system with a dummy for the last observation (see §11.8.1), so that $\widehat{l}_{t+1}$ is the restricted likelihood. On the other hand: $\widehat{\ell}_t \ngeq \widehat{\ell}_{t+1}$, as this would still require the sample size correction as employed in $\widehat{l}_t$. Note that the constant is excluded from the log-likelihood here.

(4) *Single equation chow Tests*

(a) *1-step* F*-tests* (1-step Chow-tests)
1-step forecast tests are $\mathsf{F}(1, t-k-1)$ under the null of constant parameters, for $t = M, \ldots, T$. A typical statistic is calculated as:

$$\frac{(RSS_t - RSS_{t-1})(t-k-1)}{RSS_{t-1}}. \qquad (15.23)$$

Normality of y_t is needed for this statistic to be distributed as an F.

(b) *Break-point* F*-tests* ($N\!\downarrow$-step Chow-tests)
Break-point F-tests are $\mathsf{F}(T-t+1, t-k-1)$ for $t = M, \ldots, T$. These are, therefore, sequences of Chow tests and are called $N\!\downarrow$ because the number of forecasts goes from $T-M+1$ to 1. When the forecast period exceeds the estimation period, this test is not necessarily optimal relative to the covariance test based on fitting the model separately to the split samples. A typical statistic is calculated as:

$$\frac{(RSS_T - RSS_{t-1})(t-k-1)}{RSS_{t-1}(T-t+1)}. \qquad (15.24)$$

This test is closely related to the CUSUMSQ statistic in Brown, Durbin and Evans (1975).

(c) *Forecast* F*-tests.* ($N\uparrow$-step Chow-tests)
Forecast F-tests are $\mathsf{F}(t-M+1, M-k-1)$ for $t = M, \ldots, T$, and are called $N\uparrow$ as the forecast horizon increases from M to t. This tests the model over 1 to $M-1$ against an alternative which allows any form of change over M to T. Thus, unless $M > k$, blank graphs will result. A typical statistic is calculated as:

$$\frac{(RSS_t - RSS_{M-1})\,(M-k-1)}{RSS_{M-1}\,(t-M+1)}. \tag{15.25}$$

(5) *System Chow tests*

(a) *1-step* F*-tests* (1-step Chow-tests)
This uses Rao's F-approximation (see §11.8), with the R^2 computed as:

$$1-\exp\left(-2\widehat{l}_{t-1}+2\widehat{l}_t\right), \quad t = M, \ldots, T. \tag{15.26}$$

(b) *Break-point* F*-tests* ($N\downarrow$-step Chow-tests)
This uses Rao's F-approximation, with the R^2 computed as:

$$1-\exp\left(-2\widehat{l}_{t-1}+2\widehat{l}_T\right), \quad t = M, \ldots, T. \tag{15.27}$$

(c) *Forecast* F*-tests* ($N\uparrow$-step Chow-tests)
This uses Rao's F-approximation, with the R^2 computed as:

$$1-\exp\left(-2\widehat{l}_{M-1}+2\widehat{l}_t\right), \quad t = M, \ldots, T. \tag{15.28}$$

The statistics in (4) and (5) are variants of Chow (1960) tests: they are scaled by one-off critical values from the F-distribution at any selected probability level as an adjustment for changing degrees of freedom, so that the significance values become a straight line at unity. Selecting a probability of 0 or 1 results in unscaled statistics. Note that the first and last values of (15.23) respectively equal the first value of (15.25) and the last value of (15.24); the same relation holds for the system tests. When the system tests of (5) are computed for a single equation system, they are identical to the tests computed under (4).

15.6.1 Dynamic forecasting

Dynamic (or multi-period or *ex ante*) system forecasts can be graphed. Commencing from period T as initial conditions:

$$\widehat{\mathbf{y}}_t = \sum_{i=1}^{m} \widehat{\boldsymbol{\pi}}_i \widehat{\mathbf{y}}_{t-i} + \sum_{j=0}^{r} \widehat{\boldsymbol{\pi}}_{j+m+1}\mathbf{z}_{t-j} \quad \text{for } t = T+1, \ldots, T+H, \tag{15.29}$$

where $\widehat{\mathbf{y}}_{t-i} = \mathbf{y}_{t-i}$ for $t-i \leq T$.

Such forecasts require data on $(\mathbf{z}_{T+1} \ldots \mathbf{z}_{T+H})$ for H-periods ahead (but the future values of ys are not needed), and to be meaningful also require that $\mathbf{z}_t$ is strongly exogenous and that $\mathbf{\Pi}$ remains constant. Dynamic forecasts can be viewed with or without 'error bars' (or bands) based on the equation error-variance matrix only, where the variance estimates are given by the $(n \times n)$ top left block of:

$$\begin{aligned} \widetilde{\mathsf{V}\left[\mathbf{e}^*_{T+1}\right]} &= \widetilde{\mho}, \\ \widetilde{\mathsf{V}\left[\mathbf{e}^*_{T+2}\right]} &= \widetilde{\mho} + \widehat{\mathbf{D}}\widetilde{\mho}\widehat{\mathbf{D}}', \\ &\ldots \\ \widetilde{\mathsf{V}\left[\mathbf{e}^*_{T+H}\right]} &= \sum_{i=0}^{H-1} \widehat{\mathbf{D}}^i\widetilde{\mho}\widehat{\mathbf{D}}^{i\prime}. \end{aligned} \tag{15.30}$$

Optionally, parameter uncertainty can be taken into account when computing the forecast error variances (but not for h-step forecasts): this is allowed only when there are no unrestricted variables. Using the companion matrix, which is $(nm \times nm)$:

$$\widehat{\mathbf{D}} = \begin{pmatrix} \widehat{\boldsymbol{\pi}}_1 & \widehat{\boldsymbol{\pi}}_2 & \cdots & \widehat{\boldsymbol{\pi}}_{m-1} & \widehat{\boldsymbol{\pi}}_m \\ \mathbf{I}_n & \mathbf{0} & \cdots & \mathbf{0} & \mathbf{0} \\ \mathbf{0} & \mathbf{I}_n & \cdots & \mathbf{0} & \mathbf{0} \\ \vdots & \vdots & \ddots & \vdots & \vdots \\ \mathbf{0} & \mathbf{0} & \cdots & \mathbf{I}_n & \mathbf{0} \end{pmatrix} \quad \text{and} \quad \widetilde{\mho} = \begin{pmatrix} \widetilde{\boldsymbol{\Omega}} & \mathbf{0} & \cdots \\ \mathbf{0} & \mathbf{0} & \cdots \\ \vdots & \vdots & \ddots \end{pmatrix}, \tag{15.31}$$

see §11.5.2.

Thus, uncertainty owing to the parameters being estimated is presently ignored (compare this to the parameter constancy tests based on the 1-step forecasts). If $q > 0$, the non-modelled variables could be perturbed as in 'scenario studies' on non-linear models, but here with a view to assessing the robustness or fragility of *ex ante* forecasts to possible changes in the conditioning variables. If such perturbations alter the characteristics of the $\{\mathbf{z}_t\}$ process, super exogeneity is required.

It is also possible to graph h-step forecasts, where $h \leq H$. This uses (15.29), but with:

$$\widehat{\mathbf{y}}_{t-i} = \mathbf{y}_{t-i} \quad \text{for} \quad t - i \leq \max(T, t-h). \tag{15.32}$$

To be consistent with the definition of h-step forecasts in §11.5, what is graphed is the sequence of $1, \ldots, h-1$ step forecasts for $T+1, \ldots T+h-1$, followed by h-step forecasts from $T+h, \ldots T+H$. In other words: up to $T+h$ are dynamic forecasts, from then on h-step forecasts up to $T+H$. Thus, unless there is available data not used in estimation, the h-step forecasts are just dynamic forecasts up to the value of h: this data can be reserved by using a shorter estimation sample, or setting a non-zero number of forecasts. After h forecasts, the forecast error variance remains constant at $\sum_{i=0}^{h-1} \widehat{\mathbf{D}}^i\widetilde{\mho}\widehat{\mathbf{D}}^{i\prime}$. For example, 1-step forecasts use $\widehat{\mathbf{y}}_{t-i} = \mathbf{y}_{t-i}$ for $t - i \leq \max(T, t-1)$, and hence never use forecasted values (in this case $\max(T, t-1) =$

$t-1$, as $t \geq T+1$). The 1-step forecast error variance used here is $\widetilde{\mathbf{\Omega}}$, which differs from (15.17) in that it ignores the parameter uncertainty. Selecting $h = H$ yields the dynamic forecasts.

To summarize, the following graphs are available:

(1) *Dynamic forecasts* over any selected horizon H for closed systems, and the available sample for open (with non-modelled variables, but no identities).
Graphs can be without standard errors; or standard errors can be plotted as the forecast ±2SE, either error-variance based or parameter-variance based (i.e., full estimation uncertainty, if no unrestricted variables).

(2) *h-step forecasts* up to the end of the available sample, which is dependent on the presence or absence of non-modelled variables. In the former case, data must exist on the non-modelled variables; in the latter, the horizon $H \geq h$ is at choice. Graphs can be without standard errors; or error-variance based standard errors can be plotted as the forecast ±2SE.

The forecasts and standard errors can be printed. Although dynamic forecasting is not available for a system with identities, it can be obtained by mapping the system to a model of itself and specifying the identity equations.

15.6.2 Dynamic simulation and impulse responses

The system can be dynamically simulated from any starting point within sample, ending at the last observation used in the estimation. Computation is as in (15.29), with $T+1$ replaced by the chosen within-sample starting point. Given the critiques of dynamic simulation as a method of evaluating econometric systems in Hendry and Richard (1982) and Chong and Hendry (1986), this option is included to allow users to see how misleading simulation tracks can be as a guide to selecting systems. Also see Pagan (1989). Like dynamic forecasting, dynamic simulation is not available for a system with identities, but can be obtained by mapping the system to a model of itself and specifying the identity equations.

Let y_t, $\widehat{y}_t$, $\widehat{s}_t$ denote respectively the actual (that is, observed) values, the fitted values (from the estimation) and the simulated values of the selected equation, $t = M, \ldots, M+H$. H is the number of simulated values, starting from M, $1 \leq M < T$.

Four different types of graph are available:

(1) *Actual and simulated values*
This is a graph showing the simulated ($\widehat{s}_t$) and actual values (y_t) of the dependent variable over time.

(2) *Actual and simulated cross-plot*
Cross-plot of $\widehat{y}_t$ against $\widehat{s}_t$.

(3) *Fitted and simulated values*
$\widehat{y}_t$ and $\widehat{s}_t$ against time.

(4) *Simulation residuals*
Graphs $(y_t - \widehat{s}_t)$ over time.

Impulse response analysis disregards the non-modelled variables and sets the history to zero, apart from the initial values $\mathbf{i}_1$:

$$\widehat{\mathbf{i}}_t = \sum_{i=1}^{m} \widehat{\boldsymbol{\pi}}_i \widehat{\mathbf{i}}_{t-i} \quad \text{for } t = 2, \ldots, H, \tag{15.33}$$

where $\widehat{\mathbf{i}}_1$ are the initial values, and $\widehat{\mathbf{i}}_t = \mathbf{0}$ for $t \leq 0$. This generates n^2 graphs, where the jth set of n graphs gives the response of the n endogenous variables to the jth initial values. These initial values $\mathbf{i}_{1,j}$ for the jth set of graphs can be chosen as follows:

(1) unity
$\mathbf{i}_{1,j} = \mathbf{e}_j$: 1 for the jth variable, 0 otherwise.
(2) standard error
$\mathbf{i}_{1,j} = \widetilde{\boldsymbol{\sigma}}_j$: the jth residual standard error for the jth variable, 0 otherwise.
(3) orthogonalized
Take the Choleski decomposition of $\widetilde{\boldsymbol{\Omega}}$, $\widetilde{\boldsymbol{\Omega}} = \mathbf{P}\mathbf{P}'$, so that $\mathbf{P} = (\mathbf{p}_1 \ldots \mathbf{p}_n)$ has zeros above the diagonal. The orthogonalized initial values are $\mathbf{i}_{1,j} = \mathbf{p}_j$. Thus, the outcome depends on the ordering of the variables.

Graphing is optionally of the accumulated response: $\sum_{t=1}^{h} \widehat{\mathbf{i}}_t$, $h = 1, \ldots, H$.

15.7 Dynamic analysis

After estimation, a dynamic analysis of the unrestricted reduced form (system) can be performed. Consider the system (15.2), but replace the $\boldsymbol{\pi}_{m+j+1}$ by $\boldsymbol{\Gamma}_j$:

$$\mathbf{y}_t = \sum_{i=1}^{m} \boldsymbol{\pi}_i \mathbf{y}_{t-i} + \sum_{j=0}^{r} \boldsymbol{\Gamma}_j \mathbf{z}_{t-j} + \mathbf{v}_t, \quad \mathbf{v}_t \sim \mathsf{IN}_n\left[\mathbf{0}, \boldsymbol{\Omega}\right], \tag{15.34}$$

with $\mathbf{y}_t$ $(n \times 1)$ and $\mathbf{z}_t$ $(q \times 1)$. Use the lag operator L, defined as $L\mathbf{y}_t = \mathbf{y}_{t-1}$, to write this as:

$$\left(\mathbf{I} - \boldsymbol{\pi}\left(L\right)\right) \mathbf{y}_t = \boldsymbol{\Gamma}\left(L\right) \mathbf{z}_t + \mathbf{v}_t. \tag{15.35}$$

So $\boldsymbol{\pi}(1) = \boldsymbol{\pi}_1 + \cdots + \boldsymbol{\pi}_m$, with m the longest lag on endogenous variable(s); and $\boldsymbol{\Gamma}(1) = \boldsymbol{\Gamma}_0 + \cdots + \boldsymbol{\Gamma}_r$, with r the longest lag on non-modelled variable(s). $\widehat{\mathbf{P}}_0 = \widehat{\boldsymbol{\pi}}(1) - \mathbf{I}_n$ can be inverted only if it is of rank $p = n$, in which case for $q > 0$, $\mathbf{y}$ and $\mathbf{z}$ are fully cointegrated. If $p < n$, only a subset of the ys and zs are cointegrated, see Chapter 12. If $\widehat{\mathbf{P}}_0$ can be inverted, we can write the estimated static long-run solution as:

$$\widehat{\mathbf{y}} = -\widehat{\mathbf{P}}_0^{-1} \widehat{\boldsymbol{\Gamma}}\left(1\right) \mathbf{z}. \tag{15.36}$$

If $q = 0$, the system is closed (that is, a VAR), and (15.36) is not defined. However, $\mathbf{P}_0$ can still be calculated, and then p characterizes the number of cointegrating vectors linking the ys: again see Chapter 12. $^+$ denotes that the outcome is reported only if there are non-modelled variables.

If there are no identities PcGive computes:

(1) *Long-run matrix Pi(1)-I = Po*: $\widehat{\boldsymbol{\pi}}(1) - \mathbf{I}_n = \widehat{\mathbf{P}}_0$;
(2) *Long-run covariance*: $\widehat{\mathbf{P}}_0^{-1}\widetilde{\boldsymbol{\Omega}}\widehat{\mathbf{P}}_0^{-1}$;
(3) *Static long run*: $-\widehat{\mathbf{P}}_0^{-1}\widehat{\boldsymbol{\Gamma}}(1)$;$^+$
(4) *Standard errors of static long run*;$^+$
(5) *Mean-lag matrix* $\sum \pi_i$: $\widehat{\boldsymbol{\Psi}} = \sum_{i=1}^{m} i\widehat{\boldsymbol{\pi}}_i$: only shown if there is more than one lag.
(6) *Eigenvalues of long-run matrix*: eigenvalues of $\widehat{\boldsymbol{\pi}}(1) - \mathbf{I}_n$;
(7) *I(2) matrix Gamma*: the long-run matrix of the system in equilibrium correction form, see (12.6);
(8) *Eigenvalues of companion matrix*, $\widehat{\mathbf{D}}$, given in (15.31).

Dynamic analysis is not available for a system with identities, but are available again after estimating the simultaneous equations model.

15.7.1 $\mathsf{I}(1)$ cointegration analysis

When the system is closed in the endogenous variables, express $\mathbf{P}_0$ in (15.2) as $\boldsymbol{\alpha}\boldsymbol{\beta}'$, where $\boldsymbol{\alpha}$ and $\boldsymbol{\beta}$ are $(n \times p)$ matrices of rank p. Although $\mathbf{v}_t \sim \mathsf{IN}_n[\mathbf{0}, \boldsymbol{\Omega}]$, and so is stationary, the n variables in $\mathbf{y}_t$ need not all be stationary. The rank p of $\mathbf{P}_0$ determines how many linear combinations of $\mathbf{y}_t$ are stationary. If $p = n$, all variables in $\mathbf{y}_t$ are stationary, whereas $p = 0$ implies that $\Delta\mathbf{y}_t$ is stationary. For $0 < p < n$, there are p cointegrated (stationary) linear combinations of $\mathbf{y}_t$. The rank of $\mathbf{P}_0$ is estimated using the maximum likelihood method proposed by Johansen (1988), fully described in Chapter 12 and summarized here.

First, partial out from $\Delta\mathbf{y}_t$ and $\mathbf{y}_{t-1}$ in (15.2) the effects of the lagged differences $(\Delta\mathbf{y}_{t-1} \ldots \Delta\mathbf{y}_{t-m+1})$ and any variables classified as unrestricted (usually the Constant or Trend, but any other variable is allowed as discussed below). This yields the residuals $\mathbf{R}_{0t}$ and $\mathbf{R}_{1t}$ respectively. Next compute the second moments of all these residuals, denoted $\mathbf{S}_{00}$, $\mathbf{S}_{01}$ and $\mathbf{S}_{11}$ where:

$$\mathbf{S}_{ij} = \frac{1}{T}\sum_{t=1}^{T}\mathbf{R}_{it}\mathbf{R}_{jt}' \text{ for } i,\ j = 0, 1. \tag{15.37}$$

Now solve $|\lambda\mathbf{S}_{11} - \mathbf{S}_{10}\mathbf{S}_{00}^{-1}\mathbf{S}_{01}| = 0$ for the p largest eigenvalues $1 > \widehat{\lambda}_1 > \ldots > \widehat{\lambda}_p \ldots > \widehat{\lambda}_n > 0$ and the corresponding eigenvectors:

$$\widehat{\boldsymbol{\beta}} = \left(\widehat{\boldsymbol{\beta}}_1, \ldots, \widehat{\boldsymbol{\beta}}_p\right) \text{ normalized by } \widehat{\boldsymbol{\beta}}'\mathbf{S}_{11}\widehat{\boldsymbol{\beta}} = \mathbf{I}_p. \tag{15.38}$$

Then, tests of the hypothesis of p cointegrating vectors can be based on the *trace statistic*:

$$\eta_p = -T \sum_{i=p+1}^{n} \log\left(1-\widehat{\lambda}_i\right). \tag{15.39}$$

The cointegrating combinations $\boldsymbol{\beta}'\mathbf{y}_{t-1}$ are the I(0) linear combinations of the I(1) variables which can be used as equilibrium correction mechanisms (ECMs).

Any non-endogenous variables $\mathbf{z}_t$ can enter in two ways:

(1) *Unrestricted*: they are partialled out prior to the ML procedure: denote these q_u variables by $\mathbf{z}_t^u$.

(2) *Restricted*: the q_r variables $\mathbf{z}_t^r$ are forced to enter the cointegrating space, which can then be written as $\boldsymbol{\beta}'(\mathbf{y}_{t-1} : \mathbf{z}_{t-1}^r)$, with $\boldsymbol{\beta}'$ now a $(p \times (n+q_r))$ matrix.

If lagged values $\mathbf{z}_t, \ldots, \mathbf{z}_{t-m}$ enter, reparametrize as $\Delta\mathbf{z}_t^u, \ldots, \Delta\mathbf{z}_{t-m+1}^u, \mathbf{z}_{t-1}^r$.

Output of the $\mathsf{I}(1)$ cointegration analysis is:

(1) *Eigenvalues* $\widehat{\lambda}_i$ and the log-likelihood for each rank:

$$\ell_c^* = K_c - \frac{T}{2}\log|\mathbf{S}_{00}| - \frac{T}{2}\sum_{i=1}^{p}\log\left(1-\widehat{\lambda}_i\right), \quad p = 0, \ldots, n. \tag{15.40}$$

(2) Sequence of *Trace test statistics*
The test statistics η_p for $\mathsf{H}(\text{rank} \le p)$ are listed with p-values based on Doornik (1998); $*$ and $**$ mark significance at 95% and 99%. Testing commences at $\mathsf{H}(\text{rank} = 0)$, and stops at the first insignificant statistics.
The asymptotic p-values are available for the following cases:

Hypothesis	Constant	Trend
$\mathsf{H}_{ql}(p)$	unrestricted	unrestricted
$\mathsf{H}_{l}(p)$	unrestricted	restricted
$\mathsf{H}_{lc}(p)$	unrestricted	none
$\mathsf{H}_{c}(p)$	restricted	none
$\mathsf{H}_{z}(p)$	none	none

Strictly speaking, new critical values should be computed for all other cases.

(3) $\widehat{\boldsymbol{\beta}}$ *eigenvectors*, standardized on the diagonal.

(4) $\widehat{\boldsymbol{\alpha}}$ *coefficients*, corresponding to the standardized $\widehat{\boldsymbol{\beta}}$.

(5) *Long-run matrix* $\widehat{\mathbf{P}}_0 = \widehat{\boldsymbol{\alpha}}\widehat{\boldsymbol{\beta}}'$, rank n.

15.7.2 $\mathsf{I}(2)$ Cointegration analysis

In the $\mathsf{I}(2)$ analysis, which requires at least two lags of the endogenous variables, there is potentially an additional reduced rank restriction on the long-run matrix $\boldsymbol{\Gamma}$ of the model in first differences (equilibrium correction form):

$$\boldsymbol{\alpha}_\perp'\boldsymbol{\Gamma}\boldsymbol{\beta}_\perp = \boldsymbol{\xi}'\boldsymbol{\eta},$$

where $\boldsymbol{\xi}$ and $\boldsymbol{\eta}$ are $(n-p) \times s$ matrices, see §12.5. In the analysis we have the parameter counts

s	the number of $\mathsf{I}(1)$ relations,
$n-p-s$	the number of $\mathsf{I}(2)$ relations,
p	the rank of $\mathbf{P}_0$.

The test statistics are

$$\begin{aligned} \mathsf{Q}_p &: \quad \mathsf{H}\left(\text{rank}(\mathbf{P}_0) \leq p | \text{rank}(\mathbf{P}_0) \leq n\right), \\ \mathsf{S}_{p,s} &: \quad \mathsf{H}\left(\text{rank}(\mathbf{P}_0) <= p \text{ and } n-p-s \ \mathsf{I}(2) \text{ components } | \text{rank}(\mathbf{P}_0) \leq n\right). \end{aligned}$$

For example, when $n = 4$ PcGive will print a table consisting of eigenvalues λ_{p+1}, $\lambda_{p+1,s+1}$, test statistics Q_p and $\mathsf{S}_{p,s}$, and p-values for $p = 0, \ldots, 3$ and $n-p-s = 1, \ldots, 4$ as follows:

$p =$	0	1	2	3
$n-p-s=0$	$\hat{\lambda}_1$	$\hat{\lambda}_2$	$\hat{\lambda}_3$	$\hat{\lambda}_4$
Q_p	Q_0	Q_1	Q_2	Q_3
[pval]	p	p	p	p
$n-p-s=$	4	3	2	1
$p=0$	$\hat{\mu}_{1,1}$	$\hat{\mu}_{1,2}$	$\hat{\mu}_{1,3}$	$\hat{\mu}_{1,4}$
$\mathsf{S}_{p,s}$	$\mathsf{S}_{0,0}$	$\mathsf{S}_{0,1}$	$\mathsf{S}_{0,2}$	$\mathsf{S}_{0,3}$
[pval]	p	p	p	p
$p=1$	–	$\hat{\mu}_{2,2}$	$\hat{\mu}_{2,3}$	$\hat{\mu}_{2,4}$
$\mathsf{S}_{p,s}$	–	$\mathsf{S}_{1,1}$	$\mathsf{S}_{1,2}$	$\mathsf{S}_{1,3}$
[pval]	–	p	p	p
$p=2$	–	–	$\hat{\mu}_{3,3}$	$\hat{\mu}_{3,4}$
$\mathsf{S}_{p,s}$	–	–	$\mathsf{S}_{2,2}$	$\mathsf{S}_{2,3}$
[pval]	–	–	p	p
$p=3$	–	–	–	$\hat{\mu}_{3,4}$
$\mathsf{S}_{p,s}$	–	–	–	$\mathsf{S}_{3,3}$
[pval]	–	–	–	p

Hypothesis testing normally proceeds down the columns, from top left to bottom right, stopping at the first insignificant test statistic.

15.8 System testing

15.8.1 Introduction

Many test statistics in PcGive have either a χ^2 distribution or an F distribution. F-tests are usually reported as:

```
F(num,denom)  =  Value  [Probability]  /*/**
```

for example:

```
F(1, 155)     =  5.0088 [0.0266] *
```

where the test statistic has an F-distribution with one degree of freedom in the numerator and 155 in the denominator. The observed value is 5.0088, and the probability of getting a value of 5.0088 or larger under this distribution is 0.0266. This is less than 5% but more than 1%, hence the star. Significant outcomes at a 1% level are shown by two stars.

χ^2 tests are also reported with probabilities, as for example:

```
Normality Chi^2(2)= 2.1867 [0.3351]
```

The 5% χ^2 critical values with two degrees of freedom is 5.99, so here normality is not rejected (alternatively, Prob($\chi^2 \geq 2.1867$) = 0.3351, which is more than 5%).

The probability values for the F-test are calculated using an algorithm based on Majunder and Bhattacharjee (1973a) and Cran, Martin and Thomas (1977).[1] Those for the χ^2 are based on Shea (1988). The significance points of the F-distribution derive from Majunder and Bhattacharjee (1973b).

Some tests take the form of a likelihood ratio (LR) test. If ℓ is the unrestricted, and ℓ_0 the restricted, log-likelihood, then under the null hypothesis that the restrictions are valid, $-2(\ell_0 - \ell)$ has a $\chi^2(s)$ distribution, with s the number of restrictions imposed (so model ℓ_0 is nested in ℓ).

Many diagnostic tests are done through an auxiliary regression. In the case of single-equation tests, they take the form of $T\mathsf{R}^2$ for the auxiliary regression, so that they are asymptotically distributed as $\chi^2\,(s)$ under their nulls, and hence have the usual additive property for independent $\chi^2 s$. In addition, following Harvey (1990) and Kiviet (1986), F-approximations of the form:

$$\frac{\mathsf{R}^2}{1-\mathsf{R}^2}\cdot\frac{T-k-s}{s} \sim \mathsf{F}\,(s, T-k-s) \tag{15.41}$$

are calculated because they may be better behaved in small samples.

Whenever the vector tests are implemented through an auxiliary multivariate regression, PcGive uses vector analogues of the χ^2 and F statistics. The first is an LM test in the auxiliary system, defined as $Tn\mathsf{R}^2_m$, the second uses the F approximation based on R^2_r, see §11.9.2 and §11.8. The vector tests reduce to the single-equation tests in a one-equation system. All tests are fully described in Chapter 11; we give a summary below.

[1] As recommended in Cran, Martin and Thomas (1977), the approach in Pike and Hill (1966) is used for the logarithm of the gamma function.

15.8.2 Single equation diagnostics

Diagnostic testing in PcGive is performed at two levels: individual equations and the system as a whole. Individual equation diagnostics take the residuals from the system, and treat them as from a single equation, ignoring that they form part of a system. Usually this means that they are only valid if the remaining equations are problem-free.

(1) *Portmanteau statistic*
This is a degrees-of-freedom corrected version of the Box and Pierce (1970) statistic. It is only a valid test in a single equation with strongly exogenous variables. If s is the chosen lag length and m the lag length of the dependent variable, values $\geq 2(s-m)$ could indicate residual autocorrelation. Conversely, small values of this statistic should be treated with caution as residual autocorrelations are biased towards zero when lagged dependent variables are included in econometric equations. An appropriate test for residual autocorrelation is provided by the LM test for autocorrelated residuals. The autocorrelation coefficients r_j, see (15.21), are also reported.

(2) *LM test for autocorrelated residuals*
This test is performed through the auxiliary regression of the residuals on the original variables and lagged residuals (missing lagged residuals at the start of the sample are replaced by zero, so no observations are lost). Unrestricted variables are included in the auxiliary regression. The null hypothesis is no autocorrelation, which would be rejected if the test statistic is too high. This LM test is valid for systems with lagged dependent variables and diagonal residual autocorrelation, whereas neither the Durbin–Watson nor the residual correlogram provide a valid test in that case. The χ^2 and F-statistic are shown, as are the error autocorrelation coefficients, which are the coefficients of the lagged residuals in the auxiliary regression.

(3) *LM test for autocorrelated squared residuals*
This is the ARCH test (AutoRegressive Conditional Heteroscedasticity: see Engle, 1982) which in the present form tests the joint significance of lagged squared residuals in the regression of squared residuals on a constant and lagged squared residuals. The χ^2 and F-statistic are shown, in addition to the ARCH coefficients, which are the coefficients of the lagged squared residuals in the auxiliary regression.

(4) *Test for normality*
This is the test proposed by Doornik and Hansen (1994), and amounts to testing whether the skewness and kurtosis of the residuals correspond to those of a normal distribution. Before reporting the actual test, PcGive reports the following statistics of the residuals: mean (0 for the residuals), standard deviation, skewness (0 in a normal distribution), excess kurtosis (0 in a normal distribution), minimum and maximum.

(5) *Test for heteroscedasticity*
This test is based on White (1980), and involves an auxiliary regression of the squared residuals on the original regressors and all their squares. The null is unconditional homoscedasticity, and the alternative is that the variance of the error process depends on the regressors and their squares. The output comprises $T\mathsf{R}^2$, the F-test equivalent, and the coefficients of the auxiliary regression plus their individual t-statistics to help highlight problem variables. Unrestricted variables are excluded from the auxiliary regression, but a constant is always included. Variables that are redundant when squared or collinear are automatically removed.

15.8.3 Vector tests

The present incarnation of PcGive has various formal system mis-specification tests for within-sample congruency.

(1) *Vector portmanteau statistic*
This is the multivariate equivalent of the single-equation portmanteau statistic (again using a small-sample correction), and only a valid asymptotic test in a VAR.
(2) *Vector error autocorrelation test*
Lagged residuals (with missing observations for lagged residuals set to zero) are partialled out from the original regressors, and the whole system is re-estimated, providing a Lagrange-multiplier test based on comparing the likelihoods for both systems.
(3) *Vector normality test*
This is the multivariate equivalent of the aforementioned single equation normality test, see §11.9.2. It checks whether the residuals at hand are normally distributed as:

$$\mathbf{v}_t \sim \mathsf{IN}_n\left[\mathbf{0}, \boldsymbol{\Omega}\right] \tag{15.42}$$

by checking their skewness and kurtosis. A $\chi^2(2n)$ test for the null hypothesis of normality is reported, in addition to the transformed skewness and kurtosis of the rotated components.
(4) *Vector heteroscedasticity test (using squares)*
This test amounts to a multivariate regression of all error variances and covariances on the original regressors and their squares. The test is $\chi^2(sn(n+1)/2)$, where s is the number of non-redundant added regressors (collinear regressors are automatically removed). The null hypothesis is no heteroscedasticity, which would be rejected if the test statistic is too high. Note that regressors that were classified as unrestricted are excluded.
(5) *Vector heteroscedasticity test (using squares and cross-products)*

This test is similar to the heteroscedasticity test, but now cross-products of regressors are added as well. Again, the null hypothesis is no heteroscedasticity (the name functional form was used in version 8 of PcGive).

15.8.4 Testing for general restrictions

Writing $\widehat{\boldsymbol{\theta}} = \mathrm{vec}\widehat{\boldsymbol{\Pi}}'$, with corresponding variance-covariance matrix $\mathsf{V}[\widehat{\boldsymbol{\theta}}]$, we can test for (non-) linear restrictions of the form:

$$\mathbf{f}(\boldsymbol{\theta}) = \mathbf{0}. \tag{15.43}$$

The null hypothesis H_0: $\mathbf{f}(\boldsymbol{\theta}) = \mathbf{0}$ will be tested against H_1: $\mathbf{f}(\boldsymbol{\theta}) \neq \mathbf{0}$ through a Wald test:

$$\mathsf{w} = \mathbf{f}\left(\widehat{\boldsymbol{\theta}}\right)' \left(\widehat{\mathbf{J}}\widetilde{\mathsf{V}\left[\widehat{\boldsymbol{\theta}}\right]}\widehat{\mathbf{J}}'\right)^{-1} \mathbf{f}\left(\widehat{\boldsymbol{\theta}}\right) \tag{15.44}$$

where $\mathbf{J}$ is the Jacobian matrix of the transformation: $\mathbf{J} = \partial\mathbf{f}(\boldsymbol{\theta})/\partial\boldsymbol{\theta}'$. PcGive computes $\widehat{\mathbf{J}}$ by numerical differentiation. The statistic w has a $\chi^2(s)$ distribution, where s is the number of restrictions (that is, equations in $\mathbf{f}(\cdot)$). The null hypothesis is rejected if we observe a significant test statistic.

Output consists of:

(1) *Wald test for general restrictions*, this is the statistic w with its p-value;
(2) **Restricted variance*, the matrix $\widehat{\mathbf{J}}\widetilde{\mathsf{V}[\widehat{\boldsymbol{\theta}}]}\widehat{\mathbf{J}}'$.

15.9 Progress

PcGive can be used in two ways: for general-to-specific modelling, and for unordered searches.

In the general-to-specific approach:

(1) Begin with the dynamic system formulation.
(2) Check its data coherence and cointegration.
(3) Map the system to I(0) after cointegration analysis.
(4) Transform to a set of variables with low intercorrelations, but interpretable parameters.
(5) Check the validity of the system by thorough testing.
(6) Move to the dynamic model formulation.
(7) Delete unwanted regressors to obtain a parsimonious model.
(8) Check the validity of the model by thorough testing, particularly parsimonious encompassing.

Nothing commends unordered searches:

(1) No control is offered over the significance level of testing.
(2) A 'later' reject outcome invalidates all earlier ones.
(3) Until a model adequately characterizes the data, standard tests are invalid.
(4) If the system displays symptoms of mis-specification, there is little point in imposing further restrictions on it.

PcGive does not enforce a general-to-simple modelling strategy, but it will automatically monitor the progress of the sequential reduction from the general to the specific, and will provide the associated likelihood-ratio tests.

More precisely, the program will record a sequence of systems, and for the most recent system the sequence of models (which could be empty). The program gives a list of the selected systems and models, reporting the estimation method, sample size (T), number of coefficients (k), the log-likelihood ($K_c - \frac{2}{T}\log|\widehat{\boldsymbol{\Omega}}|$). Three *information criteria* are also reported: the Schwarz criterion, the Hannan–Quinn criterion and the Akaike criterion, see §220.

Following this, PcGive will report the F-tests (based on Rao's F-approximation) indicating the progress in system modelling, as well as likelihood-ratio tests (χ^2) of the progress in modelling that system (tests of over-identifying restrictions).

Chapter 16

Cointegrated VAR

Following on from §15.7.1, it is possible to estimate a cointegrated VAR which has a reduced rank long-run matrix $\mathbf{P}_0 = \boldsymbol{\alpha}\boldsymbol{\beta}'$, or, possibly, additional restrictions on $\boldsymbol{\alpha}$ or $\boldsymbol{\beta}$.

Following estimation of a cointegrated VAR, most evaluation facilities of the unrestricted system are available, *but with the* π_i *in* (15.1) *replaced with the* $\hat{\pi}_i$ *from the restricted VAR*. Note that this is different from version 9 of PcFiml, where evaluation was still based on the unrestricted system.

All $\widehat{\boldsymbol{\beta}}$ and $\widehat{\boldsymbol{\alpha}}$ below relate to the restricted estimates, according to the selected rank p, and any additional restrictions imposed in the cointegrated VAR estimation (note that it is possible to impose no restrictions at all).

16.0.1 Cointegration restrictions

Within a cointegration VAR analysis, restrictions on $\boldsymbol{\alpha}$ and $\boldsymbol{\beta}$ can be imposed:

(1) general (non-linear) restrictions on $\boldsymbol{\alpha}$ and $\boldsymbol{\beta}'$;
(2) restricted $\boldsymbol{\alpha}$: $\boldsymbol{\alpha}_r = \mathbf{A}\boldsymbol{\theta}$;
(3) restricted $\boldsymbol{\beta}$: $\boldsymbol{\beta}_r = \mathbf{H}\boldsymbol{\phi}$;
(4) known $\boldsymbol{\beta}$: $\boldsymbol{\beta}_r = [\mathbf{H} : \boldsymbol{\phi}]$;
(5) (1) and (2) jointly;
(6) (1) and (3) jointly.

PcGive requires you to choose the rank p. For (1)–(5), the restrictions are expressed through the **A** and/or **H** matrix. The general restrictions of (6) are expressed directly in terms of the elements of $\boldsymbol{\alpha}$ and $\boldsymbol{\beta}'$. Examples of these tests are given in §12.8.

16.1 Cointegrated VAR output

Output of the cointegration estimation is:

(1) $\widehat{\boldsymbol{\beta}}$;
(2) *Standard errors of beta* but only if the restricted $\widehat{\boldsymbol{\beta}}$ is identified;

(3) $\widehat{\alpha}$;
(4) *Standard errors of alpha*;
(5) *Long-run matrix* $\widehat{\mathbf{P}}_0 = \widehat{\alpha}\widehat{\beta}'$, rank p;
(6) *Standard errors of* $\widehat{\mathbf{P}}_0$;
(7) *Reduced form beta*
Partition $\widehat{\beta}'$ as:

$$\begin{pmatrix} \widehat{\beta}'_{11} & \widehat{\beta}'_{12} \\ \widehat{\beta}'_{21} & \widehat{\beta}'_{22} \end{pmatrix}$$

where $\widehat{\beta}'_{11}$ is the top left $(p \times p)$ block of $\widehat{\beta}'$, then when $\widehat{\beta}'_{11}$ is non-singular, the reduced form matrix is:

$$-\left(\widehat{\beta}'_{11}\right)^{-1}\widehat{\beta}'_{12}.$$

(8) Moving-average impact matrix: see §5.6.

This is followed by:

(1) the log-likelihood (15.13), $-T/2 \log|\widehat{\Omega}|$;
(2) T, the number of observations used in the estimation, and the number of parameters in all equations;
(3) rank of long-run matrix p;
(4) number of long-run restrictions in excess of the reduced rank restriction;
(5) a message whether β is identified or not;
(6) a ξ^2 test for over-identifying restrictions if any have been imposed.

16.2 Graphic analysis

Some graphs additional to those listed in §15.5 are available for a cointegrated VAR.

For generality, assume that the variables $\mathbf{z}_r$ were restricted to lie in the cointegrating space. Let α_0, β'_0 denote the original *standardized* loadings and eigenvectors; α_r, β'_r are obtained after imposing further restrictions on the cointegrating space. In the unrestricted graphs, the analysis proceeds as if no rank has been chosen yet, corresponding to n eigenvectors. The restricted analysis requires selection of p, the rank of the cointegrating space, thus resulting in fewer graphs.

Write $(\mathbf{y}; \mathbf{z})$ for $(\mathbf{y}'; \mathbf{z}')$, and let $(\mathbf{y}_t; \mathbf{z}_r)$ denote the original levels of the endogenous variables and the variables restricted to lie in the cointegrating space; $\mathbf{r}_{1t} = (\check{\mathbf{y}}_{t-1}; \check{\mathbf{z}}_r)$ are the residuals from regressing $(\mathbf{y}_{t-1}; \mathbf{z}_r)$ on the short-run dynamics $(\{\Delta\mathbf{y}_{t-i}\})$ and unrestricted variables $(\mathbf{z}_u)$. For all graphs there are two variants:

(1) *Use (Y:Z)*
This uses $(\mathbf{y}_t; \mathbf{z}_r)$.
(2) *Use (Y_1:Z) with lagged DY and U removed*
This uses $\mathbf{r}_{1t}$.

The available graphs are:

(1) *Cointegration relations*
$\widehat{\boldsymbol{\beta}}_0'(\mathbf{y}_t;\mathbf{z}_r)$, or $\widehat{\boldsymbol{\beta}}_0'\mathbf{r}_{1t}$. Write the standardized i^{th} eigenvector as $(\beta_1 \cdots \beta_n\ \beta_{n+1} \cdots \beta_{n+q_r})'$, standardized so that $\beta_i = 1$. The ith cointegration relation graph is: $\sum_j \beta_j y_{jt} + \sum_k \beta_k z_{kt}$ and using concentrated components: $\sum_j \beta_j \check{y}_{jt-1} + \sum_k \beta_k \check{z}_{kt}$.

(2) *Actual and fitted*
The graphs of the cointegrating relations are split into two components: the actuals $\mathbf{y}_t$ and the fitted values $\mathbf{y}_t - \widehat{\boldsymbol{\beta}}_0'(\mathbf{y}_t;\mathbf{z}_r)$. All lines are graphed in deviation from mean. Alternatively: the $\check{\mathbf{y}}_{t-1}$ and the fitted values $\check{\mathbf{y}}_{t-1} - \widehat{\boldsymbol{\beta}}_0'\mathbf{r}_{1t}$, in deviation from mean. Considering the ith graph of actual and fitted, using the above notation for the standardized i^{th} eigenvector: y_{it} and $y_{it} - \sum_j \beta_j y_{jt} - \sum_k \beta_k z_{kt} = -\sum_{j\neq i} \beta_j y_{jt} - \sum_k \beta_k z_{kt}$ whereas using concentrated components: y_{it} and $-\sum_{j\neq i} \beta_j \check{y}_{jt-1} - \sum_k \beta_k \check{z}_{kt}$.

(3) *Components of relation*
Graphs all the components of $\widehat{\boldsymbol{\beta}}_0'(\mathbf{y}_t;\mathbf{z}_r)$ or $\widehat{\boldsymbol{\beta}}_0'\mathbf{r}_{1t}$, in deviations from their means. For the ith graph: $y_{it}, \beta_j y_{jt}\ (j \neq i), \beta_k z_{kt}$ all in deviation from their means. Using concentrated components: $\check{y}_{it}, \beta_j \check{y}_{jt-1}\ (j \neq i), \beta_k \check{z}_{kt}$ also in deviation from means.

16.3 Recursive graphics

Recursive graphics is available when the cointegrated VAR is estimated recursively. Unrestricted variables and short-run dynamics can be fixed at their full-sample coefficients, or partialled out at each sample size.

The types of graphs are:

(1) *Eigenvalues* $\widehat{\lambda}_{it}$. These are only available if no additional restrictions have been imposed.

(2) *Log-likelihood*$/T$, see (15.22).
Only available if additional restrictions was used (but this can be used without specifying any code, i.e. without any restrictions).

(3) *Test for restrictions*
The χ^2 test for the restrictions; its critical value is also shown. Only available if long-run restrictions were imposed. The p-value can be set.

(4) Beta coefficients
Recursive $\boldsymbol{\beta}$s. Only available if $\boldsymbol{\beta}$ is identified.

Chapter 17

Simultaneous Equations Model

Once a statistical system has been adequately modelled and its congruency satisfactorily evaluated, an economically meaningful structural interpretation can be sought. The relevant class of model has the form:

$$\mathbf{B}\mathbf{y}_t + \mathbf{C}\mathbf{w}_t = \mathbf{u}_t, \;\; \mathbf{u}_t \sim \mathsf{IN}_n\left[\mathbf{0}, \mathbf{\Sigma}\right], \; t = 1, \ldots, T. \tag{17.1}$$

The diagonal of $\mathbf{B}$ is normalized at unity. More concisely:

$$\mathbf{B}\mathbf{Y}' + \mathbf{C}\mathbf{W}' = \mathbf{A}\mathbf{X}' = \mathbf{U}', \tag{17.2}$$

with $\mathbf{A} = (\mathbf{B} : \mathbf{C})$ and $\mathbf{X} = (\mathbf{Y} : \mathbf{W})$. PcGive accepts only linear, within-equation restrictions on the elements of $\mathbf{A}$ for the initial specification of the identified model, but allows for further non-linear restrictions on the parameters (possibly across equations). The order condition for identification is enforced, and as discussed in §13.2, the rank condition is required to be satisfied for arbitrary (random) non-zero values of the parameters.

A subset of the equations can be identities, but otherwise $\mathbf{\Sigma}$ is assumed to be positive definite and unrestricted. When identities are present, the model to be estimated is written as:

$$\mathbf{A}\mathbf{X}' = \begin{pmatrix} \mathbf{A}_1 \\ \mathbf{A}_2 \end{pmatrix} \mathbf{X}' = \begin{pmatrix} \mathbf{U}' \\ \mathbf{0} \end{pmatrix} \tag{17.3}$$

where $\mathbf{A}_1\mathbf{X}' = \mathbf{U}'$ is the subset of n_1 stochastic equations and $\mathbf{A}_2\mathbf{X}' = \mathbf{0}$ is the subset of n_2 identities with $n_1 + n_2 = n$. PcGive requires specification of the variables involved in the identities, but will derive the coefficients $\mathbf{A}_2$.

17.1 Model estimation

Let $\boldsymbol{\phi}$ denote the vector of unrestricted elements of vec($\mathbf{A}_1'$): $\boldsymbol{\phi} = \mathbf{A}_1^{v_u}$. Then $\ell(\boldsymbol{\phi})$ is to be minimized as an unrestricted function of the elements of $\boldsymbol{\phi}$. On convergence, we have the maximum likelihood estimator (MLE) of $\boldsymbol{\phi}$:

$$\widehat{\boldsymbol{\phi}} = \underset{\boldsymbol{\phi} \in \boldsymbol{\Phi}}{\operatorname{argmax}} \, \ell(\boldsymbol{\phi}) \tag{17.4}$$

and so have the MLE of $\mathbf{A}_1$; as all other elements of $\mathbf{A}_2$ are known, we have the MLE of $\mathbf{A}$. If convergence does not occur, reset the parameter values, and use a looser (larger) convergence criterion to obtain output.

The estimated variance of $\mathbf{u}_t$ is:

$$\widetilde{\mathbf{\Sigma}} = \frac{\widehat{\mathbf{A}}_1\mathbf{X}'\mathbf{X}\widehat{\mathbf{A}}_1'}{T-c}, \tag{17.5}$$

which is $(n_1 \times n_1)$. There is a degrees-of-freedom correction c, which equals the average number of parameters per equation (rounded towards 0); this would be k for the system.

From $\mathbf{A}$, we can derive the MLE of the restricted reduced form:

$$\widehat{\mathbf{\Pi}} = -\widehat{\mathbf{B}}^{-1}\widehat{\mathbf{C}} \tag{17.6}$$

and hence the estimated variances of the elements of $\widehat{\phi}$:

$$\widetilde{\mathsf{V}\left[\widehat{\phi}\right]} = \left\{\left(\widetilde{\mathbf{\Sigma}}^{-1} \otimes \widehat{\mathbf{Q}}\mathbf{W}'\mathbf{W}\widehat{\mathbf{Q}}'\right)^u\right\}^{-1} \tag{17.7}$$

where, before inversion, we choose the rows and columns of the right-hand side corresponding to unrestricted elements of $\mathbf{A}_1$ only, and $\mathbf{Q}' = (\mathbf{\Pi}' : \mathbf{I})$.

The covariance matrix of the restricted reduced form residuals is obtained by writing:

$$\mathbf{B}^{-1} = \begin{pmatrix} \mathbf{B}^{11} & \mathbf{B}^{12} \\ \mathbf{B}^{21} & \mathbf{B}^{22} \end{pmatrix}, \tag{17.8}$$

where $\mathbf{B}^{11}$ is $(n_1 \times n_1)$. Then:

$$\mathbf{\Omega} = \begin{pmatrix} \mathbf{B}^{11} \\ \mathbf{B}^{21} \end{pmatrix} \mathbf{\Sigma}\left(\mathbf{B}^{11\prime} : \mathbf{B}^{21\prime}\right), \tag{17.9}$$

with:

$$\widetilde{\mathbf{\Omega}}_{11} = \widehat{\mathbf{B}}^{11}\widetilde{\mathbf{\Sigma}}\widehat{\mathbf{B}}^{11\prime} \tag{17.10}$$

corresponding to the stochastic equations. The estimated variance matrix of the restricted reduced form coefficients is:

$$\widetilde{\mathsf{V}\left[\text{vec}\widehat{\mathbf{\Pi}}'\right]} = \widehat{\mathbf{J}}\widetilde{\mathsf{V}\left[\widehat{\phi}\right]}\widehat{\mathbf{J}}' \text{ where } \mathbf{J} = -\left(\mathbf{B}^{-1} \otimes (\mathbf{\Pi}' : \mathbf{I})\right)^u. \tag{17.11}$$

17.2 Model output

Model estimation follows the successful estimation of the unrestricted reduced form. The sample period and number of forecasts carry over from the system.

The following information is needed to estimate a model:

(1) The *model* formulation.
(2) The *method* of estimation:

Full information maximum likelihood (FIML);
Three stage least squares (3SLS);
Two stage least squares (2SLS);
Single equation OLS (1SLS);
Constrained FIML (CFIML)
is available when selecting constrained simultaneous equations model.

(3) The number of observations to be used to *initialize* the recursive estimation (FIML and CFIML).
(4) For CFIML: the code specifying the parameter constraints.

All model estimation methods in PcGive are derived from the *estimator-generating equation* (EGE), see Chapter 13. We require the reduced form to be a congruent data model, for which the structural specification is a more parsimonious representation.

The model output coincides to a large extent with the system output. In the following we only note some differences:

(1) *Identities*
Gives the coefficients of the n_2 identity equations, together with the R^2 of each equation, which should be 1 (values $\geq .99$ are accepted).
(2) *Structural coefficients and standard errors*, $\widehat{\phi}$ and $\sqrt{(\mathsf{V}[\widetilde{\widehat{\phi}}])_{ii}}$, given for all n_1 equations.
(3) t*-value and* t*-probability*
The t-probabilities are based on a Student t-distribution with $T-c$ degrees of freedom. The correction c is defined below equation (17.5).
(4) *Equation standard error (σ)*
The square root of the structural residual variance for each equation:

$$\sqrt{\widetilde{\mathbf{\Sigma}}_{ii}} \text{ for } i = 1, \ldots, n_1. \tag{17.12}$$

(5) *Likelihood*
The log-likelihood value is (including the constant K_c):

$$\widehat{\ell} = K_c - \frac{T}{2}\log\left|\widetilde{\mathbf{\Sigma}}\right| + T\log\left||\widehat{\mathbf{B}}|\right| = -\frac{Tn}{2}(1+\log 2\pi) - \frac{T}{2}\log\left|\widehat{\mathbf{\Omega}}_{11}\right|. \tag{17.13}$$

Reported are $\widehat{\ell}$, $-T/2\log|\widehat{\mathbf{\Omega}}_{11}|$, $|\widehat{\mathbf{\Omega}}_{11}|$ and the sample size T.
(6) *LR test of over-identifying restrictions*
This tests whether the model is a valid reduction of the system.
(7) **Reduced form estimates*, consisting of:

(a) Reduced form coefficients;

(b) Reduced form coefficient standard errors;
(c) Reduced form equation standard errors.

(8) **Heteroscedastic-consistent standard errors*
HCSE for short; computed for FIML only, but not for unrestricted variables. These provide consistent estimates of the regression coefficients' standard errors even if the residuals are heteroscedastic in an unknown way. Large differences between the HCSE and SE are indicative of the presence of heteroscedasticity, in which case the HCSE provides the more useful measure of the standard errors (see White, 1980). They are computed as: $\mathbf{Q}^{-1}\mathcal{I}\mathbf{Q}^{-1}$, $\mathbf{Q} = \mathsf{V}[\widehat{\phi}]$, $\mathcal{I} = \sum_{t=1}^{T} \mathbf{q}_t \mathbf{q}_t'$, the outer product of the gradients.

17.3 Graphic analysis

Graphic analysis focuses on graphical inspection of individual restricted reduced form equations. Let y_t, $\widehat{y}_t$ denote respectively the actual (that is, observed) values and the fitted values of the selected equation, with RRF residuals $\widehat{v}_t = y_t - \widehat{y}_t$, $t = 1, \ldots, T$. If H observations are used for forecasting, then $\widehat{y}_{T+1}, \ldots, \widehat{y}_{T+H}$ are the 1-step forecasts.

Except for substituting the (restricted) reduced form residuals, graphic analysis follows the unrestricted system, see §16.2.

17.4 Recursive graphics

When recursive FIML or CFIML is selected, the ϕ and Σ matrices are estimated at each t $(k \leq M \leq t \leq T)$ where M is user selected. For each t, the RRF can be derived from this.

The recursive graphics options follow §15.6, with the addition of the tests for over-identifying restrictions.

Let $\widehat{\ell}_t$ be the log-likelihood of the URF, and $\widehat{\ell}_{0,t}$ the log-likelihood of the RRF. The tests for over-identifying restrictions, $2(\widehat{\ell}_t - \widehat{\ell}_{0,t})$, can be graphed with a line graphing the critical value from the $\chi^2(s)$ distribution (s is the number of restrictions) at a chosen significance level.

17.5 Dynamic analysis, forecasting and simulation

These proceed as for the system, but based on the restricted reduced form. Graphs are available for identity equations.

Impulse response analysis maps the dynamics of the endogenous variables through the restricted reduced form. The initial values $\mathbf{i}_{1,j}$ for the jth set of graphs can be chosen as follows:

(1) unity
$\mathbf{i}_{1,j} = -\mathbf{B}^{-1}\mathbf{e}_j$.
(2) standard error
$\mathbf{i}_{1,j} = -\mathbf{B}^{-1}\mathbf{e}_j\widetilde{\sigma}_{jj}$,
where $\widetilde{\sigma}_{jj}$ is the jth diagonal element of $\widetilde{\mathbf{\Sigma}}$.
(3) orthogonalized

$$\mathbf{i}_{1,j} = -\mathbf{B}^{-1}\begin{pmatrix} \mathbf{p}_j \\ 0 \end{pmatrix},$$

where p_j is the jth column of the Choleski decomposition of $\widetilde{\mathbf{\Sigma}}$, and it is padded with zeros for identity equations. As in the system, the outcome depends on the ordering of the variables.
(4) custum
$\mathbf{i}_{1,j} = -\mathbf{B}^{-1}\mathbf{v}_j$,
where $\mathbf{v}_j$ is specified by the user.

17.6 Model testing

The vector error autocorrelation test partials lagged structural residuals out from the original regressors, and re-estimates the model. All other tests take the residuals from the RRF, and operate as for the system.

Note, however, that application of single-equation autocorrelation and heteroscedasticity tests in a model will lead to all reduced-form variables being used in the auxiliary regression. If the model is an invalid reduction of the system, this may cause the tests to be significant. Equally, valid reduction combined with small amounts of system residual autocorrelation could induce significant single-equation model autocorrelation. The usual difficulty of interpreting significant test outcomes is prominent here.

A similar feature operates for the vector heteroscedasticity tests, where all reduced-form variables (but not those classified as unrestricted) are used in the auxiliary regression.

Part V

Appendices

Appendix A1

Algebra and Batch for Multiple Equation Modelling

PcGive is mostly menu-driven for ease of use. To add flexibility, certain functions can be accessed through entering commands. The syntax of these commands is described in this chapter.

Algebra is described in the OxMetrics manuals. Algebra commands are executed in OxMetrics, via the Calculator, the Algebra editor, or as part of a batch run.

A1.1 General restrictions

Restrictions have to be entered when testing for parameter restrictions and for imposing parameter constraints for estimation. The syntax is similar to that of algebra, albeit more simple.

Restrictions code may consist of the following components: (1) *Comment*, (2) *Constants*, (3) *Arithmetic operators*. These are all identical to algebra. In addition there are:

(4) *Parameter references*
Parameters are referenced by an ampersand followed by the parameter number. Counting starts at 0, so, for example, &2 is the third parameter of the model. What this parameter is depends on your model. Make sure that when you enter restrictions through the batch language, you use the right order for the coefficients. In case of system estimation, PcGive will reorder your model so that the endogenous variables come first.
Consider, for example, the following unconstrained model:

$$\text{CONS}_t = \beta_0 \text{CONS\_1}_t + \beta_1 \text{INC}_t + \beta_2 \text{INC\_1}_t + \beta_3 \text{INFLAT}_t + \beta_4 + u_t.$$

Then &0 indicates the coefficient on CONS_1, etc.

Table A1.1 lists the precedence of the operators available in restrictions code, with the highest precedence at the top of the table.

Table A1.1 Restrictions operator precedence.

Symbol	Description	Associativity
&	Parameter reference	
-	Unary minus	Right to left
+	Unary plus	
^	Power	Left to right
*	Multiply	Left to right
/	Divide	
+	Add	Left to right
-	Subtract	

A1.1.1 Restrictions for testing

Restrictions for *testing* are entered in the format: $f(\theta) = 0$;. The following restrictions test the significance of the long-run parameters in the unconstrained model given above:

```
(&1 + &2) / (1 - &0) = 0;
&3 / (1 - &0) = 0;
```

A1.1.2 Restrictions for estimation

PcGive allows estimation of two types of non-linear models: FIML with parameter constraints (CFIML), and restrictions on a cointegrated VAR. Examples were given in the tutorial chapters.

Parameter constraints for estimation are written in the format: $\theta^* = g(\theta)$;. First consider an example which restricts parameter 0 as a function of three other parameters, creating a model which is non-linear in the parameters:

```
&0 = -(&1 - &2) * &3;
&4 = 0;
```

Tests for general restrictions on the α and β matrices from the cointegration analysis can be expressed directly in the elements of α and β'. Consider a system with three variables and cointegrating rank of 2. Then the elements are labelled as follows:

$$\alpha = \begin{pmatrix} \&0 & \&1 \\ \&2 & \&3 \\ \&4 & \&5 \end{pmatrix}, \quad \beta = \begin{pmatrix} \&6 & \&7 & \&8 \\ \&9 & \&10 & \&11 \end{pmatrix}.$$

To test the necessary conditions for weak exogeneity, for example, set:

```
&1 = 0;  &2 = 0; &4 = 0;
```

Starting values may be supplied as follows:

```
&1 = 0;  &2 = 0; &4 = 0;
start = 1 -1 1 -1 2 4 3 5 6;
```

A value is listed for each unrestricted parameter, so &0 starts with the value 1, &3 with -1, etc. here the starting values were picked randomly. Of course, it is only useful to specify starting values if these are better than the default values.

A1.2 PcGive batch language

PcGive allows models to be formulated, estimated and evaluated through batch commands. Such commands are entered in OxMetrics. Certain commands are intercepted by OxMetrics, such as those for loading and saving data, as well as blocks of algebra code. The remaining commands are then passed on to the active module, which is PcGive in this case. This section gives an alphabetical list of the PcGive batch language statements. There are two types of batch commands: function calls (with or without arguments) terminated by a semicolon, and commands, which are followed by statements between curly brackets.

Anything between `/*` and `*/` is considered comment. Note that this comment cannot be nested. Everything following `//` up to the end of the line is also comment.

OxMetrics allows you to save the current model as a batch file, and to rerun saved batch files. If a model has been created interactively, it can be saved as a batch file for further editing or easy recall in a later session. This is also the most convenient way to create a batch file.

If an error occurs during processing, the batch run will be aborted and control returned to OxMetrics. A warning or out of memory message will have to be accepted by the user (press `Enter`), upon which the batch run will resume.

In the following list, function arguments are indicated by *words*, whereas the areas where statement blocks are expected are indicated by .... Examples follow the list of descriptions. For terms in double quotes, the desired term must be substituted and provided together with the quotes. A command summary is given in Table A1.2. For completeness, the Table A1.2 also contains the commands which are handled by OxMetrics. Consult the OxMetrics book for more information on those commands.

`adftest("`*var*`",` *lag*, *deterministic*`=1,` *summary*`=1);`

The *var* argument specifies the variable for the ADF test, *lag* is the lag length to be used. The *det* argument indicates the choice of deterministic variables:

0 no deterministic variables,
1 constant,
2 constant and trend,
3 constant and seasonals,
4 constant, trend and seasonals.

Finally, the summary argument indicates whether a summary table is printed (1) or full output (0).

`arorder(`*ar1*, *ar2*`);`

Table A1.2 Batch language syntax summary.

```
adftest("var", lag, deterministic=1, summary=1);
algebra {...}
appenddata("filename", "group");
appresults("filename");
arorder(ar1, ar2);
break;
chdir("path");
command("command_line");
cointcommon {...}
cointknown {...}
constraints {...}
database(year1, period1, year2, period2, frequency);
dynamics;
estimate("method"=OLS, year1=-1, period1=0, year2=-1, period2=0, forc=0, init=0);
exit;
forecast(nforc, hstep=0, setype=1);
loadalgebra("filename");
loadbatch("filename");
loadcommand("filename");
loaddata("filename");
model {...}
module("name");
nonlinear {...}
option("option", argument);
package("PcGive", "package");
print("text");
println("text");
progress;
rank(rank);
savedata("filename");
saveresults("filename");
setdraw("option", i1=0, i2=0, i3=0, i4=0, i5=0);
store("name", "rename"="");
system {...}
test("test", lag1=0, lag2=0);
testlinres {...}
testgenres {...}
testsummary;
usedata("databasename");
```

Specifies the starting and ending order for RALS estimation. Note that the estimation sample must allow for the specified choice.

`cointcommon {...}`

Sets the constraints for cointegrated VAR – use `rank` first to set the rank p. Two

matrices are specified, first **A** then **H**. **A** is the matrix of restrictions on α, namely $\boldsymbol{\alpha} = \mathbf{A}\boldsymbol{\theta}$. **H** is the matrix of known β, to test $\boldsymbol{\beta} = [\mathbf{H} : \boldsymbol{\phi}]$. The **A** and **H** are specified in the same way as a matrix in a matrix file: first the dimensions are given, then the contents of the matrix. Note that 0 0 indicates a matrix of dimension 0×0, that is, absence of the matrix. This can be used to have either $\boldsymbol{\alpha}$ or $\boldsymbol{\beta}$ unrestricted.
This command must appear before `estimate`.

`cointknown` { ... }
Sets the constraints for cointegrated VAR – use `rank` first to set the rank p. **A** and **H** are matrices of restrictions on $\boldsymbol{\alpha}$ and $\boldsymbol{\beta}$ for cointegration tests: $\boldsymbol{\alpha} = \mathbf{A}\boldsymbol{\theta}$ and/or $\boldsymbol{\beta} = \mathbf{H}\boldsymbol{\phi}$. The matrices are specified as in `cointcommon`.
This command must appear before `estimate`.

`constraints` { ... }
Sets the constraints for cointegrated VAR (use `rank` first to set the rank p) or for constrained simultaneous equations (CFIML) estimation. This command must appear before `estimate`.

`dynamics;`
Does part of the dynamic analysis: the static long-run solution and the lag structure analysis.

`estimate("`*method*`"=OLS,` *year1*`=-1,` *period1*`=0,` *year2*`=-1,` *period2*`=0,` *forc*`=0,` *init*`=0);`
Estimate a system. The presence of default arguments implies that the shortest version is just: `estimate()`, which estimates by OLS using the maximum possible sample, and no forecasts. Similarly, a call to `estimate("OLS", 1950, 1)` corresponds to `estimate("OLS", 1950, 1, -1, 0, 0, 0)`.
The *method* argument is one of:

`OLS-CS`	ordinary least squares (cross-section regression),
`IVE-CS`	instrumental variables estimation (cross-section regression),
`OLS`	ordinary least squares,
`IVE`	instrumental variables estimation,
`RALS`	autoregressive least squares (also see `arorder`),
`NLS`	non-linear least squares (non-linear modelling),
`ML`	maximum likelihood (non-linear modelling),
`COINT`	cointegrated VAR,
`FIML`	full information ML (simultaneous equations modelling),
`3SLS`	three-stage LS (simultaneous equations modelling),
`2SLS`	two-stage LS (simultaneous equations modelling),
`1SLS`	single equation OLS (simultaneous equations modelling),
`CFIML`	constrained FIML (constrained simultaneous equations modelling).

year1(period1) – *year2(period2)* is the estimation sample. Setting year1 to −1 will result in the earliest possible year1(period1), setting year2 to −1 will result in the latest possible year2(period2).
forc is the number of observations to withhold from the estimation sample for forecasting.
init is the number of observations to use for initialization of recursive estimation (not if *method* is RALS); no recursive estimation is performed if *init* = 0.

`forecast(`*nforc*, *hstep*`=0`, *setype*`=1);`

Prints *nforc* dynamic forecasts (when *hstep* is zero) or *hstep* forecasts. The last argument is the standard error type: 0 to not compute; 1 for error variance only (the default); 2 to include parameter uncertainty. For example, `forecast(8)` produces eight dynamic forecasts with error-variance based standard errors; `forecast(8,4)` produces the 4-step forecasts (note that the first three will coincide with 1,2,3-step respectively). Use the `store` command next to store the forecasts if necessary.

`model` { ... }

Specify the model. There must be an equation for each endogenous and identity endogenous variable specified in the system statement. An example of an equation is: `CONS=CONS_1,INC;`. Note that PcGive reorders the equations of the model into the order they had in the system specification. Right-hand-side variables are not reordered.

`module("PcGive");`

Starts the PcGive module. If PcGive is already running, this batch command is not required.

`nonlinear` { ... }

Formulates a single-equation non-linear model.

`option("`*option*`",` *argument*);

The first set relates to maximization:

option	*argument*	*value*
`maxit`	maximum number of iterations	default: 1000,
`print`	print every # iteration	0: do not print,
`compact`	compact or extended output	0 for off, 1 on,
`strong`	strong convergence tolerance	default: 0.005,
`weak`	set weak convergence tolerance	default: 0.0001,

The second set of options adds further output automatically:

option	*argument*	*value*
`equation`	add equation format	0 for off, 1 on,
`infcrit`	report information criteria	0 for off, 1 on.
`instability`	report instability tests	0 for off, 1 on,
`HCSE`	Heteroscedasticity-consistent SEs	0 for off, 1 on,
`r2seasonals`	report R^2 about seasonals	0 for off, 1 on,

The final option is for recursive estimation of cointegrated VARs:

option	*argument*	*value*
`shortrun`	re-estimate shortrun	1: re-estimate, 0: fixed.

`output("`*option*`");`

Prints further output:

option	
`correlation`	print correlation matrix of variables,
`covariance`	print covariance matrix of coefficients,
`equation`	print the model equation format,
`forecasts`	print the static forecasts,
`HCSE`	Heteroscedasticity-consistent standard errors
`infcrit`	report information criteria,
`instability`	report instability tests,
`latex`	print the model in latex format,
`r2seasonals`	report R^2 about seasonals,
`reducedform`	print the reduced form,
`sigpar`	significant digits for parameters (second argument),
`sigse`	significant digits for standard errors (second argument).

`package("PcGive", "`*package*`");`

Use this command to select the correct component (package) from PcGive:

package
`"Cross-section"`
`"Multiple-equation"`
`"Non-linear"`
`"Single-equation"`

The package arguments can be shortened to 5 letters. All models in this book require `package("PcGive", "Multiple-equation")`.

`progress;`

Reports the modelling progress.

`rank(`*rank*`);`

Sets the rank p of the long-run matrix for cointegrated VAR analysis. This command must appear before `constraints` and `estimate`.

`store("`*name*`","`*rename*`="");`

Use this command to store residuals, etc. into the database, the default name is used. Note that if the variable already exists, it is overwritten without warning. The *name* must be one of:

`residuals`	residuals
`fitted`	fitted values
`structres`	structural residuals (model only)
`res1step`	1-step residual (after recursive estimation)
`rss`	RSS (after recursive estimation)
`stdinn`	stand. innovations (after single eqn recursive estimation)
`eqse`	equation standard errors (recursive estimation)
`loglik`	log-likelihood (after recursive estimation)
`coieval`	eigenvalues (after recursive cointegration analysis)

The optional second argument replaces the default name. For example a single equation model, `store("residuals")` stores the residuals under the name `Residual`; `store("residuals", "xyz")` stores them under the name `xyz`. For a multiple equation models, say `INC` and `CONS`, the names are `VINC`, `VCONS` in the firstcase, and `xyz1`, `xyz2` in the second.

`system` { Y=...; Z=...; U=...; A=...; }

Specify the system, consisting of the following components:

- Y endogenous variables;
- A additional instruments (optional; single-equation modelling only);
- I identity endogenous variables (optional; multiple-equation modelling only);
- Z non-modelled variables;
- U unrestricted variables (optional).

The variables listed are separated by commas, their base names (that is, name excluding lag length) must be in the database. If the variable names are not a valid token, the name must be enclosed in double quotes.

The following special variables are recognized: Constant, Trend, Seasonal and CSeasonal.

Note that when IVE/RIVE are used PcGive reorders the model as follows: the endogenous variables first and the additional instruments last. This reordering is relevant when specifying restrictions.

Note that PcGive reorders a multiple-equation system as follows: first the endogenous variables and their lags: endogenous variables, identity endogenous variables, first lag of these (variables in the same order), second lag, etc. then each exogenous variable with its lags. For example, with y, c endogenous, i identity and w, z exogenous:

$$y_t \; c_t \; i_t \; y_{t-1} \; c_{t-1} \; i_{t-1} \; y_{t-2} \; c_{t-2} \; w_t \; w_{t-1} \; z_t \; z_{t-1}$$

This reordering is relevant when specifying restrictions.

`test("`*test*`",` *lag1*`=0,` *lag2*`=0);`

Performs a specific test using the specified lag lengths.

"ar"	test for autocorrelated errors from *lag1* to *lag2*;
"arch"	ARCH test up to order *lag1*;
"comfac"	test for common factor;
"encompassing"	tests the two most recent models for encompassing;
"hetero"	heteroscedasticity test (squares);
"heterox"	heteroscedasticity test (squares and cross products);
"I1"	I(1) cointegration test for VAR estimated in levels;
"I2"	I(2) cointegration test for VAR estimated in levels;
"instability"	instability tests;
"normal"	normality test;
"rescor"	residual correlogram up to lag *lag1*;
"reset"	Reset test using powers up to *lag1*.

`testgenres { ... }`

Used to test for general restrictions: specify the restrictions between { }, conforming to §A1.1.

`testlinres { ... }`

Test for linear restrictions. The content is the matrix dimensions followed by the $(R : r)$ matrix.

`testres { ... }`

Test for exclusion restrictions. The content lists the variables to be tested foe exclusion, separated by a comma (remember that variable names that are not proper tokens must be enclosed in double quotes).

`testsummary;`

Do the test summary.

We finish with an annotated example using most commands.

```
chdir("#home");              // change to OxMetrics directory
loaddata("data.in7");        // Load the tutorial data set.
chdir("#batch");             // change to back to batch file dir.

module("PcGive");            // activate PcGive
package("PcGive", "Multi");// activate the PcGive package
usedata("data.in7");         // use data.in7 for modelling
algebra
{                            // Create SAVINGSL in database.
    SAVINGSL = lag(INC,1) - lag(CONS, 1);
}
system
{
```

```
    Y = CONS, INC, INFLAT; // Three endogenous variables;
    I = SAVINGSL;          // one identity endogenous variable;
    Z = CONS_1, CONS_2,    // the non-endogenous variables; the
        INC_1,INC_2,       // lagged variables need not (better:
        INFLAT_1, INFLAT_2;// should not) exist in the database.
    U = Constant;          // the constant enters unrestricted.
}
estimate("OLS", 1953, 3, 1992, 3, 8);
                     // Estimate the system by OLS over 1953(2)-
                     // 1992(3), withhold 8 forecasts,
rank(2);             // Rank of cointegrating space.
constraints          // Cointegration restrictions, expressed in
{                    // terms of loadings (a 3 x 2 matrix) and
                     // eigenvectors (in rows, a 2 x 3 matrix).
                     // Elements 0-5 are the loadings.
    &6 = -&7;
    &9 = -&10;
}
estimate("COINT", 1953, 3, 1992, 3, 8);

rank(2);             // Rank of cointegrating space.
constraints
{
    &0 = 0;
    &1 = 0;

    &6 = 1;          // Restrictions on ECMs;
    &7 = -1;         // elements 6-8 are coefficients of 1st ECM
    &8 = 6;          // elements 9-11 of second ECM.
}
estimate("COINT", 1953, 3, 1992, 3, 8);

estimate("OLS");
testsummary;         // Do the test summary.
testgenres           // Test for parameter restrictions.
{                    // Restrictions are on the INFLAT equation:
    &12 = 0;         // coefficient of CONS_1
    &13 = 0;         // coefficient of CONS_2
    &14 - &15 = 0;   // coefficient of INC_1 - coeff. of INC_2.
}
model                // Specify the equations in the model,
{                    // including the identity.
    CONS = INC, SAVINGSL, INFLAT_1;
    INC = INC_1, INC_2, CONS;
    INFLAT = INFLAT_1, INFLAT_2;
    SAVINGSL = INC_1, CONS_1;
}
estimate("FIML");    // Estimate the model by FIML using default sample
dynamics;            // Do dynamic analysis.
constraints          // Impose constraints for constrained
{                    // estimation.
    &4 = 0;          // Delete INC_2 from INC equation.
}
```

```
estimate("CFIML");    // Estimate the constrained model by CFIML;
                      // no observations required for
                      // initialization.
progress;             // Report the modelling progress.
```

Appendix A2

Numerical Changes From Previous Versions

Changes between PcFiml 9.3 and PcGive 10

Essentially all results are unchanged, except that CFIML with unrestricted parameters now reports identical standard errors as when the same variables are entered restrictedly. PcFiml 9.3 would also not use the correct three seasonals when the database starts in Q2/Q4 (which does not affect the likelihood).

Changes between PcFiml version 8 and 9

The major change is the adoption of the QR decomposition with partial pivoting to compute OLS and IV estimates. There are also some minor improvements in accuracy, the following tests are the most sensitive to such changes: encompassing, heteroscedasticity and RESET. The heteroscedasticity tests could also differ in the number of variables removed owing to singularity. To summarize:

- QR decomposition in all regressions;
- analytical differentiation of restrictions;
- singular value based cointegration analysis;
- standard errors in (restricted) cointegration analysis take all parameters into account;
- new algorithms for restricted cointegration analysis;
- slightly improved error recovery in BFGS;
- reset every 50 observations in RLS and better handling of singular subsamples;
- recursive FIML now done backward.

References

Anderson, T. W. (1984). *An Introduction to Multivariate Statistical Analysis,* 2nd edition. New York: John Wiley & Sons.

Banerjee, A., Dolado, J. J., Galbraith, J. W. and Hendry, D. F. (1993). *Co-integration, Error Correction and the Econometric Analysis of Non-Stationary Data*. Oxford: Oxford University Press.

Banerjee, A. and Hendry, D. F. (1992). Testing integration and cointegration, *Oxford Bulletin of Economics and Statistics*, **54**. Special issue.

Bårdsen, G. (1989). The estimation of long run coefficients from error correction models, *Oxford Bulletin of Economics and Statistics*, **50**.

Berndt, E. K., Hall, B. H., Hall, R. E. and Hausman, J. A. (1974). Estimation and inference in nonlinear structural models, *Annals of Economic and Social Measurement*, **3**, 653–665.

Boswijk, H. P. (1992). *Cointegration, Identification and Exogeneity*, Vol. 37 of *Tinbergen Institute Research Series*. Amsterdam: Thesis Publishers.

Boswijk, H. P. (1995). Identifiability of cointegrated systems, Discussion paper ti 7-95-078, Tinbergen Institute, University of Amsterdam.

Boswijk, H. P. and Doornik, J. A. (2004). Identifying, estimating and testing restricted cointegrated systems: An overview, *Statistica Neerlandica*, **58**, 440–465.

Bowman, K. O. and Shenton, L. R. (1975). Omnibus test contours for departures from normality based on $\sqrt{b_1}$ and b_2, *Biometrika*, **62**, 243–250.

Box, G. E. P. and Pierce, D. A. (1970). Distribution of residual autocorrelations in autoregressive-integrated moving average time series models, *Journal of the American Statistical Association*, **65**, 1509–1526.

Britton, E., Fisher, P. and Whitley, J. (1998). *Inflation Report* projections: Understanding the fan chart, *Bank of England Quarterly Bulletin*, **38**, 30–37.

Brown, R. L., Durbin, J. and Evans, J. M. (1975). Techniques for testing the constancy of regression relationships over time (with discussion), *Journal of the Royal Statistical Society B*, **37**, 149–192.

Calzolari, G. (1987). Forecast variance in dynamic simulation of simultaneous equations models, *Econometrica*, **55**, 1473–1476.

Campbell, J. Y. and Perron, P. (1991). Pitfalls and opportunities: What macroeconomists should know about unit roots, In Blanchard, O. J. and Fischer, S. (eds.), *NBER Macroeconomics annual 1991*. Cambridge, MA: MIT press.

Chong, Y. Y. and Hendry, D. F. (1986). Econometric evaluation of linear macro-economic models, *Review of Economic Studies*, **53**, 671–690. Reprinted in Granger, C. W. J. (ed.) (1990), *Modelling Economic Series*. Oxford: Clarendon Press.

Chow, G. C. (1960). Tests of equality between sets of coefficients in two linear regressions,

Econometrica, **28**, 591–605.

Clements, M. P. and Hendry, D. F. (1994). Towards a theory of economic forecasting, in Hargreaves (1994), pp. 9–52.

Clements, M. P. and Hendry, D. F. (1998a). *Forecasting Economic Time Series*. Cambridge: Cambridge University Press.

Clements, M. P. and Hendry, D. F. (1998b). *Forecasting Economic Time Series: The Marshall Lectures on Economic Forecasting*. Cambridge: Cambridge University Press.

Clements, M. P. and Hendry, D. F. (1999). *Forecasting Non-stationary Economic Time Series*. Cambridge, Mass.: MIT Press.

Coyle, D. (2001). Making sense of published economic forecasts, In Hendry, D. F. and Ericsson, N. R. (eds.), *Understanding Economic Forecasts*, pp. 54–67. Cambridge, Mass.: MIT Press.

Cramer, J. S. (1986). *Econometric Applications of Maximum Likelihood Methods*. Cambridge: Cambridge University Press.

Cran, G. W., Martin, K. J. and Thomas, G. E. (1977). A remark on algorithms. AS 63: The incomplete beta integral. AS 64: Inverse of the incomplete beta function ratio, *Applied Statistics*, **26**, 111–112.

D'Agostino, R. B. (1970). Transformation to normality of the null distribution of g_1, *Biometrika*, **57**, 679–681.

Davidson, J. E. H., Hendry, D. F., Srba, F. and Yeo, J. S. (1978). Econometric modelling of the aggregate time-series relationship between consumers' expenditure and income in the United Kingdom, *Economic Journal*, **88**, 661–692. Reprinted in Hendry, D. F., *Econometrics: Alchemy or Science?* Oxford: Blackwell Publishers, 1993, and Oxford University Press, 2000.

Dhrymes, P. J. (1984). *Mathematics for Econometrics,* 2nd edition. New York: Springer-Verlag.

Doornik, J. A. (1995a). *Econometric Computing*. Oxford: University of Oxford. Ph.D Thesis.

Doornik, J. A. (1995b). Testing general restrictions on the cointegrating space, www.nuff.ox.ac.uk/users/doornik, Nuffield College.

Doornik, J. A. (1996). Testing vector autocorrelation and heteroscedasticity in dynamic models, www.nuff.ox.ac.uk/users/doornik, Nuffield College.

Doornik, J. A. (1998). Approximations to the asymptotic distribution of cointegration tests, *Journal of Economic Surveys*, **12**, 573–593. Reprinted in M. McAleer and L. Oxley (1999). *Practical Issues in Cointegration Analysis*. Oxford: Blackwell Publishers.

Doornik, J. A. (2006). *Object-Oriented Matrix Programming using Ox* 5th edition. London: Timberlake Consultants Press.

Doornik, J. A. and Hansen, H. (1994). A practical test for univariate and multivariate normality, Discussion paper, Nuffield College.

Doornik, J. A. and Hendry, D. F. (1992). *PCGIVE 7: An Interactive Econometric Modelling System*. Oxford: Institute of Economics and Statistics, University of Oxford.

Doornik, J. A. and Hendry, D. F. (1994). *PcGive 8: An Interactive Econometric Modelling System*. London: International Thomson Publishing, and Belmont, CA: Duxbury Press.

Doornik, J. A. and Hendry, D. F. (2006). *OxMetrics: An Interface to Empirical Modelling* 4th edition. London: Timberlake Consultants Press.

Doornik, J. A., Hendry, D. F. and Nielsen, B. (1998). Inference in cointegrated models: UK M1 revisited, *Journal of Economic Surveys*, **12**, 533–572. Reprinted in M. McAleer and L. Oxley (1999). *Practical Issues in Cointegration Analysis*. Oxford: Blackwell Publishers.

Doornik, J. A. and O'Brien, R. J. (2002). Numerically stable cointegration analysis, *Computational Statistics & Data Analysis*, **41**, 185–193.

Durbin, J. (1988). Maximum likelihood estimation of the parameters of a system of simultaneous regression equations, *Econometric Theory*, **4**, 159–170. Paper presented to the Copenhagen Meeting of the Econometric Society, 1963.

Engle, R. F. (1982). Autoregressive conditional heteroscedasticity, with estimates of the variance of United Kingdom inflation, *Econometrica*, **50**, 987–1007.

Engle, R. F. and Granger, C. W. J. (1987). Cointegration and error correction: Representation, estimation and testing, *Econometrica*, **55**, 251–276.

Engle, R. F. and Hendry, D. F. (1993). Testing super exogeneity and invariance in regression models, *Journal of Econometrics*, **56**, 119–139. Reprinted in Ericsson, N. R. and Irons, J. S. (eds.) *Testing Exogeneity*, Oxford: Oxford University Press, 1994.

Engle, R. F., Hendry, D. F. and Richard, J.-F. (1983). Exogeneity, *Econometrica*, **51**, 277–304. Reprinted in Hendry, D. F., *Econometrics: Alchemy or Science?* Oxford: Blackwell Publishers, 1993, and Oxford University Press, 2000; and in Ericsson, N. R. and Irons, J. S. (eds.) *Testing Exogeneity*, Oxford: Oxford University Press, 1994.

Engle, R. F., Hendry, D. F. and Trumbull, D. (1985). Small sample properties of ARCH estimators and tests, *Canadian Journal of Economics*, **43**, 66–93.

Ericsson, N. R., Hendry, D. F. and Mizon, G. E. (1996). Econometric issues in economic policy analysis, Mimeo, Nuffield College, University of Oxford.

Ericsson, N. R., Hendry, D. F. and Tran, H.-A. (1994). Cointegration, seasonality, encompassing and the demand for money in the United Kingdom, in Hargreaves (1994), pp. 179–224.

Ericsson, N. R. (1992). Cointegration, exogeneity and policy analysis, *Journal of Policy Modeling*, **14**. Special Issue.

Favero, C. and Hendry, D. F. (1992). Testing the Lucas critique: A review, *Econometric Reviews*, **11**, 265–306.

Fletcher, R. (1987). *Practical Methods of Optimization,* 2nd edition. New York: John Wiley & Sons.

Gill, P. E., Murray, W. and Wright, M. H. (1981). *Practical Optimization*. New York: Academic Press.

Godfrey, L. G. (1988). *Misspecification Tests in Econometrics*. Cambridge: Cambridge University Press.

Goldfeld, S. M. and Quandt, R. E. (1972). *Non-linear Methods in Econometrics*. Amsterdam: North-Holland.

Granger, C. W. J. (1969). Investigating causal relations by econometric models and cross-spectral methods, *Econometrica*, **37**, 424–438.

Haavelmo, T. (1943). The statistical implications of a system of simultaneous equations, *Econometrica*, **11**, 1–12.

Haavelmo, T. (1944). The probability approach in econometrics, *Econometrica*, **12**, 1–118. Supplement.

Hansen, H. and Johansen, S. (1992). Recursive estimation in cointegrated VAR-models, Discussion paper, Institute of Mathematical Statistics, University of Copenhagen.

Hargreaves, C. (ed.)(1994). *Non-stationary Time-series Analysis and Cointegration.* Oxford: Oxford University Press.

Harvey, A. C. (1990). *The Econometric Analysis of Time Series,* 2nd edition. Hemel Hempstead: Philip Allan.

Hendry, D. F. (1971). Maximum likelihood estimation of systems of simultaneous regression equations with errors generated by a vector autoregressive process, *International Economic Review*, **12**, 257–272. Correction in **15**, p.260.

Hendry, D. F. (1976). The structure of simultaneous equations estimators, *Journal of Econometrics*, **4**, 51–88. Reprinted in Hendry, D. F., *Econometrics: Alchemy or Science?* Oxford: Blackwell Publishers, 1993, and Oxford University Press, 2000.

Hendry, D. F. (1979). Predictive failure and econometric modelling in macro-economics: The transactions demand for money, In Ormerod, P. (ed.), *Economic Modelling*, pp. 217–242. London: Heinemann. Reprinted in Hendry, D. F., *Econometrics: Alchemy or Science?* Oxford: Blackwell Publishers, 1993, and Oxford University Press, 2000.

Hendry, D. F. (1986). Using PC-GIVE in econometrics teaching, *Oxford Bulletin of Economics and Statistics*, **48**, 87–98.

Hendry, D. F. (1987). Econometric methodology: A personal perspective, In Bewley, T. F. (ed.), *Advances in Econometrics*, Ch. 10. Cambridge: Cambridge University Press.

Hendry, D. F. (1988). The encompassing implications of feedback versus feedforward mechanisms in econometrics, *Oxford Economic Papers*, **40**, 132–149. Reprinted in Ericsson, N. R. and Irons, J. S. (eds.) *Testing Exogeneity*, Oxford: Oxford University Press, 1994.

Hendry, D. F. (1993). *Econometrics: Alchemy or Science?* Oxford: Blackwell Publishers.

Hendry, D. F. (1995). *Dynamic Econometrics.* Oxford: Oxford University Press.

Hendry, D. F. (2001). Modelling UK inflation, 1875–1991, *Journal of Applied Econometrics*, **16**, 255–275.

Hendry, D. F. and Doornik, J. A. (1994). Modelling linear dynamic econometric systems, *Scottish Journal of Political Economy*, **41**, 1–33.

Hendry, D. F. and Doornik, J. A. (2006). *Empirical Econometric Modelling using PcGive: Volume I* 4th edition. London: Timberlake Consultants Press.

Hendry, D. F. and Juselius, K. (2001). Explaining cointegration analysis: Part II, *Energy Journal*, **22**, 75–120.

Hendry, D. F. and Mizon, G. E. (1993). Evaluating dynamic econometric models by encompassing the VAR, In Phillips, P. C. B. (ed.), *Models, Methods and Applications of Econometrics*, pp. 272–300. Oxford: Basil Blackwell.

Hendry, D. F. and Morgan, M. S. (1995). *The Foundations of Econometric Analysis.* Cambridge: Cambridge University Press.

Hendry, D. F. and Neale, A. J. (1991). A Monte Carlo study of the effects of structural breaks on tests for unit roots, In Hackl, P. and Westlund, A. H. (eds.), *Economic Structural Change, Analysis and Forecasting*, pp. 95–119. Berlin: Springer-Verlag.

Hendry, D. F., Neale, A. J. and Srba, F. (1988). Econometric analysis of small linear systems using PC-FIML, *Journal of Econometrics*, **38**, 203–226.

Hendry, D. F., Pagan, A. R. and Sargan, J. D. (1984). Dynamic specification, In Griliches, Z. and Intriligator, M. D. (eds.), *Handbook of Econometrics*, Vol. 2–3, Ch. 18. Amsterdam: North-Holland. Reprinted in Hendry, D. F., *Econometrics: Alchemy or Science?* Oxford:

Blackwell Publishers, 1993, and Oxford University Press, 2000.

Hendry, D. F. and Richard, J.-F. (1982). On the formulation of empirical models in dynamic econometrics, *Journal of Econometrics*, **20**, 3–33. Reprinted in Granger, C. W. J. (ed.) (1990), *Modelling Economic Series*. Oxford: Clarendon Press and in Hendry D. F., *Econometrics: Alchemy or Science?* Oxford: Blackwell Publishers 1993, and Oxford University Press, 2000.

Hendry, D. F. and Richard, J.-F. (1983). The econometric analysis of economic time series (with discussion), *International Statistical Review*, **51**, 111–163. Reprinted in Hendry, D. F., *Econometrics: Alchemy or Science?* Oxford: Blackwell Publishers, 1993, and Oxford University Press, 2000.

Hendry, D. F. and Richard, J.-F. (1989). Recent developments in the theory of encompassing, In Cornet, B. and Tulkens, H. (eds.), *Contributions to Operations Research and Economics. The XXth Anniversary of CORE*, pp. 393–440. Cambridge, MA: MIT Press.

Hendry, D. F. and Srba, F. (1980). AUTOREG: A computer program library for dynamic econometric models with autoregressive errors, *Journal of Econometrics*, **12**, 85–102. Reprinted in Hendry, D. F., *Econometrics: Alchemy or Science?* Oxford: Blackwell Publishers, 1993, and Oxford University Press, 2000.

Hosking, J. R. M. (1980). The multivariate portmanteau statistic, *Journal of the American Statistical Association*, **75**, 602–608.

Hunter, J. (1992). Cointegrating exogeneity, *Economics Letters*, **34**, 33–35.

Johansen, S. (1988). Statistical analysis of cointegration vectors, *Journal of Economic Dynamics and Control*, **12**, 231–254. Reprinted in R.F. Engle and C.W.J. Granger (eds), Long-Run Economic Relationships, Oxford: Oxford University Press, 1991, 131–52.

Johansen, S. (1991). Estimation and hypothesis testing of cointegration vectors in Gaussian vector autoregressive models, *Econometrica*, **59**, 1551–1580.

Johansen, S. (1992a). Cointegration in partial systems and the efficiency of single-equation analysis, *Journal of Econometrics*, **52**, 389–402.

Johansen, S. (1992b). Testing weak exogeneity and the order of cointegration in UK money demand, *Journal of Policy Modeling*, **14**, 313–334.

Johansen, S. (1994). The role of the constant and linear terms in cointegration analysis of nonstationary variables, *Econometric Reviews*, **13**, 205–229.

Johansen, S. (1995a). Identifying restrictions of linear equations with applications to simultaneous equations and cointegration, *Journal of Econometrics*, **69**, 111–132.

Johansen, S. (1995b). *Likelihood-based Inference in Cointegrated Vector Autoregressive Models*. Oxford: Oxford University Press.

Johansen, S. (1995c). A statistical analysis of cointegration for I(2) variables, *Econometric Theory*, **11**, 25–59.

Johansen, S. and Juselius, K. (1990). Maximum likelihood estimation and inference on cointegration – With application to the demand for money, *Oxford Bulletin of Economics and Statistics*, **52**, 169–210.

Johansen, S. and Juselius, K. (1992). Testing structural hypotheses in a multivariate cointegration analysis of the PPP and the UIP for UK, *Journal of Econometrics*, **53**, 211–244.

Johansen, S. and Juselius, K. (1994). Identification of the long-run and the short-run structure. An application to the ISLM model, *Journal of Econometrics*, **63**, 7–36.

Judge, G. G., Griffiths, W. E., Hill, R. C., Lütkepohl, H. and Lee, T.-C. (1985). *The Theory and Practice of Econometrics,* 2nd edition. New York: John Wiley.

Kelejian, H. H. (1982). An extension of a standard test for heteroskedasticity to a systems framework, *Journal of Econometrics*, **20**, 325–333.

Kiefer, N. M. (1989). The ET interview: Arthur S. Goldberger, *Econometric Theory*, **5**, 133–160.

Kiviet, J. F. (1986). On the rigor of some mis-specification tests for modelling dynamic relationships, *Review of Economic Studies*, **53**, 241–261.

Kiviet, J. F. and Phillips, G. D. A. (1992). Exact similar tests for unit roots and cointegration, *Oxford Bulletin of Economics and Statistics*, **54**, 349–367.

Koopmans, T. C. (ed.)(1950). *Statistical Inference in Dynamic Economic Models*. No. 10 in Cowles Commission Monograph. New York: John Wiley & Sons.

Ljung, G. M. and Box, G. E. P. (1978). On a measure of lack of fit in time series models, *Biometrika*, **65**, 297–303.

Longley, G. M. (1967). An appraisal of least-squares for the electronic computer from the point of view of the user, *Journal of the American Statistical Association*, **62**, 819–841.

Lütkepohl, H. (1991). *Introduction to Multiple Time Series Analysis*. New York: Springer-Verlag.

Magnus, J. R. and Neudecker, H. (1988). *Matrix Differential Calculus with Applications in Statistics and Econometrics*. New York: John Wiley & Sons.

Majunder, K. L. and Bhattacharjee, G. P. (1973a). Algorithm AS 63. The incomplete beta integral, *Applied Statistics*, **22**, 409–411.

Majunder, K. L. and Bhattacharjee, G. P. (1973b). Algorithm AS 64. Inverse of the incomplete beta function ratio, *Applied Statistics*, **22**, 411–414.

Makridakis, S., Wheelwright, S. C. and Hyndman, R. C. (1998). *Forecasting: Methods and Applications* 3rd edition. New York: John Wiley and Sons.

Mizon, G. E. (1977). Model selection procedures, In Artis, M. J. and Nobay, A. R. (eds.), *Studies in Modern Economic Analysis*, pp. P97–120. Oxford: Basil Blackwell.

Mizon, G. E. and Richard, J.-F. (1986). The encompassing principle and its application to non-nested hypothesis tests, *Econometrica*, **54**, 657–678.

Molinas, C. (1986). A note on spurious regressions with integrated moving average errors, *Oxford Bulletin of Economics and Statistics*, **48**, 279–282.

Mosconi, R. and Giannini, C. (1992). Non-causality in cointegrated systems: Representation, estimation and testing, *Oxford Bulletin of Economics and Statistics*, **54**, 399–417.

Ooms, M. (1994). *Empirical Vector Autoregressive Modeling*. Berlin: Springer-Verlag.

Osterwald-Lenum, M. (1992). A note with quantiles of the asymptotic distribution of the ML cointegration rank test statistics, *Oxford Bulletin of Economics and Statistics*, **54**, 461–472.

Pagan, A. R. (1987). Three econometric methodologies: A critical appraisal, *Journal of Economic Surveys*, **1**, 3–24. Reprinted in Granger, C. W. J. (ed.) (1990), *Modelling Economic Series*. Oxford: Clarendon Press.

Pagan, A. R. (1989). On the role of simulation in the statistical evaluation of econometric models, *Journal of Econometrics*, **40**, 125–139.

Paruolo, P. (1996). On the determination of integration indices in I(2) systems, *Journal of Econometrics*, **72**, 313–356.

Pesaran, M. H., Smith, R. P. and Yeo, J. S. (1985). Testing for structural stability and predictive failure: A review, *Manchester School*, **3**, 280–295.

Phillips, P. C. B. (1986). Understanding spurious regressions in econometrics, *Journal of Econometrics*, **33**, 311–340.

Phillips, P. C. B. (1991). Optimal inference in cointegrated systems, *Econometrica*, **59**, 283–306.

Pike, M. C. and Hill, I. D. (1966). Logarithm of the gamma function, *Communications of the ACM*, **9**, 684.

Quandt, R. E. (1983). Computational methods and problems, In Griliches, Z. and Intriligator, M. D. (eds.), *Handbook of Econometrics*, Vol. 1, Ch. 12. Amsterdam: North-Holland.

Rahbek, A., Kongsted, H. C. and Jørgensen, C. (1999). Trend-stationarity in the I(2) cointegration model, *Journal of Econometrics*, **90**, 265–289.

Rao, C. R. (1952). *Advanced Statistical Methods in Biometric Research.* New York: John Wiley.

Rao, C. R. (1973). *Linear Statistical Inference and its Applications,* 2nd edition. New York: John Wiley & Sons.

Richard, J.-F. (1984). Classical and Bayesian inference in incomplete simultaneous equation models, In Hendry, D. F. and Wallis, K. F. (eds.), *Econometrics and Quantitative Economics*. Oxford: Basil Blackwell.

Salkever, D. S. (1976). The use of dummy variables to compute predictions, prediction errors and confidence intervals, *Journal of Econometrics*, **4**, 393–397.

Schmidt, P. (1974). The asymptotic distribution of forecasts in the dynamic simulation of an econometric model, *Econometrica*, **42**, 303–309.

Shea, B. L. (1988). Algorithm AS 239: Chi-squared and incomplete gamma integral, *Applied Statistics*, **37**, 466–473.

Shenton, L. R. and Bowman, K. O. (1977). A bivariate model for the distribution of $\sqrt{b_1}$ and b_2, *Journal of the American Statistical Association*, **72**, 206–211.

Sims, C. A. (1980). Macroeconomics and reality, *Econometrica*, **48**, 1–48. Reprinted in Granger, C. W. J. (ed.) (1990), *Modelling Economic Series*. Oxford: Clarendon Press.

Spanos, A. (1986). *Statistical Foundations of Econometric Modelling*. Cambridge: Cambridge University Press.

Spanos, A. (1989). On re-reading Haavelmo: A retrospective view of econometric modeling, *Econometric Theory*, **5**, 405–429.

Thisted, R. A. (1988). *Elements of Statistical Computing. Numerical Computation.* New York: Chapman and Hall.

Toda, H. Y. and Phillips, P. C. B. (1993). Vector autoregressions and causality, *Econometrica*, **61**, 1367–1393.

White, H. (1980). A heteroskedastic-consistent covariance matrix estimator and a direct test for heteroskedasticity, *Econometrica*, **48**, 817–838.

Wooldridge, J. M. (1999). Asymptotic properties of some specification tests in linear models with integrated processes, In Engle, R. F. and White, H. (eds.), *Cointegration, Causality and Forecasting*, pp. 366–384. Oxford: Oxford University Press.

Author Index

Subject Index